D1141165

SIR JAMES WORDIE
POLAR CRUSADER

EXPLORING THE ARCTIC AND ANTARCTIC

SIR JAMES WORDIE
POLAR CRUSADER

EXPLORING THE ARCTIC
AND ANTARCTIC

By
Michael Smith

First published in 2004
by Birlinn Limited
West Newington House
10 Newington Road
Edinburgh EH9 1QS

www.birlinn.co.uk

Copyright © Michael Smith 2004

The right of Michael Smith to be identified as the author
of this work has been asserted by him in accordance with
the Copyright, Designs and Patents Act 1988

All rights reserved. No part of this publication may be reproduced,
stored, or transmitted in any form, or by any means, electronic,
mechanical or photocopying, recording or otherwise, without the
express written permission of the publisher.

ISBN 1 84158 292 1

British Library Cataloguing in Publication Data
A Catalogue record for this book is available from the British Library

CORK CITY LIBRARY WITHDRAWN FROM STOCK

TORY TOP ROAD BRANCH

CITY LIBRARY CORK

45G 930 6

Typeset by Brinnoven, Livingston
Printed and bound by Creative Print and Design, Wales

Dedicated to
Barbara, Daniel and Nathan

CONTENTS

LIST OF MAPS AND ILLUSTRATIONS

List of Maps

List of Illustrations

Gertrude Henderson at the age of eighteen

Wordie, pictured in 1923 with his new bride, Gertrude

The *Endurance* party prepares to sail for Antarctica in October 1914

Endurance struggles against the crippling ice of the Weddell Sea, February 1915

Wordie with Sir Ernest Shackleton, in Buenos Aires shortly before *Endurance* sailed into the Weddell Sea

A cross section graphic showing the interior design and layout of the doomed *Endurance*

Wordie with Robert Clark in 'Auld Reekie' on board *Endurance*

Wordie scrubs a floor on board *Endurance* with bosun Alf Cheetham and Alexander Macklin

Endurance lurches at a crazy angle as the ice of the Weddell Sea tightens its deadly grip

After a terrible journey away from the ice, the 28 men from the *Endurance* party reached the desolate Elephant Island on April 15, 1916

The first hot drink after landing at Elephant Island

The men who spent four and a half months marooned on Elephant Island

The entire *Endurance* party re-united in Chile, September 3, 1916, after the rescue from Elephant Island

A Scottish newspaper, *The Bulletin*, gave its readers a local angle on the dramatic Elephant Island escapade

Wordie pictured in uniform after enlisting in the Royal Field Artillery, 1917

Wordie and Lethbridge at the top of Mount Beerenberg, August 11, 1921

Mercanton stands at the summit of the Beerenberg with Lethbridge

Returning from Jan Mayen, 1921

Wordie in typical pose in the Arctic during the 1920s

Heimen leaving Bergen, June 1923, on the ill-fated voyage to Greenland

ACKNOWLEDGEMENTS

A CONSIDERABLE NUMBER OF PEOPLE AND A VARIETY OF LIBRARIES and archives were consulted in the writing of this book and it would not have been possible to chronicle the extraordinarily rich and varied life of Sir James Wordie without their generous assistance. I am very grateful to everyone whose contribution, however large or small, helped me and any omissions are unintentional.

Special mention should first go to the Wordie family, who freely made available the very considerable correspondence, diaries and papers of Sir James Wordie without any pre-conditions or qualifications. I was given free access, even on occasions when my enquiries were a little awkward.

Elizabeth Clarke, George Wordie, Alison Stancer and Peter Wordie, the four surviving children of Sir James Wordie, also willingly shared memories of their father and were endlessly courteous and patient with my questions. I cannot thank them enough for their tolerance and for being so candid.

However, I must reserve particular thanks for Peter Wordie, who worked so hard to achieve his desire of having a biography written about his father. He was a constant source of optimism and understanding, who freely gave me great support and encouragement and never once sought to influence my judgement. I will always be grateful.

The generous assistance of Alan Wordie, a grandson of James Wordie, was important in obtaining access to many documents and photographs held by the family. I am very appreciative of that support.

The considered and painstakingly thorough contribution of Edward Paget-Tomlinson, a nephew of Sir James Wordie, has been essential in compiling this book and I will always be in his debt. He undertook much of the initial research, particularly into the ancestry of the Wordie family, which he gladly passed into my hands and in the best traditions of literary research kindly allowed me to form my own judgements. I owe him much.

I also owe a special debt of gratitude to Anne Savours and Harold King who, at different times, provided a great deal of constructive advice and valuable research to the preliminary work of Edward Paget-Tomlinson. This, too, was freely passed to me and I am indebted to both for their generosity.

This early research was particularly valuable because I was given access to the personal memories of Sir James Wordie provided by people who, sadly, have since passed away. Among those whose written testimonials are used in this book are Sir Vivian Fuchs, Terence Armstrong and Colin Bertram.

I am also grateful to those who allowed themselves to be interviewed by me and provided their personal recollections of Sir James Wordie or willingly supplied useful insight into relevant Polar and academic activities of the time. I wish to record my warmest thanks to Professor John Crook of St John's College, Cambridge, Tony Daltry, Barbara Debenham, the daughter of Frank Debenham, The Hon. Broke Evans, son of Teddy Evans, Sir Alexander Glen, Geoffrey Hattersley-Smith, Peter Speak, Charles Swithinbank and David Yelverton. I also owe a particular debt to Anders Mattsson for his helpful translation skills.

It is important to place on record my gratitude to the large number of archives and libraries consulted during my researches and to those who have given permission to quote from their records.

I am grateful for the help provided by the following: William Mills and Shirley Sawtell in the library and Robert Headland, the archivist, at the Scott Polar Research Institute; staff at the

Manuscripts Division of the National Library of Scotland; Vicki Ingpen at the Journals & Archives Department of the Royal Society of Edinburgh; Julie Carrington and colleagues at the archives and library of the Royal Geographical Society; Fani Karagianni and Joanna Rae in the archives at the British Antarctic Survey; Malcolm Underwood, the archivist and the Master, Fellows and Scholars of St John's College, Cambridge; Ian Riches at the National Trust for Scotland; Elma Lindsay, local history officer at Stirling Central Library; Iain MacLeod, Deputy Rector at Glasgow Academy; Moira Rankin, senior archivist at the University of Glasgow; British Library; The Glasgow Art Club; National Archives of Scotland; the National Archive (formerly the Public Record Office); Riksarkivet, the National Archives of Norway.

Peter Fuchs kindly allowed me inspect the private papers and journals of his father, Sir Vivian Fuchs, particularly his journal of the 1929 expedition to East Greenland and documents relating to the Commonwealth Trans-Antarctic Expedition. I am grateful for his help and for permission to quote freely from his father's papers.

Every reasonable effort has been made to trace the copyright holders of documents and photographs and accreditation has been given only where it can be properly established. I trust any unintentional omissions will be excused.

Finally, the support of my sons, Daniel and Nathan has been important, notably during odd periods when I struggled to overcome the demons inside my computer. But most of all I want to express my gratitude to Barbara, my wife, who was always enormously supportive and understanding.

PREFACE

THE CALL, WHEN IT CAME, WAS TOTALLY UNEXPECTED. I WAS GAZING idly at my computer terminal one day when an e-mail arrived from someone I did not know, asking a totally unexpected question. The polite enquiry was simple enough: would I be interested in discussing the possibility of writing a book about Sir James Wordie?

My immediate reaction was overwhelmingly non-committal, not from a lack of interest or disrespect, but merely a colossal ignorance of Wordie beyond knowing that he was one of the men on Sir Ernest Shackleton's dramatic *Endurance* expedition and one of those unfortunate souls marooned on Elephant Island. Beyond that I knew practically nothing.

But I was curious to find out why anyone thought that Wordie would justify a biography and did some hasty research. More importantly, I arranged to meet Peter Wordie, the son of James Wordie. Over a quiet lunch one day, Peter outlined the extraordinarily rich and varied life of his father and promised to make available his diaries and voluminous personal papers, most of which had never been seen before. I was astounded by what he told me and appalled that, as someone with a respectable knowledge of the history of polar exploration, I knew so little of James Wordie. By the time the main course arrived I had made up my mind to write the book.

What I discovered was that Sir James Wordie was a man of very many parts and that the *Endurance* adventure was merely the prelude to a remarkable and largely unknown story. Many men would have retired to the shadows after the ordeal of *Endurance*. But the shattering experience seems to have fired Wordie and ignited his own driving ambition.

The story of James Wordie is that of a prolific Polar explorer, a quiet revolutionary who changed the way that exploration was carried out, and the influential guiding light who nurtured a new generation of young adventurers and built a formidable career as an academic and administrator. He left his mark on British exploration for the best part of fifty years. Wordie was that rare Polar animal who made the successful transition from one era to another. An enormously influential moderniser, he led the way in steering exploration from the romantic and heroic age of Scott and Shackleton into the more functional mechanised and scientific age.

Few can match Wordie's active career of travelling on nine expeditions to the Polar territories. He made his final visit to the ice at the age of sixty-five when most explorers had opted for their pipe and slippers. But even fewer can claim to have been a crucial figure in shaping two of the great geographical achievements of the twentieth century – the first successful ascent of Everest and the first crossing of the Antarctic continent. His other great influence was to be the father figure of British exploration, guiding and advising many of the important expeditions which left these shores from the 1920s until the late 1950s. He became the elder statesman of Polar exploration and his steely resolve and dedication almost single-handedly ensured that the centuries-old tradition of British voyaging to the ice did not wither and die.

Wordie was in many ways as influential to exploration as men like Sir John Barrow or Sir Clements Markham. But Wordie did not have power base of either Barrow or Markham and his achievements are all the more remarkable. Few expeditions left Britain without first consulting the *éminence grise* Wordie and his wise counselling helped create and develop the next generation of Polar explorers. The list of young men who were indebted to Wordie's guidance reads like a Who's Who of modern polar exploration and includes Vivian Fuchs, Gino Watkins, August Courtauld and John Rymill.

James Wordie's power base was later extended to national institutions like the Royal Geographical Society and the Scott Polar Research Institute, and for thirty years he was one of the most significant, but under-estimated, figures in guiding British interests in the Antarctic territories, especially the diplomatically sensitive Falkland Islands.

However James Wordie was a shy, reserved figure who did not seek the limelight and was virtually unknown outside his immediate circle. He rarely gave interviews and never wrote a book about his multi-faceted and hugely influential life. This has left the history of exploration sadly incomplete, and a full biography of James Wordie is long overdue. Now, with access to his unpublished diaries and private papers, I hope that my researches will mean this omission can be corrected and a significant gap in the chronicles of Polar exploration can be filled.

Michael Smith
March, 2004

CHAPTER I

LAIRDS AND CARTS

NOTHING IN THE LONG HISTORY OF THE WORDIE FAMILY PROVIDES a clue to the twentieth-century exploits of James Mann Wordie. He was as much a rarity in the Wordie lineage as he was unusual in the ranks of explorers. The Wordies are an old-established Scots family, hailing mostly from the parishes of St Ninians Torbrex and Cambusbarron in the ancient town of Stirling, which stands geographically and historically at the very heart of Scotland. Generations of Wordies inhabited the same region where men like William Wallace, Robert Bruce, Bonnie Prince Charlie and John Knox left indelible marks on Scottish history.

The Wordies were local landowners and merchants around Stirling with deep roots in the church and an occasional flirtation with the Jacobite cause. Quietly respectable and unassuming, the family lived comfortably until the mid-nineteenth century, when the Industrial Revolution swept through Scotland and ushered in a new era of wealth and prosperity.

It is likely that the name is derived from Worthy, and later developed into Wordye; the present spelling of Wordie was probably adopted sometime in the seventeenth century. The earliest references to the family can be traced back to 1476 when a John Worthy owned a disputed tenement in the royal burgh of Stirling. A few generations later Thomas Wordye was a friar at the historic Cambuskenneth Abbey and towards the end of the sixteenth century some of the family had settled at St Ninians. It was a member of the Wordie family who in 1682 built Williamsfield House at St Ninians, which stands to this day. The distinctive initial 'W' is still visible on the lintel of various houses in the district.

By the eighteenth century, the Wordies were largely merchants and lairds around St Ninians Torbrex and Cambusbarron, a thriving area with a busy woollen industry. But as the first shoots of the Industrial Revolution emerged in the mid-eighteenth century, the family had expanded almost unnoticed into transport – the business that would become synonymous with the Wordie name for the next two hundred years.

It was a modest enough start – the humble task of carrying farm produce by horse and cart from outlying homesteads along the muddy unmade roads to the bustling market in Stirling. Before long the Wordies were loading other types of merchandise onto their carts and the seeds were sown for an enterprise which made Wordie a household name and built a sizeable fortune for generations to come. The family's first known association with cartage was in the notable year of 1745 when Thomas Wordie, clerk to the Incorporated Society of Carters of Stirling, dutifully recorded the arrival of Bonnie Prince Charlie in the town at the start of the 'Forty-five Rebellion. According to local folklore, the Young Pretender shared a cup of wine at Williamsfield House with another family member, John Wordie.

Cartage operations between Stirling and Glasgow provided a modest, but unspectacular living. One early nineteenth-century ancestor, John Wordie, even supplemented his income by running an unlawful postal service between Edinburgh and London. But he remained a small-time operator and by the 1820s debts and difficulties had piled up. In 1830 the 46-year-old John Wordie collapsed and died while taking a summer stroll, leaving his son, William, with a meagre legacy of unpaid bills and six carts.

William Wordie was only twenty when he inherited the humble operation, but he was a more astute businessman than his father and blessed with the energy of youth. Timing was also on his side and the quick-witted Wordie sensed the huge opportunities for haulage as the tide of industrialisation raced into Scotland, particularly the prospects for servicing the fast-emerging railways. William Wordie was among the first in Scotland to realise that railways urgently needed local collection and delivery of goods. In 1842 he clinched a crucial deal with the newly opened Edinburgh & Glasgow Railway to collect and forward freight from their stations; a little later he arranged a similar agreement with the Central Railway linking Stirling and Glasgow. It was an inspired move and within twenty years Wordie commanded a powerful carting network whose tentacles extended into most corners of Scotland's vibrant economy.

William Wordie also mixed business with pleasure when, a few days before Christmas 1837, he married a local woman, Janet Jeffrey, whose father was a wealthy farmer-landowner with valuable connections in transport. The Jeffrey family owned a stake in a busy ferry operation at Alloa on the Forth, which provided another important connection to the firm's network.

Around this time, the entrepreneurial William Wordie took the important decision to abandon the family's traditional home in Stirling and move closer to the heart of Scotland's burgeoning heavy industries on the Clyde. He set up home in Glasgow and began raising his own family. Between 1839 and 1853, William and Janet Wordie had seven children, two sons and five daughters.

William's eldest son, John, was born in January 1839 and firmly established at the core of the family undertaking even before his twentieth birthday. When William Wordie died in October 1874, the struggling undertaking he had inherited in 1830 was a thriving concern with a vast carting network, a stable of around 700 horses and the line of succession firmly in place.[1]

John Wordie, a solemn-looking figure with a full beard and a receding hairline, was a quiet, unassuming pillar of the community, who mixed his shrewd business dealings with a strong sense of social responsibility. He was a Justice of the Peace, a director of the City's Maternity Hospital and an elder in the Church of Scotland Hyndland Church. He also presided over the company's most expansive era and by the early twentieth century could mobilise a huge stable of around 3,000 horses pulling carts to every corner of Scotland and into parts of England and Ireland. The firm was instantly recognised by the slogan: 'You'll find Wordie & Co. everywhere you go'. William McGonagall, the poet, saluted the company's ubiquitous presence with the lines:

> Twenty horses in a row
> Every one a Wordie & Co.

John Wordie combined his relentless hard work with a lifelong dedication to thrift. He zealously guarded the family fortune and was irredeemably devoted to the cause of never wasting a penny. His wife once scolded a young member of staff who was cutting a piece of string in half. 'Never waste string,' she insisted, 'that's how my husband made his money.' The reprimand passed into folklore and anyone contemplating the frivolous waste of string at Wordie & Co. invariably faced the grim warning: 'Remember Mrs Wordie!'

John was also a strong family man, although he waited until well into middle age before finding a suitable partner. She was Jane Catherine Mathers Mann, whose well-to-do father was a merchant and exporter with the Glasgow firm, Mann, Byers & Co. Jane, at 23, was about half the age of the 43-year-old John when they married in June 1882.

It was a fertile union and their first child, William, was born two years later in July 1884. The first daughter, Jean arrived in 1887 and a second girl, Alison, was born in the autumn of 1894. The youngest son of John and Jane Wordie was born at 8.30 in the morning of 26 April 1889 at the family home at 4 Buckingham Terrace, just off Great Western Road in the Hillhead district of Glasgow. He was named James Mann Wordie.

Wordie Family Tree

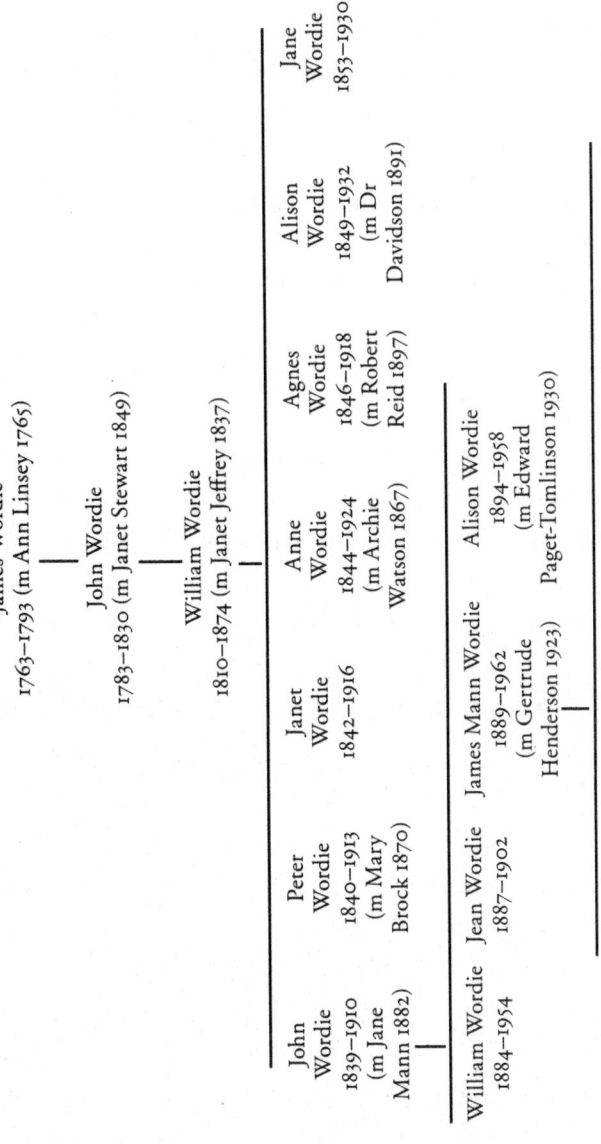

James Wordie
1763–1793 (m Ann Linsey 1765)

John Wordie
1783–1830 (m Janet Stewart 1849)

William Wordie
1810–1874 (m Janet Jeffrey 1837)

John Wordie
1839–1910
(m Jane Mann 1882)

Peter Wordie
1840–1913
(m Mary Brock 1870)

Janet Wordie
1842–1916

Anne Wordie
1844–1924
(m Archie Watson 1867)

Agnes Wordie
1846–1918
(m Robert Reid 1897)

Alison Wordie
1849–1932
(m Dr Davidson 1891)

Jane Wordie
1853–1930

William Wordie
1884–1954

Jean Wordie
1887–1902

James Mann Wordie
1889–1962
(m Gertrude Henderson 1923)

Alison Wordie
1894–1958
(m Edward Paget-Tomlinson 1930)

John Wordie
1924–1998

Elizabeth Wordie
1925–

George Wordie
1927–

Alison Wordie
1929–

Peter Wordie
1932–

Source: Edward Paget-Tomlinson

The four children enjoyed a very comfortable upbringing in a sizeable family home surrounded by servants. However, the Wordies took a fashionably semi-detached view of their offspring and followed the typical example of well-off Victorian families by handing over much of the day-to-day responsibility to a succession of nannies or governesses. John Wordie's heavy business and personal commitments ensured he was rarely visible at home, while Jane Wordie generally found motherhood a burden. She kept her children at arm's length, partly because she suffered from a lifetime of poor health.

Despite the slightly distant relationship, young James developed a deep devotion to his father. But there was less affection for his mother, who reserved her limited affection solely for her eldest son, Willie. In later life James Wordie always spoke with great fondness of his father and rarely mentioned his mother.

Jane Wordie was a remote and slightly difficult woman, who may have suffered from an aggravating kidney complaint which only increased her irascibility. She rarely left the comfort of home and spent long periods in her room, even having the servants bring her breakfast in bed away from the family. She, too, possessed a tireless passion for penny-pinching. It was customary in the Wordie household for the servants to take the remains of the family's Sunday joint for their own meal. But Jane would pointedly visit the servants' quarters and count the number of slices carved off the remnants of the joint.

Typically the children were steered into their parents' presence half an hour before dinner and it was only on a Sunday, as they endured the full rigour of the Scottish Sabbath, that the family spent any time together. It was a God-fearing household, and each sombre Sunday John Wordie force-fed the family an uncompromising diet of spiritual duties and regular services from dawn to dusk. The family spent much of Sunday on their knees. Morning prayers in the drawing room were followed by a full service at the nearby church and after lunch the children were marched off to Sunday school before being ushered back in time to attend another full service in the evening. Any spare time between services was devoted to reading 'good books', such as *The Pilgrim's Progress*. The day's proceedings were rounded off with evening prayers in the drawing room, where John Wordie invariably ordered all available household staff to dutifully line up on their knees alongside the family.

The closest person to James in his early life was Alice Barbezat, the Swiss governess, who came from Vevey on the north-east shore of Lake Geneva and formed a strong bond with the youngster. Alice was a patient, kindly soul who assumed day-to-day control of the children and effectively became a surrogate mother to James. Her presence in these formative days left a lasting impression and although she left the family when James was six, he remained devoted to Alice for years afterwards. They never lost touch and he respectfully called her 'Mademoiselle'.

However, the major influence on James Wordie was his intelligent and cultured father, who gave him a deep sense of propriety, a lifelong love of nature and a profound respect for the arts. He also picked up his father's keen business mind and the trademark partiality for being scrupulously careful with money. Perhaps the only characteristic which James did not pick up from his father was religious fervour. While respectful and conscious of his spiritual duties, James Wordie never embraced the Church with his father's commitment.

The outdoors, which was to figure so prominently in his later life, was an early feature of James's upbringing. John Wordie introduced all his children to Scotland's rugged grandeur by regularly taking a variety of large houses around Appin, a few miles south of the historic site of Glencoe. There they wold take vigorous walks among the oaks and ash. James took to the natural environment with great enthusiasm, first going on long walks and hikes with his father and later trekking independently over the hillsides. It was the start of the Lowlander's lifelong love affair with the Highlands. His fondness for walking also gave him the freedom to escape the stuffy confines of

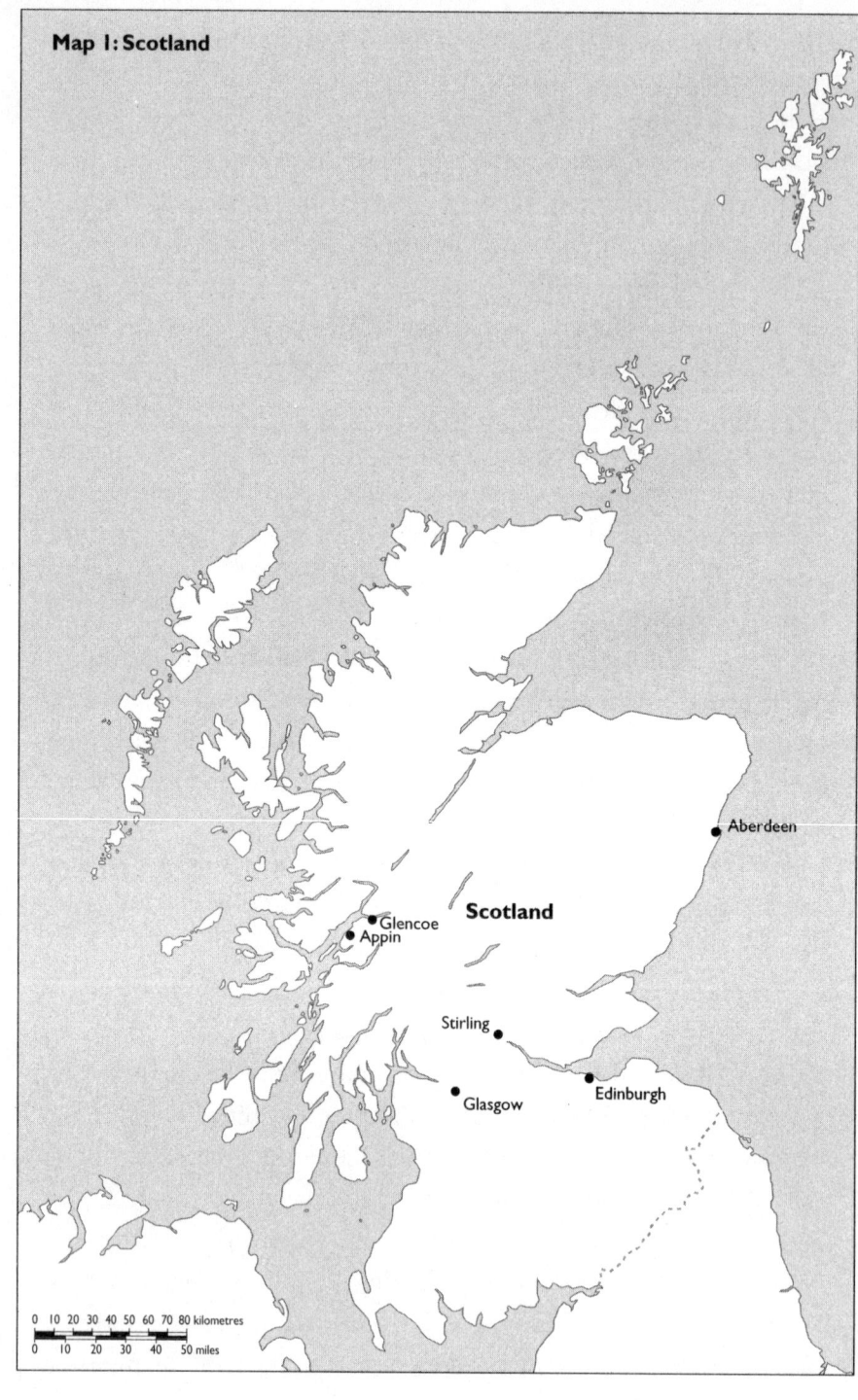

Map 1: Scotland

Aberdeen

Scotland

Glencoe
Appin

Stirling

Glasgow   Edinburgh

0 10 20 30 40 50 60 70 80 kilometres

0   10   20   30   40   50 miles

home, where the brooding presence of his mother often made him feel uncomfortable.

From an early age James Wordie also picked up many of his father's cultural interests. His father was something of an art connoisseur and a book collector, with a particular keenness for etchings and watercolours, which he picked up on frequent visits to the galleries in Paris. His collection included works by Millet, Corot and Rousseau and he owned etchings by Rembrandt, Whistler and Meryon. John Wordie was also associated with the artists who emerged in Glasgow at the end of the nineteenth century and he acted as a governor of the Glasgow School of Art from 1898 until 1905. Occasionally he supported struggling painters and frequently advised galleries on staging exhibitions. By contrast, Jane Wordie took a curmudgeonly view of her husband's interest in the arts, even going to the lengths of trying to prevent him bringing his prized works into the house. She once conceded: 'You can smuggle your books into the house easier than a new painting.'[2]

Jane Wordie's attitude was especially surprising since she came from an artistic family and was no stranger to art. Her parents were both art lovers and her brother, Alexander Mann, became an accomplished landscape painter, studied in Paris under Carolus Duran and was associated with the Glasgow school. His work, which hung on the walls of the Mann family home, was once described as 'assured and confident rather than impassioned'.[3]

The Wordies did not stay long at Buckingham Terrace and it may be that their new home was chosen because it provided a better showcase for John Wordie's expansive collections. Soon after the birth of James, the family moved to a large house named Fraisgil in Montgomerie Drive (later re-named Cleveden Drive) in the Hyndland area of Glasgow. Fraisgil was a substantial detached home with numerous rooms, a large garden and a spacious conservatory where the family grew orchids. The walls in the study were adorned from floor to ceiling with paintings and etchings and the shelves in the grand library groaned under the weight of John Wordie's books.

John's other passion was education. He spent thirteen years as a director of the distinguished Glasgow Academy and ensured that his children would have the best education that money could buy. James Wordie's first taste of schooling was a carefully chosen but unlikely setting for the youngster. At the age of five, James was taken to Westbourne School for Girls in Westbourne Gardens, Hyndland, which despite its name took in a few small boys as pupils. A classmate was Alexander Lindsay, who later graduated to become Master of Balliol College, Oxford. James spent three years at Westbourne School for Girls before being sent to the Glasgow Academy in 1897, where his elder brother Willie was already in attendance. It was an excellent choice, which propelled the gifted youngster towards the inevitable place at university.

Glasgow Academy, which was founded in 1846, had earned a formidable reputation for educational excellence, turning out a glittering array of young men destined to achieve fame in many fields. A contemporary of James Wordie was John (Lord) Reith, the first director of the British Broadcasting Corporation, and another old boy was J.M. Barrie, the author and creator of Peter Pan. By coincidence, Barrie's close friend was the Antarctic explorer, Captain Robert Scott, who named his only son, Peter, after Barrie's best-known character.

James Wordie took to school with zest, driven by his innate eagerness to learn. He excelled from the start, rising to second in his class in the first full year and quickly developing into the golden boy of the school.[4]

He never fell below second place in class overall and topped his form for six years, picking up a succession of prizes for subjects as varied as writing, gymnastics, mathematics and drawing. General knowledge, probably nourished in his father's library at Fraisgil, was a speciality. At sixteen he was appointed Dux – a now defunct title meaning academic head – of the classical section of the school. He shone at almost everything he touched. He edited *The Glasgow Academy Chronicle* and gained his marksman's badge for rifle shooting.

Even music came easily to the exceptional youngster. He took up the bagpipes, joined the Academy's Cadet Corp in 1903 as a Pipe-Corporal and within a year was promoted to the Pipe Major of the band. For some unknown reason, he regularly played an unusual set of pipes about three-quarters the size of the common adult type. About the only talent lacking in Wordie was a decent singing voice. It was one of the few vulnerable points in his formidable armoury.

Almost inevitably, there was a touch of arrogant superiority about the teenager with the Midas touch. He became an enthusiastic member of the school's Literary and Debating Society, but often ignored the theme of the debate to bang on about his own personal favourite issues. The official Academy records note that he was 'quite indifferent' to the subject of debate.

James Wordie grew up quickly in this heady academic environment and the starched surroundings at Fraisgil and there appears to have been only a brief interlude between childhood and adulthood. He was precise and proper, always impeccably dressed for the occasion and armed with the formal vocabulary of an adult. He wrote copiously and his writing, even at an early age, displayed a maturity well beyond his years.

At the age of sixteen, when most young men were contemplating somewhat more worldly topics, he chose to address the Academy's debating society on the gruelling theme of Tariff Reform. Without the merest hint of mockery, he once posed the pretentious question: 'Does Education Remove Superstition?'

The academic laurels and extramural accomplishments ensured that James Wordie frequently stood out from the crowd, although he was not always as popular with his fellow pupils as he was with his teachers. It was a trait that contemporaries would recognise in later years as Wordie became infamous for his distinctive but dictatorial style. From an early age, James Wordie sincerely believed that what was best for James Wordie was best for everyone.

Wordie's seemingly unstoppable progress was halted by family tragedy in February 1902 when his elder sister, Jean, was struck down by meningitis and died, aged only fourteen. He was devastated at the sudden loss. It is possible that John Wordie bore the tragedy in mind a year later in 1903 when he took his three surviving children, Willie, James and Alison, on their first trip abroad, a major two-month vacation to the Alps. It was a journey which opened up new horizons and was influential in changing James Wordie's life. Although the frequent visits to Appin had whetted his appetite for the outdoors, Wordie was overwhelmed by the scale and magnificent splendour of the Alps. In the following weeks among the mountains and glaciers of France and Switzerland, Wordie developed a lifelong interest in rocks and ice.

A busy schedule took the Wordie family from Geneva to Champery, La Comballaz, Clarens near Montreux and finally to Bern. The family quickly established a strict routine of long walks, odd games of tennis and dutiful visits to church. James Wordie was the model of a young Scotsman abroad, causing mild curiosity among the Swiss by proudly wearing his kilt at every occasion. On one occasion at Champery he played the bagpipes and then performed a sword-dance at a concert in aid of a local English church in the area.

Jane Wordie did not participate in the holiday. She was often excused all duties and regularly stayed behind for a quiet breakfast in bed. In the evening she would retire early to bed. Significantly, James took the opportunity to re-establish contact with his former governess, Alice Barbezat. Even though she had left Glasgow eight years earlier, Barbezat was warmly restored to the fold and played a full part in the holiday. While Jane sat quietly in her hotel room, Alice enthusiastically joined James on walks and at other functions.

James's diary of the Swiss holiday is full of references to 'Mdle Barbezat' and contains only a few mentions of 'Mother'.

After a month of regular Alpine exercise, the 14-year-old was considered fit enough to tackle his first serious climb, one of the peaks of Les Dents Blanches above Champery on the border between Switzerland and France. A local guide was hired to steer James and his elder brother Willie through the swirling mist and rain to one peak of 8,881 ft (2,664 m), the highest he had ever stood. It was bitterly cold at the top and they stayed only a few minutes. No one had remembered to wind their watches so it was impossible to say how long the climb had taken.

Wordie made a series of further climbs around Champery, Aigle and La Comballaz during his memorable summer of 1903, beginning a passion for mountaineering which would last for the rest of his life. Touched by the majestic scenery, the young man wrote in his diary: 'My power of appreciating scenery has sensibly increased after having studied day after day the mighty ridges of the mountains with glaciers plastered over their sides.'[5]

He followed up the visit to the Alps by spending more time in the Scottish hills, and in 1904 the 15-year-old embarked on his first independent excursion. It was a two-day hike with a cousin through the wet and foggy Dollar Glen, northwards past Drummond Castle and on to Crieff. Hiking and climbing became a regular routine for the teenager. He frequently rose before dawn to catch an early train for a full day trip, accompanied by Willie and Alison, cousins James and Keith Doak, and George Buchanan-Smith, a close friend from Glasgow Academy.

The attachment to the outdoors was not allowed to interfere with studies and the pursuit of a place at university. In October 1906 he matriculated at Glasgow University, having secured the James Lochhead Bursary. It was no surprise that the young man chose to read Geology.

One of the hardest talks at this time must have been to keep the exceptional youngster's feet on the ground. So far, everything he touched had blossomed and Wordie's astute father told his son that he 'must be careful to fully appreciate the responsibility that lies on you from having gained such an honour'.[6] Wordie, to his credit, fully understood his responsibilities and he took to the university, with its rich Scots traditions and scholarly dedication, with typical zeal. It was the ideal environment for the eager and outstanding young student and by chance, it also gave Wordie an early introduction to the increasingly fashionable world of polar exploration.

Wordie's main influence at Glasgow was Professor John W. Gregory, a distinguished geologist and explorer, who came close to changing the course of British exploration to the Antarctic in the early twentieth century, the heroic age. Gregory possessed all the right credentials to be one of the most significant figures in the drive to open up Antarctica. He was an eminent geologist with valuable first-hand experience of the ice, having made the first crossing of Spitsbergen with Sir Martin Conway in 1896. In 1901, as Britain was putting together the *Discovery* expedition, Gregory was a prime candidate to play a leading role in the most comprehensive attempt to explore the continent.

Initially, Gregory was asked to lead the landing party from *Discovery*, which intended to make the first serious attempt to explore the interior of the continent. The ship's party, which was not scheduled to land, would be under the leadership of an ambitious naval commander, Robert Scott. But the driving force behind the expedition was Sir Clements Markham, the elderly President of the Royal Geographical Society who wanted *Discovery* to be a naval enterprise, like the earlier British expeditions to the Arctic in the nineteenth century. Markham had been to the Arctic half a century earlier and was implacably opposed to the notion of civilian scientists like Gregory interfering with naval business. The clash of ideals between Gregory and Markham was hugely significant for Britain's exploration, a classic struggle of old school versus the modernisers.

A different outcome might have avoided the undeniably heroic but dreadful climax of this effort with Scott's tragic last expedition in 1912.

Markham, who was seventy, had learned little from his Arctic experience and resolutely clung to the old-fashioned idea of mobilising cumbersome, large-scale naval operations to explore in the hostile environment. It was a regime which obstinately refused to learn Eskimo methods of survival and involved parties of robust seamen hauling their own heavy sledges over the ice – a system which had failed so spectacularly in the past.

If Markham epitomised the Imperial arrogance of the Victorian age, Gregory had grasped the essentials of modern polar travel and urged a more progressive approach. He argued that *Discovery* should be captained by an experienced skipper from the whaling fleets, with knowledge of the pack ice, and recommended a small landing party using dog-drawn sledges to penetrate the unknown interior. A decade after *Discovery* the Norwegian, Roald Amundsen, beat Scott's navy-led party in the race to the South Pole using a small hand-picked crew and teams of dogs, while Scott and four other men died dragging their own sledges over the ice. But Markham won the political battle and Gregory resigned from the *Discovery* expedition, leaving Scott in full control of both the ship and landing party. Gregory's contribution to *Discovery* was purely symbolic – the wooden hut erected at Hut Point on Ross Island was initially known as 'Gregory's Lodge' after its designer. In the event, Scott became a household name and died in appalling circumstances, while Gregory returned to the relative anonymity of academic life. In 1904, as *Discovery* returned from the Antarctic, he was appointed to the first Chair of Geology at Glasgow University and held the post for twenty-five years until his retirement in 1929.

Gregory's knowledge and experience were an inspiration to young men like Wordie, his intellectual prowess knitting perfectly with practical and impressive direct experience. He was the ideal mentor for Wordie, a bright young man with a keen interest in mountains and glaciers and a growing interest in exploration.

Wordie flourished at Glasgow, helped by Gregory and his own eagerness to learn. His talents were soon rewarded with the William Hunter Medal in geology and a First Class certificate in mathematics. In 1909 he won a medal in Advanced Geology and a First Class certificate in Natural Philosophy, graduating a year later with an MA with distinction in Geology.

The degree was not enough for Wordie, who wanted to continue his studies elsewhere. He turned his attention to Cambridge, where he applied to be taken on as an advanced student, backed by the heavyweight support of Gregory and Edwin Temple, Rector of the Glasgow Academy. In October, 1910 Wordie was duly admitted to St John's College, Cambridge to read natural sciences as an advanced student. It was a life-changing decision.

CHAPTER 2

FROM GOLD
TO ICE

St John's, Cambridge was the turning point in James Wordie's life. By tradition he should have been preparing to follow earlier generations into the prosperous family haulage business. However, carting and geology were simply incompatible to the talented 21-year-old.

His perceptive father also sensed that his youngest son was destined for bigger things than carting. He re-arranged his affairs to ensure that the firm was placed in safe hands and then gave full rein to his gifted son. Wordie & Co., under John Wordie's assured guidance, had grown rapidly in the late Victorian and early Edwardian era, even expanding away from its established Scottish base into the larger English and Irish markets. As he entered his sixties, John passed day-to-day control of the empire to his eldest son, Willie, and to Archie Watson, a nephew who was sixteen years older than Willie and possessed considerably more haulage experience. This left James Wordie without obligation to the family and free to pursue his academic career and chosen profession of geology.

It was one of the last acts which John Wordie performed for his family. Within months of James going up to St John's, both his parents were dead. John Wordie had struggled with ill health in his later years, but his condition deteriorated markedly towards the end of 1910 following a tiring journey to look at some works of art in Canada. He died on Boxing Day 1910, aged seventy-one. Less than five weeks later, on 30 January 1911, a second misfortune struck when James's mother Jane died after a long struggle with illness. She was only fifty-two.

John Wordie left his three children with a sizeable legacy. His estate was valued at almost £186,000 (around £9 million in today's terms), but well over half was tied up in the carting business and not immediately accessible. The remainder was held in bonds and shares, including a small stake of forty shares in the Glasgow Academy. The family home, Fraisgil, and John Wordie's admirable collection of paintings, etchings and books were valued at £7,300, or about £350,000 at today's values.[1]

The canny John Wordie divided up his estate to ensure that his wealth was well spent. James and sister Alison were awarded sizeable sums of money to accommodate their lives outside the family company, while Willie's bequest was to retain the lucrative role at the centre of the wealthy business.

James's bequest was a cash sum of £32,000 (about £1,500,000 today), a generous bounty which would allow him to pursue his academic career in security. Alison was awarded £16,000, worth around £750,000 today.

Alison, who was just sixteen years old, was the most vulnerable to the double loss and Wordie quickly grasped the nettle. With little fuss he quietly by-passed the older Willie and assumed the role of notional head of the family, taking Alison under his wing. It was a role he held for the rest of his life. The pair quickly developed a very close relationship, spending considerable time together walking or skiing. Even when apart they kept in touch through a constant flow of letters, with Wordie exercising a gentle fatherly influence. In contrast, Willie remained the outsider.

Aside from family affairs, Wordie rose to the challenge at Cambridge, claiming more academic honours and demonstrating an insatiable desire to learn. In 1912 he earned a BA when graduating in Part II of the Natural Sciences Tripos and was awarded the Harkness Scholarship in Geology. At the same time he took the first step towards become a tutor in his own right by occasionally assisting John Marr, the renowned Geology lecturer, in supervising young students.

Wordie punctuated his academic development with an increasing enthusiasm for climbing, both at home and abroad. In 1907 he had made a return journey to the Alps and climbed the 12,300ft (3,690 m) Piz Morteratsch, the highest peak so far attained. At home his appetite for climbing rose steadily and while still a teenager he managed to scale about fifty Scottish peaks. On occasions he joined parties led by Professor Gregory and during 1911 he formalised his hobby by joining the Scottish Mountaineering Club.

Wordie gained another honour, an unofficial graduation in 'University Alpinism'. This was the dangerous pastime of climbing the ancient steeples of Cambridge, which, while much frowned upon by the authorities, has proved an irresistible pastime for students down the ages. 'University Alpinism' had initially developed as a means for students to get back into the colleges at night long after the doors had officially been closed. The hazardous practice of scaling the college walls and scrambling over the roofs in pitch darkness later became known as night-climbing and a powerful sense of bravado drove young men to extraordinary feats. Accomplished climbers like Wordie took the peculiar custom to new levels, scaling the most perilous of buildings and concealing their clandestine activities in a strict code of secrecy. Only the climbers themselves were supposed to know of each other's achievements. Such was the exacting code that night-climbs were only regarded as valid if undertaken during term when the alpinists faced summary expulsion if caught. However, the alpinists diligently followed each other's exploits; once in later life Wordie was sitting next to the headmaster of Gordonstoun School at a function and astonished the man by asking how he had managed a particularly difficult manoeuvre on a night-climb some twenty years earlier. The man, a former student of Wordie, had never mentioned the climb and was amazed to discover that anyone knew about his feats.

Wordie developed a special flair for ascending the seemingly sheer outside walls of various university buildings. A particular favourite was a daunting climb up the vertical tower of the College Chapel at St John's. He was in good company since two of the men most associated with 'University Alpinism' were later involved with the biggest ascent of them all – Everest. It was said that the first person to ascend the Chapel wall at St John's was Jack Longland, a highly proficient climber who was a member of the 1933 Everest expedition. Wilfred Noyce, who graduated from college walls to become a member of the successful 1953 expedition, was regarded as the most capable man to tackle the sheer face of St John's Chapel.

Soon after formally graduating from St John's, Wordie went to the Sedgwick Museum of Geology to continue his research, and before long he had gained his first experience of the polar landscape. An early part of his research programme took Wordie to Canada for the 13th International Geological Congress in Toronto during the summer of 1913. Part of the programme involved numerous excursions and field trips and Wordie signed up for an opportunity to visit the mountainous Yukon Territories. He was not disappointed and soon became enthralled by the awesome natural beauty of the endless mountains and the immense Malaspina Glacier, which pours into Yakutat Bay.

It was also a moment to get a foretaste of the hazards of exploration. While steaming up Yakutat Bay towards the Russell Fjord, the party's ship ran aground on a hidden reef. The ship was stuck fast near Disenchantment Bay, an inhospitable place given its uninviting name by the seventeenth-century navigator, Malaspina, who wrongly believed it to be the exit channel from the North West Passage. The passengers were fortunate that the ship struck the reef close to low tide. Had it struck at high tide, the ship would probably have toppled over as the water level fell, leaving the party stranded many miles from civilisation.

Wordie enjoyed the brush with danger. In a telling letter to Alison he offered a light-hearted observation which, only two years later, would have sounded highly apposite. He wrote:

> You must try and imagine me a hardy navigator of the good old days, wrecked while pushing westward the boundaries of empire. Here, stranded on an inhospitable coast with my last efforts I draw a chart on a piece of sealskin and use my own blood for ink.[2]

Thankfully the returning tide enabled the ship to escape the reef and the geologists resumed their trip.

The next stop was an opportunity to visit the old gold-rush sites of the legendary Klondike. Wordie was even tempted to try his hand at panning for gold. But he was no luckier than most old-time gold diggers. The Klondike was the last of the great gold rushes; it erupted in 1897 and fizzled out within about two years. Over 100,000 wild-eyed fortune-seekers poured into the remote region, suffering appalling hardship and misery in the stampede to strike it lucky. But only a few hundred fortunate souls found gold in any reasonable quantities and only a handful managed to hang onto their money long enough to live the high life. Wordie, to the surprise of no one, failed to find 'pay-dirt' in his brief quest for gold and joined the multitudes of disappointed prospectors who left the Yukon empty-handed. However, the Yukon trip reinforced his intention to spread his wings further and embark on more serious exploration. The opportunity was waiting for him in the quiet study rooms of Cambridge.

TO THE ANTARCTIC

Wordie returned to Cambridge in October 1913 to discover that Polar exploration was the main topic of conversation. Word of Captain Scott's tragic South Pole expedition did not reach Britain until February 1913 and there was a major public appeal for funds to compensate the dependants of the five dead men. In addition, there was fresh speculation that Sir Ernest Shackleton was poised to return to the Antarctic. Cambridge was bristling with polar interest at this time. The university was both home to survivors of the Scott disaster and the place where Shackleton came to recruit scientific staff for his planned journey. Wordie suddenly found himself at the centre of events.

First-hand accounts of the Scott debacle were freely available from four survivors of the expedition who were at Cambridge busily collating data and writing up their own scientific papers. The men – the geologists Frank Debenham, Raymond Priestley and Thomas Griffith Taylor, and the physicist and glaciologist Charles Wright – quickly struck up a rapport with the eager Wordie. Wordie formed a particular affinity with Priestley, who seemed to match his own ambition of mixing adventurous voyaging with a sound academic career.

The 27-year-old Priestley, the son of a headmaster from Tewkesbury, was already a veteran of two Antarctic missions and had packed more escapades into his few years than most achieve in a lifetime. He joined Shackleton's *Nimrod* expedition in 1907 when he was only twenty and travelled with Scott in 1910, surviving an incredible ordeal with a splinter group of six who spent the vicious Antarctic winter in a 12ft by 9ft ice cave. His introduction to exploration was a cameo of the typically cavalier approach to expeditions which characterised – and romanticised – the early era of Polar discovery. Priestley had been studying for his degree at Bristol University when his brother Bert told him that Shackleton was in another room desperately trying to persuade a reluctant man to enlist as geologist on the *Nimrod* expedition. Bert Priestley casually asked his brother:

'How would you like to go to the Antarctic, Ray?'

'I'd go anywhere to get out of this damned place,' Priestley replied.[1] Shackleton subsequently invited Priestley for an interview and floored the apprehensive young man by asking him two perplexing questions: could he sing and would he recognise gold if he saw it? A puzzled Priestley said no in both cases and thought his chance of adventure had evaporated. A few weeks later he received a brusque telegram from Shackleton demanding to know why his new assistant geologist was not preparing to depart for the Antarctic.

Priestley was also the man with some inside knowledge of Shackleton's forthcoming expedition. Shackleton wanted to take Priestley on his new trip and Wordie began to wonder if he, too, had a chance of venturing south. He chatted at length with Priestley, Debenham and Wright and the idea grew in its appeal. His resolve was further strengthened when Griffith Taylor confidently predicted that Shackleton's voyage would be the 'last big expedition to go south'.

Shackleton's plans for a new Antarctic trip were officially announced during the 1913 Christmas break and Wordie, away with the family in Scotland, had little doubt that he wanted to enlist as a geologist. He took long walks in the hills with Willie and Alison, effectively seeking family approval to join the endeavour. Both gave their blessing, despite some reservations about a journey which might keep him away for at least two years. On 17 March 1914 he formally applied to join Shackleton.

It is likely that all concerned would have had serious reservations had they first studied Shackleton's highly ambitious plans. Shackleton's bold plan was to march across the entire Antarctic continent, a distance of around 1,800 miles (2,800 km), deploying two ships and two separate teams of men on either side of the continent, one from the Weddell Sea and another from the Ross Sea. The grandly titled Imperial Trans-Antarctic Expedition was the most audacious Polar enterprise ever attempted and represented a potent blend of Shackleton's natural self-confidence and his desperation for adventure.

The year 1913 was a highly unsettling time for Shackleton, a restless man who always had his eye set firmly on the next great voyage. He was haunted by the ghost of the martyr Scott and tainted by his flaky brother, Frank Shackleton, who was convicted of fraud at a highly publicised trial at the Old Bailey. Age was also against Shackleton. At thirty-nine, his days as an explorer were clearly numbered, and as he approached his fortieth birthday he admitted to being 'a bit weary'. The urge to escape to the wide open spaces of the Antarctic had never been greater.

A further irritant was the publication of Scott's poignant diaries, which heaped yet more attention on his rival and further eclipsed Shackleton as the nation's most famous explorer. Shackleton and Scott had become bitter adversaries after the *Discovery* expedition and Wordie was among those who witnessed the lingering ill-feeling which continued even after Scott's death.

Lady Kathleen Scott, his widow, attended a dinner at Cambridge in March 1914 where the conversation was dominated by Shackleton's forthcoming expedition. She openly disliked Shackleton and urged Wordie and the others not to join him. Wordie, respectful and in awe of Shackleton's reputation, was taken aback by the depth of feeling. He recalled: 'Shackleton is certainly not "persona grata" with Lady Scott, who tried to dissuade all would-be candidates from the thought of going.'[2]

Shackleton was also concerned at the prospect of other explorers stealing what Polar glory remained. The Austrian Dr Felix Konig had announced plans to explore from a base in the Weddell Sea and in Britain a man called J. Foster Stackhouse had drawn up his own scheme. Stackhouse, a Quaker with a loose connection to the Scott entourage, had a hazy plan to visit King Edward VII Land which, he announced, demanded the 'finest qualities of British endurance'. However, Stackhouse failed to raise money for his expedition and was subsequently drowned in 1915 when the passenger liner *Lusitania* was sunk by a German submarine.

Shackleton's defiant riposte to the encircling adversity was the coast-to-coast trek. It had first been proposed in 1908 by the Scottish explorer, William Speirs Bruce. But Bruce was an outsider who was never accepted by the Polar establishment and he failed to generate enough interest in his scheme. However, Bruce generously supported Shackleton's plan to undertake the journey. Shackleton's proposal was greeted with disbelief in some quarters. Hugh Robert Mill, the much respected librarian at the Royal Geographical Society and a good friend of Shackleton, regarded it as too dangerous and the RGS itself had grave reservations. Douglas Freshfield, the RGS President, would later describe the venture as 'audacious in the extreme'. But the most venomous attack came from Sir Clements Markham, who had sponsored Scott's Polar ambitions and loathed Shackleton. He saw the expedition as an absurd idea designed solely for self-advertisement and accused Shackleton of falsifying accounts of his earlier exploits to win support for his scheme. In a confidential note to the RGS, Markham declared that the expedition would be 'useless and a deplorable waste of money' and that Shackleton was at least ten years too old to undertake the mission.

The catalogue of risk was truly daunting. Shackleton's principal ship, *Endurance*, had to navigate the precarious pack ice and hundreds of miles of uncharted water in the Weddell Sea to find a suitable spot to land a party that would over-winter before embarking on the trans-continental journey. At least half that journey was across unknown territory.

Robert Mossman, a member of Bruce's *Scotia* party, which had successfully penetrated the Weddell Sea in 1903, summed up the potential difficulties of navigating a safe pathway through the ice. In a newspaper article at the time, he concluded: 'The vital point bearing on the success of Shackleton's expedition is not what he will do when he reaches his base in 78° S; the main difficulty lies in his getting there through perhaps 1,000 miles of pack ice.'[3]

The intended spot for Shackleton's base was Vahsel Bay on the edge of the Filchner Ice Shelf, an area which had only been seen from afar and where no one had landed before. It was not known if a safe harbour could be found at Vahsel and even more worrying was the uncertainty of the surrounding pack ice, which might block off the ship's escape route in the following year. After over-wintering at Vahsel Bay, Shackleton intended to lead a party of six men across 900 miles (1,400 km) of uncharted mountains and ice fields to the South Pole. From the Pole the group planned to retrace Scott's steps back to his old base camp at Cape Evans in the Ross Sea, a further distance of 900 miles.

Shackleton's party would be incapable of carrying enough food and fuel for the four-month journey and the success of the mission depended entirely on plans to lay a line of supply depots along the final stages of the route from Cape Evans in the Ross Sea towards the Pole. A second ship, *Aurora*, was scheduled to land another group of men at the Ross Sea. While Shackleton was travelling from Vahsel Bay to the Pole, the depot-laying party was expected to build vital caches of food and fuel, quite literally a lifeline for the trans-continental party.

Shackleton was pinning his faith on dog teams to haul his sledges for most of the journey. But his men had only limited experience of driving teams and his schedule for the crossing was wildly optimistic. Shackleton's plan was to achieve the 1,800-mile crossing in only a hundred days – a phenomenal feat for men with very little familiarity of the art of dog driving. Amundsen needed ninety-nine days to complete the 1,860-mile (2,900 km) return journey to the Pole in 1911–12, but his party included several expert dog handlers and a Nordic ski champion. In 1958 the Commonwealth Trans-Antarctic Expedition under Vivian Fuchs also took ninety-nine days to cross the continent, but by this stage explorers were driving motorised tractors and Sno-cats – not unruly dogs.

However, the complex plan contained an even bigger element of doubt for the men, like Wordie, who would be left behind conducting scientific studies while the trans-continental party was marching across the interior.

Shackleton's plans for the expedition, which were outlined to the RGS in London, did not commit the party to a specific winter base. The only clue the outside world had to the location of the winter station was Shackleton's commitment to 'try and land . . . in latitude 78 degrees south'. Vahsel Bay was simply the preferred site and if conditions drove them elsewhere the only news of the alternative base would be carried by *Endurance*. The loss of the ship would be fatal to the men left behind.

Despite uncertainties and obvious hazards, Wordie became increasingly determined to join the enterprise, which he believed offered the chance for adventure and geological work. He called on some influential friends to help, including Gregory who gave a glowing reference to Shackleton. Another useful supporter was Dr Marr, the Cambridge lecturer who once unsuccessfully applied to go with Nordenskjold's *Vega* expedition.

But the key was Priestley. Shackleton had initially turned to the experienced pair of Priestley and Debenham for his geological team. Both declined, Priestley with considerable regret. But he gave a timely recommendation in support of Wordie.

The day before Wordie's application arrived at the expedition's offices in London, Priestley wrote to Shackleton personally suggesting that he should take him. Wordie soon discovered that he was among a deluge of about 5,000 hopefuls applying to join the expedition. Applications were quickly assembled into three piles labelled, 'Mad', 'Hopeless' and 'Possible'. One optimistic bid came from 'three sporty girls' who cheerfully promised to wear men's clothes, ' if our feminine garb is inconvenient'.

Wordie's application was also helped by the fact that Shackleton's scientific resources at this point were virtually non-existent. Shackleton's attitude to science was, at best, casual and it did not rank highly on his list of priorities. He readily admitted that the 'first and foremost' objective of the enterprise was to cross the continent from sea-to-sea.

Despite his own lack of interest, Shackleton recognised that a cogent scientific plan was essential to gain official backing from authoritative bodies like the RGS. Without formal approval raising funds for the expedition would be almost impossible. However, he regarded the RGS as 'hide-bound and narrow' and was content to economise with the truth if it meant finding suitable backing for his enterprise. A year before setting out, he blithely told Bruce: 'I do not mind how much you enlarge on the value such an expedition would be to science.'[4] He quickly promised Wordie that the expedition would incorporate an extensive scientific programme and even asked if he knew any other geologists who might be willing to enlist in the enterprise.

The outline aim of the scientific operations was to send parties from the Weddell Sea base on parallel journeys into the unknown areas in the east and west of Vahsel Bay. But, like the main thrust of the expedition itself, the plans for the scientific programme were vague and highly risky.

Wordie was earmarked for a three-man party that was to travel west along an uncharted area – known today as the Filchner Ice Shelf and Ronne Ice Shelf – to Graham Land at the tip of the long Antarctic Peninsula. The aim was to establish whether the mountains of Graham Land were part of the chain first discovered by Shackleton and Amundsen on their great journeys towards the Pole. It was a highly precarious round-trip of at least 1,000 miles (1,600 km), over mostly unknown territory and by far the longest overland journey Wordie had ever undertaken. Another group, including a geologist and a glaciologist, was due to head eastwards into the enormous void of central Antarctica towards Enderby Land, while two other men would remain at the Weddell Sea base camp to study the weather and fauna in the area.

At the RGS Shackleton had been forced to defend himself against critics who felt the expedition was adventure-for-the-sake-of-adventure. He also embroidered the issue for public consumption without ever going into too much detail, telling reporters that the scientific staff was 'probably the best that has ever left this country'.

But the RGS needed more substance and soon found that Shackleton's plans were focused almost entirely on the trans-continental crossing. In haste, he began to enlarge on his sketchy outlines and proposed a wider programme of geological, biological, hydrographical and meteorological work.

Shackleton, however, was on weak ground when it came to providing detailed answers. In the absence of precise information he threw up a smokescreen of evasive and vague answers to questions from sceptical RGS members. One recalled the 'impossibility of getting any clear answers' out of Shackleton. Even the specific number of scientists going on the expedition was unclear. At one stage he promised that the combined expedition – the Weddell Sea and Ross Sea parties – was planning to take four geologists, two biologists and a meteorologist and to supplement their work with the support of the 'laymen of the expedition.'

Aware that funding a large-scale scientific programme was beyond his means, Shackleton even tried to use the meeting with the RGS as a platform to attract more backing which, he claimed, would be used to expand the scientific effort. Without too much conviction,

CITY LIBRARY CORK

he said: 'If there is anybody . . . who is ready to put up £10, £20, £30 or £40,000 to aid the scientific side of the expedition, I will take as many geologists as they are ready to provide me with.'[5]

In the event, the burden of Shackleton's expansive scientific agenda in the Weddell Sea fell on the shoulders of only four scientists – the geologist Wordie, the meteorologist Leonard Hussey, the biologist Robert Clark and Reginald 'Jimmy' James, a physicist and friend of Wordie from St John's College, Cambridge.

More surprisingly, Shackleton told the RGS that one of the six-man trans-continental party would be a 'trained glaciologist and geologist', to study ice formations and the mountains ranges likely to be seen for the first time on the journey. 'This man will represent science,' he told the RGS with great enthusiasm. 'Every step taken into the unknown, apart from the sentimental reasons, is an advance to geographical science.'

Shackleton had hinted privately to Wordie that he might take a geologist on the crossing party. But with barely any scientific staff on the books at this stage, the prospect of joining the trans-continental party was probably a simple inducement to recruit Wordie to the expedition and he never seriously intended taking him.

Although Wordie certainly fitted the bill as mountaineer and geologist, Shackleton had already identified the men who would undertake the long march. In an early expedition prospectus, he revealed that five of the party would be Frank Wild, George Marston, Bernard Day, Aeneas Mackintosh and himself. The only clue to the unidentified sixth person was that he had been south before with either Scott or Shackleton. This ruled out Wordie and pointed clearly to one of Priestley, Debenham or Tom Crean. But after Priestley and Debenham declined his invitation to join the expedition, Shackleton re-shaped the six-man trans-continental party as: Wild, Crean, Frank Hurley, Marston, Alexander Macklin and himself.

Despite the paucity of scientists and general indecision Shackleton waited until the eleventh hour before finally approving Wordie's appointment. Indeed, he waited so long that he almost lost his only geologist. Wordie was unaware of Shackleton's manoeuvring and attempts to raise money and without a clear signal of acceptance he began to look elsewhere for an alterative expedition. The chance came at Cambridge. In early 1914, Wordie was given a new post as Demonstrator in Petrology at the university. Soon after he was asked to go to Easter Island in the Pacific with a party under Fred Corry. It was a tempting offer but after due consideration he decided to wait for Shackleton. Corry travelled without Wordie, but was subsequently injured in transit to the Pacific and never reached Easter Island.

Shackleton waited until late June, only a month before the party was due to sail, before confirming the appointment of Wordie as his sole geologist of the Weddell Sea party. But the good news was tempered by a disappointing postscript. In the absence of the more experienced Priestley or Debenham, the ambitious Wordie hoped to be appointed the expedition's chief of scientific staff. But Shackleton gave the job to another geologist, Professor Garwood. Only a few weeks later, however, Garwood withdrew from the expedition and *Endurance* was destined to sail without a head of scientific staff.

Shackleton's response to Garwood's resignation was to decree that there would be no chief of scientific staff. No one, he decided, would have overall responsibility for the elaborate programme and each scientist would be his own master. Wordie swallowed his disappointment and hurried off to make arrangements for the departure of *Endurance*. In Scotland he said his farewells to Alison and Willie, while in London he met his new colleagues, an intoxicating mixture of adventurers, old sweats and earnest academics.

Wordie stood out from the crowd, partly because of his extensive climbing and trekking experience. He was, in fact, almost a model of what the far-sighted Gregory had suggested a Polar explorer should be. Few of the Shackleton party had first-hand knowledge of the ice and crucially, only one other – a marine officer, Thomas Orde-Lees –

had any experience of mountaineering. The only men in the Weddell Sea party with experience of the Polar regions were Shackleton, the two Antarctic veterans Frank Wild and Tom Crean, artist George Marston, and Frank Hurley, the Australian photographer who had been south with Douglas Mawson. Most were scientists, doctors or ordinary seamen who had merely signed up for the round-trip to the Antarctic. The lack of mountaineering experience was a critical deficiency in many Polar expeditions of the time, and Wordie, a seasoned climber, was among the few to recognise the flaw. Many years later, he told friends that Shackleton 'would have got on better if he had been a better mountaineer'.[6]

Wordie's fitness and physique would be important factors on the expedition. At the age of twenty-five, Wordie had filled out, helped by the routine of regular and strenuous exercise in the hills and mountains. Although only standing 5 ft 8½ inches tall, he was a solid broad-shouldered figure endowed with considerable reserves of strength and a firm inner resolve, which would be needed as much as physical fitness in the hostile wilderness. The firmly set jaw gave a slightly forbidding appearance and only the ever-present spectacles – he was short-sighted and wore glasses all his life – offered any hint of weakness. To everyone, Shackleton was known as 'the Boss'. Wordie, compact, neat, bespectacled and with a soft Glaswegian accent, was immediately christened 'Jock'.

Travelling on *Endurance* was to be the greatest adventure of his life and in some ways a means of fulfilling a dream. While he cherished his spells in the Alps and wilder landscapes like the Yukon, Wordie longed for something on a grander scale, and this Shackleton's expedition seemed to offer. He once spent a month poring over Charles Darwin's journal from the *Beagle* journey. In the pages of Darwin's great chronicle he saw his own destiny of one day undertaking a similar voyage of epic proportions. 'I have learnt far more than I ever expected, notably the advantages of making one long sea voyage sometime or other,' he mused.[7]

CHAPTER 4

'THE FATES ARE AGAINST US . . .'

FAR BIGGER ISSUES THAN ANTARCTIC EXPLORATION WERE AT STAKE as *Endurance* was made ready for the long voyage south. In the weeks leading up to departure, Europe had moved inexorably towards war. Archduke Ferdinand, the heir to the Austrian throne, was assassinated in Sarejevo on June 28 and the slow countdown to the Great War started.

Endurance sailed from the Thames on 1 August, the day that Germany declared war on Russia and armies throughout Europe were being mobilised. Shackleton assembled the ship's crew at Margate and announced that anyone who wished to enlist in the services was free to leave. He also cabled the Admiralty, placing the ship and its crew at the government's disposal. Within an hour Shackleton received a laconic, one-word reply to his offer: 'Proceed'. In a detached almost surreal atmosphere, *Endurance* sailed around the coast of southern England, first to Eastbourne then to Plymouth. On 4 August Britain and Germany were officially at war and on 8 August *Endurance* finally left Plymouth for the Antarctic, steaming slowly across the Atlantic towards Buenos Aires.

In charge was Frank Worsley, the New Zealander sailing master. Wordie, Shackleton and several others were travelling independently to South America. Alison thoughtfully gave her brother a reminder of Scotland to take on the voyage. Her farewell present was a Cameron tartan plaid, traditionally worn over the shoulder and breast, which she probably felt would double-up as an extra blanket on freezing nights in the south. Another reminder of his roots which

Wordie took south was a sledging flag emblazoned with St Andrew's cross. By coincidence, the 3ft (1 m) flag was made by Kenning & Co, the Glasgow firm which had made a similar flag for Henry 'Birdie' Bowers from Greenock, one of the men who died with Scott on the return march from the South Pole.

Wordie finally sailed from Liverpool on 19 September, bound for Buenos Aires on the Houlder Line's cargo ship, *La Negra*. Only nine passengers were on board, including Shackleton's deputy, Wild, and the physicist James, plus about seventy dogs destined for the continental crossing. Houlder Line generously gave the men free passages and in return they signed on as 'dog attendants' at a nominal salary.

Alison had flirted with the notion of joining her brother for the long trip to South America. But wiser counsel prevailed and the 19-year-old was persuaded to remain behind. British and German warships were already gathering off the coast of South America in the early days of the war and it was necessary to arm the *La Negra* against possible attack. Initially a squad of Territorials came on board to man the guns, but shortly before sailing two trained gunners from the list of naval reservists were drafted in.

It was a largely uneventful but slightly uncomfortable trip. The 'dog attendants' were kept busy by their noisy, quarrelsome charges, who fought each other constantly and kept their masters awake at night with endless barking. Much of the day in open seas was spent hosing down the filthy decks and keeping a watch for enemy ships. Buenos Aires was finally reached on 11 October, and they found *Endurance* already berthed there.

Shackleton arrived a few days later and immediately began imposing his own discipline and weeding out unruly members of the crew, including the cook. Five seamen were dismissed and Charles Green, a willing merchant-navy cook, was hired. More importantly, Shackleton formally took over the captaincy of *Endurance* from Worsley.

The 42-year-old Worsley was a first-rate sailor but a light-hearted character prone to impetuous behaviour and with little grasp of naval discipline. He was not a natural leader. Heavy drinking among the officers and crew had threatened to get out of control during the trip down to Buenos Aires and at one stop-over in Madeira four men were thrown into jail for wrecking a café in a drunken brawl. Shackleton's decision to take command was well received among the more serious-minded individuals on *Endurance*, including Wordie. He commented: 'It is a much needed change; the ship's crew would have gone to pieces otherwise.'[1]

A more diverting issue was that Shackleton had run out of money. The expedition's finances, like most of Shackleton's money matters, were decidedly shaky. Shackleton's colourful life was littered with half-baked money-making schemes and a scattering of unpaid bills. He once planned to divert a Polar expedition to search for a pirate's buried treasure on a tropical island. In 1909 the government handed over £20,000 (almost £1,000,000 in today's terms) of tax-payers' money to settle a catalogue of outstanding debts from the *Nimrod* expedition and the administration of the Imperial Trans-Antarctic venture had a familiar uncomfortable feel.

In the absence of hard cash, Shackleton usually resorted to his winning charm, great powers of persuasion and a flurry of seemingly plausible promises. James said he was a 'mixture of personal magnetism, bluff and blarney that could be irresistible'. Somehow he had managed to arrange for many of the expedition's supplies to be taken on board without arranging proper payment and the expedition's London offices slowly accumulated more and more bills.

The chaotic financial mess must have appalled Wordie, who was more accustomed to Scots prudence and had a strong family aversion to debts. He once wrote: 'I doubt if he [Shackleton] would ever have made a businessman or been able to run whaling ventures with any success.'[2] But Wordie was a generous spirit. On the eve of sailing he was informed that *Endurance* badly needed more money to buy coal for the voyage; without hesitation he kindly offered to help. In his diary he reported: 'I had an important talk with Shackleton after breakfast and made an offer to advance him some money as more had been done in port here than he bargained for. He accepted my offer on the understanding that I can get the money drafted over. It does not amount to very much but will get him out of a hole without raising trouble in London.'[3] The sum – estimated to be $25 – was insignificant compared to the overall costs of the expedition. But it demonstrated that, on the eve of departure, the expedition's affairs were still in a highly precarious state and strangely dependent on a modest $25 money-order from a benevolent member of the party.

However, even this simple transaction was not straightforward and the British Consul in Buenos Aires was called in to help smooth things over. Wordie was excused all ship's duties and despatched to town to have his signature witnessed by the Consul and to finalise details of the money transfer. While waiting for the paperwork to be completed, Wordie slipped away and bought some extra geological hammers. Freed from immediate financial worries, final preparations were made for early departure.

The weather, which would have a major bearing on the trip south, was the main preoccupation as *Endurance* prepared to sail. Constant rain, which the locals said was abnormal for that time of the year, had dogged their stay in Buenos Aires and did not bode well for the journey through the Weddell Sea. Wordie remembered the warning of Mossman, one of the few to have sailed into the Weddell. In a prophetic entry, he wrote in his diary: 'The people here say it is most unusual weather. Mossman's explanation, of course, is that it is due to the ice not having broken out of the Weddell Sea this season and if his theory correct, it may quite easily prevent our getting down to Coats Land (on the Antarctic mainland) this season.'[4]

At one of the last celebratory dinners, the expedition was given a painful reminder of the perils of Polar exploration when they met

Colonel David Brainard, an elderly American with a salutary tale to tell. Brainard was one of only seven survivors from the twenty-six members of the horrific Greely expedition to Ellesmere Island in the Arctic in the early 1880s. Putting Brainard's grim story, which featured lingering starvation, a summary execution and dark suspicions of cannibalism, to the backs of their minds, the expedition set sail.

The original plan was to sail *Endurance* to the Falkland Islands and pick up the last supplies before heading into the Weddell Sea. But a build-up of German battleships elsewhere in the South Atlantic prompted a change of plan. The expedition, with twenty-seven men on board, left Buenos Aires on 26 October and turned towards South Georgia, the most southerly point in the Empire. In search of an appropriate send-off, a thoughtful Argentine band played a rousing rendition of 'It's a Long Way to Tipperary'. 'We fully expect heavy seas to come washing over the bows and the waist of the ship,' Wordie told his diary in a classic understatement of the trials of crossing the dangerous Southern Ocean.

On the third day out, a stowaway was discovered in a locker. The young man was Percy Blackborrow, a 19-year-old steward fresh from the White Star Line's *Golden Gate*, who had attempted to join the ship in Buenos Aires but was turned down. It was too late to turn back and Shackleton's dark warning to Blackborrow was that stowaways were always the first to be eaten if the expedition ran out of food.

The Imperial Trans-Antarctic Expedition party now stood at twenty-eight explorers, sailors, scientists and a stowaway. But after months of preparation, the entire party was delighted that the enterprise was finally under way in earnest. Wordie captured the optimistic mood when he wrote: 'What a difference there is in the feelings of everyone, now that we have gone to seas! Crean and Marston have begun to sing at their work and there is an end to all complaints.'[5]

South Georgia, with its bustling whaling stations, was the ideal place to pick up last supplies and gather valuable information about ice conditions in the Weddell Sea, which blocked their path to the Antarctic mainland. The whalers, who had first arrived on the island a decade earlier, had more knowledge and experience of the local ice than anyone alive. But the wisdom they dispensed was unpalatable. At the port of Grytviken, surrounded by the natural theatre of majestic black mountains and reeling from the gut-wrenching stench of rotting whaleflesh, the men listened as the whalers delivered a bleak warning. The ice in the Weddell, they said, was heavier and packed further north than anyone could remember. The unmistakeable threat was that *Endurance* risked becoming trapped in the ice if the expedition sailed into the Weddell.

The Weddell Sea is a vast basin of mostly impenetrable ice, surrounded on three sides by Coats Land, the Filchner and Ronne ice shelves and the spindly Antarctic Peninsula, which stretches out towards the tip of South America. It is a graveyard for ships. Previous forays into the treacherous waters had suffered badly. Otto Nordenskjold's *Antarctic* was lost off Paulet Island in 1903 and only two years before the *Endurance* expedition, in 1912, Wilheim Filchner's ship, *Deutschland*, was trapped in the ice for nine months before breaking free.

Currents from the east drive the seas in a clockwise direction, slowly churning the ice south to the Flincher Ice Shelf and west up the long peninsula before resuming the drive down the eastern flanks of the continent. Sir Joseph Hooker, the botanist who had first experienced the seas with Sir James Clark Ross in the 1840s, described the Weddell as 'repellent'. The sea was first discovered in 1823 by the Scottish naval captain, James Weddell, who originally named it after George IV. By the time it was given Weddell's name in 1900, the waters had earned a ferocious reputation and even today modern ice-breaking ships rarely penetrate the Weddell. But as 1914 drew to a close the wooden barquentine *Endurance* was poised to enter the ice without the benefit of accurate charts and little scope for rescue if anything went awry.

Endurance, a 300-ton sailing ship with auxiliary power, was built in 1913 at the Norwegian whaling port of Sandefjord and was designed for Arctic waters. The vessel was born on the back of an optimistic business scheme and was now poised to make her maiden voyage in another equally optimistic venture. Originally named *Polaris*, the ship was the creation of a Norwegian shipowner, Lars Christensen, and the Belgian explorer, Adrien de Gerlache. They had devised an ambitious scheme to run Polar 'safaris' to places like Spitsbergen and East Greenland for well-heeled amateur adventurers in search of the ultimate trip or game hunting. But the idea fell flat and Shackleton snapped up the redundant vessel. He changed her name to *Endurance* to reflect his family's motto – *Fortitudine Vincimus* (By endurance we conquer).

Shackleton was impatient to get under way, heedless of the warnings about the ice conditions. Ignoring the whalers' advice, *Endurance* sailed from Grytviken at 8.45 in the morning of 5 December 1914, severing the last links with the outside world. Tucked away among his personal gear and scientific equipment, Wordie had packed a neatly folded flag of the Scottish lion. Two hours after *Endurance* disappeared over the southern horizon the mail ship, carrying the last letters from home, steamed into Grytviken.

After weeks of delay and hanging around, the men were glad to be finally under way and any lingering apprehension about entering the Weddell seemed to have disappeared. Wordie, too, seemed oblivious to the imminent danger, writing, 'We bowl along at a good pace and feel that as regards weather we are very lucky.'[6]

Flat-topped tabular icebergs were spotted only two days into the journey south, and on the third the loose pack loomed out of the sea to present a tricky pathway directly ahead. Shackleton, apparently forgetting the whalers' warnings, expressed surprise to find the pack ice so far to the north. Across the horizon on the same day, British and German warships were engaged in the bloody Battle of the Falklands and the expedition's decision to avoid the area by sailing direct to South Georgia seemed an inspired choice.

Progress south was slow until early January, when the ice began to break apart and Coats Land, first discovered a decade earlier by Bruce, came into view on 10 January. Two days later they passed Bruce's 'furthest south' and Wordie cheerfully recorded that the party was 'in great spirits.' Optimism spread further at the exhilaration of entering virgin waters and catching sight of previously unseen land. Shackleton named it the Caird Coast after Sir James Caird, the philanthropic Dundee jute millionaire whose personal fortune and great generosity had largely paid for the expedition.

This was the decisive moment in the Imperial Trans-Antarctic Expedition. As *Endurance* edged along the imposing white cliffs of the Caird Coast, a possible landing place was spotted. There was a natural bay formed by a 400 ft (120 m) high glacier spewing out from the mainland which offered a safe haven for the ship.

Worsley urged Shackleton to seize the moment and establish his winter base camp in the bay. While Shackleton fully recognised that it would be an excellent choice, he resisted the temptation to land. Instead, he wanted to make for Vahsel Bay, about 200 miles (320 km) further south, largely on the grounds that it would cut 200 miles off the proposed trans-continental crossing. Hindsight shows that it was a mistake and the turning point in the *Endurance* saga.

The ship battled south, struggling to steer clear of the giant bergs on all sides. Wordie estimated the length of one mighty floating island at over 20 miles (32 km). But the immediate problem was the strong north-east wind, which was inexorably driving the ice – and *Endurance* – towards the land. There was little concern. Vahsel Bay, at the southern tip of Coats Land, was just 80 miles (128 km) away, close to the start of the Filchner Ice Shelf. In normal seas, it was less than a day's sailing. Most men anticipated landing in a day or two and supply boxes were being labelled 'ship' and 'shore'. Wordie optimistically had his hair cut short on the grounds that he would be too busy unloading supplies and equipment in the next few days and would have little time for niceties.

The following day *Endurance* came to a halt in the heavy pack ice. The ship initially sheltered among a scattering of smaller floes, but the strong north-easterly wind was still driving the ice towards land. Caught in the middle between the ice and the land was *Endurance*. During the night ice closed in all around the ship and from the crow's nest the view on the morning of 19 January was a bleak one of unbroken ice as far as the eye could sea. All lanes of open water had disappeared and *Endurance* was stuck fast. Wordie noted that 'the fates are still against us'. He formally recorded their position as 76° 34′ S, 31° 18′ W. Another interpretation was that *Endurance* and its crew of twenty-eight were 1,500 miles (2,400 km) from the nearest human settlement and surrounded by about 1,000,000 square miles of freezing seas.

'Being tied up so near our goal is very disappointing,' Wordie wrote. Hurley, the photographer, said the idea of being ice-bound was 'extremely unpleasant', but he was optimistic they would soon be released and return to open waters in the north. 'Spent most of the day letter writing in anticipation of the ship returning to South Georgia,' he wrote on 20 January. On the same day Orde-Lees came to the conclusion that, with the temperature at the fairly high level of 29° F (-2° C), there was 'no fear' of getting frozen in.

By an ironic quirk of fate, *Endurance* was actually drifting slowly towards the party's goal of Vahsel Bay. Although stuck firmly in the ice, the ship was carried southwards in the direction of Vahsel by the underlying currents of the Weddell. From the crow's nest it was possible to glimpse the landing spot, only 60 miles (95 km) away. At one point it was suggested that the men should abandon *Endurance* and trek across the ice to Vahsel, erect the hut and sit out the winter. But a round trip of 120 miles (190 km) with tons of supplies across the broken, hummocky ice was quickly ruled out as hopelessly impractical. *Endurance* was not equipped with lightweight kayaks, which could be carried on sledges and used to cross any open lanes of water they might meet on the journey. Without kayaks they risked getting marooned.

Slowly it began to dawn on the men that they were stranded. A gloom began to descend on the party and Wordie noted 'a wave of depression seemed to come over everybody on board: it was soon noticed that it was best not to get in the Boss's way. It certainly looked as if we might not get out of this flow before the winter and might spend the next nine months drifting north.'[7]

Shackleton, in public at least, was more optimistic and on 14 February he ordered a major attempt to break out from their imprisonment. The ship raised steam and the men took to the ice with picks and saws to cut a channel through to a nearby pool of young ice which offered a slim chance of escape. It was, Shackleton noted, 'terrific labour', but 400 yards (365 m) of stubborn ice still separated the ship from freedom. Every opening soon froze over in the low temperatures and reluctantly the work was abandoned.

In more typical weather, *Endurance* might have struggled free. But the warmer temperatures had given way to colder weather and by late February, when the waters ought to have been more navigable, the ice was already a foot thick. A few days later the ice-bound ship drifted past the longitude of Vahsel Bay, some 60 miles (95 km) to the south and on 22 February *Endurance* reached the latitude of 77° S – the expedition's most southerly point. Wordie said most of the men were 'reconciled to the prospect' of spending the winter drifting along in the ice and a few days later on 1 March he said the hope of being freed 'has now been given up'. Reconciled or not, it was a depressing prospect.

Endurance ceased to observe ship's routine and a thorough review of food and fuel supplies was ordered. Men scoured the ice for seals and penguins and the resourceful carpenter, Henry 'Chippy' McNish, built kennels on the ice for the dogs, which were soon known as 'dogloos'. The scientists, for the most part, continued their work, examining the ice, taking weather readings or depth soundings. But there was little work for a geologist on a drifting ice-floe and Wordie soon adapted himself to other tasks like studying the behaviour of ice. Anxious to keep busy, he also found time to assist Clark in taking depths or testing water samples.

Shackleton understood the need to keep the men busy, regardless of their qualifications. All hands participated in hunting for food and general tasks around the ship, while regular games of football were played during the daylight hours and lusty sing-songs were heard after dinner, helped by the energetic banjo-playing of Hussey.

However, there was some tension between the crew and the scientists. Many of the seamen were rough trawlermen or crusty seafarers who had few points of reference with academic types like Wordie, James or Clark. The cramped quarters below decks made matters worse and, only two weeks after *Endurance* was beset, Hurley casually observed that the crew were 'not altogether partial to the scientists'.

Shackleton's handling of the motley collection was remarkable and he deployed his superb man-management skills to defuse any tension. Always attentive, he somehow succeeded in making each man feel he was as important as the next and that there were no favourites. Everyone ate the same food and when winter clothing was distributed Shackleton made sure the crew were supplied before the officers and scientists. At night he would readily chat with either sailor or scholar.

All hands, from trawlerman to geologist, were required to do their share of menial tasks like scrubbing the floors, and at one point Shackleton himself set an example by helping to lay some linoleum. The scientists shared the mundane chores and occasionally the seamen helped take scientific readings. Hurley took an illuminating photograph one day, which showed the egalitarian nature of life on board. In the picture three men are on their knees energetically scrubbing the floor – the scholarly Wordie, the surgeon Alexander Macklin and Alf Cheetham, an old sweat who was making his fourth voyage to the Antarctic.

The marooned men rubbed along together, more or less in unison. The diaries written at the time reflect a general air of harmony, punctuated only by brief displays of bad behaviour, invariably nipped in the bud before they blossomed into anything more serious. Certainly the initial rancour some of the crew felt towards the scientists was never allowed to develop. Meals were held at regular times to preserve some degree of discipline; each man's birthday was celebrated in style; all types of entertainment, ranging from nightly sing-songs to lavish concert parties and lantern slide lectures, were arranged to keep minds active.

Wordie's diary provides one of the most comprehensive and detailed accounts of the expedition. Although not as frank and personal as the journal kept by the eccentric Orde-Lees, it is more detailed and thorough. Wordie was accustomed to keeping records and the diary – he called it the Weddell Sea Log – is an important record of the expedition. (See Appendix, page 276.) One typical entry – made in February 1915 – discusses matters as varied as Shackleton's mood, the thickness of the ice and the feral behaviour of the dogs, before concluding with a list of the men and positions in the two football teams who played a match on the ice that day. Even the names of the referee and linesmen are faithfully recorded.

On 3 April Wordie's diary recorded a largely unnoticed but significant change of orders from the Boss. On that day, Shackleton handed the responsibility for the care and exercise of the remaining sixty dogs to six hand-picked men – Wild, Crean, Marston, McIlroy, Macklin and Hurley. The significance of the order was not lost on Wordie, who noted, 'Change the Boss for one of these and I think the personnel of the transcontinental party will be complete.'[8]

At this point, Shackleton still clung to the belief that *Endurance* would emerge after the winter entrapment and that the coast-to-coast crossing could be resurrected the following year. In preparation he had nominated five of the six destined for the trek, with James McIlroy the doctor temporarily standing in for himself in the dog-handling party. Any half-hearted notions of taking the geologist Wordie on the journey had been officially dumped. However, Wordie's noting of the decision suggests that his desire to tackle the Antarctic's western territories was still alive.

Wordie made another noteworthy diary entry on 3 April. He had been on watch at 4 o'clock in the morning when he detected faint rumbling noises from underneath the ship. It was the first sign of ice pressure slowly building up around *Endurance* and he wrote, 'I was convinced that heavy pressure was going on and was able to verify this afternoon that such had been the case.'[9] Wordie had detected the first clear indication that *Endurance* was now under threat from the slow build-up of pressure from the ice. Luckily, he added, the pressure was 'some little distance from the ship'.

CHAPTER 5

CAST ADRIFT

Endurance WAS TRAPPED LIKE A TWIG FROZEN IN A WINTRY POND. The difference was that the Weddell Sea was constantly on the move. The ship, snared by the ice, drifted slowly, first in a south-westerly direction along the face of the mainland and then northward in a mazy journey which ran in parallel with the Antarctic Peninsula. The initial concern was that, unless released, the great mass of ice would start to jam against the landmass and *Endurance* would be smashed like a matchwork model in the pressure. *Endurance's* gradual journey north was a torture, especially for the scientists and doctors, who found time passed very slowly without the demands of regular work. Naturally enough, these men – Wordie, Clark, James, Hussey and the two doctors, McIlroy and Macklin – tended to gravitate towards each other.

Wordie was particularly close to James and Clark. The three academics had much in common and were drawn together by their middle-class backgrounds and a shared familiarity with life in university cloisters. With his fellow Scot, Clarke, Wordie occupied a tiny cubicle on *Endurance*, which was christened 'Auld Reekie', the Scots slang for a foul-smelling hovel.

Robert Selbie Clark, the shrewd 32-year-old biologist, was a dry Aberdonian of few words with an unquenchable appetite for his work. He spent hours with dredging nets or dissecting specimens and came to the expedition on the positive recommendation of Bruce. Clark was a last-minute addition to the party. Shackleton had great difficulty finding a biologist and only managed to persuade him to take up the post shortly before *Endurance* sailed from Plymouth to Buenos Aires. Wordie's sardonic comment was that Clark was a 'pier-head jump at Plymouth'. Earnest and thoughtful, he was animated only by his work. On one occasion the crew tricked him into great excitement by secretly placing spaghetti into a jar of formaldehyde and telling him they had discovered something weird. Despite the all-round hilarity, Clark was not amused by the incident.

The physicist, Reginald 'Jimmy' James came from Wordie's own college of St John's. James was a brilliant but serious and reserved scholar who had spent his adult life buried in academia and lacked worldly wisdom. The youthful James, peering anxiously from behind his heavy spectacles, was often easy prey for the old salts with their honours degrees in the university of life. Wordie was especially fond of the 23-year-old James, who was another to join *Endurance* after a baffling interview with Shackleton which had centred on whether James enjoyed good circulation. When James replied that he had a little finger which went dead in cold weather, Shackleton casually asked if he would seriously mind losing it. Not once did he ask about physics.[1]

Shackleton had no gut feeling for science – unlike his rival Scott – and he did not naturally warm to the scientists, which may explain his unusual style of interviewing candidates. Yet he once held the post of secretary to the Royal Scottish Geographical Society and on *Discovery*, his first trip to the Antarctic, was briefly in charge of taking water samples. James, a perceptive observer of character, said that Shackleton had 'very little sympathy with the scientific point of view and had no ideas about scientific methods'. According to James, he had little patience with the academic mind and 'would openly ridicule it'. James admired Shackleton's leadership but was irritated by his habit of playing practical jokes on the scientists, which created 'something of an antagonism' between the seamen and the scholars. 'This kind of thing can be overdone and I sometimes think that Shackleton sometimes overdid it,' James concluded.[2]

Wordie understood the flaw in Shackleton's make-up but was more obliging. He once wrote, 'In the case of an exploration journey, the journey itself is science and any discoveries which can be made should be treated as scientific.'[3] It may be, however, that dour Scots – Wordie and Clark – and serious-minded scholars like James had little in common with a restless cavalier like Shackleton and it would be wrong to assume he disliked all scientists. One of Shackleton's oldest friends was Hugh Mill, a distinguished meteorologist and geographer as well as being head librarian at the RGS. Shackleton was more comfortable with the Polar hard-nuts and explorers like Wild and Crean or lifelong seafarers like Worsley. It is no surprise that Shackleton's book on the Imperial Trans-Antarctic Expedition, *South*, contains only five cursory mentions of Wordie and even fewer of Clark and James.

Others took a more considerate view and found Wordie's even temper and gentle humour useful assets in the close confines of the ship, where idleness and boredom could cause friction. Orde-Lees, an oddball marine captain who joined the expedition as a ski expert, said that Wordie possessed 'a most amiable temperament and a wonderful fund of very dry humour'. He concluded: 'Taking him all round he is at once the most inoffensive and one of the most popular of our members. He has no use of cliques, which have unfortunately developed a little and are well known to be the bane of expeditionary life.'[4]

Orde-Lees had great sympathy for Wordie, the geologist trapped at sea. Wordie had not seen as much as a pebble since leaving South Georgia and was the most pitied man on the expedition, according to the sardonic Orde-Lees. Wordie, he explained, had access only to 'a small stone or two found in an iceberg and the contents of the penguins' stomachs.' He added: 'In default of rocks to vent his spleen on "Jock" has made a great study of glaciology and I have no doubt that with his keen philosophical judgement he will produce a book of great merit upon this interesting and little known subject.'[5]

Living quarters were cramped but made comfortable by little additions such as bookshelves and a 'bonded' section where Wordie and Clark stored their precious hoard of tobacco and matches. Above his bed Wordie pinned reminders of the family – photographs of his father and Alison.

While the imprisonment was deeply frustrating, the men were well fed and reasonably comfortable. Poor or inadequate food and uncomfortable living quarters were potential causes of discontent during the confinement and Shackleton knew the value of keeping his men happy. He knew there would be few complaints from adequately-clad men with full stomachs. Wordie, with typical thoroughness, recorded a typical day's diet, which seems more suitable for heavy labour or the torture of man-hauling sledges over the ice:

Breakfast:

9.0 a.m.   Porridge with milk and sugar.
            Fish, or curry, or seal-steak, or liver and bacon, etc.
            Bread; butter; jam; tea and coffee.

Lunch:

1.0 p.m   Hoosh, varying from day to day: either of seal, pea soup, etc; many vegetables always; sometimes a little pemmican put in as well.
            Ship's biscuit; bread; jam; Golden syrup (No butter except at breakfast; we are short).

Tea:

3.45 p.m   Tea and biscuits: (a whack of 2 per man if these are 'Digestive')

Dinner:

6 p.m.   Meat: potatoes, preserved or roasted; vegetable. Dough or rice or vermicelli or bottled fruits, etc. (Syrup only with dough).
            Tea or cocoa. (Cake and spirits on birthdays).'[6]

To the naked eye, *Endurance* was stationary, locked in a dry dock of endless ice. Only the sightings of James and Worsley told a different story of the slow daily drift to the north. In bed one night Wordie read Leopold McLintock's *Voyage of the Fox*, the expedition which partly solved the mysterious disappearance of Sir John Franklin's party of 129 men and two ships in the Arctic during the 1840s. The *Fox* was trapped for eight months in the ice of Baffin Bay and Wordie saw other gloomy parallels with *Endurance*. The *Fox* contained twenty-six men compared with *Endurance*'s twenty-eight and Wordie confided to his diary: 'There are the same expectations of early freedom during the first month's imprisonment, the same anxiety about cracks forming near the ship and similar dread of stranded bergs.'[7]

Both expeditions also shared concerns about the slow build-up of ice pressure. McLintock described the sounds of mounting pressure as the 'continued roar of distant surf' or as if 'trains of heavy wagons with ungreased axles were slowly labouring along'. Wordie contented himself with the hope that the men on *Endurance* might have 'as safe a winter' as McLintock.

Winter in the Weddell Sea brought a distinct worsening in the weather conditions. By early June, the depth of winter, temperatures had dropped sharply and winds had increased, occasionally screeching to 70 mph. At the same time, the combination of currents and wind began to dislodge the ice, replacing solid pack ice with a broken jumble of ice blocks and mounds which piled up on each other like the toy bricks of a child.

The grinding movement of the ice, making eerie sounds that echoed across the white landscape, caused a slow build-up of pressure during the winter months. Wordie heard the 'ungreased axles' in the distance and noted that a 9 ft (2.7 m) ridge of ice had formed not far from the ship. Hurley said it was difficult to believe the ship, stuck fast, was drifting in the heart of the Weddell. But drifting it was, slowly north. Since becoming trapped six months earlier, the ship had drifted almost 700 miles (1,100 km) with the current and the grinding, rumbling pressure was getting perceptibly stronger. On

23 July an emergency stack of sledging provisions was placed on deck in case the ship became nipped in the ice and toppled over.

Pressure began to crack the floe which encased *Endurance* and on 1 August the men rushed on deck to watch the drama as the ship was lifted bodily out of the water. Shackleton said mighty blocks of ice jumped up like cherry-stones squeezed between thumb and forefinger.

The sides of *Endurance* began to give under the strain and the linoleum, which Shackleton had helped to lay only a few months earlier, crinkled up at the edges as the walls of the ship were pressed inwards. For the first time the men began to ponder the awful prospect of abandoning the ship. Under attack from the pressure, *Endurance* was tilted at a 10° angle and McNish placed pictures of his loved one inside his Bible. It was exactly one year to the day since *Endurance* sailed from London Docks full of hope and expectation.

Miraculously, the weather improved and the pressure eased. By the end of August, with spring approaching, some optimism had returned and a few men were cheerfully taking bets on when the ship would be released. Shackleton now calculated they were perhaps only 250 miles (400 km) from the nearest land and 500 miles (900 km) from the nearest outpost of civilisation on the Antarctic Peninsula, where the whaling ships from South Georgia were regular visitors. The calculations were slightly illusory, however. Land may have been within reach, but the only way to find it was by abandoning the ship and trekking over hundreds of miles of broken ice. It was an appalling prospect. 'I hoped fervently that we should not have to undertake a march across moving ice-fields,' Wordie wrote in his diary.

Towards the end of September the grinding ice began to strike again and *Endurance* shook under the intense strain. On board, the mood swung again and became increasingly pessimistic. Wordie was particularly exasperated by the confinement and boredom. In one entry he wrote wearily that 'We have practically nothing to show' for the year away. He added: 'Had we been favoured with a successful year – gone sledging, opened up new country – I suppose it would have been different, but I confess to a certain feeling of shame at our failure.'[8] It was a gloom shared by James, who wrote, 'I'll be blowed if I want to see any more ice as long as live!'

In early October, *Endurance* remained locked in the drifting ice while all around small open leads of water appeared. Hopes of an early release were dashed a few days later when a huge build-up of pressure struck, lifting the ship out of the water like a model. *Endurance* lurched at a crazy angle of 30° and dogs, supply boxes and men were scattered across the decks. Towards the end of October, the timbers on *Endurance* began to buckle under the strain and water poured into the holds. McNish knew enough about the sea to conclude that it was 'all up with the ship'.

Below decks, men toiled up to their waists in freezing water, trying to plug the leaks and others began gathering up food, clothes and the three small lifeboats in preparation for abandoning the ship. Worsley grabbed all the charts and maps he could lay his hands on and even ripped pages from the library of Polar books which might contain odd clues to the local geography. The end was approaching and Shackleton wrote that the ship was the 'embodiment of helpless futility'. Wordie simply recalled, 'In a few minutes we were preparing for the worst.'[9]

The pressure intensified and timbers snapped with a sound like gunshots, sending torrents of cold water pouring into the stricken ship. On the ice, the men watched an extraordinary scene – a group of eight emperor penguins shuffled alongside and began wailing a strange lament. No one had heard penguins make such a sound before and Tom McLeod, a deeply superstitious Scots seaman, solemnly warned it was a signal that none of the men would ever see their homes again.

The final assault on *Endurance* was brutal. The stern was pushed upwards, the decks and keel began to buckle and snap and water flooded in, rendering the pumps utterly useless. Wordie recalled the scene:

> At 2.0 pm the pressure started which has given the ship its death blow. It drove us along the crack athwart the bows, raising the stern clean out of the water: the rudder and propeller were buried in a maze of pressure blocks – a sorry sight they were in.
>
> Then came the news – the water was gaining on us, though all three pumps were working. Orders given to put dogs out on the floe: we then knew that matters were serious. And so till 4.45 when we had a spell off for tea.[10]

Pumping was stopped soon after and at around 5 o'clock in the evening of 27 October, Shackleton gave the order to abandon ship. It was a timely move because soon after the ice moved in for the kill. Worsley wrote in his diary, 'The ship was not abandoned one hour too soon, for shortly after we had camped on the floe we could hear the crushing & smashing of her beams & timbers.'[11]

Wordie said that 'everything had come too quickly to make us pause to regret' and predicted that the work ahead would be 'frightfully hard'. Sitting in a tent on the ice that night, he added: 'The programme of the future is simple: to discard all unnecessary gear – my gold watch may have to go; to sledge and boat westwards to the land; and once there to try and make Snow Hill.'[12]

Endurance's position was 69° 5′ S, 51° 32′ W, an area of sea where no ship had ever travelled before. Hundreds of miles away to the immediate west was the unknown area of the Antarctic Peninsula and about 350 miles (560 km) to the north-west were the uninhabited Snow Hill and Paulet islands, two tiny specks at the tip of the Peninsula where it was known a hut and supplies were stored. Beneath their feet the ice-floe offered only a flimsy sense of security. The thickness of the floe was between 3 ft and 10 ft (1–3 m) and underneath lay the black chilly depths of the Weddell Sea. Clark's last sounding, taken exactly a month earlier on 28 September, had established the depth in the area at 1,876 fathoms – 11,256 ft (3,430 m) or more than two miles.

Few managed a decent sleep on the first night on the ice. It was, said Wordie, an 'uneasy . . . awful night of suspense'. Several times during the night the men were forced to move camp because worrying cracks appeared on the ice. The thought of two miles of ocean beneath their sleeping bags was not conducive to gentle slumber. Only five tents were available for the twenty-eight men and Wordie was crammed into a small hoop tent with Wild, McNish and McIlroy. Unhappily there were only eighteen of the warm reindeer-fur sleeping bags and the others had to make do with woollen bags, which offered less protection against the cold and held the damp. Shackleton wisely drew lots to select the unlucky ten.

A short distance away *Endurance* was clearly in her death throes, the timbers groaning and crackling under the weight of the assaults from the pressure. At 7 o'clock in the morning the main mast came crashing down. The imminent demise of *Endurance* was a devastating blow, both to the sailors who mourned the loss of their ship and to Shackleton, whose ambitions were being ground to matchwood by the Weddell Sea.

But the peril of their position and the urgent need to take harsh decisions left little time to dwell on the loss. Initially it was proposed to haul two of the ship's three lifeboats across the ice towards the Roberston Island area, which lay about 250 miles (400 km) to the north-west. By travelling progressively west it was hoped to counter the northerly drift and bring the castaways somewhere close to Graham Land at the top of the Peninsula. It was, by any standards, an optimistic scheme, which offered little but the dire prospect of months of back-breaking labour over appalling terrain. It also meant some heartbreaking choices.

Shackleton told the men that nothing was of value if it worked against their survival, which meant that everything but essential supplies had to be ditched to save weight. Each man was given a new set of winter clothing and allowed to carry only 2 lb (0.9 kg) of personal possessions. Shackleton set the mood by tossing his own gold watch and a few gold sovereigns onto the snow. He ripped a single page from the ship's Bible, which contained a highly pertinent verse from the Book of Job:

> Out of whose womb came the ice?
> And the hoary frost of Heaven, who hath gendered it?
> The waters are hid as with a stone.
> And the face of the deep is frozen.

What Shackleton did not spot was McLeod, who considered it bad luck to throw away a Bible. When no one was looking, McLeod picked up the Bible and tucked it inside his jacket. There were official exceptions to the rule. Hussey was allowed to keep his banjo, the doctors held onto their surgical instruments and McNish kept a few important tools. Those who kept diaries, like Wordie, were permitted to keep them.

All around, the ice was littered with books, unwanted clothing, personal keepsakes and boxes of gear. Wordie tossed away the new geological hammers bought in Buenos Aires. To emphasise the point that only the strongest would survive, the weakest dogs were shot. Mrs Chippy, McNish's much-loved ship's cat, was also destroyed on the grounds that the remaining dogs would rip the animal to pieces when their own food began to run out.

McNish was a tower of strength, working slavishly to attach strengthened sledge runners beneath the two lifeboats, which it was hoped would glide over the ice. On 30 October the boats were loaded and Shackleton drew loud cheers when he shouted: 'Now we start for Roberston Island, boys.'[13]

The men were split into three parties of trail-breakers, haulers and dog handlers. Wordie, with his valuable climbing experience, was selected for the pioneering party who went ahead, breaking the ground and attempting to make the broken surface as smooth as possible for those hauling the boats. Alongside were Shackleton, Hussey, and the engineers Rickinson and Kerr. Behind came two dog teams followed by a gang of fifteen men yoked in a harness dragging the heavy boats. The procession of men, dogs and boats stretched in a line about half a mile over the ice. Hacking a path was difficult enough, but the boat haulers struggled the hardest, dragging the first boat a few hundred yards and then returning to repeat the slog with the second. Often the men sank deep into the snow and collapsed exhausted after only a few hundred paces.

The toil was far harder than anyone expected, partly because the men were out of condition after months of idleness. Wordie summed up the work: 'Deep soft snow; hard going.'[14] It was also a futile exercise. It was calculated at the outset that up to five miles (8 km) a day might be managed. At best, this implied almost two months of punishing work to cover the 250 miles (400 km) to Robertson Island. At the end of the first day it was discovered that the party had covered barely one mile (1.6 km). Next day brought another huge physical effort and the shattering realisation that they had advanced only another mile. Next morning the march was abandoned. Wordie wrote, 'To sledge to the land dragging the boats will be too big a task.'[15]

While the enormous effort may have been fruitless, Shackleton's motives have perhaps been misunderstood. He was desperate to keep up morale and badly needed to demonstrate that, despite their grim plight, the party were capable of survival. The boat-hauling journey not only kept their minds off their predicament, it also gave some hope that the men could influence their own destiny.

After abandoning the boat march, the men began to build a more stable, permanent home on the ice. Parties went back to the broken *Endurance* to salvage any food or gear and the third lifeboat was also recovered. Even a few books were retrieved and Wordie optimistically concluded that 'things look more promising'.

One item salvaged from the ship was the tartan plaid which Alison gave Wordie shortly before he left Britain. The plaid's decorative role was now at an end and Wordie saw a more practical purpose for the garment. Helped by the resourceful McNish, he made a shirt and trousers from the cloth. With the colder weather approaching, he admitted that 'any extra clothing will be only too welcome'.

The party was now in a quandary. On the one hand, they could wait for the northerly drift to carry them to open waters. Their new home, called Ocean Camp, would suffice while the northerly drift carried them slowly into warmer waters, where the boats could be launched for Snow Hill or Paulet Island at the tip of the Antarctic Peninsula.

On the other, there was the option of using the dense pack ice as a pathway to freedom. This would involve leaving the boats behind and marching due west to the Graham Land area with lighter sledges. It all hinged on the stubborn ice remaining unbroken. Worsley admitted it was a 'risky' notion. But Wordie was horrified at the prospect of traversing completely unknown territory and running the terrible risk of finding large leads of open water blocking the way west. The party might get caught in no-man's-land and Wordie concluded, 'I hope it will never happen.'

Before the choice was made the party had to contend with the psychological blow of losing *Endurance*. To many the ship was a symbol of defiance. But the end came shortly before 5 p.m. on 21 November and Wordie recorded the sombre moment: 'The stern went right up till she almost made an angle of 45°; but her head was going down all the time and about ten minutes after the first alarm, the last of the stern sank from view. So she completes her first and last voyage and sinks beaten in fair fight only after a fine struggle.'[16]

A few days later an air of maritime normality was restored when the three lifeboats were christened and crews were selected for the moment when it was hoped they could be launched. The largest, which had been built in London to Worsley's specifications, was called the *James Caird* after the expedition's principal benefactor.

Next came the *Dudley Docker,* which bore the name of the Midlands industrialist who had made a significant contribution to the expedition's costs. The smallest was the *Stancomb Wills,* named after Janet Stancomb-Wills, the elderly adopted daughter of the Wills tobacco millionaire who had succumbed to Shackleton's charm and generously donated money to the cause.

But without a dramatic break-up of the ice, a boat trip remained a remote possibility. Shackleton sensed that a long spell of idleness at Ocean Camp, waiting for the drift to carry them to open water, was a recipe for disaster. After talks with Wild it was agreed that a further spell of hard work was necessary and that the party would start the march westwards to Graham Land.

Wordie, who was not a member of Shackleton's inner circle of confidants, assumed the real reason for the march was to offset a noticeable change in the drift to a more easterly direction. The fear, he said, was that the northerly drift was being checked and the slight alteration of course would take the party away from Paulet Island and other islands at the top of the Peninsula. It was desperately heavy labour. Shackleton's optimistic assumption was a march of two to three miles (3.2 to 4.8 km) a day. Once again, only two boats were taken and a hopeful message was left in the *Stancomb Wills,* which revealed details of their plans to reach Paulet Island. It ended on the singularly optimistic note: 'All well'.

Paulet Island was almost 250 miles (400 km) away and the daily struggle gave precious little hope of ever reaching it. On 29 December a quick study of the immediate surroundings showed a bleak outlook. The ice ahead, in Shackleton's words, was 'quite unnegotiable'. Even more disturbing was the sight of some areas of thin ice and narrow leads of water which were either too fragile to bear the weight of a boat or too narrow for a vessel to navigate safely. Shackleton promptly abandoned the march and retreated half a mile to firmer ice.

The march had taken a heavy toll of the men and brought the first signs of mutiny. McNish, recognising the futility of the boat-hauling, once refused Worsley's order to continue the pointless slog and threatened the first serious breakdown of discipline. Shackleton had to quell the mutiny before it spread and hurriedly assembled the entire party on the ice. McNish argued that he was no longer obliged to obey orders because the ship had been sunk. Shackleton insisted that disobedience would be 'legally punished' and that, regardless of the sinking, the men would still be paid. The rebellion was snuffed out at a stroke and McNish was left in no doubt that 'legal punishment' for mutineers meant he would be shot if there was a repeat of his insubordination.

Wordie had begun with great respect for Shackleton. But the events of the past few days, including the boat-hauling episode and his reluctance to retrieve the *Stancomb Wills*, had begun to change his mind. He found it difficult to accept some of Shackleton's decisions and began to question his leadership. In his diary one night Wordie wrote: 'The floes have not really opened much, but the Boss at any rate has changed his mind yet once again; he now intends waiting for leads, and just as firmly believes he will get them, as he did a week ago that the ice would be fit for sledging the boats at the rate of ten miles a day.'[17]

By this stage Ocean Camp had degenerated into a filthy slushy mess and a new camp was established nearby. It was intended to be their home until the northerly drift brought open water and appropriately was called Patience Camp. The new situation demanded an urgent decision about the future of the dogs. By mid-January 1916, the stock of seal meat for the animals had fallen sharply and four of the teams were shot by Wild. It was a necessary decision, but Wordie saw another consequence. Without the dog teams, he reasoned, it would be very hard to cross the ice on foot, which probably meant an end to the hazardous scheme to march to Graham Land.

But there was also the awful possibility that the pack might never open up. Shackleton, too, feared that the pack would stay unbroken despite the northerly drift, which meant they would be carried past the land and out into the vast expanses of the Southern Ocean. Wordie was more optimistic about the break-up and was even prepared to put a date on the time when they would be released. He wrote, '. . . not until the end of February should we give up hope of getting away in the boats.'[18]

With the march to the west now ruled out, the lifeboats assumed critical importance and few at Patience Camp could understand Shackleton's reluctance to fetch the *Stancomb Wills,* which had been left on the ice at Ocean Camp. Worsley argued strongly that it would be a 'practical impossibility' to pack twenty-eight men into two small lifeboats for the sea journey. Wordie shared his pessimism and slowly Shackleton came round to the general point of view. 'Its importance is obvious,' Wordie wrote. 'It has taken a long time to persuade the Boss to this move and I doubt if he would have done it had it not been for the general feeling in camp.'[19]

The *Wills* was duly retrieved. But the next day, when Crean, Worsley and Macklin set off towards Ocean Camp to forage for any remaining scraps of food and supplies, they were halted by sizeable leads of open water. Had they waited another twenty-four hours to recover the *Wills* the only way out of the Weddell would have been the 'practical impossibility' of jamming twenty-eight men into two small lifeboats.

The drift continued, taking the castaways almost directly opposite the end of the Peninsula and close to the farthest reaches of the Weddell Sea. By mid-February Snow Hill and Paulet were only 100 miles (1,600 km) away across the frozen landscape, though there were no open sea lanes. At the end of February, Wordie noted that Paulet was only 86 miles (137 km) away, adding: 'So near, yet so far.' Conversation was dominated by speculation about the course of the drift and when the ice would free the men. But James concluded that 'a bug on a single molecule of oxygen in a gale of wind would have the about the same chance of predicting where he was likely to finish up'.

Excitement rose on 9 March when all hands felt a sudden movement in the ice-floe. 'It may well be a swell,' Wordie wrote, sensing that the drift had finally carried them to open water. His assumption was correct and open water was not far away. Two days later large leads began to appear and they all began to wonder about how quickly they could launch the boats. But it was misplaced optimism and was soon replaced by news that blubber stocks had fallen to a worrying level. In the circumstances, they began to eat pemmican set aside for the dogs.

Behind the concerns about food was another far more serious issue – the potential onset of scurvy. Scurvy, which develops through a lack of vitamin C, was the scourge of sailors and Polar explorers down the ages and is lethal if not treated. As the body can only store vitamin C for a few months, it needs to be replenished through intakes of fresh foods like meat and vegetables. But a large part of the rations at this point was not fresh. While fresh seal or penguin steaks were available, the strong taste did not appeal to everyone. Often the men preferred tinned food or pemmican, the dried meat paste that was mixed with water to make a porridge-like mush called 'hoosh'. Both diets lacked the necessary vitamin intake.

Shackleton, who had narrowly escaped death from scurvy in 1909, knew the risks but chose not to discuss the matter openly in case it caused panic. Those who understood the potential danger – such as Wild, Crean or the two doctors Macklin and McIlroy – were urged join to him in a conspiracy of silence. Wild had first-hand experience of scurvy with Shackleton in 1909 and knew enough to see that it lay behind the Scott disaster. He once told Wordie: 'There is very little doubt that the Polar party died of scurvy.'[20] Macklin was also aware of the potential risks and shared Wild's belief that scurvy was the real cause of Scott's death, not the lack of food or fuel which had been offered to the public as the reason for the deaths of the five men. Macklin feared that, without precautions, it might strike at the *Endurance* party and he later wrote:

Shackleton . . . in our hard-up days used to tell all hands that this was a complete and wonderful ration containing meat and drink and all that was required to maintain health and vigour.

This of course was not the case . . . I was terribly afraid of scurvy in those days but Shackleton told me to keep my mouth shut and say nothing.[21]

The immediate problem was that as winter approached, the stocks of seals and penguins began to dwindle, which meant a loss of fresh meat and a more serious loss of the fatty blubber that was used as fuel for the stoves. Towards the end of March only ten days of blubber remained for fuel, which meant cutting back to only two hot meals a day and fewer hot drinks. Dinner, Wordie observed, was washed down with cold water to conserve fuel.

In the circumstances, any fresh food was leapt upon. One day Wild shot a giant sea leopard. On gutting the beast, the men found about sixty undigested fish in its stomach and that night they enjoyed the rare luxury of 'fresh' fish. 'White, sweet flesh and very agreeable,' Wordie announced.

Food was the main topic of conversation. Mealtimes not only broke the monotony but provided a brief feeling of warmth in the damp, cold conditions. As the soothing effects of a hot meal wore off, the men usually retired to their sleeping bags to keep warm. In some cases, they resorted to clumsy gallows humour. Worsley and another seafarer, Lionel Greenstreet, often mocked Marston, the well-built artist, with hints that he was ideally built if the men had to resort to cannibalism. They implored the cherubic Marston not to lose weight and even speculated about which parts of his ample frame would provide the men with the tastiest cuts. In the circumstances it was a poor attempt at humour and after a while Marston found his own way of dealing with it. He would simply turn and walk away if he saw Worsley and Greenstreet approaching.

Food and drink assumed colossal importance to the cold, weary men. Once, Greenstreet spilt his mug of hot milk during a minor argument with Clark. Greenstreet, a mature merchant-navy officer, was close to tears as he stared at the floor and contemplated the loss of a precious hot drink. In a second, Clark leant across and tipped some of his milk into Greenstreet's mug, followed by Worsley, Macklin, Kerr, Rickinson, Orde-Less and Blackborrow, who all did the same. Everyone understood.

The 'fresh' fish offered an exceptional change in the diet, which now relied heavily on dog food and occasional slivers of seal or penguin flesh. Wordie recorded the worsening situation in his diary:

> The fire is on in the morning only about ¾ pint of hot milk per man; for breakfast each man is served out with ½ lb of cold dog-pemmican: what he has over he eats for lunch with a biscuit and three lumps of sugar. The night hoosh consists of three flakes of meat, with generally soup squares or turtle cup added: it will not be fully cooked, only so to speak made palatable.
>
> There is talk of the dog-pemmican ration being reduced by half, but this has not happened yet: however it seems very probable, as we have only about a week's ration of that sort.[22]

It was an uninviting regime, but Wordie nevertheless reckoned that a combination of the sledging provisions and seal meat would last the men for six months.

Shackleton, however, ordered the men not to stockpile food or blubber. Wordie was among those astounded at the baffling decision. On contemplating the blubber shortage, he scornfully rounded on Shackleton and wrote: 'For this shortage bad management is to blame, as for months past many of us have urged the prudent course of laying in more meat while it was available.'[23]

On the surface Wordie was correct. But he miscalculated Shackleton's reasoning. Shackleton believed that stocking up food sent the wrong signals, particularly to the pessimistic sailors. It implied no escape or, at best, another year living on the ice.

His philosophy was that it was better to live on the margin and instil hope.

It is a surprising fact that, despite the apparent abundance of wildlife, the trapped men relied mostly on the rations brought down with the ship and killed a comparatively small number of seals and penguins for their own consumption. Worsley kept a record of the slaughter, which shows that only fourteen Weddell seals were killed in the 15-month period from mid-December 1914 – when *Endurance* first entered the pack – until they left the floe in April 1916. A further forty of the lighter Crabeater seals were also butchered. In contrast, 810 Emperor and Adelie penguins were slaughtered, though a typical 850-lb (385-kg) Weddell seal provided at least sixty times the meat and blubber obtained from an average 10-lb (4.5-kg) Adelie carcass.[24]

The hopes of the men did rise in March when the mountain tops of Joinville Island, which is among the last islands in the archipelago at the tip of the Antarctic Peninsula, came into view. It was the first land seen in fifteen months. But it also meant that the drift had carried them passed Snow Hill and Paulet islands, their original targets.

There was further excitement at the end of the month when large cracks in the ice opened close to their camp and all hands were on constant alert to launch the boats. At night the men slept fully clothed. Temperatures began to drop as March gave way to April and the first days of winter began to descend. Darkness reigned for around twelve hours, but there was enough light to see the mountains of Joinville Island disappear to the south. On 30 March the last remaining dogs were shot. Tension on the floe rose markedly as the ice began to break up. Once large crack opened only 18 ft (5 m) from the galley and Shackleton ordered everyone to make ready. Immediately afterwards another crack opened under the *James Caird* and the men scrambled to drag the boat to safety before it was carried away in the swell.

The break-up was enormously welcome, but it was still far too dangerous to launch the boats in the ice-strewn waters. At the same time, the floe, which had been their home for so long, was slowly disintegrating into a slushy mess. The men had little sense of anything firm underfoot and no hope of escaping to the water.

Attention now switched to the nearest dry land, the two small islands about a hundred miles to the north, Clarence and Elephant, two lonely outposts of rock which lie at the far-eastern end of the South Orkneys' chain. But even this optimism was tempered by fears that the drift might carry them past those islands too. Beyond Clarence and Elephant islands was the vast open expanse of the South Atlantic. Wordie voiced the worries of all when he wrote: 'At present we are in great fear lest the ice should carry us through the gap between Elephant Island and King George Is., for beyond that there is only the open sea.'[25]

The night of 8 April brought fresh turmoil, with the floe pitching and rolling and chunks of ice crashing against each other. The floe split on a number of occasions and the twenty-eight men were left contemplating their fate. The slab of ice which accommodated Patience Camp had now been whittled down to a mere 100 yards (90 m) across and escape was becoming urgent. Around mid-morning on 9 April a large crack sliced diagonally through the floe and across Shackleton's tent. It was the final warning shot and the order to launch the boats was given. A last lunch was hurriedly prepared and at 1 p.m. the boats were made ready. Worsley's log put the position at 61° 56′ S, 53° 56′ W.

It was over fifteen months since *Endurance* had become trapped in the ice and the semi-circular drift had carried the castaways close to 2,000 miles (3,200 km) around the Weddell Sea. Wordie scribbled in his diary: 'One felt it was high time we were away.'[26]

CHAPTER 6

THE OPEN BOAT
JOURNEY

THE *Dudley Docker* WAS FIRST INTO THE WATER. ALL HANDS HURRIED to load stores and supplies. Next the little *Stancomb Wills* was lowered off the ice and filled with stores. Finally the *James Caird* was launched and loaded. The *Caird,* with Shackleton at the tiller, was the most seaworthy of the vessels, and the crew had been chosen to incorporate a suitable mixture of the dependable and the not so dependable. In the first category were Wild, the genial Irish seaman, Tim McCarthy and the cook, Charles Green. But the *Caird* also contained three men – McNish, Hurley and the troublesome trawler-hand, John Vincent, whom Shackleton felt it necessary to keep close tabs on.

For different reasons, Shackleton also felt compelled to keep the scientists under his watchful eye and Clark, Hussey, James and Wordie completed the eleven men packed into the *Caird*. It is possible that Shackleton felt their sheltered, comfortable backgrounds left them ill-prepared for the hardships of an open-boat journey through the icy waters which lay ahead. Certainly nothing in their backgrounds could have prepared them for the ordeal. Shackleton, above all, put the safety of his men first and his consideration for scientists was the same as that for seasoned trawlermen, who probably understood the severe difficulties which lay ahead. But a closer inspection would have shown that Wordie and James, in particular, were among the most robust of the entire group.

The open-boat journey away from the ice was the most difficult and testing phase of the entire expedition. The three craft were painfully inadequate, many of the men unsuited for the task and the ominous weather cast a horrible shroud of doubt over proceedings. From the start, the odds were stacked heavily against the boat parties. The heavily-laden vessels were not designed for navigating the icy waters. At nearly 23 ft (7 m), the whaler *James Caird* was the largest and the *Stancomb Wills*, at just over 20 ft (6 m), the smallest. The *Docker*, with the experienced small-boat skipper, Worsley, in charge, was a 22-ft (6.6-m) cutter. McNish had performed minor miracles by raising the gunwales of the *Caird* and *Docker*, which helped keep out the oncoming waves but also made rowing very difficult.

But the *Stancomb Wills*, with a tiny mainsail, was a liability – too small to keep pace with the other vessels and forced dangerously low in the water by the burden of eight men and piles of supplies. Waves poured over the sides and bailing became frantic. The crew was also a major problem. In charge, nominally, was the navigator Hubert Hudson. But Hudson had struggled to cope with confinement on the ice and then developed severe frostbite and a nasty, debilitating abscess on his bottom, which contributed to his confused state. Before long, command of the *Stancomb Wills* passed to the imposing Crean, an indestructible and optimistic character on his third Antarctic voyage. Another passenger was Blackborrow, the stowaway, whose feet had developed acute frostbite.

Rowing was intensely hard work, particularly as the men were clearly unfit for heavy labour after months languishing on the ice floe. They rowed in spells, one group struggling to cope with the choppy seas and the remainder bailing continuously or fending off threatening chunks of ice. Freezing spray lashed their faces and each passing wave brought a fresh soaking. The flotilla threaded its way through the floating chunks of ice and lumpy seas until around 6 o'clock in gathering dusk, when it was decided to rest for the night. A suitable floe, about 50 yards (45 m) across, was found but the tired men took an hour to unload the three vessels. They had come about 10 miles (16 km) and by good fortune a seal was basking on the floe.

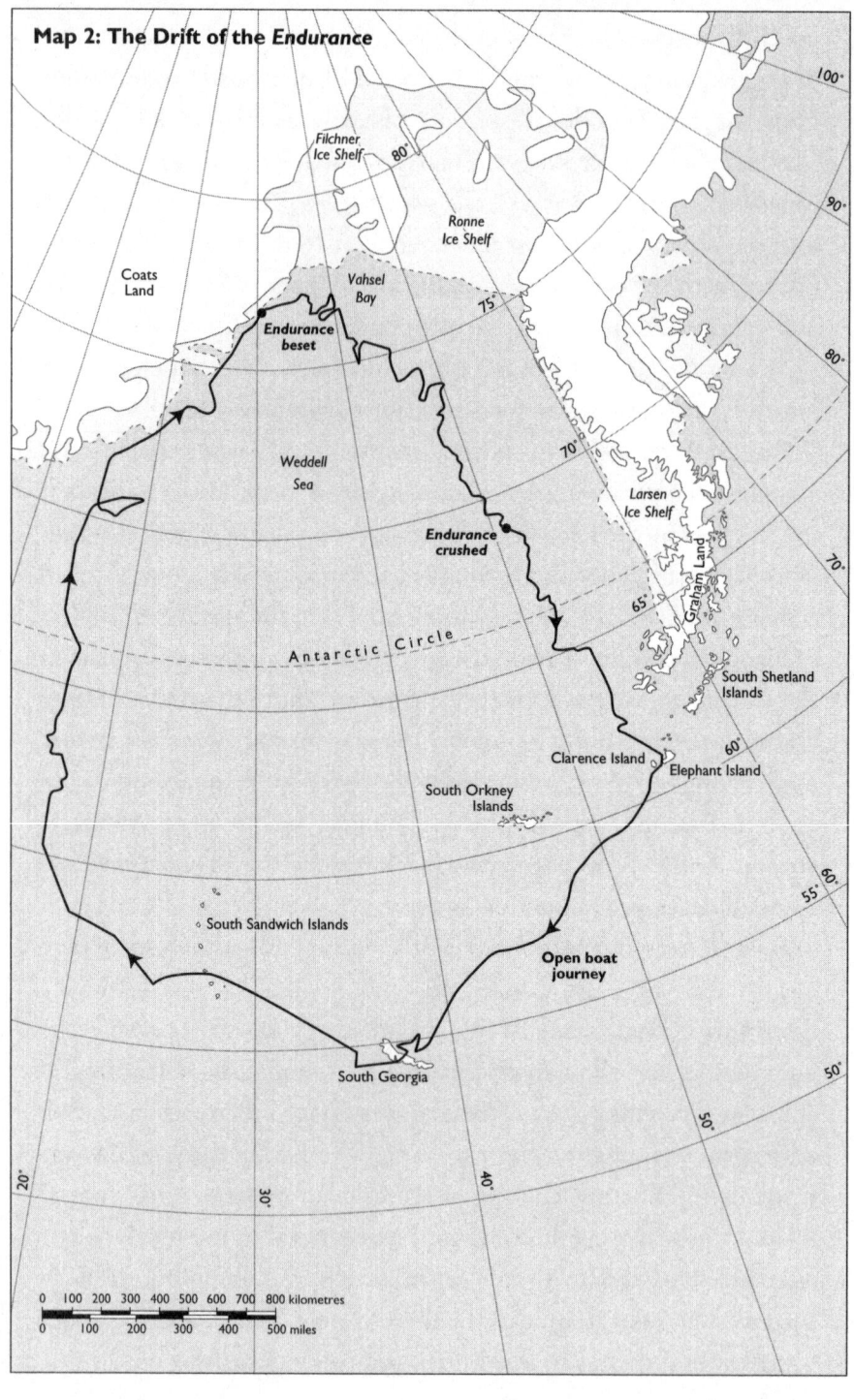

Map 2: The Drift of the *Endurance*

Filchner
Ice Shelf

Ronne
Ice Shelf

Coats
Land

Vahsel
Bay

**Endurance
beset**

Weddell
Sea

Larsen
Ice Shelf

**Endurance
crushed**

Antarctic Circle

South Shetland
Islands

Graham Land

Clarence Island

Elephant Island

South Orkney
Islands

South Sandwich Islands

**Open boat
journey**

South Georgia

0   100 200 300 400 500 600 700 800 kilometres

0   100 200 300 400 500 miles

But the well-earned rest was rudely interrupted in the middle of the night when the floe suddenly split, tipping two men into the water. Shackleton's tent and the *Caird* were separated from the others in the turmoil. In the pitch blackness, the *Wills* was hurriedly launched to recover Shackleton and the whaler before they drifted off into oblivion. Tents were quickly hauled down and the men spent a miserable freezing night pacing up and down watching for further splits in the ice and waiting for the dawn. It was a long, cold night.

The little fleet resumed operations early next day and soon ran into fresh pack ice, which halted their progress to the north. Sails were raised to take advantage of freshening winds and suddenly the pack broke away and the three vessels found themselves in open water – the first free-flowing seas they had encountered since leaving South Georgia sixteen months earlier.

It was a great sense of freedom, but the joy was soon interrupted by the grim reality of the seas around them. Emerging from the protective shield of the pack, the three boats were immediately struck by the ferocity of the wind and heavy breaking seas which tossed them around like corks. The flotilla was close to the far-eastern end of the Bransfield Strait, which links the fearsome Drake Passage to the northern tip of the Weddell Sea. These are treacherous waters where winds blow in one direction and the current flows in another. As they tried to steer a north, north-easterly course, the *Caird* fared best. But the *Wills* and *Docker* struggled badly against the powerful winds blowing directly in their faces. Wordie said conditions were 'none too pleasant' and Hurley pronounced 'all wet, cold & miserable'.

During the day a makeshift lunch of cold dog-pemmican was dished out. 'Positively nauseating', Orde-Lees declared. Violent seasickness afflicted almost everyone in the rolling seas, even salty veterans of the oceans. In the face of insurmountable odds, Shackleton reluctantly took his armada back into the protection of the ice. The irony of prisoners from the pack ice returning to their dungeon for safety was not immediately apparent to all.

By darkness, tiredness had swept over most men and it was decided to risk another night on a floe. They had not slept properly for forty-five hours and fatigue had pushed the previous night's incident of the splitting floe to the back of their minds. 'So much can exhaustion do,' Wordie observed dryly.

Despite the exhaustion, cold and nausea, Wordie somehow managed to maintain the discipline of writing up his diary at the end of each day in the boat. The entries were hastily scribbled scraps of information, which provided a running commentary on the unfolding drama. 'A few words each day on a slip of paper are all I have to go by in writing this narrative,' he explained. It was a predicament which did not demand literary flourish. One typically terse summary of the bleak situation simply read: 'A thick day: land at no time visible: we have no idea where we are.'[1]

The condition of the men was causing Shackleton grave concern. Only a few days into the boat journey he was seriously questioning whether they would all pull through. It was, he remembered, a 'terrible night and I doubted if all of the men would survive it.' Survive the night they did but by morning the men were again imprisoned. A heavy gale from the north-east had driven loose pack all around their small floe and whipped up the seas, making a launch improbable. 'Boats could not live among heaving ice like this,' Wordie said, 'it was swaying like a switchback.'

However, the battering from the seas was slowly carving away at the floe and the party spent an anxious few hours desperately hoping that the pack would drift away before the floe broke up. It was not possible to get back into the water until early afternoon, leaving only a few hours of daylight to make progress. But the strong north-easterly wind still blocked their passage and the islands of Clarence and Elephant remained out of reach.

Under pressure, Shackleton altered course and directed the three vessels to turn south-east to King George Island about eighty miles (130 km) away. From there, it was hoped the party could island-hop to Deception Island. Deception was the 'capital' of the whaling industry in the South Shetlands and the hope was that they might intercept one of the visiting ships. The desperation was such that someone recalled that a small wooden church stood on Deception Island. It was suggested if no whaler could be found, the house of worship should be ripped down to build a boat.

But Deception Island was a particularly forlorn hope as the three vessels set their new course. The *Wills* was unable to keep pace, limping along far behind the *Docker* and *Caird* in the lumpy waters. The task of keeping tabs on the *Wills* became Shackleton's primary concern and Worsley took the *Docker* back to fetch the labouring vessel. As the light began to fade, the journey was abandoned for the night.

It was only at the end of each day that the effects of the appalling journey could be fully appreciated. The lack of sleep and the penetrating cold exacerbated the physical effects of widespread frostbite, seasickness and the painful salt-water boils which had begun to strike many of the men. Nor was there much relief from the paltry rations. Indeed the gruesome food only intensified the feelings of despair. Wordie's scraps of diary recalled the daily allowance: 'The day's food: ¼ lb dog-pemmican and a biscuit for breakfast; nut food and biscuit for lunch; breakfast ration and a biscuit for supper. So far we have always managed hot milk in the morning.'[2]

Spirits were hit further when Shackleton refused to land on a floe that night. The bitter experience of the two previous evenings meant the three boats were tied up along a floe and only Green, the imperturbable cook, was allowed to disembark to knock up an evening meal. From the boats twenty-seven pairs of eyes stared longingly at the stove. 'A sight not to be forgotten was the blaze of the blubber stove in the darkness,' Wordie wrote.

After 'dinner' the boats resumed their journey to the south-west, rowing slowly and carefully in the darkness. It was bitterly cold and snow fell, sticking to their clothes. Occasionally, killer whales surfaced to investigate the intruders.

When rowing was no longer possible, the boats tied up together and the men tried to snatch some badly needed rest. Sleep was haphazard and broken in the cramped boats. Men huddled together for warmth and cursed anyone who moved and allowed the cold air to seep into the gaps between the bodies. In the *Caird*, Wordie wrote: 'It proved a wet and miserable night: to sleep in the bottom of the boat on rough cases with wet feet and damp clothes was only possible owing to our being tired.'[3]

The cold night gave way to a startling new dawn of glowing sunshine and clear skies. No one could recall the last time they had seen the sun. Green was hurriedly landed on a floe where he brewed piping hot and instantly invigorating mugs of milk.

But the mood of quiet optimism was shattered when Worsley took a sighting, the first since leaving Patience Camp. It showed that three days of hard labour and suffering had yielded nothing. The position of the three boats was about thirty miles (48 km) east of Patience Camp, despite their westerly course. Currents, which they had evidently under-estimated, were propelling them in the opposite direction to their goal to the north-west.

Disbelief gripped the men. Some concluded that Worsley, despite his reputation as a highly accomplished navigator, had somehow made a terrible mistake. Later in the day he took another sighting and revealed that Joinville Island, which they had passed while on the floe a few weeks earlier, was now only about eighty miles (128 km) away to the south-west.

Shackleton responded to the alarming development by once again changing course. The new goal was Hope Bay, about 130 miles (210 km) away at the very apex of the Antarctic Peninsula. Three members of Nordenskjold's party had spent a desolate winter at Hope Bay in 1903–4 living on the abundant stocks of Adelie penguins which colonise the area. 'Hopeless Bay', someone quickly christened it.

Towards nightfall the boats ran into some patches of lumpy broken ice, which threatened a damaging collision. In haste, the boats were tied to a small floe and welcoming hot drinks were made. But the peace did not last long and the wind shifted strongly to the south-west, forcing the boats to leave their sanctuary. The ties were cut and the boats once again made for open seas. The wind, driving from the Polar mainland, sliced through the cold, wet and desperately tired men huddled together in the boats. After a while, the vessels drew up alongside each other and in temperatures well below freezing the men tried to grab a little sleep. 'A very cramped and cold night,' Wordie recalled. Water froze on the oars and ice clung to the sides of the boats like a suit of armour. A film of ice began to form on the water and their clothing, dusted with a white shroud of frost, stiffened. Men shivered uncontrollably throughout the night, keeping each other awake.

Dawn broke on 13 April to reveal that all twenty-eight had survived a terrible night. But the strain was deadly apparent, with each man showing the outward signs of cold and exhaustion. Lips were cracked and their beards had turned white with frost. Frostbite and salt-water boils disfigured them all.

The internal damage was more difficult to discern, though Shackleton said 'most of the men were now looking seriously worn and strained.' In the half-light of daybreak, the boats pulled away. It was quickly apparent that they were lower in the water under the weight of the ice which had accumulated overnight. The wind picked up, powering once again from the icy reaches of the Polar landscape. For the fourth time, Shackleton changed direction, this time re-setting course for Elephant Island about 100 miles (160 km) to the north, driven by the strong south-westerlies.

By now the boats were on the very edge of the pack and, as a precaution against the more turbulent open seas ahead, some surplus stores were dumped and the men were given the small luxury of eating as much pemmican and biscuit as they wanted for breakfast.

'No stinting of food,' Wordie commented. The only proviso was that it was to be eaten cold.

The raw pemmican dog-food tasted dreadful and caused debilitating outbreaks of diarrhoea. It was a humiliating ordeal for men who were also experiencing severe sea-sickness. In both cases, the only relief came from over the sides of the rocking boat and enduring a soaking from freezing spray. To clean themselves they broke off small chunks of ice. An ugly side-effect of the sickness and diarrhoea was worsening dehydration. The convoy had emerged from the pack faster than expected and there was not enough time to take sufficient ice on board as they pulled into more open waters. The cold itself was another source of their dehydration, since freezing temperatures increase urine production, even if liquid intake is low. While sucking lumps of ice gave some immediate relief to the thirst, drinking ice-cold water merely accelerated the loss of body heat. To compensate for the thirst, men chewed slices of raw seal meat and swallowed the blood. Others, including Orde-Lees, took the big risk of drinking sea water. 'No ill after-effects at all,' he reported.

By noon the convoy had broken free from the last remnants of the pack but the seas, as expected, were far rougher and the men suffered horribly from a fresh bout of sea-sickness. At the margin of discomfort, the *Caird* was the most secure of the three vessels. James said the *Caird* men were 'fairly comfortable' compared with the 'pretty critical' state of affairs on the *Docker* and the *Wills*.

In the *Wills*, Hudson had collapsed and Crean, having assumed full command, found it impossible to keep up with the two larger craft. The *Wills* and the *Docker* also suffered badly in the swell, taking on dangerous amounts of water. Once the *Wills* almost sank when a heavy wave swept over the boat. Luckily the next wave slammed into the craft, tipping it over and sending gallons of water rolling overboard.

Some of the men were now in a critical condition and Worsley urged Shackleton to push on through the night and get to Elephant

Island as fast as possible. But Shackleton was more worried that the three boats would become separated in the darkness and it was obvious that the *Wills* was unlikely to survive alone in the open seas.

As darkness fell, a sea-anchor was improvised and the three boats hove to. But the winds picked up and temperatures dropped sharply. Spray froze as soon as it splashed over the boats and their clothing was quickly encased in ice.

'And so we settled down to a very cold stormy night,' – the night of 13 April – which, as Wordie wrote, 'proved terrible enough'. Some simply put their heads in their hands and wept. Penetrating cold gripped the men, sores had developed on their buttocks from long spells of rowing and their feet had turned a sickly off-white colour from the constant wetness. Blackborrow lost all feeling in his feet.

On the *Caird,* Wordie's only protection from the bitter cold was an overcoat draped over his head. His discomfort was increased by a splinter in his hand which turned septic and blew up into an ugly blister. The blister later burst, leaving Wordie with a nasty bag of surplus skin which, he reasoned, would make a very good mitten.

On the boats the thin line of rope tying the *Caird* and the *Wills* together – quite literally, a lifeline – was strained to breaking point in the night's vigorous swell. Had it broken, the *Wills* and its crew would have been lost. One man fell overboard and was very lucky to be rescued before the boats drifted away in the darkness.

The only crumb of comfort was that food remained plentiful. Marston chipped in with occasional bursts of singing, which was incongruous enough in the circumstances to relieve a little of the anxiety. Shackleton kept a close watch on the behaviour of his men, acutely aware that any breakdown in discipline would endanger the whole party. On one occasion Shackleton brushed against the surly boatswain, Vincent, and felt something hard in his breast pocket. Shackleton thrust his hand into Vincent's pocket and discovered his own gold watch, which had been thrown away on the ice weeks before. Shackleton was furious and threw the watch into sea, yelling, 'No, by God, you shall not have it.'[4]

The seventh day at sea broke with glorious news. Dead ahead in the far distance were the unmistakably clear outlines of the mountains on both Clarence and Elephant Island, about thirty miles (48 km) away. The sun suddenly broke through the scudding clouds and Wordie recorded that 'everybody was smiling'.

A straightforward run to the islands was interrupted around noon when the wind dropped. Sails were useless and the desperately tired and thirsty men were forced back to the oars like galley slaves. Wordie noted: 'But the rowing was none too brisk – we had no water, had been 24 hours without a drink. But fortunately we had on board a sack of seal meat, and this we started to eat raw for the water it contained – nearly 60 per cent of the whole, so the Boss said.'[5]

Progress was pitifully slow and many were on the brink of collapse. Some, according to Shackleton, said they simply wished to die. No one had slept properly for at least 72 hours and Wild casually reckoned that several were 'insane . . . simply helpless and hopeless'. Wordie, more diplomatically, said there was 'no life in the rowing'.

Fortunately, the sight of land ahead seemed to invigorate some on board and the boats slowly came within about ten miles (16 km) of Elephant Island. In the circumstances, the dark, brooding snow-topped mountains and precipitous cliffs looked positively inviting. However, the currents were less predictable and despite a monumental effort with the oars, the boats were making no progress and darkness was approaching. Luckily, winds from the south-west picked up again and sails were quickly raised.

The target was Cape Valentine on the north-east point of Elephant Island, where it was hoped a suitable landing place might be found in the lee of the land, away from the constant howling gales. Worsley felt it prudent for each boat to make independent attempts at landing, but Shackleton refused to allow the vulnerable

Wills to be left to the mercy of the seas. Once again, a line was fixed between the *Caird* and the *Wills*.

It was a minor miracle that the *Wills* had survived for so long. Many thought the vessel was doomed and Hurley recalled that when all hope appeared gone, a dark shape would suddenly appear against the white spume and through the tumult would come a 'faint but cheering hail' from the redoubtable Crean. As darkness fell, the winds picked up and temperatures dropped sharply in the worsening seas. Shackleton said the 'general discomfort' could scarcely have been increased. 'It was a fearful night and much water came on board,' Wordie said as the two vessels battled howling winds and a constant deluge of freezing spray. Temperatures sank to 20° below freezing.

On the *Wills*, men were often up their knees in icy water and four of the eight men in the boat had virtually collapsed. On the *Caird*, the imperturbable Wild admitted it was the worst night he had ever known. In the raging storm the old-stager Cheetham seriously believed that the *Docker* would break its back. Much to Shackleton's alarm, the *Docker* became separated from the two other vessels during the fearful night and there were concerns that the craft had been lost.

By early morning the *Caird* and the *Wills* had gathered near the extreme eastern end of the island and hurriedly managed to scramble around to the northern side, where there was welcome shelter from the winds. But the land, said James, was a 'most uncompromising type' of sheer cliffs, glowering mountains and treacherous glaciers. Sailing alongside the bleak cliff face, they found a small sheltered bay about a mile along the coast called Cape Valentine. Shortly afterwards the *Docker* suddenly re-appeared amidst the rolling waves.

The first priority was water. Nearby chunks of ice, which had broken off from the island's glaciers, drifted alongside the boats and the men eagerly grabbed pieces to slake their thirst. It had been forty-eight hours since they had last had a proper drink.

Shackleton decided to take the *Wills* closer to inspect the land, reasoning that he did not want to risk losing his largest vessel. He quickly joined Crean on board and prepared to make landfall, noticing that a menacing reef of rocks stuck out from the rollers, blocking their path to the beach.

The *Wills* roamed up and down searching for a path through the rocks and after a while a narrow channel was located. Slowly the boat was lined up at the head of the opening, waiting for an incoming wave to help carry them through the gap. With suitable precision the next wave caught the *Wills* and carried the vessel forward until it finally ground to a halt on the pebbly beach. It was 497 days since the men from the *Endurance* had last felt firm ground beneath their feet. Not since 1830 had anyone set foot on Elephant Island.

Using the *Wills* as a tender, Crean went back and forth carrying men and stores from the two other boats and depositing them on the beach. Wordie was among the few men still fit for work, helping to carry cases up the beach and away from the shoreline. Some stumbled about on rubbery legs as though drunk, while others gleefully ran stones through their fingers. Some shivered uncontrollably. James said that most 'hardly knew whether to laugh or cry'. Green, the cook, briefly lost control, manically slaughtering ten seals with what Orde-Lees described as 'all the primitive savagery of a child killing flies'.

The seven days in the open boats had exacted an appalling toll on the men. Even Shackleton was gaunt and haggard, though Wild seemed almost unaffected by the ordeal. They were exhausted and freezing and suffering from a combination of acute dehydration, frostbite, cracked lips, swollen tongues and boils. The worst casualties were those in the *Docker* and in particular, the *Wills*. Wordie said only two men from the *Wills* – one was Crean – were fit to do anything. Among the crew of the *Wills*, McNish declared that Hudson had 'gone of [sic] his head', Blackborrow and Stephenson had to be helped ashore, while Rickinson is thought to have developed heart problems.

Shackleton gloomily concluded that 'about ten of the party were off their heads' and Wordie reported that Blackborrow's feet were so bad that 'some toes of one foot may have to be amputated'. After surveying the rest of the human wreckage scattered on the shore, he wrote:

> Some fellows moreover were half crazy: one got an ice axe and did not stop till he had killed about ten seals: another began eating raw limpets and dulse (seaweed), although during the last two days there has been absolutely no restriction to food. None of us had suffered like this in the *Caird* and to us it now fell to do most of the work.[6]

The three boats and cases of stores were brought onto the beach as fast as the men's exhausted condition would allow. 'We had got a footing on the land but not much more,' Wordie observed. 'Three shingle beaches are backed by steep cliffs and screes, up which there is no escape should a storm come.' Wordie's instant description was apt. The uninhabited Elephant Island is among the world's most inhospitable places. It is no spot to be marooned.

First discovered in 1819 when the English skipper, William Smith, was blown off course in a storm, the island is remote and bleak in the extreme. It lies at the north-eastern end of the South Shetland Islands and is around 600 miles (1,000 km) from the nearest civilisation at the tip of South America or in the Falklands. The island is a mountainous outcrop, about twenty-three miles (37 km) long, jutting out of the Southern Ocean. Towering mountains make the interior uninhabitable and the only shelter can be found on narrow strips of beach, which are under constant onslaught from the wind. Nor was Elephant Island on any known shipping lanes, so the men could not expect rescue.

The only salvation was the abundance of wildlife. Wordie recorded seeing seals, penguins and many different types of birds. Remarkably, he had the presence of mind to collect a few rocks to study, not realising that he would have ample time for geology. Cape Valentine characterised the innate bleakness and hostility of the island and unmistakable tide marks on the cliff face indicated that the beach might be swamped at high tide. It was evidently only a temporary refuge and next day two parties were sent to find an alternative campsite.

Wordie and Hurley walked along the shore in search of a safer harbour. 'Our quest was useless,' Wordie reported after finding that they risked getting cut off by the tide. A little later Wordie and Orde-Lees, the only climbers in the party, tried to reach the cliff tops and find a more hospitable place to camp by climbing up some loose rocks. The pair, weak from the boat journey and without proper crampons or ropes, found it a perilous climb up the hazardous scree and Wordie almost plunged to his death. He described the excursion as a 'stiff climb' up about 300 ft (100 m). 'A less enjoyable scree I have never been on,' he concluded. On the top he slipped and only saved himself by the quick-thinking use of the ice axe. 'In the neighbourhood of Cape Valentine there is no safe camping place,' Wordie decided. Climbers, he reckoned, could certainly reach the top, 'but certainly not such a party as ours'. Orde-Lees simply reported: 'Nothing doing'.

The alternative was to find a new beach. The pick of those still capable of another sea voyage – including Wild, Crean and Marston – took the *Docker* on a scouting mission to the west, and returned after dark with some cheerful news of a more suitable spot about six or seven miles (10 km) along the coast.

All three boats were launched at 6 o'clock the following morning for the comparatively simple journey. But little is simple on Elephant Island and it was not until 5 p.m. that all boats and cargo were successfully beached on the new home. It was hardly a sight to fill them with joy. 'Our first remark on landing was that this looked a very windy spot,' Wordie wrote in his diary. It had looked better in the sunshine the day before, Wild insisted.

Shackleton called the place Cape Wild after his deputy. But it quickly became known as Cape Bloody Wild. Cape Wild – the precise location is 61° 06'S 54° 52'W – is an uninviting spit of rock thrust into the foaming seas with a sheer ice-cliff at its back and a cluster of huge boulders at each end. Shackleton said it was 'rough, bleak and inhospitable' and Hurley described the area as 'like the courtyard of a prison only 250 yards by 50 yards wide'.

The prison courtyard, in fact, was even smaller than Hurley estimated. According to Wordie's calculations the level part of the spit was 'almost exactly 100 yards (91 m) in length, the breadth not quite 40 yards (36 m)'. At the end of the spit was what Wordie described as a 'rocky knob' of 95 ft (28 m), which was called Lookout Point or Penguin Hill. To their backs were the Furness Glacier and sheer cliffs leading up to South Mountain, a 1,100-ft (330 m) peak which was later named Mount Houlder.[7]

The weather blasted out a ferocious greeting to the new inhabitants of Cape Wild. As the party was making camp, a storm hit the beach with a stunning ferocity. Two tents were ripped in the turmoil and at one point the *Docker* was lifted from the beach and thrown around by the violence. Shackleton was blown off his feet. Bags of clothing and precious parts from the aluminium cooker were torn from the camp and swept out to sea.

The battering was a severe blow to the already low levels of morale. Hurley said a 'fair proportion' of the men would starve or freeze if left their own devices. Moreover, he had little sympathy for the weaker ones who, he said, had conducted themselves in a manner 'unworthy of gentlemen & British sailors'.

Wordie was more considered, but no less challenging. He concluded, 'About 8 of the party are broken down and unable for work, some of course merely disheartened by the bad weather.'[8] More serious was that many had lost all hope. Wordie gloomily reported that 'dejected men were dragged from their bags and set to work'. Even Green, who had served the party so well with his monumental performances at the stove, was declared 'quite incapable' by Wordie. In the face of a complete breakdown of the party, Shackleton acted.

On 20 April he announced that a party of six men would take the *James Caird* and sail to the whaling stations of South Georgia, where the journey of the *Endurance* party had begun almost seventeen months earlier. It was a trip of approximately 800 miles (1,300 km) and a desperate gamble that only desperate men could possibly contemplate.

The remaining twenty-two men left behind on Elephant Island had little hope to cling to. At best, rescue was improbable and at worst downright impossible. Winter was approaching in the southern hemisphere and Shackleton could have elected to wait until the spring before launching the *Caird*. But months sitting around on the beach at Elephant Island held no appeal for the restless Shackleton. A more chilling concern was the dreadful condition of some men. Hurley's grim warning that 'a fair proportion' of the men would starve or freeze to death had a horrible ring of truth about it. It was a fear echoed by McNish, who concluded there would 'not be many survivors' after a winter on the beach.

South Georgia was the only logical place to go for help, even if it meant a longer journey than to Tierra del Fuego in South America or Port Stanley in the Falklands, which lay about 600 miles (1,000 km) away. Both South America and the Falklands lay across the fearsome Drake Passage and beating against the prevailing westerly winds in a 23-ft whaler was impossible. In contrast, Worsley spoke of 'fair gales and favouring currents' to South Georgia, where whaling stations were manned all year round. The nearest rescue ship would be found at South Georgia.

At this point Shackleton made what Wordie considered was his most crucial and difficult decision – the choice of who would accompany him on the boat journey. Wild, loyal and resolute, was an obvious choice for the voyage of the *James Caird*. But Shackleton needed a strong and reliable character to take charge of those left behind on Elephant Island and it was essential that the man carried the respect of the castaways. Such a man was Frank Wild.

Map 3: Elephant Island

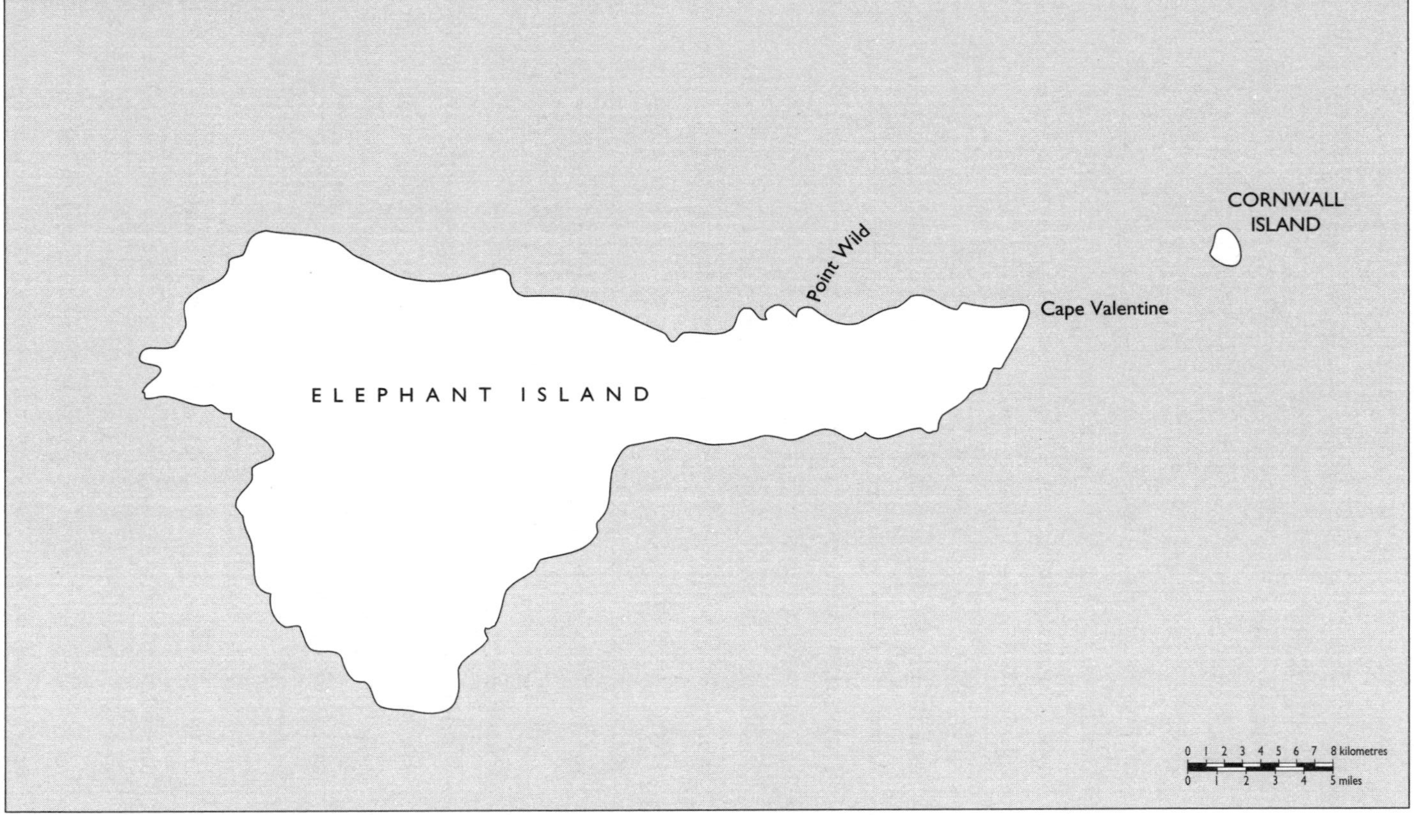

CORNWALL
ISLAND

Cape Valentine

Point Wild

ELEPHANT ISLAND

0 1 2 3 4 5 6 7 8 kilometres
0 1 2 3 4 5 miles

Shackleton insisted on leading the boat party and Worsley, whose peerless navigation had succeeded in getting the men from the ice floe to Elephant Island, was a certainty for the trip.

Crean, too, was ideally suited for the *Caird*'s voyage. But Shackleton badly needed at least two people he could rely on to take charge of affairs on the island and he asked Crean to stay behind to support Wild. Tom Crean was a formidably dependable and loyal lieutenant to Shackleton, having first met him on *Discovery* in 1901. Crean's courage and endurance were immense. He earned the Albert Medal, the highest award for gallantry, for saving the life of Lieutenant Teddy Evans on Scott's last expedition in 1912. He was undeniably a man for a tight corner. But his temperament was more suited to surviving the rigours and dangerous waters of the Southern Ocean than managing a bunch of despairing castaways. He begged to join the *Caird* party and Shackleton changed his mind.

Selection of the other men was difficult. He briefly considered taking Blackborrow, whose feet had deteriorated badly and who now needed an operation to amputate some toes. But this was dismissed as impractical and instead he picked the dependable McCarthy and the potentially disruptive pair of McNish and Vincent, probably because he saw them as likely troublemakers for Wild during the long idle days on Elephant Island.

The first task was to make the *Caird* more seaworthy and all those capable of work were immediately deployed. Timbers were stripped from the *Docker* to make decking, and when the wood ran out, a length of canvas was stretched over the void. But the canvas was frozen solid and only became workable after being held over the flames of the blubber stove to thaw out.

An ingenious piece of improvisation was conjured up to caulk the vessel and make it as watertight as possible. The seams of the *Caird* were slowly filled with an unlikely combination of cotton lamp wick and Marston's oil paints before being finished off with smears of seal's blood. McNish showed his great skills as a shipwright by meticulously raising the *Caird*'s gunwales and jamming the mast from the *Wills* into the hull for added strength. Others filled bags, made from old blankets, with stones and sand to act as ballast. Appalling weather made the task very demanding and most were nipped by frostbite. Hussey estimated that the winds screeched to 120 mph at one point and some suffered cuts from flying stones and lumps of ice.

By the morning of 24 April the weather had cleared a little and the *Caird* was ready for the trip. The empty boat was rowed out beyond the reef and the *Wills* ferried food, cooking facilities and other supplies out to the vessel. Shackleton took four weeks of rations, though a confident Hurley calculated that the journey would take only fourteen days. 'How we shall count the days,' he added. Wordie was equally optimistic. He predicted the men would return before the end of May, about five weeks hence. With luck, he said, they might get back sooner. 'She faces a journey of abut 800 miles to South Georgia through the stormiest belt of seas: should all go well we expect relief in a month's time.'[9]

But it was Orde-Lees who sounded the most sober note. He did not expect Shackleton to make a rapid return: 'What with the difficulty of getting a ship and soon, I don't expect he will be able to relieve us much before next spring, say September.'[10]

The *James Caird* set sail at 12.30 p.m. on 24 April, carrying the full expectations of its six-man crew and the twenty-two left standing on the beach at Elephant Island. On shore, the men gave three hearty cheers, which were immediately drowned out by the sounds of crashing rollers and howling winds. Occasionally, the men on the little boat gave an optimistic wave before the *Caird* finally disappeared behind the dark rolling waves.

It was difficult to know which group faced the greater danger – the crew of the *Caird* at the mercy of the Southern Ocean or the castaways on the bleak weather-beaten spit at Elephant Island. Wordie wrote of the *Caird*, 'She is our only hope.'[11]

CHAPTER 7

MAROONED ON ELEPHANT ISLAND

WITHIN TWENTY-FOUR HOURS OF THE *Caird's* DEPARTURE, LOOSE drift ice closed in and blocked off all escape routes from the island. Any delay in finishing work on the boat or deterioration in the weather would have prevented the party getting away at all. Wordie concluded, 'The *Caird* did not sail a day too late.' However, there was no time for pondering the imponderable and Wild, in a decisive assertion of his leadership, summoned all hands to spell out the three main priorities for the twenty-two men – shelter, food and the men's health. A fourth, less clear-cut matter, was a contingency plan for the Elephant Island party if the *Caird* was lost in the Southern Ocean.

The burden of leadership on the narrow shoulders of Frank Wild was truly enormous. Wild, a small wiry man of less than 5 ft 5 ins, had 'celebrated' his forty-third birthday on the second day of the terrible boat journey from the ice. He was, in every sense, a veteran of Antarctic exploration, having travelled with great distinction on four Polar voyages with three of the prominent figures of the age, Mawson, Scott and Shackleton. Wild, who came from Yorkshire, claimed to be a direct descendant of Captain James Cook. His loyalty and respect for Shackleton were unequivocal; it was a relationship which went far deeper than mere friendship. During the horrendous 'furthest south' journey with Shackleton in 1909, Wild and Shackleton reached rock bottom together when their food virtually ran out. In the tent one night, Shackleton kindly gave the starving Wild his last biscuit. Wild later insisted that no one could realise how much generosity and sympathy were shown by the act, and he insisted, 'I do by God, I shall never forget it.'

His leadership, naturally enough, followed the astute example set by Shackleton and earned him unwavering respect among the assorted ranks of castaways. Indeed, some found him easier and more down to earth than the occasionally flamboyant Shackleton. Wordie, who had little in common with Wild, nevertheless recognised his qualities of leadership. Like everyone else, he readily accepted orders from a man with only a fraction of his education and intellect who, surprisingly, had never achieved a high rank in a chequered naval career. Yet Wild somehow managed the unusual feat of simultaneously being 'one of the boys' and the commanding officer. He did his share of the chores around the camp and willingly joined in the morale-raising sing-songs at night. Indeed, his fine baritone was the pick of Elephant Island's choristers.

He was a patient, level-headed leader who exercised his authority in an unhurried straightforward manner without ever seeming to do anything demonstrative. Wild led by example and Wordie wrote, 'He has the confidence of all hands, his reputation during the boat journey being enhanced twofold.'[1]

Wild followed the example set by Shackleton of keeping the men as busy as possible and always found time to pay attention to each man's little quirks or worries. He also managed to instil belief that Shackleton would work a miracle by fetching rescue. Each day he roused the party with the optimistic command: 'Lash up and stow, boys, the Boss may be coming today.'

The appalling weather made it difficult to be optimistic. With winter approaching, it was difficult to imagine a more inhospitable place. Even to Wild the weather was simply 'hellish'. Winds were the main problem, often tearing down at hurricane force, lifting stones and chunks of ice into the air. Men were regularly blown off their feet, either by the horribly cold south-westerlies or damp north-easterlies.

However hellish, the weather on Elephant Island was relatively mild compared with the lower temperatures and wilder climate which they endured on the ice-floe further south while drifting through the Weddell Sea. The island lies north of the colder currents which sweep through the Weddell and the customary depressions epitomising the vicious Antarctic climate, though this was of little consolation to those under the relentless battering. Temperatures on Elephant Island rarely fell much below -20° F (-28° C) and in many cases hovered around 32° F (0° C). In contrast, far lower temperatures down to around -35° F (-37° C) were recorded in the Weddell Sea.

However, the severe wind-chill made the exposed beach feel significantly colder. Winds regularly raced to over 100 mph in the first few weeks on the island. In temperate climates the winds would have uprooted trees. The spit was highly vulnerable to the violent winds, lying at the bottom of a narrow gully with open sea on two sides. Winds rushed down the gully, gathering pace as they squeezed into the slender gap before hitting the beach with full ferocity.

In the circumstances, adequate shelter was the biggest concern. The tents had been largely shredded by the winds and the initial solution was to chisel a habitable space from inside a nearby ice cave. Wordie spent his twenty-seventh birthday laboriously hacking away at the ice-face before it dawned on the men that those inside would get soaking wet when temperatures rose because of cooking or even the combined body heat of twenty-two souls.

Marston and Greenstreet came up with a sensible alternative: to build a makeshift hut by upturning the *Docker* and the *Wills* and installing living quarters underneath. Wild agreed and some large stones were used to construct a foundation and two small walls, about 4 ft high (1.2 m) and 19 ft (5.7 m) apart. The boats were then laid upside down, side-by-side and lashed to the rocks. Two blankets were employed as a makeshift entrance. Some spare timbers were laid across the boats from keel to keel and the remnants of a tent were stretched over the top and secured by guy ropes. It was appropriately named Frankie Wild's Hut.

Inside the twenty-two men toiled to find some space in the dimly-lit, cramped quarters, which measured about 19 ft x 10 ft (5.7 x 3 m). No one could stand up when inside. While it offered shelter, the 'hut' was a dark, dank dungeon built on a former penguin colony, which reeked of guano and the embedded filth of the men themselves.

Four men were stretched out on the thwarts of the *Wills* and three on the *Docker*. The remainder found space on the floor. It was so badly overcrowded that James and Hurley initially declined the invitation and fled to Shackleton's old tent. But they quickly returned when a fresh storm hit the beach.

Kerr, the engineer, made a chimney from the tin lining of a biscuit case to allow smoke to escape from the blubber stove and a dim light was made from old sardine cans with thin strips of surgical bandages for wicks. The murky lighting allowed the men to ease the boredom by reading the 'library' of six books, including two volumes of the *Encyclopaedia Britannica* and a penny cook-book provided by Marston.

The improvised lamp burned continuously, partly to prevent people stepping on each other at night and partly to conserve the precious stock of dry matches. It was a prized luxury for Wordie, whose bag was stationed alongside the flickering light; he manoeuvred himself within 12 inches (30 cm) of the flame to snatch a few extra hours of reading.

At night the men would often break into song, helped by Hussey's ubiquitous banjo. Once a week, Wild ordered a more formal concert party, which at least gave them something to look forward to. James even composed a song which defiantly mocked their predicament. Sung to the traditional tune of *Solomon Levi*, the chorus went:

My name is Frankie Wild-o and my hut's on Elephant Isle
The wall's without a single brick and the roof's without a tile,

Yet, nevertheless, you must confess by many and many a mile
It's the most palatial dwelling place you'll find on Elephant Isle.

Food, initially at least, was not a problem. The island, which was named after its colonies of elephant seals, offered ample stocks of penguin, though few seals were apparent as the autumn months turned to winter. However, there was usually enough food for at least two good meals a day from slices of penguin or seal and the party's ample supplies of biscuits, pemmican, peas, barley and dried milk. Although boringly repetitive, the diet of fresh meat was at least sufficient to ward off scurvy.

All the available penguins were slaughtered in the early days. On some occasions up to a hundred a day were butchered. Occasionally, they caught birds which looked similar to ptarmigans and became known as Paddies. Once the hunters caught over twenty birds in a single day and each man enjoyed the rare luxury of eating a whole bird for dinner. Seals were scarce, though especially valued because of their bulk. A single seal provided about the same meat and blubber for fuel as the slaughter of sixty penguins.

The first decline in the stocks of food also caused the first serious outbreak of dissent. Orde-Lees, who was in charge of supplies, clashed with Wild over the necessity of storing food for emergencies. Orde-Lees, a marine captain adrift in unfamiliar naval surroundings, was passionate about the need to slaughter all available wildlife and build up food reserves for the winter months. He was among those who did not expect Shackleton to make a quick return to the island and could not understand Wild's reluctance to stockpile, the same reluctance shown by Shackleton on the ice floe. But Wild was adamant. He followed Shackleton's example and insisted that the stock-building of food gave the wrong signal to the beleaguered men, implying that the *Caird* had failed to reach South Georgia. Removing the hope of rescue would be fatal, he reasoned. It was a feud which simmered throughout the stay on the island.

As the supplies of fresh meat began to dwindle, a different crisis arose when Wild discovered that some food had been stolen. Pilfering was easy for any light-fingered soul because food cases were left partly open. But a breakdown in discipline, leading to anarchy, was the worst nightmare and Wild was determined to stop this antisocial behaviour before it got out of hand. He assembled the men and delivered the clear message that he would readily execute anyone found stealing food. Wild possessed a gun and was evidently prepared to use it to maintain discipline. The meaning was abundantly clear to all the men and Wordie wrote at the time, 'Very strong measures may be necessary.'[2] Years later Greenstreet described the incident somewhat more graphically and commented, 'He [Wild] was a strict disciplinarian and when men were stealing the meat he threatened to shoot them – and would have.'[3]

Aside from food, the condition of the men – physically and mentally – was a permanent cause of concern. Blackborrow's frostbitten feet were now struck by gangrene and Rickinson's heart problems needed constant observation. Others were also struggling.

According to Wordie, the worst case was Hudson, who had collapsed during the boat journey and was suffering the debilitating physical and emotional effects of the severe abscess on his buttocks. 'In addition to frost-bitten hands, a general breakdown has set in,' Wordie noted. What Wordie did not know was that the poisonous pus from the abscess was causing delirium and that the unfortunate Hudson was also suffering from painful necrosis of the spine.

Minor ailments were also a matter of concern in the wretched conditions and the doctors, Macklin and McIlroy, were kept busy in perhaps the most rudimentary surgery on earth. On one occasion Macklin had to remove one of Kerr's teeth without anaesthetic. 'Not much refinement here,' Macklin explained. Although some chloroform remained, pulling a tooth was not considered serious enough to justify its use.

Wordie was among those threatened with the unpleasant prospect of an operation without anaesthetic during the first few weeks on the island. In early May a tendon in his right hand became infected and blood poisoning set in. The infection was painful enough to prevent him writing his precious journal for three weeks. Macklin was initially concerned that the wound was taking too long to heal and proposed an exploratory operation. Fortunately, the problem cleared up and Wordie avoided painful surgery. However Wordie did not escape altogether: some weeks later Macklin was called upon to extract one of his teeth without a painkiller or sedative.

No such escape was possible for young Blackborrow, whose gangrenous left foot was now beyond repair. One reason why Shackleton had not waited until the spring to launch the *Caird* was Blackborrow's condition. The doctors, hoping that Shackleton might return by the end of May, waited until mid-June before deciding to operate. On 15 June it was decided to amputate his toes.

Everyone except the other patients – Hudson and Greenstreet – was ejected from the 'hut' and Macklin and McIlroy boiled their instruments in a cooking pot. There was enough chloroform to put Blackborrow under for fifty-five minutes while all the toes from his left foot were cut off. Afterwards Macklin pronounced, 'The poor beggar behaved splendidly & it went thro' without a hitch.'

Blackborrow's emergency surgery carried a different sort of message to the men. Had the doctors expected Shackleton to return, they would have delayed the amputation. But the *Caird* had been gone for seven weeks as Blackborrow went under the knife and the clear signal was that rescue would not be quick.

Each day since the *Caird*'s departure the men scanned the horizon, searching for plumes of smoke or a distant dark shape. It was invariably the last duty before darkness fell. The view from the spit was not encouraging. Ice was everywhere, though not always packed tightly. But it was thick and dangerous enough to prevent ships getting close to the island, or making their escape. As a result, the hopes of the men on the beach rose and fell, depending on whether the gales blew the ice towards the shore or alternatively drove the pack away from the immediate vicinity.

Wordie had begun with the hope that rescue would arrive about one month after the *Caird*'s departure, the last week in May. But the ice conditions were crucial and slowly he came to the conclusion that the castaways were doomed to wait until the spring. On 5 June, a week after he anticipated Shackleton's return, Wordie finished his journal entry with the prophetic lines: 'Still no relief. We conclude that the Boss has been down and finding close pack has returned. At that rate we can hardly expect a ship before August.'[4]

***

Wordie was perfectly correct. The tiny *James Caird*, under Worsley's extraordinary navigation skills, had achieved one of the great maritime feats and made landfall at South Georgia on 10 May. The *Caird* took seventeen tortuous days to cover the 800 miles (1,300 km) from Elephant Island to South Georgia and endured hurricane-force winds, constant threats of capsizing and the desperate hardship of raging thirst and exposure.

Worsley said it was an 'ordeal by water'. The ordeal was far from over when they made landfall. The *Caird* had landed on the southern side of the island and it was impossible to sail the vessel against the currents to get around to the manned whaling stations located on the northern shores. In desperation, Shackleton, Crean and Worsley decided to walk across the frozen, mountainous interior of the island. No one had crossed South Georgia before. But after thirty-six hours of marching without proper rest, the three men achieved the impossible and reached the Norwegian whaling station at Stromness on 20 May, the first outside human contact by the *Endurance* party for 532 days.

No cablehead existed on South Georgia for Shackleton to summon help to rescue the marooned Elephant Island party. Grabbing anything they could, Shackleton, Crean and Worsley left South

Georgia on 23 May in the small steam whaler, *Southern Sky* – almost a month to the day since the *Caird* had sailed from Elephant Island. Because the English owners could not be contacted in time, they simply 'borrowed' the vessel.

However, the *Southern Sky* was not an ice-strengthened ship and only carried enough coal for ten day's steaming. Heavy pack ice was encountered about 70 miles (110 km) from Elephant Island which, said Shackleton, formed an 'impenetrable barrier' to the rescuers. Reluctantly, the rescue was abandoned and the *Southern Sky* turned back towards the Falklands, where Shackleton felt he could find a more suitable ship and also cable news of the expedition to the outside world.

Shackleton's telegram reached London late on 31 May, the first word of the lost *Endurance* expedition for almost eighteen months. Although far weightier matters were preoccupying minds in Europe – the Battle of Jutland was being fought at the same time – news of the lost explorers was splashed across the front pages. The *Daily Chronicle* thundered: 'Sir Ernest Shackleton Safe'. A little further down the page was the news: '22 Companions Left In A Hole On Island'.

Shackleton provided an outline of the remarkable story, explaining that the twenty-two men had been left 'in a hole in the ice cliffs' on Elephant Island. 'At the time of leaving the island, all were well but in urgent need of rescue,' he concluded. The cable confirmed the worst fears in London, where concern had risen about the party's safety in the months leading up to Shackleton's return. In March, word reached Britain that the other expedition ship, the *Aurora,* which was carrying the depot-laying party to the Ross Sea, had broken free of its moorings, leaving ten men stranded at Cape Evans with a minimum of supplies and equipment.

With no word of Shackleton's Weddell Sea party, there was talk of sending rescue parties to the Ross Sea and to the Weddell in search of the two groups of men. In May 1916 a memorial to Scott's party was unveiled at St Paul's Cathedral and the *Daily Chronicle* used the occasion to lead calls for urgent action. An editorial pointed out: 'It would show ill on us as a nation if, while erecting memorials to the heroic dead, we fatally lagged in our duty towards the heroic living.'[5] The King responded to Shackleton's safe return by sending a personal telegram, which said: 'Rejoice to hear of your safe arrival in Falkland Islands and trust your comrades on Elephant Island will be rescued soon.'

Shackleton threw himself into the task of finding a new ship capable of breaking through the encircling ice around Elephant Island, though this proved far more difficult than expected. But hopes rose when the government of Uruguay offered the free loan of a stout trawler, *Instituto de Pesca No 1*.

The ship sailed from Port Stanley on 17 June – two days after Blackborrow's amputation – with the anxious trio of Shackleton, Crean and Worsley on board. Although the weather was again heavy, the steam-driven vessel made good progress and on the third day out, the peaks of Elephant Island were clearly visible on the horizon as the rescuers steered within 20 miles (32 km) of their goal.

On the island a screen of fog had descended and the men on the spit could not see the plumes of smoke. However, the mid-winter ice conditions around the island were formidable and the ship's fuel stocks were perilously low. It was apparent that the risks of getting trapped were very high and for the second time Shackleton gave the order to turn back to Port Stanley. The *Instituto de Pesca No 1* arrived on 25 June with her bunkers almost empty and engines stuttering ominously.

***

'All anxiously and longingly await relief,' Hurley wrote on 12 June as the *Instituto de Pesca No 1* was being made ready for the journey south. It was precisely seven weeks since the *Caird* had left. However, the entry routes to Elephant Island were now effectively closed until the spring by the menacing pack ice. Hopes of an early rescue had virtually disappeared. Monotony took over and talk of Shackleton coming back began to fade from the conversation. Orde-Lees considered the subject was 'practically taboo' and that it was quite obvious that 'no one really dare say what they really do think'.

Wordie's diary reflected the changing mood and increasing decline in morale. As the weeks passed by, references to rescue in his diary began to evaporate and finally disappear altogether. Wordie had come to terms with his longer than anticipated imprisonment and now accepted that rescue would not happen until late August or September. Others soon came round to the same view. Orde-Lees and Hurley, in particular, saw mid-August as the likely date when the rescue ship would come. Wild was more precise, informing Orde-Lees that 25 August was the day he expected Shackleton to return. Many expected the *Aurora*, the ship which carried the Ross Sea party to the other side of the continent, to be their rescuer.

Physically, the men were in a deplorable state, living in squalid semi-darkness and haunted by fears that stocks of penguins and seals would dry up. They had not washed or changed their clothes for around nine months and the soot from the blubber stove and blood from the slaughter caked their beards and hair. They were frequently soaked and battered by the fierce winds that chilled them to the bone.

Orde-Lees said the time spent on Elephant Island was 'one long nightmare' and added: '. . . the most that can be said for it is that it might have been worse, but could not possibly have been very much worse.' Only Wild remained outwardly optimistic, though this was undoubtedly for reasons of morale. Privately, he knew the odds were stacked against the *Caird* party and he had to plan for his own escape. This meant only one thing – Wild leading his own open-boat journey across the Southern Ocean.

Shackleton's parting message in April was that, if he did not return, the Elephant Island party should attempt to reach Deception Island, which lay about 250 miles (400 km) to the south-west. From

Deception it was hoped a passing whaler might be spotted. In the circumstances, it was a highly optimistic goal.

Some of the men, like Hudson and Blackborrow, were probably unfit for such a trip while others probably lacked the will to tackle another testing boat journey. It was equally improbable that those left behind on Elephant Island would survive further months of isolation awaiting a second rescue attempt. Some were already in serious decline, wracked by a combination of frostbite and the gathering ennui. The longer hours of winter darkness only added to their woes. By mid-June, as two rescue attempts were failing, the light lasted little more than six hours a day. The growing sense of despair was reflected in the conditions around the spit, which were becoming more primitive as the weeks passed. The daily routine of set mealtimes began to slip, the living quarters were noticeably less clean and many spent the entire day in their sleeping bags. Even the cooking pots were not cleaned. Orde-Lees reported that, 'indifference as to what is going to happen is very marked lately'. Wordie also sensed the deteriorating mood and noted: 'Very little pleases us nowadays; an extra 3 lumps of sugar caused a little sensation.'[6]

Tobacco was the only real luxury on Elephant Island, although most of the seamen had recklessly smoked their own personal allowance without attempting to ration supplies. By June many men, especially the sailors who were accustomed to heavy smoking and the free flow of tobacco, were getting desperate. On one occasion, those with a few remaining ounces of tobacco – Wordie, Wild, Marston and Hurley – kindly donated a small share of their personal allowance to the distressed seamen. According to Orde-Lees, it was an act of 'extraordinary self sacrifice'.

Wordie became a minor legend during this period, his ability to eke out his tobacco astounding everyone. He performed the small miracle of making his tobacco last for weeks longer than anyone else, and when everyone else had puffed their last pipe Wordie somehow conjured up enough scraps to make a comforting smoke.

With little else to ponder, a few addicts descended on Wordie like a wolf-pack. Some went to the lengths of scouring the beach for any faintly interesting specimen of rock which might arouse his attention and hopefully get swapped for a pipe-full of tobacco. Though Wordie routinely combed the narrow spit of beach on a daily basis to inspect the stones, his inherent curiosity invariably got the better of him and he gladly bartered a half-pipe or even a pipeful of the precious weed in exchange for a potentially interesting stone or two.

Bill Bakewell, one of the seamen, recalled an incident when Wordie somehow scraped together enough tobacco to make a single cigarette. Bakewell was helping Wordie clean a piece of sealskin to mend his fur boots and gazed longingly at the prized possession. Without hesitation, Wordie generously gave the tobacco to Bakewell, insisting that smoking did not bother him. Bakewell made a cigarette with toilet paper and shared the smoke with his pals, Walter How and Wild, hidden away from prying eyes behind the big rock at the end of the spit. 'It surely tasted good,' said Bakewell. 'We were like kids stealing a smoke.'[7]

Some resorted to bizarre alternatives in the search for a smoke. McLeod was among those who tried to improvise by stuffing his pipe with sennegrass, the grassy insulation from the inside of his boots. The habit duly caught on, though James said the smell of the smoking grass was more like a prairie fire than tobacco. Other strange concoctions included dried seaweed and scrapings from the sleeping bags, while Bakewell went to the lengths of breaking up a few old pipes and boiling them in water mixed with slivers of sennegrass. When dried and shredded the mixture resembled tobacco but the smell was positively overpowering.

Slight relief to their predicament came in the shape of a ghastly drink made from a combination of sugar and milk or water mixed with methylated spirits from the primus stove. The potion received a mixed reception from the customers, but it clearly had the desired effect. Wordie declared some of those who enjoyed the drink became 'very merry' in the process.

The crude hooch did little to blot out the reality of the situation. On 25 July Wordie wearily recorded that Shackleton had now been gone for three months and added the plaintive cry: 'Anything for a drink!' It was the hundredth day on the desolate spit and he added: '. . . methylated was served out to the thirsty ones, now reduced to half a dozen.'[8]

Four days earlier Shackleton had abandoned his third attempt to reach Elephant Island in the 75-ton wooden schooner, *Emma*. The vessel had struggled to within 100 miles (160 km) of the island on 21 July and spent some days cruising up and down the pack, looking for a way through. But *Emma* was too light for the task and Shackleton cabled news of the abortive rescue back to London, saying: 'It is evidently a very bad season in the south.'

As the *Emma* returned to the Falklands in early August, the food situation on Elephant Island began to deteriorate. Food stocks had been generally good, notably the continued presence of penguins, which provided both meat and fuel for the blubber stove. But as winter bore down, the wildlife dwindled and Wild made a bad mistake in early August when he decided not to slaughter all the available birds.

Wild believed that seals, which had been scarce in the winter, would soon start to return as the spring weather improved. It was an optimistic assumption and the seals returned only in small numbers. The decision inflamed the already delicate relationship between Orde-Lees and Wild. Orde-Lees was perhaps the only man who challenged Wild's leadership, dismissing him on one occasion as being 'as great an optimist as Sir Ernest himself & that is saying a good deal'. Wild was constantly irritated by Orde-Lees' nagging and in response reportedly threatened to shoot him unless he kept his mouth shut.

It hardly mattered that Orde-Lees was probably right. By August, the men had resorted to scavenging because food was in such short supply. They scrapped limpets off the rocks at low tide and, in the absence of fresh seal meat, were reduced to eating slices of half-rotten penguin flesh killed two months earlier or even scraps of birds. The meat, Wordie recalled was 'distinctly high'.

One night they celebrated the delights of stew made from boiled backbone and a seal's head. 'A very savoury stew all told, especially the head parts,' was Wordie's culinary judgement. However, the absence of penguins in mid-August was causing growing unease and an unrepentant Orde-Lees reported that 'everyone is concerned' about the lack of fresh meat. Shortly afterwards the party was down to one decent meal a day.

The ample supplies of food, particularly fresh seal or penguin meat, had managed to relieve many of the earlier tensions on Elephant Island. A full stomach worked wonders for morale. While there had been occasional cut-backs, no one so far had gone hungry. But as the party approached their fifth month of captivity, the men were faced with the reality of short rations and increasing hunger – and no sign of rescue.

Towards the end of August the situation was critical. Only a few days' food remained and penguins and seals seemed to have disappeared. The only remaining drink was a few servings of Bovril. Orde-Lees blithely concluded that the food problem was 'serious, not grave but serious'. The meagre breakfast that day consisted of three half-rotten penguin legs and Wordie wrote: 'There is a chance of going short of meat unless the pack clears away.'[9]

On 29 August, Wordie's diary records that only six penguins had been killed in the previous two days. Very little food was now left and he added: 'this is causing us a little anxiety, as our meat store is now considerably reduced: we begin to regret not having killed the penguins which visited us a fortnight ago.'[10]

The condition of the men was also giving grave cause for concern. A number had lost heart altogether and others were close to reaching the end of their tether. Hussey observed that towards the end of

August 'everyone except Wild had become listless'. By now even the repugnant topic of cannibalism had arisen. A few crass jokes about eating the first person to die were a poor attempt at humour and received a mixed reception. 'There's many a true word spoken in jest,' said a wary Orde-Lees, the outsider and most disliked member of the party.

With no sign of a ship, thoughts turned increasingly towards the unhappy prospect of the boat journey to Deception Island. Wild had spent some weeks quietly preparing for the trip, having ordered that all scraps of rope and nails should be tracked down and stored. Timing was important. The all-too familiar ice conditions around the island probably meant delaying the trip for at least another six weeks until mid-October. Wild indicated that he wanted to set out on 5 October. It would have been wiser to delay the journey until the warmer days of November or even December, but a later start risked missing the period when the whalers were due to visit Deception.

Wild took the two doctors, Macklin and McIlroy, into his confidence and discussed breaking up the 'hut' and using one of the boats, probably the *Docker*, to sail to Deception. It was expected that he would take a party of five men, leaving the remaining seventeen to cope under only one upturned boat and with an uncertain supply of fresh seal or penguin meat.

It was a hopelessly impractical idea which only desperate men could possibly consider. Few had much confidence that the patched up *Docker* could survive the 250-mile (400 km) journey in the face of the prevailing strong south-westerlies. All the best sailing materials had been given to the *Caird*. An old tent cloth would have to make do as a mainsail and the *Docker* had only five oars. There was no proper mast.

Wild's only hope was to make his way slowly and cautiously under the lee of the land from island to island and pray that the little vessel would not run into foul weather. He estimated that the boat would be capable of making only a few miles a day and the island-hugging voyage would take anything from four to six weeks. It was not a cheerful prospect. Orde-Lees judged the voyage a 'big undertaking' while the more realistic Hussey admitted it would be 'a hopeless journey'.

***

Over the horizon to the north, Shackleton, Crean and Worsley were embarking on the fourth attempt to rescue their despairing comrades. Enraged by the delay in sending a rescue ship from Britain, Shackleton, Crean and Worsley travelled to Punta Arenas in Chile, where they asked the local naval commander if he would release a vessel called *Yelcho* for another try to reach the men. The generous Chileans agreed and the *Yelcho* sailed through the Straits of Magellan on 25 August, crewed by Shackleton, Crean, Worsley and a handful of enthusiastic volunteers from the Chilean navy. The skipper, Luis Pardo, allowed Worsley to navigate. The undistinguished *Yelcho* was hardly an inviting prospect. The steel-built vessel, weighing about 150 tons, was employed as a humble tender running supplies to local lighthouses and hardly suitable for a battle with the ice. Shackleton felt obliged to promise the Chilean government that he would not take the *Yelcho* into the pack.

Fortunately, luck was on *Yelcho's* side in the marginally more clement weather of August. Conditions to the south of Cape Horn were blissfully calm and the waters were mostly free of ice as the *Yelcho* steamed southwards. Good progress was made until late in the evening of 29 August, when a blanket of fog descended over the seas. Normally, the *Yelcho* would have waited for the fog to lift to avoid the risk of a nasty collision with the ice. But these were not typical circumstances. Shackleton did not trust the conditions to remain favourable for long, fearing that the pack would surreptitiously close around them in the dark.

The *Yelcho* was still blessed with open seas and Shackleton decided to push his luck. He assumed command of the ship and steered blindly onwards in the dense fog. Luckily the fog began to lift in the early morning and by around 10 a.m. the familiar snow-capped peaks of Elephant Island suddenly came into view. Worsley's navigation, for the second time in 1916, had been flawless. Small chunks of ice clung to the shallow reefs dotted around the island, a reminder that the *Yelcho* was not free from danger. The pack, they felt, might not be too far away and the risk of getting trapped remained. Speed was of the essence.

***

The morning of 30 August was like any other on Elephant Island. Some men spent the time shovelling away snow from outside the hut and others trawled the shore looking for limpets. The lunch menu was to be a stew of seal bones and limpets, liberally garnished with seaweed. Alone among the twenty-two men, the frugal Wordie still possessed a few precious scraps of tobacco in his pouch.

Hurley and Marston were the last two left on the beach at around 1 o'clock when they noticed a dark object in the far distance. It seemed a curiously shaped berg, vaguely resembling a ship. As they gazed casually into the mist the image suddenly took shape and materialised into the *Yelcho*. 'Ship O,' someone screamed and pandemonium broke out.

The cooking pot was knocked over in the rush to get outside and men began to leap up and down in wild excitement. James put his boots on the wrong feet in the commotion. Orde-Lees performed an act of quiet kindness by carrying the invalid Blackborrow outside to witness the joyous scene.

Marston demanded that a smoke signal be made to signal the ship and Hurley rounded up some rotting blubber and bits of sennegrass. A hole was punched in one of the few remaining cans of paraffin, but the pile of rubbish burst into flames without creating any smoke. Macklin had the presence of mind to rip off his Burberry jacket and tie it to one of the *Docker*'s oars which had been turned into a makeshift flagpole. But in the rush he was only able to hoist his jacket halfway up the mast.

On the *Yelcho*, Shackleton, Crean and Worsley stared at the frenzied activity through binoculars. They were shocked at the sight of the 'flag' flying at half-mast, which they interpreted as a signal that some men had died. Shackleton counted out loud as the dark figures scurried around in a state of near delirium, first two, then four, six, eight and at last he cried out: 'They are all there. Every one of them. They are all saved.'

Yelcho came to within 500 yards (450 m) of the beach and a boat was hurriedly lowered. Standing up in the front and clearly visible from the shore were the striking frames of Shackleton and Crean. Wild admitted that he 'felt jolly like blubbing'. As the rowing boat came within hearing distance, an anxious Shackleton called out: 'All well?' The apprehension caused by seeing the Macklin's coat at half-mast was evident. 'We are all well, Boss,' Wild replied.

Shackleton and Crean threw cigarettes and tobacco to the men, who descended upon the treasures like street urchins scrambling for crumbs. But there was no time to celebrate. Shackleton, still fearful that the pack might have the last word, urged the men to climb aboard the boat before the weather closed off their exit route. Within an hour, the twenty-two castaways and their few meagre possessions had been plucked off the beach and ferried out to the *Yelcho*. Shackleton even turned down the chance to make a fleeting visit to the 'hut' under the boats. Wordie remembered:

> The end was rather a hurry: none of our rescuers ever saw the hut; the weather seemed changing for the worse; it was best to cut and run. And so all my beach exotics are left behind; the only rocks I have are in situ; But can one complain ? My notes are safe and every man is safe.[11]

It was 138 days – almost four and a half months – since the *James Caird*, *Dudley Docker* and *Stancomb Wills* had made their first landing on Elephant Island.

CHAPTER 8

CLOSING RANKS

TOBACCO AND CIGARETTES, WORDIE RECALLED, 'circulated like water' on the *Yelcho*'s return voyage to South America. At night, Hussey played his banjo as he had done so many times before until sheer weariness drove the men to their bunks.

One oddity was that the Chilean crew of the *Yelcho* seemed reluctant to get too close to the survivors. It took a little time for the men to realise that the stench of their body odour and clothing was almost overwhelming. The survivors had not washed properly for over ten months and had worn the same filthy blood-soaked and grease-stained clothing since abandoning *Endurance*.

The main topic of conversation, inevitably, was the war. The men from *Endurance* were probably the only people on earth who were unaware of the momentous events taking place in Europe. The retreat at Mons, disaster at Gallipoli, the sinking of the *Lusitania*, the titanic naval battle at Jutland and the slaughter on the Somme – all had passed them by. The war had been Shackleton's first question to the Norwegians on reaching the whaling station at Stromness and his colleagues now devoured every scrap of shocking information from the few English-language newspapers on board *Yelcho*. 'On all sides we hear of nothing but the terrible war news,' Wordie wrote.

The ship re-entered the Straits of Magellan on 2 September and, soon after, a harbour was found close to Punta Arenas where Shackleton could cable news of the rescue to the outside world. The telegram simply announced: 'Punta Arenas, September 3 – All saved. All well – Shackleton.'

Their arrival at Punta Arenas ignited an explosion of celebrations and festivities among the local Chileans and other visitors in the cosmopolitan port. Even the few German and Austrian ships in the harbour sounded their horns and flew their flags. Shackleton did not waste the opportunity for a public relations coup. He asked the men not to shave off their scruffy beards or cut their hair until they had assembled for photographs outside the Royal Hotel in Punta Arenas. Soon afterwards they luxuriated in their first bath and change of clothing.

Days of intense festivities followed as the men were relayed from one party to another, fêted as celebrities. Worsley left a lavish dinner one night to snatch some fresh air and was promptly confronted by armed guards, who insisted that 'no sober *gringo* leaves the building'. On another day a charity football match was arranged between a Punta Arenas team and the aptly-named Elephant Island Wanderers.

But the partying had no appeal for Wordie. Within days of landing at Punta Arenas, he slipped away from the bustle and embarked on a brisk eight-mile walk, the first time he had managed to stretch his legs properly since leaving South Georgia almost two years earlier.

By mid-September, the *Yelcho* had taken the party up the coast to Valparaiso and the nearby Chilean capital, Santiago, for another round of celebrations. At Valparaiso an estimated crowd of 30,000 well-wishers thronged the streets to greet the men. A little later the party crossed the Andes by train to the east and visited Montevideo in Uruguay and Buenos Aires in Argentina. The festivities came to an end in the first week of October, with most of the party anxious to return to Britain and join the war effort.

Wordie was given some unexpected news as he prepared for the journey home. First, Shackleton's money problems were so severe that he asked Wordie to defer collecting his salary. The money was not important to someone as comfortably off as Wordie, though it confirmed that Shackleton's skills with the expedition's finances did not come anywhere near matching his leadership. As one of his biographers later commented, it demonstrated that while Shackleton's men found it hard to trust him with their money, they could undeniably trust him with their lives.

However, the decision was sweetened with the news that Wordie was finally to be given the position of responsibility he had sought at the outset of the expedition. In tying up the enterprise's loose ends, Shackleton suddenly appointed Wordie as chief of scientific staff – both for the *Endurance* and for the Ross Sea party. The appointment, made on the day before the expedition members began to disperse, gave Wordie 'full power' to prepare and publish all the scientific results of the voyage. In handing over responsibility, Shackleton made two conditions: that he alone should retain copyright on all published material and second, that, for an unspecified reason, no geological or biological specimens should be given to the British Museum.[1]

In the circumstances, the geographical results of *Endurance* were modest and added little to the discoveries of Bruce and Filchner beyond a short stretch of the newly-found Caird Coast. But Wordie was not among those in the Polar establishment, including Mill, who believed that *Endurance* should never have sailed. The Weddell Sea journey, he once declared, 'paved the way for others . . . and not to have made it would have been against the whole tradition of exploration in general'.

The scientific results of the expedition were inevitably patchy and mostly inconclusive. All the records and specimens from the expedition were lost with the ship and the official papers were drawn up from an assortment of soiled field notebooks and scraps of paper which had somehow survived the ten-month ordeal after the sinking of *Endurance*.

Wordie was not deterred and quietly pulled together all the available data, encouraging Clark, James and Hussey to contribute papers on various specialist subjects such as oceanography, meteorology and even whales. Most valuable, however, were Wordie's own studies of the movement and nature of the sea ice in the Weddell, which provided invaluable assistance to later travellers in the difficult waters.

Wordie subsequently delivered a general summary of events to the RGS in December 1917 but the official papers were not published in the Society's *Geographical Journal* until 1921. James, Clark, Hussey and Wordie all contributed brief summaries of their work as appendices to Shackleton's own book on the expedition, *South*, which was published to great acclaim in 1919.[2]

Miraculously, Wordie produced a sound geological paper for the RGS, despite the obvious impediment of being a geologist adrift at sea or marooned on a tiny spit. Although the results were based on the most flimsy of observations, the outcome was nevertheless a triumph of improvisation over adversity.

The only firm land encountered during the expedition was South Georgia at the outset and Elephant Island at the conclusion. Although the ship had skirted the Antarctic coastline of Coats Land for some time, Wordie was unable to study the geology because the entire region was covered in a blanket of snow. Even the tops of mountains were too distant to monitor with any accuracy. 'No bare rocks were seen,' he freely admitted.

Without a geologist's raw material, Wordie ad-libbed, basing his geological conclusions on the odd rock or stone brought up from the bottom of the Weddell Sea by Clark's depth-sounding apparatus during the early stages of the *Endurance*'s drift. On one occasion the apparatus yielded two large boulders, one weighing an impressive 70 lb (32 kg). 'Here was a treasure indeed,' the frustrated geologist wrote in his diary.

Another minor source of information was the accumulation of dirt embedded in passing icebergs. While on *Endurance*, Wordie was able to melt fragments of this 'dark ice' with the aid of the wardroom kettle and examine the very small residues of mud and granules of stone. More improbably, he was also able to draw some further conclusions from a few tiny pebbles retrieved from the stomachs of slaughtered penguins. Although his ingenious use of penguin innards was excluded from the official papers on the voyage, Wordie later confirmed that he had gone to extraordinary lengths to fulfil his obligations as the expedition's geologist. In an interview some years later he divulged: 'Geologically, we had to confine our research to examining the contents of penguins' stomachs. They have a grinding mechanism in their crop and large pieces of rock can be recovered.'[3]

The results of his improvisation were understandably inconclusive. But he did make a useful contribution to the issue of whether the Graham Land peninsula was attached to the Antarctic continent, though it did not resolve the matter. Wordie's judgement – based partly on the unwitting contributions of numerous penguins – was that the land beneath the Weddell Sea was similar to the terrain around the Ross Sea region on the other side of the continent. He concluded that the rocks were considerably different to those near Graham Land, which he decided was an extension of the South American Andes.

One of the few definite conclusions from the expedition was that the controversial Morrell Land, which had been rumoured to exist in the western reaches of the Weddell Sea for almost a hundred years, was a mirage. The vexed question of Morrell Land had divided the Polar experts for the best part of a century. Even Shackleton believed it existed before the *Endurance* voyage. By contrast, Mawson dismissed Morrell's theory of land in the Weddell Sea as 'humbug' and 'tosh' while Rudmose Brown, who was among the few to have sailed in the Weddell Sea, was more supportive of the notion. However Wordie's formal papers brought the debate to an abrupt end by revealing that *Endurance* had drifted right across the previously unknown seas where Morrell Land was supposed to be located.

Overall, the results of the scientific papers were received with great understanding, even if they added only fragments to knowledge of the region. But the scientific community fully understood the difficult conditions under which the fragments of knowledge were secured and it was widely accepted that Wordie had performed a small miracle in producing anything meaningful in such gruelling circumstances.

Gregory, Wordie's mentor at Glasgow, said the findings showed the 'most indefatigable industry and enterprise' and Mawson paid tribute to his agility in transferring his research efforts from land to sea. Alfred Harker, the eminent geologist, said that by ordinary standards the observations were 'fragmentary and inconclusive' but nevertheless had made a 'valuable contribution' to knowledge of the region. Even warmer praise came from Frank Debenham at Cambridge. Debenham said the papers reflected a 'fine spirit of research' and suggested that Wordie 'might well become the leading authority' if he concentrated on a prolonged investigation of the Polar sea-ice.

***

The *Endurance* expedition came to a formal close in the early morning of 8 October 1916 on an undistinguished railway platform in Buenos Aires. There were few witnesses and no ceremony, just simple handshakes as the men went their separate ways. Shackleton and Worsley went to Australia and then back to Antarctica to discover the fate of the *Aurora* and the Ross Sea party. But most were heading back to Britain, where the war was at its height.

The rump of the *Endurance* expedition sailed back to England on board the *Highland Laddie*, whose owners, the Nelson Line, generously paid their passage home. On deck, there was an immediate foretaste of the war as watchful crewmen permanently manned the ship's two guns. Despite the incredible strain of the previous two years, there were no plans for even a short period of recuperation. The stark contrast with today's post-trauma stress counselling or relaxing holidays could not be more dramatic as the *Highland Laddie* steamed towards the full inferno of war.

Fortunately, it was an uneventful journey, except for Hussey. Apart from the *Endurance* party, there were only five passengers on board the *Highland Laddie*, including two young women. By the time the ship docked the banjo-playing meteorologist was engaged to one of the women, though the engagement was later broken off.

Wordie's sister Alison met him at London's Albert Dock in early November, well over two years since she had seen him off. But the joy of coming home was tempered by bad news. Wordie discovered that numerous friends and acquaintances had already been killed in the war. Among them was his oldest pal, George Buchanan-Smith, who died from wounds inflicted at Loos in 1915.

What he pointedly did not do was tell Alison the true facts of what occurred on Elephant Island. Indeed, the full horrors of what occurred on the forbidding spit at Elephant Island will, in all probability, never be fully told. In each case the men imposed an informal degree of self-censorship, which almost certainly obscured the worst excesses and the more grisly details of the primeval living conditions of men clinging to life at the extremes. Even in later life the old hands from *Endurance* quietly closed ranks and ensured that some things, at least, would remain a secret forever. A variety of men kept diaries during their long ordeal – including Hurley, James, Macklin, Orde-Lees and Wordie – and others, like Wild and Bakewell, wrote accounts at a later stage. But it is unlikely that even these diaries reveal the full story.

Wordie's diary, although comprehensive and highly informative, does not betray all the secrets, least of all his own private feelings. Only occasionally his entries offer a glimpse of the grim reality. However, he was also hard on the other diarists. Once he scribbled a terse verdict on three of the diaries kept during the expedition. He wrote: 'James is good, Hurley is turgid, Orde-Lees is lengthy.'[4]

In later life he rarely spoke about the confinement on Elephant

Island, not even to his closest family. His own children recall that it was not until the final two or three years of his life that Wordie even mentioned the expedition in any detail.[5] He rarely strayed from providing a broad-brush account of events, preferring to keep the darker moments and his personal feelings obscured.

One of the few occasions when he allowed the mask to slip came many years later in a private document which was never published. Writing thirty years after the ordeal, Wordie commented: 'Food supply proved very precarious and it was merely by very good fortune that we were able to keep going as we did through the unexpected habits of the Gentoo penguin. Survival at Cape Wild proved a very near thing.'[6]

One of the most sensitive issues was the apparent mental breakdown of some men. Shackleton told his wife in a letter that, after the boat journey to Elephant Island, 'about 10 of the party were off their heads' and Hussey remembered that 'six of the party went off their heads'. Some had collapsed to the point which, said Hurley, inevitably meant they would 'starve or freeze if left to their own resources' on the island.

However, other survivors, like Wordie and Macklin, were emphatic in later years that only two of the party had truly broken down. But neither discussed the matter publicly, preferring to avoid bringing any distress to old comrades.[7]

The most delicate subject was, of course, the issue of cannibalism, which, according to rumour, involved a plot to kill the unpopular figure of Orde-Lees. But the story has gained little credence over the years, and even in later years, old men from *Endurance* would brush off all suggestions that men had contemplated such a heinous act. 'It was an absolute lie,' Greenstreet bluntly declared in the 1970s.

Nor was there much mention of the cliques which inevitably formed. Wordie, for example, remained close to fellow spirits, Clark and James. It was a group which, although given little credit afterwards, coped outstandingly well, given that they were all cultivated men trapped in unfamiliar conditions of overwhelming squalor. In some respects, it might be considered that the academics were the least well equipped for the ordeal. In the event, Wordie, James and Clark showed great resolve and set an example to others, while never once causing disciplinary problems for either Shackleton or Wild.

Wordie, in fact, was among the strongest at the end of the dreadful open-boat journey to Elephant Island. On landing he was still capable of work and performed an invaluable role in helping to carry stores and equipment from the water's edge to safety up the beach. However, Wordie was never particularly close to either Shackleton or Wild, which may explain why his role was under-estimated.

Shackleton turned mainly to Wild for advice and guidance and occasionally to Hurley, and when Wild needed support on Elephant Island he usually spoke to Hurley or McIlory. In his first press interview after the escape, Wild did not once mention the solid reliability of Wordie during the time on Elephant Island. The only individuals he singled out for credit were Macklin, McIlroy, Hurley, Hussey, Kerr, Rickinson and How, whose 'energy and ability' he praised.[8]

But Wordie held Wild in high regard. His respect for Wild had increased during the expedition, first on the trip to Elephant Island and then through his astute leadership on the island, which had held the disparate group together and prevented any serious breakdown in discipline. Wordie summed up Wild's remarkable performance when he wrote that, apart from the expedition leaders, 'no other Antarctic figure has so impressed himself on so many of the rank and file' as Wild. Using language which was unusually expansive for Wordie, he added: 'No one was more liked and loved and his attraction, apart from his feats, lay partly in his simple and confiding nature, but also in his being the complete confidence-giving companion without fear.'[9]

Another insight into Wordie's thinking about events on *Endurance* came in the late 1950s with the publication of a new book on the expedition by Alfred Lansing. The book, called *Endurance*, was the last major work on the subject to be compiled after interviewing survivors. Among those who gave first-hand accounts to Lansing were Bakewell, Greenstreet, Hussey, James, Macklin, McIlroy and Wordie.

Lansing said that most survivors submitted to 'long hours, even days of interviewing with courtesy and co-operativeness'. He concluded that through these recollections he was able to form 'as true a picture of the events as we could collectively produce'.[10] Wordie's judgement, which he scrawled on the inside of his personal copy of Lansing's book, was brief and unambiguous. The inscription reads: 'Inaccurate throughout'.[11]

An incident at a reunion of the survivors also provided a clear hint of Wordie's determination to keep certain matters private. In 1955, Walter How, who had signed on as a sailmaker on *Endurance*, was reminiscing aloud about events on Elephant Island almost forty years earlier. How, a chirpy Cockney, was entertaining a small crowd of enthralled listeners after an agreeable dinner in London. Wordie overhead the conversation and stepped in, promptly cutting How short with the abrupt comment, 'What's going on here, How? Not telling stories out of school, I hope.'[12] How obediently stopped chatting with the brisk reply, 'No, sir.'

It is always possible that Wordie's comments were meant to be light-hearted. One witness to the scene said it was a good-humoured remark which did not imply any rebuke to the genial How. But whatever the tone, Wordie's intervention brought How's conversation to an immediate halt. As Orde-Lees said on Elephant Island: 'There's many a true word spoken in jest.'

CHAPTER 9

THE WESTERN FRONT

WORDIE WASTED NO TIME JOINING THE WAR. Within a week of arriving home from the Antarctic, he was at the War Office for interviews and a medical examination. In early December 1916, Wordie informed the Cambridge Board of Military Studies of his intentions, suggesting it would be best if his 'mathematical and scientific qualifications could be utilised'. The point was not lost on the War Office, which noted: 'This is quite a good man. He is just back from Shackleton's Antarctic Expedition. I had intended to take him for the RFA (Royal Field Artillery).'[1]

Wordie was duly called up in mid-January, underwent preliminary training at the Topsham Barracks, Exeter and completed his preparations at the Royal Artillery Barracks, Bordon in Hampshire. In late May 1917, he was formally posted to 3/4th Lowland (Howitzer) Brigade, part of the Royal Field Artillery, at the rank of 2nd Lieutenant. In between bouts of military training, Wordie was increasingly preoccupied with the affairs of *Endurance*, collating data and preparing publication of the official papers for the Royal Geographical Society of London. But before his work was competed he received shocking news.

Shackleton returned from the Antarctic in February 1917 with disastrous word of the Ross Sea party, the other less-remembered half of the Imperial Trans-Antarctic expedition. The ten-man party had suffered an ordeal of similar hardship to the men from *Endurance* and three of the party died in terrible circumstances, thus demolishing the myth that Shackleton never lost a man.

The Ross Sea party, which knew nothing about the crushing of *Endurance,* had been cut off for two years, faithfully laying depots for Shackleton's trans-continental party who never came. But the men were poorly equipped and struck down by the deadly combination of scurvy and malnutrition on a marathon sledging expedition which covered over 1,500 miles (2,400 km). The Ross Sea party's immense depot-laying journey, however futile, was the last great episode of man-hauling sledges during the heroic age of Polar exploration. One of the survivors was Frank Wild's brother, Ernest, who was awarded the Albert Medal for his bravery.

Wordie also received a medal. In 1918, Shackleton recommended Wordie for the Polar Medal in recognition of his services to the expedition, though not everyone was so fortunate. Shackleton used the honours system to settle a few old scores, which meant that four *Endurance* men – McNish and three trawlemen, Vincent, Holness and Stephenson – did not receive their Polar Medals.

It was a vindictive swipe at men whom he considered had fallen short of his own standards. The snub did no credit to Shackleton and was particularly severe on McNish, who had paid dearly for his one brief moment of mutiny on the ice. McNish was undoubtedly a spiky character and something of a barrack-room lawyer, but there is little doubt that his impressive carpentry skills in modifying the *James Caird* for the journey to South Georgia were crucial in making the trip possible. The niggardly rebuke of withholding the Polar Medal remains an open wound in the history of the *Endurance* expedition.

Even some of Shackleton's men were surprised at the treatment of McNish. Because there was no official ceremony, news of the exclusion did not emerge for some time. When it did, Macklin condemned the rebuke as a 'grave injustice' to McNish. However there was little sympathy for Vincent, the disruptive and unpopular trawler hand. When in later life he fell on hard times, the normally generous Wordie uncharacteristically declined to help. In a letter about Vincent's appeal for help, he commented:

Vincent was by nature of cowardly disposition . . . I do not think many of Shackleton's men would be as anxious to help Vincent as they would others of the party.[2]

For much of 1917 Wordie juggled the affairs of the expedition with his military commitments. A week before Christmas, he travelled from Bordon to the RGS in London to deliver his paper on *Endurance*. It was his final act before being shipped to the Western Front.

In February 1918 Wordie joined D Battery in the 11th Army Brigade stationed around Armentières on the border between France and Belgium. Initially it was a leisurely introduction to combat. For the first few weeks, Wordie found time away from his new duties to maintain a steady stream of correspondence from his billet, tidying up the formal affairs of *Endurance* with the RGS and others, seemingly unconcerned at the tumult elsewhere along the Western Front. In one letter to Arthur Hinks, the secretary of the RGS, he cheerfully reported: 'Splendid weather out here and very little doing.'[3]

But Wordie had entered the war at precisely the moment the conflict had entered its decisive final phase. The most significant event was Russia's withdrawal from the war. In early March, Russia signed the Brest–Litovsk Treaty with Germany, which released numerous divisions from the Eastern theatre for duty on the Western Front.

At the same time, thousands of American troops were starting to pour into Europe following the US entry into the conflict in 1917. Among those escorting American soldiers to the front during the spring of 1918 was Shackleton. The German commander, General Erich Ludendorff, was intent on smashing the Allies into submission before the full weight of fresh US battalions could be assembled and he prepared a massive new assault on the Western Front, aiming to drive the British from the Somme and the French from the Aisne.

Germany's great offensive began on the morning of 21 March when more than 6,000 heavy guns began bombarding the Allied lines. Initially the German divisions made good progress at the centre, smashing forward around the strongholds of St Quentin and Cambrai. But the resistance soon proved far greater than expected and Ludendorff was forced to switch the focus of the attack to the north of the front around Ypres and Armentières on the River Lys. Among those waiting for the attack near Armentières was Lt Wordie's D Battery.

The Battle of Lys, which began on April 9, was a mass German attempt to scythe through the British lines towards Mount Kemmel and the strategic railway junction at Hazebrouck, about 20 miles due east of Armentières. It was the first stage of a bold scheme, code-named Georgette, to break through to the vital coastal ports of Calais and Dunkirk and disrupt the Allies' ability to re-supply their armies. Ludendorff had chosen his target with care.

The line near Lys was thinly defended, partly by battle-weary British forces shifted from combat elsewhere and partly by a cluster of reluctant Portuguese troops with no stomach for the fight. Early morning mist hung over the trenches at the start of a massive 4½-hour German bombardment. Hundreds of guns opened up and over 2,000 tons of deadly gas were released. Ludendorff then hurled fourteen divisions at the defenders strung out along a 10-mile front, and soon a 3½-mile gap in the line was opened as the Portuguese defences disintegrated under the onslaught.

Wordie was among the first casualties of the battle. He was caught in the open during the early morning bombardment and was highly fortunate not to be killed by the blanket shelling. Wordie's field-gun, being pulled by a team of two horses, was manoeuvring into position when a shell exploded nearby. Wordie was riding the horse on the left of the carriage and he survived only because the shell landed on the right of the team, killing the riderless horse. But the explosion blew Wordie off his mount and the dead horse fell on top of him, badly breaking his leg. He would probably have been killed had he been riding the other horse. In a letter to Hinks he explained:

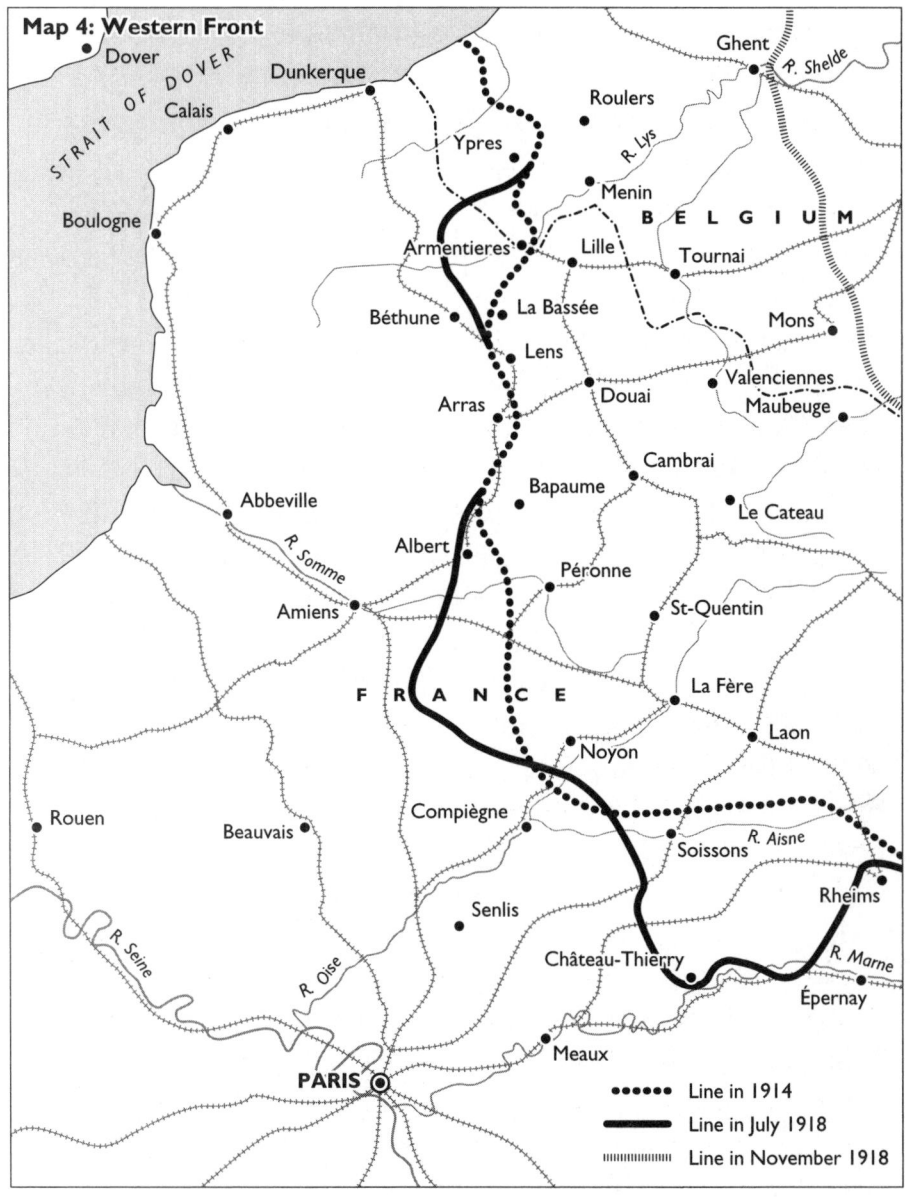

Map 4: Western Front

Dover

STRAIT OF DOVER

Calais

Dunkerque

Boulogne

Ghent

R. Shelde

Roulers

Ypres

Menin

R. Lys

B E L G I U M

Armentieres

Lille

Tournai

Béthune

La Bassée

Mons

Lens

Valenciennes

Arras

Douai

Maubeuge

Abbeville

Bapaume

Cambrai

Le Cateau

R. Somme

Albert

Péronne

Amiens

St-Quentin

F R A N C E

La Fère

Laon

Noyon

Compiègne

Rouen

Beauvais

Soissons

R. Aisne

Rheims

R. Seine

Senlis

R. Marne

R. Oise

Château-Thierry

Épernay

PARIS

Meaux

●●●●●● Line in 1914

━━━━━ Line in July 1918

ııııııııı Line in November 1918

I suppose I should be considered lucky. I was on horseback near Armentières when a shell dropped beside me and by one of those strange chances gave me a few grazes only; and as these things have a habit of happening quickly, I could not get away before the falling horse broke my leg.[4]

However the break was more serious than first expected. He was shipped back to Britain where doctors at the military hospital in Bristol told Wordie that the injury was so serious that he might not regain the full use of the leg. 'At present, the surgeons say no, but I have hopes to the contrary,' he wrote.

Wordie was luckier than many of the men engaged in the Battle of Lys, which cost the lives of around 50,000 men. Ludendorff was astonished by the fierce resistance shown by the British troops in one of the great defensive actions of the war. He was equally alarmed at his own enormous casualties and on April 29, after almost three weeks of bitter fighting, the offensive in the northern sector was called off. Among the thousands of captured German prisoners was a regimental band assembled specially to play the victorious Germans into the town of Béthune, a few miles to the south of Armentières.

Wordie's second stroke of luck on the Western Front was that, contrary to the doctor's early warning, his leg made a near full recovery. After leaving the military hospital in Bristol, he went back to Scotland for a period of recuperation. He spent some time with Alison at Banavie, near Fort William. Slowly regaining his strength, he made frequent trips into the hills. On one occasion Wordie climbed the 4,406-ft (1,343-m) Ben Nevis, Britain's highest mountain, while still using crutches. But the lingering effects of the injury prevented him rejoining his regiment and Wordie was still unfit for duty when the war came finally to an end on 11 November 1918. Two months later, on 9 January 1919, he was demobbed. In recognition of those who were less fortunate, he donated £60 (approximately £1,300 today) to a permanent memorial for the war dead in the grounds of the Glasgow Academy.

Among those lost were old colleagues from the Imperial Trans-Antarctic Expedition. From a combined party of fifty-six who went south on *Endurance* and the *Aurora*, three were killed in action and five were wounded, some badly. Tim McCarthy, the popular Irishman who had sailed in the *James Caird*, was killed at his gun in the Channel in 1917 and Alf Cheetham, a veteran of four Antarctic voyages, was torpedoed only a few weeks before the Armistice. Frank Wild's brother, Ernest, a survivor from the Ross Sea party, died off the coast of Malta in 1918. McIlroy, like Wordie, was badly wounded during the Ypres campaign and subsequently invalided out of the army.

Wordie had used his long convalescence to reflect and plan the next stage of his life. Despite the rigours of *Endurance*, his appetite for exploring remained stronger than ever.

CHAPTER 10

WITH BRUCE TO SPITSBERGEN

PICKING UP THE THREADS OF NORMALITY, WORDIE RETURNED TO Cambridge, where he found a comforting air of familiarity about the place. Ray Priestley was in residence and Frank Debenham was lecturing in geography and floating an idea which appealed to Wordie.

Debenham's proposal was to establish a permanent Polar research organisation in Cambridge. He found a willing ally in Priestley and before long Wordie too became an enthusiastic supporter. Debenham had chosen his moment to propose a polar institute with perfect timing. With the two Poles reached and a large portion of the landscape mapped, exploration was poised to move from an era of discovery into a more broader scientific phase and a new Polar institute was a natural addition to the new age.

The idea of forming a dedicated Polar research facility in Britain was first discussed by Debenham, Priestley and Wright in late 1912 during the melancholic final days of Scott's expedition. While sitting out a blizzard at Cape Royds – Shackleton's base for the *Nimrod* expedition in 1908–09 – Debenham jotted down a few outline plans for a 'Polar Centre'. He saw it as both a centre of Polar excellence and a fitting memorial to his old leader, Scott.

During the days at Cape Royds, Debenham's jottings were left lying around the hut and someone crossed out the proposed name, 'Polar Centre' and replaced it with the title of 'A Polar Institute'.[1] Plans began to crystallize at Cambridge immediately after the war and by 1920 the trio of Debenham, Priestley and Wordie had drawn up a detailed prospectus for the proposed new Polar Institute, which they submitted to the trustees of the Scott Memorial Fund.

The Scott Memorial Fund, originally known as The Lord Mayor's Fund, was set up in 1913 in the wake of the Polar tragedy and raised almost £76,000 (approximately £3,500,000 in today's terms) from public donations, almost double the cost of the expedition itself. After making payments to the dependents of the five dead men and other related causes, a residue of about £10,000 was set aside 'in aid of Polar research' which perfectly suited Debenham's purpose.

The Cambridge explorers were pushing at an open door. Two of the key trustees of the fund were Sir Francis Younghusband, President of the RGS and J.J. Thomson, President of the Royal Society. Both could see the merit of a specialist organisation, separate from their own, which could accommodate Polar data under one roof and undertake new research, as well as providing a dedicated library and archive.

Towards the end of 1920, the Memorial trustees accepted the proposal and gave an initial grant of £6,000 (approximately £115,000 today). The Scott Polar Research Institute (SPRI), with Debenham installed as the first director, was soon housed in an undistinguished attic in Cambridge's Sedgwick Museum. The modest Institute at this stage was little more than a club, where explorers and scientists gathered informally. There were not enough funds to employ full-time staff and the Institute initially relied on the support of friends within the Polar community and Cambridge University. Debenham cheerfully called SPRI's early period the 'attic years'.

The Institute gradually began to collect records and equipment from past expeditions, notably those of Scott and Shackleton. Wordie's most telling contribution at this point was to recruit Shackleton, the most famous living British explorer, as a supporter of the Institute. Wordie also secured Shackleton's approval for important records from the Imperial Trans-Antarctic Expedition to be donated to the fledgling organisation. Wordie's role as chief of scientific staff meant that he had accumulated numerous diaries and papers from the expedition and he was anxious to ensure that these records should be preserved. He once told Shackleton that storing the documents at SPRI would allow material to be 'very get-at-able and not liable to be knocked about as at present'.[2]

SPRI's fortunes moved onto a different footing in 1925 when the Scott Memorial Fund was formally wound up. In handing over the residue of money to Debenham's organisation, the Fund laid down an important condition: that the money should finance a permanent home for the Institute. A management committee, which included Wordie, Priestley and Debenham, met for the first time that year and began the laborious task of findng a suitable location. It proved to be a far longer process than anyone anticipated. The Institute's new building, at Lensfield Road in Cambridge, was not formally opened until 1934, the ceremony being performed by the Prime Minister, Stanley Baldwin.

Aside from helping with the birth of SPRI, Wordie was anxious to resume his active career in the field and his first step was to approach the notable Scottish explorer, William Speirs Bruce, who was planning to take an expedition to Spitsbergen. It was Wordie's first voyage above the Arctic Circle.

Bruce, a 52-year-old naturalist and oceanographer, was travelling to Spitsbergen in the hope of establishing commercial coal mining or oil fields in the area and needed geologists. Professor John Horne of Edinburgh University, the expedition's scientific adviser, was consulted about Wordie and readily gave him a glowing recommendation. Horne had known Wordie since his arrival at Cambridge and told Bruce that Wordie was, 'a good geologist, health excellent, a most genial man.'

The recommendation was good enough for Bruce and Wordie was immediately hired at a salary of £240 (about £5,000 in today's terms) for the three-month voyage. By comparison, Bruce earned

£600 (£12,600 today) and the more experienced geologist, George Tyrell, was paid some £320 (£6,700).

Explorers can generally be separated into two distinct types: the romantic adventurer like Shackleton in search of new frontiers or the scientist eager to broaden the horizons of human knowledge. Bruce came from the latter school. Bruce was a passionate believer in scientific endeavour. He was among the few living British explorers with knowledge and experience of both the Arctic and Antarctic, but his prickly nature and overt Scottish nationalism left him isolated from the Polar establishment. Despite almost thirty years of highly commendable work, he never received the Polar Medal.

Bruce's first venture to the ice was a pioneering trip to the Weddell Sea in 1892–3 with the Dundee whaler, *Balaena*, and he spent a year in the Arctic with the Jackson-Harmsworth expedition to Franz-Joseph Land in 1896–7. He was initially short-listed for the *Discovery* expedition in 1901, but Gregory, later Wordie's mentor at Glasgow, rejected his application. The snub inspired Bruce to return to the Weddell Sea in the *Scotia* in 1902–04, making a significant new addition to the map of Antarctica by discovering an extensive slice of new coastline, which he named Coats Land after the Scots industrialists, Andrew and James Coats, who financed the expedition. In 1903 Bruce established a weather-monitoring centre on Laurie Island in the South Orkneys, the first scientific station built in the Antarctic. It was Bruce who in 1908 first proposed making a full crossing of the Antarctic continent from coast to coast, an idea freely adopted a few years later by Shackleton.

Bruce was someone who liked to swim against the tide. While British Polar activity around the turn of the twentieth century was centred largely on conquering the Antarctic, Bruce turned his attention north to the Arctic and began a lifelong fascination with Spitsbergen. His first trip to Spitsbergen was in 1898 and over the next few years he made ten separate journeys to the region, mapping the area and focusing increasingly on his plans to open profitable mining or oil operations. He even tried to persuade Britain to annexe the uninhabited island, whose sovereignty at this point had not been claimed.

Bruce had developed a mild obsession with Spitsbergen and by 1909 had persuaded a group of Edinburgh businessmen to set up the Scottish Spitsbergen Syndicate to finance his ambitions for the El Dorado of the north. He was keen to return after the war but suddenly discovered that rival prospecting companies from Britain, Norway, America and Russia had moved into the area. Spitsbergen, Europe's Arctic outpost, became a repository for old Antarctic hands who had gravitated north as the heroic age of Shackleton and Scott drew to a close. As Wordie prepared to sail with Bruce, he discovered that Wild and McIlroy from *Endurance* had joined the rival Northern Exploration Company, while Herbert Ponting, Victor Campbell and Michael Barne, who had been south with Scott, were also associated with the NEC.

Bruce had a reputation for taking only the most accomplished men on his expeditions. He once recruited Hjalmar Johansen, the tough Norwegian who participated in both Fridtjof Nansen's epic 'furthest north' journey and Amundsen's South Pole expedition.

Wordie now found himself alongside experienced men like Tyrell, the distinguished surveyor John Mathieson and the highly-regarded geographer-botanist, Robert Rudmose Brown, plus a selection of bright young graduates from the universities of Edinburgh and Glasgow. Bruce's new expedition was a sizeable gamble for the Syndicate, which was prepared to invest £25,000 (£500,000 today) to fund the search for economic deposits of coal or oil. It was a substantial enterprise, which involved hiring the 1,000-ton *Petunia*, a surplus war vessel, at a cost of £600 a month and assembling a large team of miners, surveyors, naturalists and nine geologists.

Under Bruce the expedition was a typically Scottish affair. In 1904 a kilted piper from his *Scotia* party had been famously photographed in Coats Land and the *Petunia* was given a suitable send-off when the party sailed from Leith on 15 July 1919. A piper was playing and St Andrew's Saltire flew from the mizzenmast. It hardly seemed to matter that Bruce, in fact, was born in London and only developed ardent Scottish nationalism in his twenties after studying at Edinburgh University. Wordie, for one, was not very impressed with Bruce's flag-waving chauvinism, despite his own deep Scottish roots. He preferred the low-key approach to exploration and never embraced the Scottish nationalism of men like Bruce. In his diary, he simply wrote: 'The nationality idea is a bit overdone.'[3]

The *Petunia* sailed north to Spitsbergen, dropping off parties to the Syndicate's estates at Prins Karls Forland and at the head of Isfjorden in Spitsbergen. Wordie and Bruce went up to the Stor Fjord, where in 1909 Bruce claimed to have smelt oil, and where he believed that the hopes of riches were at their strongest. 'It was a remarkable smell,' he once said. 'Reeking, real reeking!'

He called it the 'Broxburn smell' after the Broxburn Petroleum Company, which had managed to extract oil from shale deposits near Edinburgh. Though the smell certainly existed, Wordie was highly sceptical of finding oil and he found the optimistic claims of Bruce less than convincing. In one scornful entry to his diary, Wordie said: '. . . has Jules Verne anything so exciting and romantic as this of a broken man forcing his mind back ten years so as to guide others to the treasure. We fairly romped back to the ship, planning a novel of the Jules Verne, John Buchan, etc type.'[4]

Wordie's doubts were well founded and the 'oil' proved to be worthless bituminous shale. In his official report Wordie concluded that the geology of the country was 'extremely unfavourable' to locating oil. Indeed, the fruitless search for oil summed up the huge disappointment of the 1919 expedition and the Syndicate's costly but failed gamble.

The expedition returned to Scotland empty-handed but Bruce was adamant and refused to be shifted from his belief in Spitsbergen's potential. He pushed for another search in 1920, with Wordie earmarked as a key member of the team.

The year 1920 was a busy time for Wordie. In March he received the prestigious Back Grant from the RGS for his much-admired work in rescuing some meaningful scientific data from the *Endurance* expedition and before long he was confronted with the choice of returning to the Antarctic or going back to Spitsbergen with Bruce.

Another diversion came when Wordie was reunited with a scattering of old *Endurance* hands, including Wild, Crean, James and Orde-Lees, who gathered together for Shackleton's hundredth lecture on the expedition at the Philharmonic Hall, London. Hussey also turned up, playing his banjo and leading the motley ensemble in a nostalgic rendition of the song which James composed during their imprisonment. However the song, 'My name is Frankie Wild-o, My hut's on Elephant Isle . . .' sounded oddly out of place when delivered in refined surroundings by clean-shaven men in pressed suits, polished shoes and neat collars and ties.

Painful memories of a different sort were aroused when a member of the audience asked the explorers a seemingly innocent question: 'Was there not any use for a proper trained nurse?' Shackleton diplomatically glossed over the two years of sexual deprivation and simply pointed out that, so far, women had not taken part in Antarctic exploration.

Soon after the reunion Wordie agreed to join Bruce for a second visit to Spitsbergen, which meant turning down the opportunity of enlisting on the proposed new expedition to the Antarctic with the hapless British Imperial Expedition. The expedition was, on paper at least, an attractive proposition. It was heading for the Hope Bay region of the Graham Land Peninsula under the leadership of John Cope, a surgeon who was among the survivors of Shackleton's Ross Sea party. Also involved was a 19-year-old Cambridge geology student, Thomas Bagshawe, and the pioneer aviator, Hubert

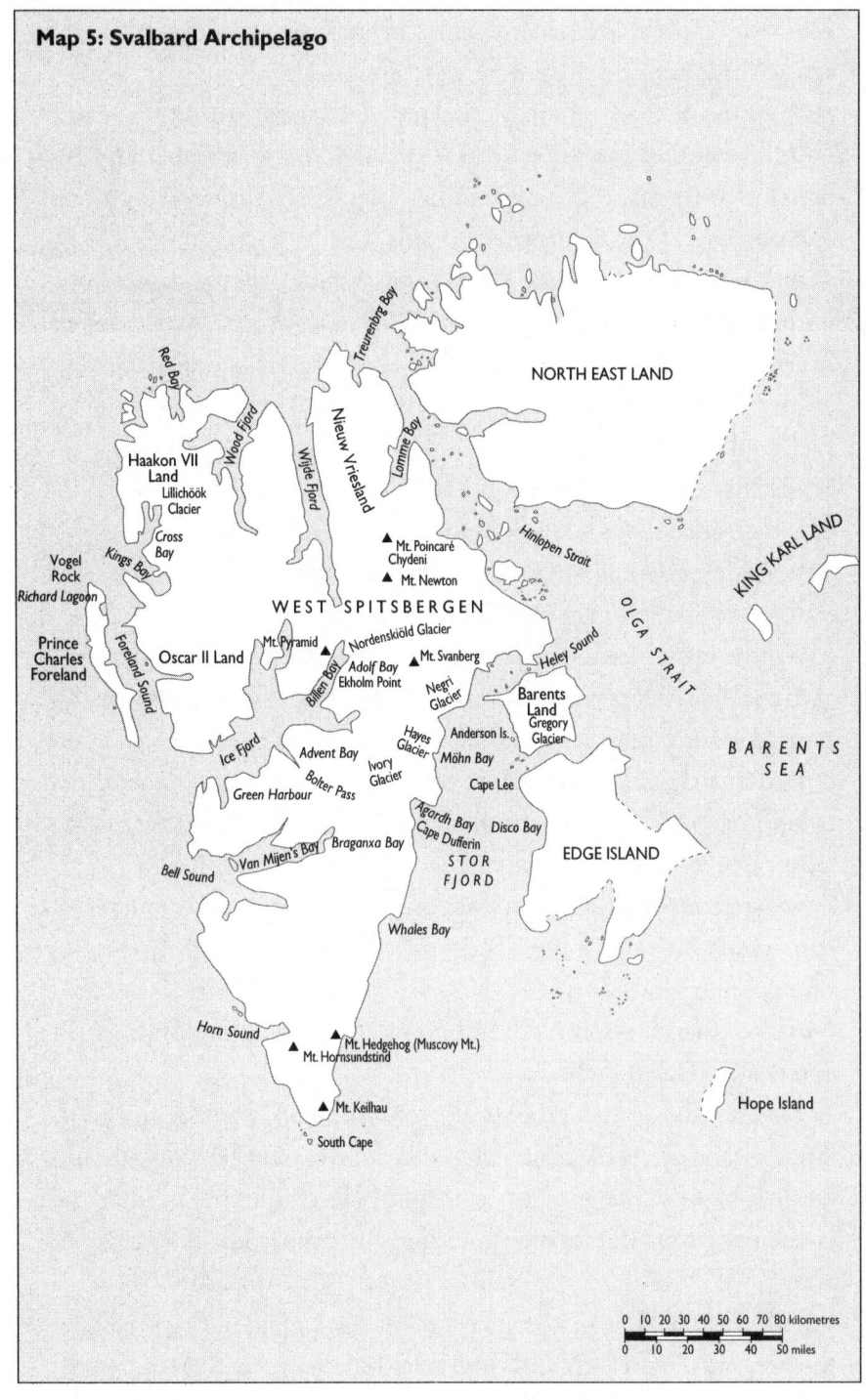

Map 5: Svalbard Archipelago

NORTH EAST LAND

Red Bay

Treurenbrg Bay

Wood Fjord

Nieuw Vriesland

Lomme Bay

Wijde Fjord

Haakon VII
Land
Lillichöök
Glacier

Hinlopen Strait

KING KARL LAND

Cross
Bay

Kings Bay

Mt. Poincaré
Chydeni

Mt. Newton

Vogel
Rock

Richard Lagoon

WEST SPITSBERGEN

OLGA STRAIT

Prince
Charles
Foreland

Foreland Sound

Oscar II Land

Mt. Pyramid

Nordenskiöld Glacier

Mt. Svanberg

Heley Sound

Billen Bay

Adolf Bay
Ekholm Point

Negri
Glacier

Barents
Land
Gregory
Glacier

BARENTS
SEA

Ice Fjord

Advent Bay

Hayes
Glacier

Anderson Is.

Möhn Bay

Ivory
Glacier

Cape Lee

Boher Pass

Green Harbour

Agardh Bay
Cape Dufferin

Disco Bay

EDGE ISLAND

Bell Sound

Van Mijen's Bay

Braganxa Bay

STOR
FJORD

Whales Bay

Horn Sound

Mt. Hedgehog (Muscovy Mt.)

Mt. Hornsundstind

Hope Island

Mt. Keilhau

South Cape

0 10 20 30 40 50 60 70 80 kilometres

0 10 20 30 40 50 miles

Wilkins, who entertained thoughts of making the first-ever flight across the Antarctic. But there were doubts about the organisation and the RGS soon officially disclaimed the venture. In the event Wordie's caution proved to be well placed and he avoided another dreadful Antarctic ordeal, which saw two men marooned for a year and nothing of consequence achieved.

By the summer of 1920, Wordie was back in the familiar Arctic territory of Spitsbergen, although one important item had changed. Bruce's health had deteriorated since the last voyage and leadership of the expedition passed to the experienced Mathieson, one of the syndicate's founding shareholders. Mathieson's entourage of geologists, engineers, surveyors and miners made up a large party of fifty men spread across three ships: *Autumn*, *Eastonian* and *Lady of Avenel*. It represented another chunky investment of £25,000 (about £500,000 today) for the syndicate.[5]

Wordie was placed in charge of a party of twelve men on the *Lady of Avenel*, his first taste of command in the field. His light touch and assured leadership, picked up at the feet of the master Shackleton, proved quietly efficient. Despite very poor weather, testing working conditions and a young inexperienced team, Wordie was able to report '. . . all fellows are happy'.

Spitsbergen in 1920 was an undemanding and relatively unhurried trip, which included a brief and final visit to the area by the ailing Bruce. Little more than a year later, Bruce was dead at the age of fifty-four and the long-standing ambitions of the Scottish Spitsbergen Syndicate were all but exhausted.

The results of the geological work in 1920 were depressingly familiar and it was Wordie who was called upon virtually to end any hopes of a bonanza for the syndicate. Profitable mining, he concluded, was 'out of the question' on properties at Ferrier. At Stor Fjord, Wordie and Tyrell also established that the 'Broxburn smell' was not due to the presence of oil and they reported that the area was 'extremely unfavourable' for oil deposits. Wordie told

Mathieson: 'I do not think that free oil will ever be found on the Syndicate's properties in the Stor Fjord area.'[6]

However, Wordie still considered that at least one more trip would be needed to complete the geological examination of the syndicate's properties, although he had decided against making a third visit to the area in person. Instead he restricted his role to that of casual adviser to Mathieson. Privately Wordie was not optimistic, a judgement which proved to be perfectly correct. While further reconnaissance was made over the next three decades, no mining ever took place on the syndicate's properties in Spitsbergen and the business was finally wound up in 1953.

However, Wordie emerged from the Spitsbergen venture with something more personally valuable. In Bruce, a man from the more romantic but declining age of discovery, he saw the future of exploration.

CHAPTER II

CONQUERING THE BEERENBERG

THE OPPORTUNITY TO RETURN TO THE ICE CAME FROM AN unexpected quarter. Shortly after his return from his second voyage to Spitsbergen in the autumn of 1920, Wordie received a surprising approach from Shackleton, who was planning to mount another expedition. Shackleton, in fact, was planning something of an old boys' reunion and Wordie was one of nine men from the Imperial Trans-Antarctic Expedition whom he aimed to recruit for his latest venture.

The initial plan was to lead a party to the Arctic, the first time that Shackleton had turned his attentions to the north. But when this proposal ran into difficulties, Shackleton turned his attention back to his old stamping-ground in the Antarctic.

He intended to draw the bulk of the party from the Imperial Trans-Antarctic venture. All the men invited – Wild, Worsley, Stenhouse, Hussey, Macklin, McIlroy, James, Crean and Wordie – had served on either *Endurance* or *Aurora*. He was so confident that his old comrades would re-enlist that he named the men in a formal proposal submitted to the Admiralty asking for public money to support the new expedition. Shackleton told the Admiralty in September 1920 that his nine old comrades were the 'proposed scientific staff and also personnel earmarked as ready to join'.[1] What is not clear is how many of the men Shackleton had asked to join him before their names were submitted to the Admiralty.

Shackleton was a lost soul after returning from *Endurance*. By 1920 he was forty-six years of age, in declining health and flitting aimlessly from one project to another in pursuit of fresh pastures or some means of making a quick buck. In neither case was he successful. Wordie once said that Shackleton was a man who 'just had to keep going with exploration' and in the end was 'willing to explore anywhere'. James concluded that 'Shackleton afloat was a more likeable character than Shackleton ashore.'

The new expedition was originally intended to map the largely uncharted Beaufort Sea above the Arctic Circle which, Shackleton said, was 'the last unknown sea of the world'. In a bid to encourage a reluctant government into funding the venture, he also threw out the vague possibility of striking out from the Beaufort Sea and reaching the North Pole. In doing so, he hoped to lay to rest finally the lingering dispute about whether Robert Peary or Frederick Cook had actually reached the Pole over a decade earlier.

However, the climate for funding large-scale Polar expeditions was decidedly frosty in the more austere post-war years. Even Canada, which had considerable national interest in clarifying the nation's claims to the Beaufort Sea, was reluctant to commit funds. Negotiations dragged on for months and by the middle of 1921 it was too late to mount an expedition in the north during that year.

In haste, Shackleton abruptly turned his plans on their head and launched a typically expansive scheme to return south. His new proposal was to circumnavigate the Antarctic continent. The journey, according to the more florid press reports, would involve a round-trip of 30,000 miles (48,000 km), more than a circumnavigation of the globe itself.

Both Wordie and James had initially indicated their willingness to join Shackleton for his voyage to the Beaufort Sea. But going back to the Antarctic was a major commitment of time, lasting at least one and possibly two years. This clashed with Wordie's increasing responsibilities at Cambridge. At the back of his mind, Wordie was also evidently concerned about Shackleton's indifference to science. Helped by his two voyages with Bruce, Wordie was now firmly committed to expanding his role as an explorer-scientist. Wordie's reservations about Shackleton's attitude to science had first surfaced on *Endurance* and nothing he heard about the proposal to circumnavigate the continent offered much hope of a change of heart. Although Wordie kept his concerns private, his apprehensions emerged in a letter to Shackleton's friend, Hugh Mill. He wrote: 'Impress on him the need for doing any amount of oceanography: he has a very hazy idea of what it is and <u>hates</u> water samples.'[2]

Fortunately, there were other options. While considering Shackleton's proposals, Wordie was invited to join two different expeditions to the Arctic, which suited his purpose and had the added attraction of not interfering with his professional duties at Cambridge. With little further consideration, he turned down Shackleton's appeal and went north. Indeed, neither Wordie nor James was on board Shackleton's ship, *Quest*, when the expedition finally sailed for the south in late September 1921. Nor was the reliable Crean.

Wordie's choice lay between joining an Oxford University party to the well-known terrain of Spitsbergen or visiting the largely unknown Jan Mayen Island with a team from Cambridge. The Oxford party, which was organised by George Binney, wanted to exploit Wordie's extensive knowledge of the area and help guide a mainly untried team of young university volunteers. Although primarily a study of the island's bird life, the Oxford trip offered ample scope for geological work and Wordie was tempted. But Wordie was an undiluted Cambridge man and the clinching factor was the opportunity to visit new land.

Jan Mayen, the Cambridge expedition's target, was something of a mystery and there was no record of any geological study ever having been carried out on the island. It is an uninviting volcanic island of lava and rock about 35 miles (56 km) long, located in remote Arctic waters north of Iceland and about 300 miles (480 km) off the east coast of Greenland. The opportunity to visit the island arose in early 1921 at the same time as Shackleton's Arctic plans were slowly dissolving. James Chaworth-Musters, a keen 19-year-old botanist at Caius College, expressed an interest in exploring Jan Mayen's plant and wildlife and floated the idea of extending the team to include some geology. Chaworth-Musters, the son of a wealthy land-owning family from Nottingham, knew of Wordie's exploits with Bruce and Shackleton and invited him to come along.

It was an attractive proposition, both scientifically and personally. The trip would be the first attempt to make geological studies of the island and to establish whether the volcano was still active. But what appealed most to Wordie was the prospect of climbing the 7,470 ft (2,277 m) Mount Beerenberg, the unconquered volcanic peak which dominates Jan Mayen Island.

By a stroke of good fortune, it was discovered that a group of Norwegians were also hoping to reach Jan Mayen that summer to erect a weather station and build a radio transmitter on the island. Wordie and Chaworth-Musters seized the moment and asked if they could accompany the party.

Hagbard Ekerold, the leader of the Norwegian party, generously agreed to take the Cambridge men, but told them that his expedition was entirely dependent on Norway's government financing the venture. With no other realistic prospect of a lift to Jan Mayen, the Cambridge group were at the mercy of Norwegian bureaucracy. After a lengthy delay of several months, Ekerold finally secured the necessary backing and the expedition began to take shape. Unlike his Spitsbergen journeys, Wordie would not be paid for the Jan Mayen trip. Instead he paid his own expenses and arranged to borrow some scientific equipment – compasses, a sextant and a hypsometer – from his new-found connections at the RGS.

Preparations for the trip were moving quickly and smoothly until Ekerold inadvertently disclosed word of Wordie's plan to climb the Beerenberg to a Swiss mountaineer, Paul-Louis Mercanton. Mercanton, a professor at Lausanne University and an accomplished climber, had his own long-standing ambitions to scale the Beerenberg. The war had interrupted his initial attempts to reach the island and news of the British attempt on the mountain sent him into a flurry of excitement. Mercanton immediately asked Ekerold for a berth on the ship taking the Cambridge party to Jan Mayen that summer. Ekerold agreed and the multi-national group of Norwegian, Swiss and five Britons finally left the port of Alesund on 1 August in two wooden sealers, the 24-ton *Polarfront* and the 54-ton *Isfuglen*. Six days day later, the vessels skirted the coast of Jan Mayen after a very rough passage in which Mercanton was almost thrown overboard by the wild seas.

The sudden burst of activity around Jan Mayen must have baffled most observers. Voyagers had largely ignored the desolate wind-swept island since its discovery in 1607 by Henry Hudson, who called it Hudson's Tutches. In 1614 a Dutch captain, Jan Cornelis May, claimed territorial rights for Holland and the island was named after him. A team of Austro-Hungarians under Lieutenant von Wohlegemuth was the first to over-winter on the remote island during the International Polar Year of 1882–3. Strangely, the party had spent almost a year stationed on Jan Mayen but they had not bothered to include a geologist in the team.

There were no harbours on Jan Mayen and landing the men and equipment was especially difficult in the face of steep cliffs, a hefty swell and constantly shifting volcanic sand. Fotherby, an English captain who landed in 1615, graphically described the island's crystalline surface as 'like unto a smiths sinders both in colour and forme'.

By August 9 the Cambridge men and the Swiss climber had scrambled ashore and established base camp while the Norwegians had gone their own way. Chaworth-Musters turned to the island's wildlife, but Wordie and Mercanton began to weigh up the assault on the imposing Beerenberg.

The Beerenberg, a huge dormant volcano, dominates the landscape

Map 6: Jan Mayen Island

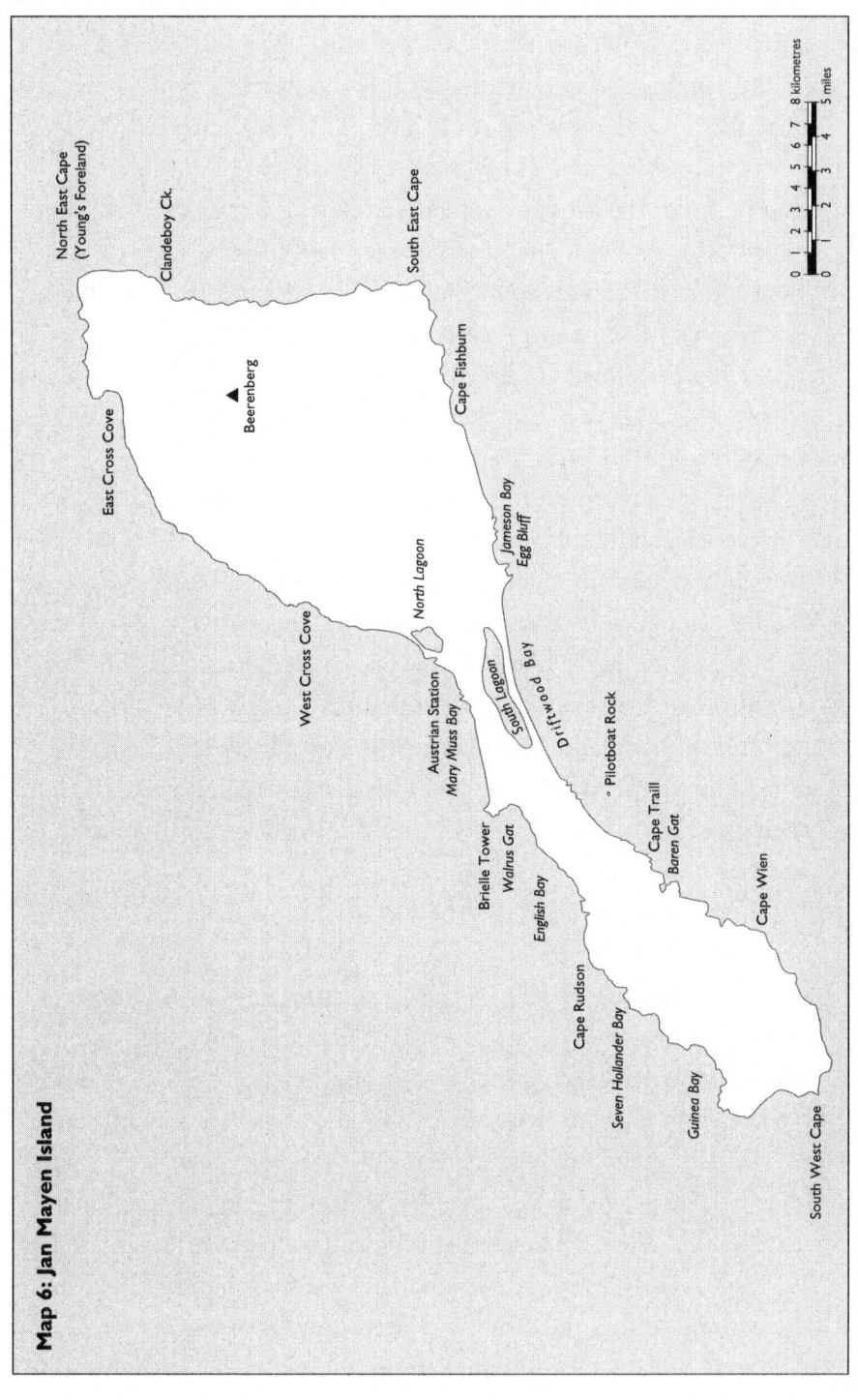

North East Cape
(Young's Foreland)

Clandeboy Ck.

East Cross Cove

Beerenberg

West Cross Cove

North Lagoon

Austrian Station

Mary Muss Bay

South East Cape

Cape Fishburn

Jameson Bay

Egg Bluff

South Lagoon

Driftwood Bay

Pilotboat Rock

Brielle Tower

Walrus Gat

English Bay

Cape Traill

Baren Gat

Cape Wien

Cape Rudson

Seven Hollander Bay

Guinea Bay

South West Cape

0 1 2 3 4 5 6 7 8 kilometres
0   2   3   4   5 miles

of Jan Mayen's northern region. It is more than 30 miles (48 km) around the base of the mountain and the dazzling white cone is topped by a yawning crater about 3,000 ft (1 km) across. Only two previous known attempts had been made to scale the peak. Naval officers from the Austro-Hungarian expedition – the peak was named after Lt Beer, one of the party – were forced to turn back about 2,000 ft (700 m) from the summit and a private party made an unsuccessful attempt to reach the top in 1911. The ascent did not appear too formidable to an experienced climber like Wordie. He relished the challenge. But there were other problems, notably the uneasy relationship with Mercanton.

Wordie took an instant dislike to the energetic little Swiss, whose frenetic behaviour and constant fussing irritated him. Mercanton, a small man with a pronounced moustache, jarred on Wordie's nature. Wordie, thoughtful, reserved and precise, contrasted starkly with the bustling and hasty Mercanton, who, he considered, was guilty of not thinking things through. For the meticulous Wordie, little was ever done in haste and Mercanton's impulsive and erratic behaviour grated. In his personal diary Wordie dismissed the Swiss as the 'worthy professor' and mocked him as 'a scientist greedily collecting perfectly useless data'.

On one occasion he found the Swiss taking a bath upstream in a river which lower down the slope provided the men with their source of drinking water. Wordie was infuriated by Mercanton's thoughtlessness and coolly observed: 'Mercanton, I see that you are washing your private parts in our drinking water.'

Mercanton had his own reservations about the Cambridge team. He insisted their climbing equipment was very poor and airily concluded that Wordie's group possessed only 'slender knowledge' of climbing. Wordie had been climbing for almost fifteen years at this stage, but Mercanton declared that the Scot had followed his instructions around the camp with 'encouraging obedience'.[3]

Despite his serious misgivings, Wordie took the baffling decision of asking Mercanton to take charge of the climb. 'I regretted it afterwards – he had not a good eye for the best route and wastes time most abominably,' Wordie confided to his diary.[4] Mercanton's version of events was slightly different. He said the two groups had 'agreed without the slightest hesitation' to pool resources for the climb. 'I had the choice of route, of the time of starting and of the companion who was to make up our equipage of three,' he recalled.

The summit party – Wordie, Mercanton and Tom Lethbridge, a 20-year-old Cambridge student with no climbing experience – found the climb comparatively easy in fairly good weather. Without too much difficulty, the trio made it to the summit on 11 August after a routine ascent lasting about eight hours.

Wordie, with his solid mountaineering experience and a jaundiced view of Mercanton, believed the relatively modest climb up the Beerenberg took two or three hours longer than necessary because the route chosen by Mercanton was needlessly difficult. The outcome only added to his contempt for the Swiss.

The last straw for Wordie came in the final stages of the climb. As the three men came within 100 ft (30 m) of the summit, Mercanton turned to Wordie and suddenly blurted out: 'Switzerland is such a small country – I must be first to the top.' He then dashed ahead, leaving Wordie and Lethbridge behind and scrambling up the final few feet to ensure that he could claim to be first at the top. Mercanton said reaching the summit was a 'priceless moment' in his life and proclaimed: 'My dream of ten years has become true.'

But his personal account of the climb made no mention of his selfish dash to the top or the simmering discontent with Wordie. 'Generous and sporting, my British friends allowed the White Cross the place of honour on the staff,' he wrote.[5] Wordie was appalled at Mercanton's behaviour and lack of respect for his fellow climbers. He observed: 'The little man never had a ghostly chance getting there had we not mothered him.'[6] He watched in astonishment when

Mercanton deposited at the summit a cylinder containing a list of their names, a Swiss ten-centime coin and a tooth from his only child. He added fresh insult to Wordie's sensibilities by insisting that the Swiss flag flew above the Union Jack. Wordie, unimpressed and resentful, ridiculed the little ceremony as 'sheer comedy'.

The first ascent of the Beerenberg did not go unnoticed in Britain. On reaching Norway, Wordie broke news of the ascent by cabling Hinks at the RGS: 'Expedition from Jan Mayen very successful. Reached summit Beerenberg. Please inform any interested.'[7] *The Times* was certainly interested but completely ignored the contribution of Mercanton to the ascent and the undeniable fact that the Swiss had reached the top first. Instead the climb was attributed solely to Wordie and the feat described as 'the mountaineering success of the year'.[8]

Most notably Wordie established that the Beerenberg was not, as commonly thought, an active volcano and he took particular delight in pointing out an erroneous reference to its activity in the *Encyclopaedia Britannica*. Away from the Beerenberg, Wordie completed the first proper geological study of the island. The findings were far from startling, cautiously concluding that the island was comparatively young and that it was impossible to date the most intense volcanic activity. Remembering his experiences with Bruce on Spitsbergen, he dismissed any hopes for commercial mining on the island.

The expedition had nevertheless been a great success for the Norwegians, whose weather-station and radio communications were soon fully operational. Ekerold's mission was a triumph, which provided invaluable weather information for Norway's important fishing fleets and later helped many nations in handling the fast-growing commercial air traffic across the North Atlantic. Ekerold's expedition also paved the way for the island to be proclaimed part of Norway in 1929. By coincidence, Chaworth-Musters went on to become British vice-consul in Bergen, and during the Second World

War he was awarded Norway's Freedom Medal after escaping from the Nazis and reaching Britain by fishing-boat.

But there was little sense of achievement for Wordie, perhaps because he was not the undisputed leader of the party and perhaps because the friction with Mercanton had taken the gloss off the episode. However Jan Mayen had reinforced Wordie's intention to broaden his horizons. As *Polarfront* headed back to Britain, Wordie was already planning his next expedition, and he had twin ambitions in mind. One target was Greenland, the world's largest island. The other, far more ambitious project, was Mount Everest, the world's largest mountain.

CHAPTER 12

A NEW
ERA

IN HIS OWN CONSERVATIVE AND UNDEMONSTRATIVE MANNER, JAMES Wordie was a man of profound ambition. He was driven by a powerful inner desire to be the best in his field. While there was nothing theatrical or attention-seeking about Wordie, his ambition knew no boundaries.

Soon after returning from Jan Mayen, Wordie turned his attentions towards Everest, one of the last great geographical challenges. During the autumn of 1921, Wordie approached the RGS, asking for his name to be put forward for the 1922 expedition.

His first port of call was Hinks, the dictatorial RGS secretary who quietly wielded great influence from behind his desk at the Society's headquarters in Kensington. Wordie asked Hinks if he stood a chance of joining the expedition. Hinks responded positively to the initial approach and Wordie was happy to put his application in writing. He told Hinks, 'I have always been keen to join the Everest expedition and your letter indicating that I should apply is very welcome news.'[1]

The 1922 expedition would be the first major attempt to scale Everest. The mountain, named after Sir George Everest, the Surveyor General of India, was not seen by Westerners until the 1850s. But political difficulties with the neighbouring countries of Nepal and Tibet and the war had hampered all previous attempts to reach the mountain.

Interest in the mountain was revived after the First World War and in 1920 a joint initiative by The Alpine Club and RGS led to an approach to the Dalai Lama in Tibet seeking permission to enter the country. Months of delicate negotiations followed before permission was given shortly before Christmas 1920. A few weeks later the Alpine Club and the RGS set up the Mount Everest Committee. The secretary in charge of day-to-day affairs was the formidable Hinks.

Wordie could hardly fail to be caught up in the mild euphoria surrounding the bid to reach the roof of the world. Under the all-knowing direction of Hinks, the Everest Committee had quietly assumed proprietorial rights over the mountain and the British public naturally assumed that the nation had acquired exclusive rights.

The committee drew up plans for a two-year programme to conquer Everest. The first year, 1921, was given over to general reconnaissance of this mostly unexplored area of Tibet and to finding a suitable route to the top in the following year. It was typical Imperial adventure, which captured the public imagination. The total cost was put at £10,000 (about £200,000 today), provided by wealthy members of the Alpine Club and RGS, newspaper sponsorship and some private donations. King George V gave £100 (£2,000). Even a minor inconvenience – a thief absconded with £717 of the expedition's funds – did not halt the expedition's progress.

The exploratory mission was led by Lieutenant Charles Howard-Bury, an Old Etonian and decorated army officer. It contained only four recognised climbers but achieved far more than anticipated. Two of the climbers, George Mallory and Guy Bullock, reached an impressive height of 23,000 ft (7,000 m), which took them near to the highest that humans had ever reached and proved that Everest was not unbeatable. Prior to 1921, the record was the 23,385 ft (7,128 m) Trisul, which Tom Longstaff's party had conquered in 1907.

Wordie was a sound candidate for the next more deliberate attempt on Everest. His climbing experience, although mostly limited to the Alps and Scotland, was extensive. He had never climbed in the Himalayas but his powers of endurance, which would be essential to reach Everest's 29,035-ft (8,850-m) peak, had been amply demonstrated with Shackleton.

Wordie was confident of winning a prized place on the team, even if it interfered with his duties at Cambridge. To make the long overland journey to Tibet, Wordie would have to leave Cambridge in early March when the university was in full swing. However, St John's College was accommodating and happily gave him permission to take extra time off to join the climb. The next step was a medical examination and in mid-November Hinks sent him to London's Harley Street for a routine check-up. It was the nearest that Wordie ever came to joining the 1922 Everest expedition.

The physician, Dr Larkins, was concerned at Wordie's blood pressure and summarily concluded that he was not fit enough to undertake a high-altitude climb. Wordie was shocked. Larkins decided that Wordie was fit only for 'moderate hard work' despite fifteen years of regular climbing and a presence on four rigorous Polar expeditions. Larkins added a further disturbing parting shot for Wordie when he concluded: 'You ought not to be asked to undertake arduous and prolonged climbing.' On Larkins' unambiguous recommendation, the Everest Committee turned down Wordie's application to join the expedition.

Hinks, sensing the disappointment for Wordie, tried to soften the blow by suggesting that he contemplate travelling to the Himalayas with the party as a geologist. But he also urged him to be cautious about 'living at high altitudes'. Wordie was deeply disappointed at the doctor's diagnosis and was worried that his days of exploring might be numbered. With his ambitions under threat, Wordie told Hinks: 'I hope it is not going to prevent other expeditions.' However, Wordie did not allow the doctor's verdict to obstruct his plans and soon afterwards he began to formulate alternative plans. Instead of moping over the loss, he put Everest behind him and turned instead to Greenland.

The last rites of the heroic age of Polar exploration were being read during the time Wordie was attempting to join the Everest expedition. The heroic era, which began in 1895 with the first landing on the Antarctic mainland, came to a quiet end in the autumn of 1921 with Shackleton's unfortunate expedition on the *Quest*, the endeavour that Wordie had turned down. The expedition, which sailed from London a few days after Wordie returned from Jan Mayen, was the last of its type and the final voyage for Shackleton, a compelling character who most symbolised the heroic age.

The *Quest* sailed with ten old hands from *Endurance* on board – including Wild, Worsley, Macklin and McIlroy – and reached South Georgia in the first few days of 1922. With the ship anchored in the well-known surroundings of Grytviken Harbour, Shackleton suffered a fatal heart attack and died on 5 January, aged only forty-seven. Although the dependable Wild immediately took control, the *Quest* expedition achieved little and limped home nine months later, effectively lowering the curtain on the heroic age. It was also Wild's fifth and last polar expedition. Wordie was among those who recognised the significance of Shackleton's passing. Even before Shackleton's death he saw that Polar exploration was changing.

Endurance had provided him with a haunting and highly personal memory of the heroic age's finest hour. But the post-*Endurance* journeys to Spitsbergen with Bruce and with the Cambridge party to Jan Mayen demonstrated that there was a new, more modern way to explore and Wordie, in his quiet and determined manner, resolved to be in the vanguard of the revolution.

The precise date of Wordie's renaissance is open to question. In public he always insisted that the germ of the idea dated from 1919 and 1920, when he saw at first-hand the methods of Bruce on the two voyages to Spitsbergen. However this overlooks an earlier inspiration. In fact, Wordie's idea for the new style of exploration was formulated in 1915 when *Endurance* was trapped in the ice and drifting slowly through the Weddell Sea.

During the long dark nights in the Weddell, Wordie used the

endless periods of idleness to study most of the modern Polar literature on board. Most notably he read an account of Amundsen's historic first navigation of the North West Passage in the *Gjoa* between 1903–06. Buried in Amundsen's arid, pedestrian prose was the origin of the idea which helped change Britain's entire approach to Polar exploration.

Amundsen was the most professional and single-minded of all Polar explorers, and Wordie saw the advantages of adopting similar techniques to his own plans, even if Amundsen virtually ignored the scientific side of exploration on his epic journeys. Amundsen had gone into the Arctic ice in 1903 with a small vessel and a team of only seven experienced explorers, though he wisely provisioned *Gjoa* for five years. In addition, Amundsen's men were fully confident of being able to adapt to the environment like native Eskimos and to live off the land by shooting game.

Wordie sensed he could repeat the process by deploying small, hand-picked teams of scientists in the Arctic, supplied by a small ship and capable of living off the land. Unlike Amundsen, he had no intention of over-wintering in the Arctic and instead planned to take lightweight teams to the field for only the two or three months of the summer season. Over-wintering, he believed, was costly and unnecessary. But he always took enough back-up provisions for a winter in case of emergencies.

He began to flesh out the idea while stranded in the Weddell in the depths of 1915. In his diary he wrote: 'One has only to read the scientific works of the Franklin Search Expeditions to feel how much there is to do up there on modern lines; and in a small ship, such as the *Gjoa,* much could be done very cheaply.'[2] He had learned other lessons from both *Endurance* and Bruce, particularly on equipping small expeditions and on paying more careful attention to packing food and other supplies. He understood that more efficient use of space would, if necessary, extend voyages.

On *Endurance,* for example, Orde-Lees had unpacked all food tins from their wooden boxes, thus saving vital space in the holds. Wordie drew lessons from both men and concluded: 'It struck me that if regard were paid to the proportionate bulk of articles, it should be quite easy to provision a ship like [*Endurance*] with a small company for at least 3 years. Small ships with not many mouths to fill seem the best suited for polar work.'[3]

However, Wordie turned to Bruce for another source of inspiration for his future expeditions. It was Bruce who had broken the mould in 1919 by picking his scientific team largely from the Scottish universities and adding Wordie from Cambridge. Wordie now intended to follow suit, though his parties would be drawn largely from Cambridge. Wordie had no doubts about the significance of Bruce in leading the change of style. Bruce, the scientist, was effectively Wordie's mentor for the new age of scientific exploration, even if he picked up the germ of the idea from Amundsen and crucial pointers on leadership from Shackleton.

Wordie was loyal and utterly supportive of Shackleton and over the years did much to enhance his reputation. But Shackleton's qualities, particularly his outstanding leadership, marked him out largely for the age of geographical discovery. 'There could be no better teacher of the art of exploration,' Wordie once said of the Boss. 'Shackleton, indeed, possessed the faculty of leadership to a pre-eminent degree,' he added.

But Bruce set a new approach which appealed to Wordie's own twin disciplines of exploration and science. He saw in Bruce the ideal mixture of talents. He once told a meeting of the RGS: 'I should never have felt properly equipped for the Arctic if I had not also been associated with Dr W.S. Bruce. I went with him to Spitsbergen shortly before he died and it was from him I learned the methods and arts of summer exploration.'[4]

A wider significance of the change of style was that the national focus of Britain's Polar exploration was being switched from the Antarctic to the Arctic. The Arctic, by tradition, was the main theatre of British Polar operations, an association which dated back to the Elizabethan adventurers Frobisher and Davis and continued into the nineteenth century to Parry and Franklin. But Scott's *Discovery* expedition in 1901 marked a clear change of direction towards the Antarctic and in the first two decades of the twentieth century the Arctic was largely ignored by the British. Bruce, through his repeated visits to Spitsbergen, was among the few to keep the country's flame burning in the Arctic territories.

Size and speed were the key ingredients of Polar activity which Wordie envisaged and saw develop between the two wars. The small-scale scientific expeditions of the 1920s and '30s were admirably suited to the Arctic. It was possible to take a handful of men for a brief three-month voyage during the summer months – the universities' long vacation – and return to Britain before the winter ice trapped their ships. Over-wintering, the darkest feature of the heroic age and a necessity for the Antarctic, was unnecessary. It was a scheme which also allowed him to combine an academic career with regular experience of exploration.

The type of expedition proposed by Wordie was significantly smaller than earlier voyages, which had captured so much public attention. Some involved as few as two men, although typically the expeditions numbered between six and eight. They rarely took more than ten people. By comparison, 129 men sailed on Sir John Franklin's catastrophic attempt to navigate the North West Passage in 1845 and Scott's *Discovery* expedition between 1901–04, the first major attempt to open up the Antarctic, initially involved forty-nine naval officers, seamen and scientists. Shackleton's *Endurance* and *Aurora* parties numbered a combined fifty-six and there were twenty-one men on *Quest* in 1921 for the last hurrah of the heroic age.

Arctic exploration enjoyed a minor boom in the period immediately after the Great War. Freed from the constraints of war, the 1920s saw a flurry of activity above the Arctic Circle, driven initially by the Danes. But before long Russia, Norway, Germany, Sweden, Canada and America sent parties north, mostly on science-based missions. Britain, too, was caught up in the movement and Wordie soon emerged as among the country's most influential figures.

Wordie was one of the key people who between the wars modelled the new approach to British expeditions and developed a vibrant school for emergent explorers. Together with men like George Binney, Gino Watkins and Alexander 'Sandy' Glen, Wordie's prodigious efforts were essential in prolonging the country's Polar operations after the end of the heroic age. Wordie, slightly older and more experienced than the others, bridged the gap between the two eras of exploration. He was the link between the old heroic age and the new mechanised and scientific age which blossomed in the 1920s and '30s.

It is reliably estimated that Britain despatched around sixty separate expeditions to the Polar regions between 1919 and 1939, deploying more than 260 men – and a handful of women – mostly recruited from the campuses of Cambridge, Oxford and the Scottish universities.[5]

Wordie was directly engaged in 10 per cent of these voyages and played a crucial part in advising countless other expeditions. By the late 1920s, few expeditions left Britain without first consulting the knowledgeable, experienced and ever willing Wordie. It is entirely possible that, without the university-dominated expeditions of Wordie and his colleagues, the nation's interests in Polar affairs might have withered altogether and Britain's long-standing influence in the area, would probably have been lost forever. Terence Armstrong, the Arctic authority of the 1950s and '60s, concluded that the university expeditions had 'kept alive in British universities the interest in polar exploration' in the inter-war years. He stressed that the importance of these voyages was 'out of all proportion to their size'.[6]

Wordie's genius was in realising that by the early 1920s the basic geography of the Polar regions had been established and that the focus was now on scientific understanding. With the aid of new technology – radio communications, motor vehicles, aircraft, etc. – explorers were equipped for different advances. Although many gaps in the map still existed and some vague outlines had to be clarified, the need for lengthy voyages of exploration had passed.

As a result, the new generation of explorers turned increasingly towards geology, glaciology, meteorology, zoology, botany and archaeology. Even on *Quest*, Shackleton had recognised that a new mechanised and technologically-driven era was dawning. He took an 8-horsepower monoplane, and among the new gadgets on board was an electrically-heated crow's nest to provide a modest degree of comfort while threading a path through the ice. But the 21-man party contained only one geologist, a single naturalist and a meteorologist.

The modern expeditions had other characteristics which marked them out from earlier exploration. Staffed mostly from the universities, they were far cheaper and often low-profile undertakings, which generated little publicity.

J. Gordon Hayes summed up the difference between the traditional approach and the new university-led school of exploration in the 1930s when he wrote: 'While not unadventurous, this [new] type is academic in character, benevolently monarchical in government and desirous in avoiding heroics.'[7] In more expansive mood, Hayes once wrote to *The Times* declaring that the university explorers would return from their expeditions 'laden with scientific data of greater value than all the gold of Ophir'.

The make-up of the parties also ensured that the new expeditions were noticeably more egalitarian than the earlier enterprises. Until the 1920s, exploration was traditionally dominated by the Royal Navy, with its heavy reliance on blind obedience and total deference to rank. The new expeditions featured non-military men of equal status, who were invariably experts in their own field. Leadership was exercised with a light touch and each person was left to his own devices to complete his chosen tasks. The men were also ready to muck in and share the mundane tasks. Hierarchy, in the old naval sense, ceased to exist. Glen once said that the keynote of the expeditions was to be found in the reliance on every member playing his part to the best of his ability. The personnel, he said, was 'all important' and explained: 'Besides being scientifically qualified, it must be a team which can work together.'[8]

Wordie's considerable experience also set him apart from the majority of the new school, who were mostly complete novices. As Binney noted when planning his 1921 Spitsbergen voyage: 'None of us . . . had previous experience of the Arctic.' By the end of 1921 Wordie had been on four expeditions and was planning many more.

Bruce first employed the system of using university graduates or undergraduates on his Spitsbergen voyages. But Wordie took the practice to new levels. His own presence on Bruce's 1919 trip ensured the first Cambridge involvement with the new style of Polar expeditions and in 1920 he was joined by C.M. Pollock, a geology student from Trinity College. The first major expedition under the Cambridge banner was the 1921 voyage to Jan Mayen, which included Bristowe, Chaworth-Musters, Lethbridge and Wordie from the university.

However, the new ventures were notably inconspicuous affairs compared with the well-known expeditions of Scott or Shackleton. The expeditions of the heroic age had relied heavily on being in the public gaze to help to raise money to fund the ventures. In most cases, the exclusive film or press rights to the story of the expedition were sold in advance to help meet costs.

On *Endurance* Shackleton had insisted in advance that each man sign away all rights to publication of books, diaries or photographs as an important means of cashing in on the expedition's media potential, and the first news of the castaways on Elephant Island was given to the *Daily Chronicle* under an exclusive contract. But the no-frills, low-profile style of exploring appealed to Wordie. He was basically a shy man who was often uncomfortable in crowds and preferred to remain out of the limelight.

Without the need for hefty public funding, the Arctic explorers of the 1920s and '30s generated little interest in the press. In turn, this was reflected in the modest later accounts of the voyages. Many parties returned home almost unnoticed in the general media and very few books were ever published about their exploits. Quite often, their public profile was restricted to humdrum lectures at formal venues like the RGS or routine reports in a variety of technical journals.

Some men were reluctant to publish results of their season's work or were simply too busy on their return to devote much time to writing post-expedition reports. To encourage a better output of written material, research degrees or lectureships were awarded, and at Cambridge the Scott Polar Research Institute set aside space specifically for returning students.

Of course, the university-led expeditions rarely touched the heights of drama of the Scott or Shackleton undertakings, and the safe arrival in Britain of a few graduates was thought insignificant when measured against the headline-grabbing events surrounding the death of Scott's South Pole party or the *Endurance* rescue. Another factor behind the lack of publicity was that the new expeditions were mostly private and not directly affiliated with the government or even official bodies like the RGS or the Royal Society, who had sponsored earlier expeditions.

Scott was part-funded by the Government on both his expeditions and he was heavily influenced by the RGS, while even a self-appointed adventurer like Shackleton needed some official blessing to mount his *Nimrod* and Imperial Trans-Antarctic expeditions. In the 1920s and '30s organisations like the RGS had a more arms-length relationship with the new generation of explorers and their role was often limited to giving advice or lending items of equipment.

The private nature of the new expeditions also ensured that costs were kept to a minimum. In most cases, the voyages were funded by the academic explorers themselves or by hand-outs from their wealthy parents. Only occasionally were they supported by official sources, although bodies like the RGS and the Royal Society frequently provided small grants.

Nor did the universities play a major role in setting up or managing the voyages. While the explorers operated with the full support of the universities, the journeys were initiated and administered entirely by dedicated individuals like Wordie at Cambridge or Binney at Oxford. Individual members of the expeditions usually paid all their living and equipment expenses for the voyage out of their own pockets, which meant that exploration was restricted to those with adequate private means or generous backers. For many, as Hayes noted, Polar exploration was 'an expensive hobby'.

The costs were very small compared with the huge cost of launching the much larger expeditions of the heroic age. The short Arctic expeditions in the 1920s and '30s typically cost less than £5,000, or roughly £125,000–£150,000 in today's terms. The main item of cost, after ignoring the personal expenses of the individuals, was in hiring a ship for two or three months. Oxford University's short four-week trip to Spitsbergen in 1923 was estimated to have cost just £250 (£6,500 today) and one of Wordie's later voyages to Greenland cost only £1,700 (£45,000 today). By contrast, Scott's last expedition had cost over £40,000 in 1910, which is close to £1,900,000 in today's terms. It was estimated that Shackleton's Imperial Trans-Antarctic Expedition had cost around £80,000 or some £2,500,000 today.

The personnel were mostly academics like Wordie or young undergraduates and graduates of the two universities. Most were in their twenties, generally from wealthy backgrounds or blessed with specialist skills. Chaworth-Musters was only nineteen years old when he proposed the Jan Mayen expedition in 1921, and one of Binney's Oxford party was Andrew 'Sandy' Irvine, the young undergraduate who died on Everest with George Mallory in 1924.

Another was Noel Odell, a Cambridge geologist and the last man to see the pair alive near the summit.

But the Oxbridge expeditions also recruited outside their immediate environment. Tom Longstaff, the accomplished mountaineer, once accompanied Wordie to the Arctic and in 1924 Binney managed to recruit the legendary Helmer Hanssen, one of the select band of Norwegians who stood at the South Pole with Amundsen in December 1911.

Wordie took a close interest in the personnel. He had learned much from the outstanding leadership of Shackleton, which, among other things, relied heavily on fostering harmony among the group. Splits or disagreements were a serious issue in the confined spaces of an expedition tent and it was essential that people rubbed along together. The fractious Jan Mayen trip with Mercanton was a salutary warning.

One of Wordie's great talents was communicating with others and nurturing talent. He possessed a happy knack for choosing the right people and instilling them with confidence and the vital ability to work together in the field as a team. Wordie understood that in claustrophobic living conditions even small everyday mannerisms or idiosyncrasies can cause awkward friction among the men. Explaining the delicate selection process for expedition members, he once said: 'We chose the men who had the best scientific qualifications and who we also thought would get along together.'9

Vivian Fuchs, who travelled with a Cambridge expedition under Wordie at the age of twenty-one and graduated to Polar greatness, applauded the 'quiet judgement and steady enthusiasm' of Wordie's leadership. According to Fuchs, Wordie's advice to young explorers was 'invaluable' and he possessed a 'clear understanding of each man's peculiarities and limitations'.

There was also considerable cross-fertilisation between the two universities. Wordie frequently advised his counterparts at Oxford and men from opposing universities regularly went on each other's expeditions. Both Wordie and Binney were always on standby to help if another's expedition ran into trouble and did not return to Britain on schedule in the autumn. The rivalry that characterised exploration in the heroic age had largely evaporated by the 1920s.

Nor did the new teams of explorers restrict their activities exclusively to the Arctic or Antarctic environment. Men like Irvine, Odell, Longstaff and Jack Longland were in the forefront of early Himalayan climbing and the first attempts to scale Everest. In addition, African explorers of the age included men like Fuchs, Kenneth Sandford and Cuthbert 'Jumbo' Wakefield.

The biggest single contribution of the expeditions was the huge advances in the topography and structure of the Polar regions. In the era before large-scale aircraft or satellite reconnaissance, the new breed of explorers helped produce the most accurate and in-depth maps then available. Whereas the earlier voyages of discovery had concentrated largely on breaking new ground at the expense of detailed mapping or geology, the expeditions in the post-war era deliberately chose to focus their efforts on localised and intensive studies of fairly small areas. The outcome was the emergence of far more comprehensive and detailed maps and where necessary, the correction of earlier errors. Areas like the Spitsbergen archipelago, the east coast of Greenland and some Canadian coastal territories were among those selected for detailed study.

The Arctic was a particularly useful training ground for the new generation of geologists and glaciologists in the 1920s and '30s. Only a limited amount of surveying in the Arctic had been undertaken before the First World War, mainly by Knud Rasmussen, J.P. Koch, Ludvig Mylius-Erichsen and Otto Svedrup in Greenland and the Canadian Arctic, and by Bruce in Spitsbergen. But the post-war expeditions offered a golden opportunity for young geologists, including Pat Baird, Harald Drever, Fleming and Sandford, to fashion their skills on the landscapes of the Canadian Arctic, Greenland, Iceland and Spitsbergen.

The summer season excursions also brought considerable advances for glaciologists. It was this generation – including Glen – which first delved into the Arctic ice-caps and began the process of establishing the history and evolution of glaciers. Extensive work was carried out in Greenland, Iceland and Spitsbergen and several long-term ice monitoring stations were built in pursuit of a better understanding of the life cycle of glaciers. Biologists and naturalists were able to study the delicate balance between plants and animals in the Arctic and pave the way for a later generation of conservationists.

From Chaworth-Musters on Jan Mayen, the new generation of ornithologists and animal-behaviour specialists included men such as Charles Elton, David Lack, Brian Roberts and Colin Bertram, who helped lay the foundations for the development of today's ecological studies. Archaeology also flourished in the years between the two wars, thanks to keen young men like Tom Lethbridge and Dick Feachem, whose diligent excavations of abandoned sites shed new light on the living habits and the origins of the Eskimo people.

The Arctic expeditions also encouraged the use and development of newer technologies such as radio, and inevitably brought a significant expansion of meteorological observations. Binney's expedition to North East Land in 1924 was the first to include a wireless transmitter and receiver on a sledging journey, although it was not a great success. The only trained operator became ill and the 40-lb (18-kg) apparatus was an extra weight to be dragged on a sledge. But this did not deter the later development of radio as a crucial aid to exploration. One of the most famous early exponents of the wireless was Professor Robert Watson-Watt, the Scottish physicist whose early work on short-wave radio transmissions above the Arctic Circle helped lead him to the development of radar in the mid-1930s.

Studying the weather became progressively more important to Arctic expeditions, particularly with the growth of airline traffic, which demanded more accurate forecasting. The growing importance of understanding the weather was underlined in the 1932–3 International Polar Year when more than ninety-four meteorological stations were established, seven times more than had operated in the 1882–3 Polar Year. As meteorology became a standard feature of expeditions, men like Gino Watkins devoted more resources to the science and Alfred Stephenson and Quintin Riley were among those who also achieved fame in their own right.

Overall the era brought a quiet revolution. The style of exploration changed, techniques improved and additional knowledge was gained. In addition, a new school of explorers was nurtured. Behind all this effort was the neat figure of Wordie, directing operations and finding time to lead from the front with his own expeditions.

CHAPTER 13

BOTH ENDS OF
THE WORLD

WORDIE'S ASSOCIATION WITH SHACKLETON DID NOT END WITH THE death of the most charismatic and romantic figure from the heroic age. Within months of his passing, Wordie was actively engaged in administering his affairs and ensuring that Shackleton would be properly commemorated.

Shackleton's knack of letting money slip through his fingers had left his family's financial position in an uncertain state and some close associates wanted to arrange sensible provision for his widow, Emily, his three children and his widowed mother, Henrietta Shackleton, who was in her late seventies. Under the influence of Hugh Mill and the RGS, it was agreed to set up the Shackleton Memorial Fund and Wordie was called in to help. A committee was established which included political grandee Lord Curzon, Shackleton's brother-in-law Charles Sarolea, former supporters like Dame Janet Stancomb-Wills and John Rowett and the loyal Frank Wild. Wordie was appointed secretary to the fund, effectively in charge of day-to-day affairs.

It was a delicate position, with Wordie caught between the conflicting ambitions of the Shackleton family and the political machinations of the RGS. It is always possible that someone at the RGS saw the task as a test of Wordie's mettle.

Shackleton was estimated to have left sizeable debts of around £40,000 (about £1,000,000 today) and Emily Shackleton put some pressure on the committee to raise a large sum to wipe the slate clean and secure the family's long term future. In the event, only £3,000 (about £75,000 in today's terms) was raised, but the family's financial situation improved dramatically in the mid-1920s. Others had made adequate provision for Shackleton's dependants and in 1926 Henrietta Shackleton died. For once, a venture associated with Shackleton had a surplus to its name. It was decided that the spare money should be spent on a permanent statue of Shackleton. The statue, sculpted by Charles Jagger, was unveiled on 9 January 1932 – the anniversary of Shackleton's 'furthest south' in 1909 – and still stands on the outside wall of the RGS in Kensington Gore, London. A small residue from the fund, about £100 (about £2,500 today), was donated to the RGS as an endowment to keep the statue in good order.[1]

Behind the scenes, Wordie performed another useful act for the lasting memory of Shackleton. He always took a faintly paternalistic view of Shackleton, despite being fifteen years younger, and was keen to preserve his image as a great explorer. As late as the 1950s, he urged James and Margery Fisher, his biographers, to delete references to personal matters between Shackleton and his wife Emily.

Soon after Shackleton's death in 1922 it became obvious that a biography of his colourful life was certain to be written. Those close to him wanted to see the matter placed in the correct hands and handled with care, perhaps because of Shackleton's messy financial affairs and perhaps because they did not want any muck-raking of his personal relationships with other women.

Wordie moved quickly to put the issue beyond doubt and was partly responsible for ensuring that the author would be Hugh Mill, a long-standing confidant and occasional father-figure to Shackleton. Mill was keen to write the book and Wordie urged Emily Shackleton to support him. Emily's backing was essential and Wordie recognised that if Mill was given the task it would effectively close off the project to anyone outside the preferred circle. Emily Shackleton accepted Wordie's argument, and in response she told him: 'I am indeed grateful to you for your advice – and I value it. I do hope that Dr Mill will be the one.'[2]

Mill, with Emily Shackleton's close co-operation, duly wrote the first biography of Shackleton and contributed the profits from the book to her. The scholarly, thoughtful book, *The Life of Sir Ernest Shackleton,* was published in 1923 and remains essential reading for anyone studying Shackleton or early Antarctic exploration.

Wordie's services to the cause reflected his huge admiration for Shackleton. The reservations expressed while under immense strain in the Weddell Sea were long-forgotten and it was Wordie who most notably likened Shackleton to the great Elizabethan explorers, Drake and Raleigh.

James and Margery Fisher, who wrote a more comprehensive and authoritative biography of Shackleton in the 1950s, said it was Wordie, better than anyone, who captured the 'particular flavour' of Shackleton's personality. Wordie wrote his own eloquent and formal judgement of Shackleton, which was delivered in an obituary that he wrote for the *Geographical Journal* in 1922. It read:

> Caution and shrewdness were combined, however, with invincible optimism; this made him a trying partner at card games, and was also responsible for a continual hankering after and belief in hidden treasure. The latter feature was but another instance of his romantic nature. It was perhaps this which first suggested to his intimates a likeness to Raleigh. Then his friends found that he was a Raleigh in many ways – courtier, poet, explorer, and lover of his country. In an age which is producing modern Elizabethans Shackleton will surely be reckoned as most true to type.[3]

A more informal reflection of his high regard came in private correspondence. 'Shackleton', he said, 'continually rose in my estimation and forced one to overlook his shortcomings.' Writing to Mill shortly after Shackleton's death, Wordie added the personal postscript: 'Scots boys brought up on Carlyle are all hero worshippers and also very difficult to satisfy in their heroes.'[4]

A romantic age of a different type had crept up on Wordie in 1923.

To the surprise and astonishment of most who knew him, Wordie suddenly revealed that he was engaged to be married. Women had played little part in Wordie's early life, perhaps because he was continually engaged on expeditions or fulfilling a busy schedule of academic responsibilities. More likely it was because his innate shyness made him something of a wallflower.

His wife-to-be was Gertrude Mary Henderson, the bright and attractive 22-year-old daughter of a prosperous shipping executive. She was studying medicine in London, and Wordie was only a few weeks from his thirty-fourth birthday when the pair were married on 21 March 1923 at St Columba's Church in Pont Street, London. In the context of Wordie's measured and cautious approach to life, the engagement and marriage to Gertrude was almost a whirlwind romance. The pair had only known each other for about a year before the wedding, though the two families had been close for many years. Wordie and Gertrude, in fact, were distant cousins by marriage.

The Hendersons were a wealthy Scots family with an envied position in shipping circles and an unfortunate history of personal tragedy. The wealth came from Victorian times, when a member of the family married into the owners of the flourishing White Star Line of Aberdeen. George Henderson, Gertrude's father and one of sixteen children, joined the business at the age of fourteen and worked his way up to become head of the firm's important operations in London.

Gertrude was one of six children – three boys and three girls – born to the Hendersons in late Victorian or early Edwardian London. But tragedy struck the family, and in the space of only a few years George Henderson lost all three sons. One died from a brain tumour at the age of seven, his eldest son was only eighteen when killed in the war, and a third died from tuberculosis. It was said that Henderson was so devastated by the terrible losses that he donated half his considerable wealth to charity. However, George

Henderson himself was also a victim of the family's misfortune, dying from a kidney complaint at the age of forty-seven only a year after Gertrude's marriage to Wordie.

Gertrude's personal links with the Wordies went back some years and both were related to the Doak family in Scotland. Wordie had been to Glasgow Academy with members of the Doak family and James Doak was best man at their wedding. In her youth, Gertrude spent some time looking after the Reverend Andrew Doak, the minister who was married to Wordie's aunt, Julia Mann. By her twenties Gertrude had decided to study to be a doctor. She went to King's College, London but she abandoned her studies after accepting Wordie's proposal of marriage.

The rapid courtship was not universally popular in the Wordie family. Alison, who saw her brother as something of a father figure, was uneasy about Gertrude Henderson. It may be that the two women, for entirely different reasons, were competing for the attention of the same man. The uncomfortable relationship between Alison and Gertrude placed Wordie in a difficult position. The outcome was that the close bond between Wordie and his younger sister began to weaken as the years passed and the relationship never fully recovered after his marriage to Gertrude.

Wordie's marriage did not get off to an especially romantic start. He informed his new bride that a traditional honeymoon would have to wait a few days until he completed an archaeological dig in Suffolk. The diversion had no lasting impact on the relationship and the marriage would last thirty-nine years. She always called him Hamish – Gaelic for James – but Wordie stuck to formality and never called her anything other than her full name of Gertrude.

Wordie settled easily into married life and the couple moved into a small house in Wordsworth Grove, Cambridge. In 1925 they moved into Coton End, an exclusive nine-bedroom house in nearby Grange Road, set in grounds of 1¼ acres and overlooking St John's sports fields. The grand house, which was rented cheaply on a long lease from St John's College, was to remain their home for almost three decades.

Gertrude readily accepted the prospect that her husband's full-time commitments to Cambridge and to Arctic exploration would inevitably lead to lengthy periods of separation. The honeymoon episode was the first of many times when work took precedence. But Wordie approached the tricky problem with the same meticulous care and preparation he devoted to most issues. In a bid to balance his professional responsibilities with the demands of family life Wordie found a suitable compromise.

The arrangement involved creating a unique three-year life cycle which, in theory, gave him the scope to continue exploring, fulfil his academic duties at Cambridge and devote adequate time to his family. The three-year format allowed him to spend one summer season exploring, another devoted to responsibilities at Cambridge and a third spent with Gertrude. It was a delicate balancing act which needed the full co-operation of the authorities at Cambridge and the personal support of Gertrude. Almost inevitably, the delicate arrangement soon came under pressure.

Wordie's academic duties had expanded, first in 1921, when he was made a Fellow of St John's College and shortly after his wedding in 1923, when he was appointed Tutor. The appointment coincided with the preparation for a new expedition to the Arctic and a happy new domestic issue. In the summer of 1923, as Wordie was putting the finishing touches to his next expedition, Gertrude revealed that she was pregnant.

The most immediate commitment was Wordie's planned trip to Greenland, his fourth and most ambitious Arctic project to date. The aim was to reach the rarely penetrated east coast of Greenland. The original idea for a trip to Greenland had germinated at Cambridge in 1922 but there was no suitable ship available and Wordie could not attract what he regarded as the correct people for the trip. After talks at Cambridge with Tom Lethbridge and the botanist peer,

Lord Cawdor, it was agreed to make the voyage in the summer of 1923, only three months after his marriage.

The 1923 journey was almost entirely a Cambridge University expedition. Six of the seven-man party – Cawder, C.C. Duchesne, Lethbridge, Bobby Maclaren, L.S. Mayne and Wordie – were Cambridge men. The only 'outsider' was H.E. David, a friend of Lethbridge.

However, the enterprise almost failed before it began because Wordie ran into severe difficulties trying to find a suitable ship. Months of tedious negotiations failed to secure a vessel and it was June, a few weeks before the scheduled departure date, before a ship was finally booked. The relief was audible when the party finally hired the 72-ton motor-driven sealer, *Heimen*, which sailed under Captain Lars Jakobsen, a noted ice navigator from the Arctic port of Tromso in Norway. Because of the delay, all the gear and food for the two-month journey to the ice were assembled in a frantic ten days of hyper-activity.

It was an elaborate mission considering that the party expected to be gone for barely ten weeks. The aim was to complete the mapping of Greenland's east coast, explore the mighty Franz Josef Fjord, conduct geological and archaeological work and repeat the pendulum gravity experiments made on the Clavering-Sabine expedition a hundred years earlier. The Royal Society, which paid some of the expedition's expenses, lent Wordie a pendulum apparatus that had been used on Scott's last expedition.

The *Heimen* sailed from Tromso in mid-July, a little late in the season. But hopes were high and the party even took time off to make a brief stop at Jan Mayen Island to visit the Norwegian radio station. Two days later the ship entered the pack ice off Greenland's east coast and weather conditions, particularly the persistent fog, worsened dramatically.

Greenland can be compared with Antarctica as a hostile wilderness with a formidable ice-sheet, which averages 5,000 ft (1,500 m) thick and covers 85 per cent of the land. It is over 1,600 miles (2,600 km) long and the 24,400-mile coastline is roughly the equivalent of the Earth's circumference. The island was first reached by Norsemen over 900 years earlier. The fortune-hunter Eric Thorvaldsson – better known as Eric the Red – persuaded his fellow citizens to establish colonies on the west side of the island by giving the island its misleading name. Most of the island's subsequent development over the following centuries took place in the south and west where ice conditions were more favourable and navigation invariably easier than in the east.

By contrast, the east coast remains a highly dangerous region of notoriously difficult pack ice, which had prevented many ships entering the area and restricted the large-scale exploration and development seen in the west. Even maps in the east were incomplete as Wordie set sail for the area.

British sailors had been among the most frequent visitors, despite the early association with Norsemen. Henry Hudson was credited with the first sighting of the east coast in 1607 and the Scoresbys, father and son whalers from Yorkshire, visited the area many times between 1803 and 1823, though they rarely got closer than thirty miles to the mainland. Only once in twenty years were the Scoresbys able to penetrate the ice and reach land.

Captains Douglas Clavering and Edward Sabine in HMS *Griper* mapped a large part of the coastline from a distance in 1823, and numerous Danish and Swedish explorers were able to make significant new territorial discoveries over the following century, notably in the north-east. But ice conditions in the surrounding waters were always the major limiting factor.

The ice conditions were especially severe off Greenland in 1923 and the *Heimen* soon ran into problems. In the same waters that summer the Norwegian sloop, *Teddy*, was crushed by the ice and the crew drifted over 700 miles on a floe. The *Anni,* another Norwegian ship, suffered a worse fate, disappearing with all hands.

The *Heimen* ran into difficulties about 30 miles (48 km) off the coast during the night of 27 July when the vicious pack ice closed in around the ship. Captain Jakobsen was sufficiently alarmed to wake Wordie's party in the early hours with the stunning news that the ship risked being crushed. Large blocks of ice gathered beneath the *Heimen*, lifting the ship out of the water and toppling it over to a list of 15°. The parallels with the *Endurance* only eight years before were starkly evident and Wordie recorded: 'It looked extremely ugly, for the ice was of the heaviest and nastiest.'⁵

But there was one significant difference between the plight of the *Endurance* crew and the men on the *Heimen* in 1923. In 1915 the *Endurance* party was able to leave the sinking ship and set up temporary home on a huge ice floe drifting in the Weddell Sea. The colder Weddell was an almost unbroken field of ice, but to his horror Wordie quickly realised that the pack in the Arctic Ocean was more fragmented. There were no suitable floes offering a safe haven for the *Heimen*'s party if the ship lost the battle with the ice. But the more broken ice also offered the hope of break-out, and at the moment when the predicament looked its most bleak, the men had a stroke of good fortune. Patches of open water suddenly appeared nearby and the capable Jakobsen found enough open lanes to manoeuvre the ship away from immediate danger.

The threat was not entirely past and *Heimen* spent almost a month dodging and weaving through the ice, constantly searching for leads of open water. Wordie said it was the heaviest pack he had ever encountered and the position was made worse by the blankets of thick fog which hampered all attempts to break through to land.

Jakobsen's skills prevented the ship getting trapped but his caution often infuriated the more eager Wordie. He once reported a 'noticeable lack of effort' by Jakobsen and exchanged angry words with the ship's mate for wanting to 'tie up unnecessarily' in open water. Another of the crew, said Wordie, was 'chicken-hearted' and he bluntly warned Jakobsen that his solid reputation as an ice-master was at stake if other ships managed to reach east Greenland that summer.

However, the pack remained heavy and by 10 August Wordie was writing that 'we are losing the chance of doing any work at all this summer'. Four days later the mission was effectively abandoned when Jakobsen took the ship south of the proposed landing place into the less hostile waters around Scoresby Sound. But even in the south the pack remained just as impenetrable and Wordie gloomily recorded: 'There is no doubt that is an exceedingly bad ice year.'

Jakobsen was not prepared to risk his ship and had little alternative but to withdraw. After almost a month of avoiding the ice and with the season advancing, it was reluctantly decided to wrap up the expedition and run to the friendlier haven of Iceland. Dry land was reached at the Icelandic port of Seydisfjord on 19 August and the *Heimen* was back in Aberdeen by 29 August. It was a frustrating and largely fruitless journey and Wordie's diary ended with the wistful comment: 'How different would have been our feelings had we arrived back in Aberdeen after a successful voyage!'[6]

Nevertheless, it had been a lucky escape, thanks largely to the expertise of Jakobsen. Wordie never elaborated further on the failed trip or sought to draw unhappy parallels with *Endurance*. But in his official report to the RGS, which was written in the formal and restrained language of the day, Wordie readily conceded the abortive trip was 'a narrow escape from disaster'.[7]

Wordie retreated into academic and family life at Cambridge for the next two and a half years, as ordained by his unofficial lifestyle agreement. Official duties at the university absorbed much of his time and work on the Shackleton Memorial Fund was a further diversion. At home, Gertrude produced their first child with admirable precision almost exactly nine months after their marriage. A son, John, was born on 15 January 1924 and a daughter, Elizabeth followed less than two years later in October 1925.

Another departure from the routine was Wordie's quiet entry into the shadowy world of international diplomacy and politics through the innocently-named Discovery Committee. The committee was ostensibly a scientific body charged with important research in the Antarctic and surrounding islands. But behind the learned façade it concealed a hidden agenda of British territorial ambitions in the region. The committee, officially established in 1923, was the vehicle employed by Britain to fortify its interests in the Antarctic, involving the Graham Land Peninsula, the Falkland Islands, South Georgia, the South Orkneys and other smaller island territories in the region.

The future of the Antarctic and its immediate area had been exercising official minds for some years after the exploratory exploits of Bruce, Scott and Shackleton. While the subject was mostly pushed into the background during the war, plans for the peacetime environment in the Antarctic were already being drawn up in 1917, a year before the end of hostilities. Matters moved quickly after the Armistice; an inter-departmental committee was set up to consider the best way to proceed, and Wordie became involved immediately after.

Wordie's association with the Discovery Committee began in 1922 when the Colonial Office discreetly approached the RGS looking for someone with 'actual experience' of the Antarctic. The request passed across the all-seeing desk of Hinks, who gladly recommended Wordie; Winston Churchill, the Colonial Secretary, personally approved his nomination.

Hinks had struck up a solid working relationship with Wordie, first with the *Endurance* papers and the Shackleton Memorial Fund, and later with his Arctic activities. They were like peas in a pod. Hinks, a large and imposing figure approaching his fifties, was a demanding purist with the clear and precise mind of an exceptional mathematician. He was also authoritarian and impatient with those he perceived as possessing a lesser intellect. 'Always rubbing people up the wrong way,' the mountaineer Odell once concluded. 'He considered his word should be taken as gospel – and sometimes it wasn't gospel.'[8] In the meticulous and thorough Wordie he had discovered a like-minded soul who spoke the same language. Both were occasionally abrasive and both were Cambridge men. Hinks lived at Royston, only a few miles away from Wordie. Hinks did not recommend people lightly and the decision to submit Wordie's name to Churchill carried a hidden honour. With it came the formal acknowledgement that Wordie had been adopted into the inner reaches of the RGS.

The Discovery Committee, which was chaired by Rowland Darnley of the Colonial Office, was the ideal platform for Wordie. The scientific work centred mainly on how best to conserve stocks of whales, but it soon expanded into areas like oceanography, mapping and geology and into preparations for an exploratory voyage.

The appointment also introduced Wordie to the eminent zoologist, Dr Stanley Kemp, who was appointed the Committee's first Director of Research. Kemp was another academic purist with an intense dislike of publicity. He even questioned the need to conduct surveying of the region in case it interfered with the principal task of collating data about whales.

But behind the perfectly valid scientific research was an almost unspoken Colonial Office agenda of territorial rights. Argentina and Chile led the rival claims to the region but Australia, France and New Zealand were also interested in establishing a foothold and Britain intended to deploy the Discovery Committee to assert its authority.

Britain's claims to the region dated from the earliest Antarctic exploration, from Cook in the eighteenth century through to Bransfield and Weddell in the nineteenth and to Bruce, Scott and Shackleton in the early twentieth century.

Few nations bothered to challenge Britain's rights in the area, even though American, Norwegian, German and Swedish parties had mapped large parts of the area and sealing and whaling ships from many nations moved freely through southern waters. It was at the big Norwegian-owned Grytviken whaling station in 1916 that Shackleton, Crean and Worsley had first reached civilisation with news of Wordie and the other castaways on Elephant Island.

The whaling fleets enjoyed a phenomenal boom in the first decades of the twentieth century, which some likened to the Californian or Klondike gold rushes. Britain turned the bonanza to its political advantage and exercised control over the region by operating a system of licensing the whalers.

Wordie soon proved to be an influential member of the committee, firstly through his invaluable recent experience of the area and secondly by exploiting his impressive network of contacts in the Polar community. Wordie's advice centred on various matters like ice conditions and weather patterns and on finding a suitable ship and personnel to undertake the committee's first expedition south. For intimate knowledge of sledging across the Antarctic landscape he was able to consult Cambridge colleagues Debenham and Priestley and elsewhere he trawled the Polar community in search of a proper expedition ship.

The choice of ship was crucial and Wordie examined a veritable who's who of Polar vessels in search of a reliable craft capable of tackling the ice. Among the ships considered and rejected was Scott's *Terra Nova*, the *Belgica* which survived the first over-wintering in the Antarctic and the Norwegian-built *Fram*, which had been in the Arctic with Nansen and on the momentous South Pole voyage with Amundsen. After lengthy consideration, he came down in favour of Scott's old ship, *Discovery*, a specialist ice-ship built in the former whaling port of Dundee. The ship was duly purchased in 1923 and Joseph Russell Stenhouse, who skippered *Aurora* on Shackleton's Imperial Trans-Antarctic Expedition, was subsequently installed as captain for the first voyage.

Wordie was the key figure in selecting the experienced Stenhouse, even though other notable Polar skippers were available. Among others considered for the post was Worsley from *Endurance* and Campbell, who was marooned with Priestley in 1912 on Scott's Northern Party. Worsley was at a loose end in 1923 and was very keen on getting the job. He wrote to Wordie, insisting that he was the 'most suitable, fit and proper person' for the task. 'If not,' he added, 'your Scottish gore will dye the heather.'[9]

But the post went to Stenhouse, whose initial expedition sailed in 1925 and began a monumental effort of scientific endeavour which continues until this day. The expedition was the first of thirteen voyages to the region master-minded by the Discovery Committee in the years running up to the war in 1939, beganning a process which mapped large areas of the Southern Ocean for the first time. Discovery's work, despite some claims that events had been mishandled, also made an important contribution to providing a better understanding of Antarctic whaling which, in the long run, laid the foundation for the International Whaling Convention of 1946 that finally exerted some control over the slaughter.

The Discovery Committee was also the start of Wordie's close association with the fate of the Antarctic region. He served on the Committee unbroken for twenty-six years and oversaw the creation of a new organisation, the Falkland Islands Dependencies Survey, which later evolved into today's British Antarctic Survey.

ON GREENLAND'S
UNKNOWN SHORES

Ice conditions had improved markedly in the summer of 1926 when Wordie went back to the east coast of Greenland. He had faithfully stuck to his three-year cycle and was determined to finish the task wrecked by the ice in 1923. He selected the 64-ton sloop *Heimland*, which had been built for Amundsen's Polar drift a few years earlier and was originally named *Svartisen*. But the ship had been rejected as being too small for the task, and Lars Jakobsen, the Norwegian ice-master whose family owned the steam-driven vessel, was again the ship's captain.

The *Heimland* followed in the best traditions of Polar exploration, weighed down with boxes of supplies and equipment packed in every inch of the vessel. The ship sailed from Aberdeen on 30 June, a little earlier than in 1923 and with hopes of avoiding the dangerous pack. Gertrude travelled from Cambridge to say farewell and another welcome visitor was former *Endurance* shipmate, Clark.

The 1926 voyage was typical of the new breed of expedition, a small-scale affair with costs kept to a minimum and members drawn exclusively from the reservoir of talent at Cambridge. It slipped out of Britain virtually unnoticed. Total costs were estimated at just £1,700 (£45,000 today), with the RGS chipping in £150 (£4,000) and the eight-man party contributing a total of £1,200 (£32,000) from their own pockets.

Wordie's all-Cambridge team covered a mixture of scientific disciplines. Lieutenant P.F. White and G. Manley were in charge of surveying, M.A. Barnett organised the radio and Dr D. McI.

Johnson came along to study the ethnology of the Eskimo people. Charles de Bunsen was responsible for photography, while the equipment and stores were under the stewardship of J.H. Bell. The youngest member was 21-year-old August Courtauld, a member of the wealthy textile family, who had longed to join the adventurous ranks of Polar explorers. By coincidence, the Courtauld family home in Essex was a only a few miles from the village of Gestingthorpe, where the grand manor house was owned by the family of Captain Lawrence 'Titus' Oates, the most tragic figure from Scott's last expedition. Courtauld eagerly gave Wordie £100 (approximately £2,700 today) to cover his expenses for the trip. Less fortunate was another enthusiastic Cambridge student, Gino Watkins, who applied to join the expedition but was disappointed to learn that all the places had been filled. His turn would come.

It was a typically multi-skilled and egalitarian group, who willingly shared the everyday duties and cheerfully assisted each other. An important issue was that the men also learned how to live off the land, routinely sharing the hunting and developing great precision in the search for food. In under two months the party killed a total of ten bears, thirty-two musk-oxen and a mixture of hares, ducks and other birds. Wordie, a fine shot, was among the most proficient hunters.

Wordie, now on his fifth Arctic voyage, had developed his own style of leadership. The men selected for the voyage were deliberately picked as experts in their own field and there was little fear of clashing egos or rivalry for the leader's attention. In the circumstances, few orders were necessary and Wordie seemed merely to guide affairs. It was an easy style of leadership which appealed to all ages. The younger students revelled in the informality and even an experienced traveller like Longstaff admired Wordie's light touch. He once wrote: 'As a leader he never seems to give an order, he only makes suggestions but they always get carried out.'[1]

The 1926 Cambridge party spent barely seven weeks in Greenland but achieved a great deal, helped by generally good weather and an enormous appetite for work. Compared with the necessarily long drawn out operations in the Antarctic, the 1926 Cambridge expedition resembled a lightning guerrilla raid. The ship navigated the ice with unexpected ease and the men were landed for a few hyperactive weeks of work, followed by a rapid departure before the ice trapped the vessel. The men were constantly busy and precious little time was wasted. It was so hectic that normal patterns of life were abandoned in the near-24-hour daylight of the summer season and the men slept only when they needed to. Boredom, which gnawed at many over-wintering Polar ventures, was never a factor.

The coastal survey of parts of east Greenland was completed, new territory was explored at Granta Fjord to the west of Clavering Island and old abandoned Eskimo settlements were examined for the first time. Fossil trees and charred wood indicated a more temperate past for the region, and at the summit of Mount Huhnerberg Courtauld found a brief note written in 1870 by Professor Copeland from the *Germania* expedition.

Wordie also achieved his ambition of making the first penetration of the imposing Franz Josef Fjord since its discovery in 1899 by the Swede, Professor Nathorst. At the head of the fjord it was possible to see an impressive chain of mountains to the west, notably the towering Petermann Peak about twenty miles away. For Wordie the Petermann offered the enticing prospect of scaling another unconquered peak in the Arctic.

However, the route to the Petermann across the Nordenskjold Glacier looked treacherously difficult and Wordie's party did not have enough time to reach the mountain and return to the ship before the ice took grip. Captain Jakobsen was also reluctant to risk taking the *Heimland* too far into the fjord where Wordie reported a 'perfect phalanx of bergs' up to 80 ft (24 m) high. Even if Jakobsen withdrew to safer waters while a party travelled to the mountain, there was no guarantee the ice would allow them to re-enter the fjord and pick up the men.

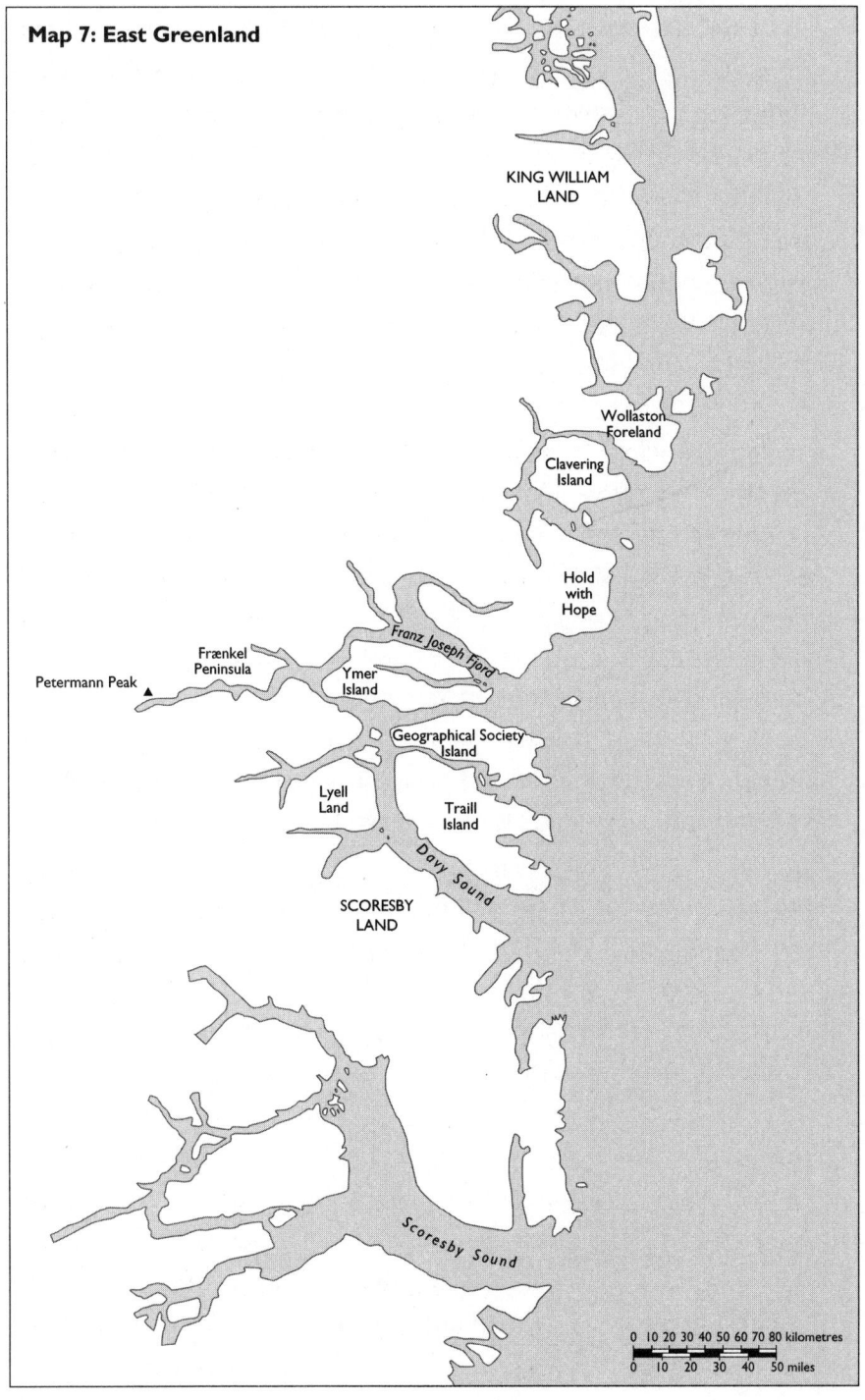

Map 7: East Greenland

KING WILLIAM
LAND

Wollaston
Foreland

Clavering
Island

Hold
with
Hope

Frænkel
Peninsula

Franz Joseph Fjord

Petermann Peak ▲

Ymer
Island

Geographical Society
Island

Lyell
Land

Traill
Island

Davy Sound

SCORESBY
LAND

Scoresby Sound

0 10 20 30 40 50 60 70 80 kilometres

0   10   20   30   40   50 miles

In the circumstances, Wordie abandoned his plans to scale the Petermann and agreed to stay in the area for only five days. But they did not waste their time and instead launched a rapid assault on a cluster of nearby mountains. A number of mountains – subsequently named the Cambridge Peaks and ranging from 6,000–7,000 ft (1,800–2,100 m) – were scaled in a hectic five days of climbing. The pace was so rapid that on one occasion two separate parties climbed the same mountain unknown to each other. Wordie also cut things fine by taking only six days' food, which left little margin for error if conditions worsened or an accident occurred.

The breathtaking tempo of work continued until 19 August, when the party packed up and departed southwards, mapping three small previously unknown islands – the Ymer, Geographical Society and Traill – in the region of 73°N. A more sombre task was to keep a sharp lookout for any survivors of the 1923 wreck, *Anni*, who were lost in the ice. But no trace was found.

Heimland's homeward trip was interrupted by a brief visit to a newly-established Eskimo colony at Amdrup's Havn in Scorseby Sound, where they found Dr Lauge Koch, the influential Danish explorer and Greenland's greatest surveyor of the age. Wordie hoped to make a short trip to the interior with Koch. But Jakobsen was still anxious about ice conditions and the plan was abandoned. The *Heimland* prepared to return home.

The *Heimland* brought an unusual cargo back from Greenland: a live polar bear and a musk-ox calf. The bear, which was thought to be about four years old, was captured by lasso while climbing an ice slope on Little Pendulum Island and was eventually caged on the *Heimland*'s decks after a violent struggle with her captors. Wordie felt very uncomfortable about capturing the bear, which was destined to be imprisoned in a zoo. He had previously turned down several requests from a number of zoos to bring home live animals from the Arctic and although he freely admitted shooting bears for food, he disliked the idea of taking them out of their own environment. This time Wordie relented and agreed to bring home a bear from the expedition and the animal was eventually given to London Zoo. The bear, which was named Susie, became a major tourist attraction. But to his dying day Wordie deeply regretted his action and despite many requests, never once visited the animal in captivity. *Heimland* reached Aberdeen on 8 September, though most attention centred on their captive bear. A small crowd lined the pier to catch sight of the animal and the bear gave full value by diving into the sea and swimming round the ship.

However, the more pertinent results of the 1926 East Greenland expedition did not go entirely unnoticed and a few months later Wordie received a flattering compliment from the distinguished Mill, who unexpectedly compared him to Shackleton. Mill told a meeting of the RGS in London that Wordie had caught 'something of the spirit of Shackleton' on his expedition. He added: 'I do not think I have ever heard of any other small expedition turning to such good account every minute of favourable weather.'[2]

Recognition of a different sort came from the Royal Society of Edinburgh. He was made a Fellow of the Society in 1922 after choosing to publish the *Endurance*'s scientific papers in the society's journal and in 1926 was singled out again. This time Wordie was awarded the society's first-ever Bruce Memorial Medal for his much-admired 'geological and oceanographical work in the Arctic and Antarctic regions'. Wordie was especially pleased to be associated with Bruce. Shortly before his death, Bruce designed the medal and insisted that it should be awarded to someone making a notable contribution to natural science and – perhaps more pertinently for Bruce – a Scot. Wordie qualified on both grounds.

By the mid 1920s, Wordie had developed into one of the foremost explorers in Britain, someone with almost unrivalled experience of Polar travel. At thirty-seven years of age, he could already boast six expeditions to the ice in only ten years and was already making preparations for a seventh. Yet he was almost unknown outside the crusty Polar establishment or the arcane academic world of Cambridge. Wordie was the opposite of the earlier generations of explorers, whose feats propelled them to celebrity-style status and turned them into household names. He was anonymous to the general public. Thousands of well-wishers thronged the streets of London in 1909 to greet Shackleton on his return from the 'furthest south' journey. Only seventeen years later those gathered on the dockside at Aberdeen paid more attention to the antics of a polar bear than to the returning explorer, Wordie.

But no one at this stage could challenge Wordie's experience in both the Antarctic and Arctic, while his senior role at Cambridge added to his authority. Cambridge, with its combination of the university and the Scott Polar Research Institute, was at the heart of Polar exploration. As a result, few explorers left Britain for the Polar regions from the mid-1920s onwards without first consulting Wordie.

What they discovered was a kindly, considerate man, always willing to offer advice on areas to explore or to recommend the right person for the right task. He could tap into his rich pool of Polar contacts to arrange the loan of items of equipment or provide the odd research grant. At the outset, Wordie's advisory role was strictly informal. But by the early 1930s the task became more formalised and he was soon sitting on numerous official expedition committees guiding parties of explorers to the Polar territories.

Wordie's informal advisory role had another important side-effect. In assisting so many young people to travel with his expeditions or to arrange their own voyages, Wordie helped build an unofficial school for young explorers and create a new dynasty of Polar explorers in Britain.

A notable number of young men from the universities graduated from junior roles on early voyages to become leading players in later expeditions, including Vivian Fuchs, Gino Watkins, August Courtauld, Edward Shackleton, Brian Roberts, Andrew Croft, Alexander Glen, Tom Lethbridge, Pat Baird, Quentin Riley and F.

Spencer Chapman. At least nine of the new school were subsequently knighted for their efforts while others achieved great distinction as academics and Wordie's friend, Launcelot Fleming, became a bishop and was later appointed Dean of Windsor.

Two of Wordie's most accomplished Polar 'graduates' at this time were Henry George Watkins, a dapper fresh-faced student from Trinity College known as Gino, and John Rymill, an Australian surveyor. Both careers were heavily influenced by their associations with Wordie.

Watkins was only twenty years old when he first approached Wordie to join his 1926 party and in a tragically short life earned a remarkable reputation as an explorer. He was a likeable and enthusiastic figure, who became attracted to exploration after listening to a lecture by the knowledgeable Priestley. Soon afterwards, Priestley introduced Watkins to Wordie. But Watkins was impatient and could not wait for Wordie's next scheduled voyage in 1929. Watkins, who possessed a slice of Shackleton's dashing spirit, decided instead to launch his own expedition and turned to Wordie for advice. Wordie was happy to help.

The target was Edge Island, a small unexplored island off the east coast of Spitsbergen. Wordie was typically generous with his advice and according to Watkins' biographer, 'Mr Wordie helped enormously.'[3] Wordie's hand could be also seen in Watkins' ability to raise money from both the RGS and the Worts Fund of Cambridge. In addition, Watkins' ship for the voyage was the *Heimen* from Norway, captained by the experienced Jakobsen. Wordie was also on hand in 1929 when Watkins assembled an expedition to Greenland, sailing in Shackleton's old ship *Quest* with a party that included eight men from Cambridge. Among the men on board was Rymill. But in the early 1930s the 25-year-old Watkins died in a boating accident.

John Rymill had sailed with Watkins in 1929 and Wordie now eagerly supported his proposed expedition to Antarctica's Graham

Land peninsula, a plan originally attributed to Watkins. Wordie and Debenham willingly served on the expedition's planning committee and they recommended Rymill's scheme over a rival expedition to the area proposed by a former member of Mawson's entourage, James Martin. Wordie was much impressed with Rymill and when asked about his suitability for the task, he simply replied: 'I have the very highest opinion of his capabilities as an explorer and leader.' Wordie encouraged the RGS to provide £1,000 (about £32,000 today) and advised Rymill to take sledging parties to the lesser known west side of Graham Land. Helped by Wordie's direction, the 1934–37 Rymill expedition carried out the most comprehensive geographic and scientific programme so far undertaken in the Antarctic. Rymill's party deployed a combination of sledging parties, dog teams and an aircraft, and finally established that Graham Land was a peninsula and not an archipelago.

Vivian Fuchs, who was given his first opportunity to explore by Wordie, said his style was to trust the good intuition of the individual unless that trust was abused. Wordie also understood an individual's limitations but always insisted that a man should stand on his own two feet. His advice, Fuchs judged, was 'invaluable'. He rarely, if ever, turned down even the most frivolous plea for help. Even those without the money to pay their expedition expenses were given proper consideration and rarely dismissed out of hand.

On one occasion Wordie was approached by a man with one arm who wanted to join an expedition to Greenland to conduct some work on the breeding habits of Arctic birds. While many people might have dismissed the request as impractical, Wordie had the courtesy to meet the man and discuss his plans, though he did not take him on the expedition.

The eagerness of Polar recruits was shown by another man who boasted a first-class degree in physics and useful experience in sledging and dog-driving. The man offered to work either on high altitude atmospherics or to serve as expedition cook. But Wordie did not suffer fools gladly and he never allowed sentiment to blur his judgement. Fuchs once noted: 'Underdogs and lost causes were perhaps deserving of sympathy, but seldom of support.'

Wordie does not appear to have taken a conscious decision to become the father-figure to the younger generation of Polar explorers. But it was the type of back-seat driving which suited him. He was not a natural leader in the mould of Shackleton who, quite simply, inspired people. While Shackleton led from the front, Wordie was someone who exercised his power and influence quietly from behind the scenes. Wordie was more *éminence grise* than cheerleader. Nor was he a natural administrator or bureaucrat, preferring to dispense his wisdom in private and putting very little in writing. One colleague remembered that he appeared to have no filing system and instead relied on a formidable memory for detail.

His office at Cambridge was a disorganised jumble of papers and books and odd relics of previous expeditions, including ice-axes, rucksacks and even musk-ox skins. It more closely resembled an expedition campsite than an academic's study. 'His room was full of books and papers and you were lucky to find a free chair to sit,' an old student remembered. However he could always find what he wanted among the turmoil. He never carried a briefcase and all the necessary papers were stuffed into the pockets of his double-breasted suits. But in his reserved, mildly chaotic but highly effective manner Wordie had become the elder statesman of Polar exploration in Britain.

PERILS ON
PETERMANN PEAK

WORDIE WENT BACK TO CAMBRIDGE IN 1926 AND QUIETLY SETTLED into the next stage of his three-year schedule, where family matters suddenly assumed increasing importance. A second son, George, was born in July 1927, and in February 1929 Gertrude gave birth to a second daughter, Alison. The arrival of Wordie's fourth child coincided with the planning for a new expedition to Greenland, which aimed to complete the mapping of the eastern coast and fulfil his ambition of scaling the unclimbed Petermann Peak.

The expedition was slightly larger than the previous two voyages to Greenland, partly because two late additions to the party – the doctor, J.F. Varley and wireless operator, P. de Dykes – were made less than a fortnight before the team sailed from Aberdeen. The nine-strong company was again composed entirely of Cambridge.

Only Courtauld and the geographer, Vernon Forbes, who been with Watkins on Edge Island in 1927, had any previous experience of the ice. Cuthbert 'Jumbo' Wakefield was a surveyor and Walter Whittard, a research student, helped Wordie with the geology. Two students from St John's College, Mervyn 'Park' Parkinson and 21-year-old Vivian Fuchs, also went as geologists. Fuchs, who was always known as Bunny and went on to become the country's most acclaimed explorer, later recalled that his maiden trip to the ice in 1929 'led to my lifetime of expedition work'.

Wordie stuck with the tried and tested formula of using Norwegian ships and he again hired the *Heimland* from Tromso. The ship was fresh from taking part in the search for Amundsen, who disappeared

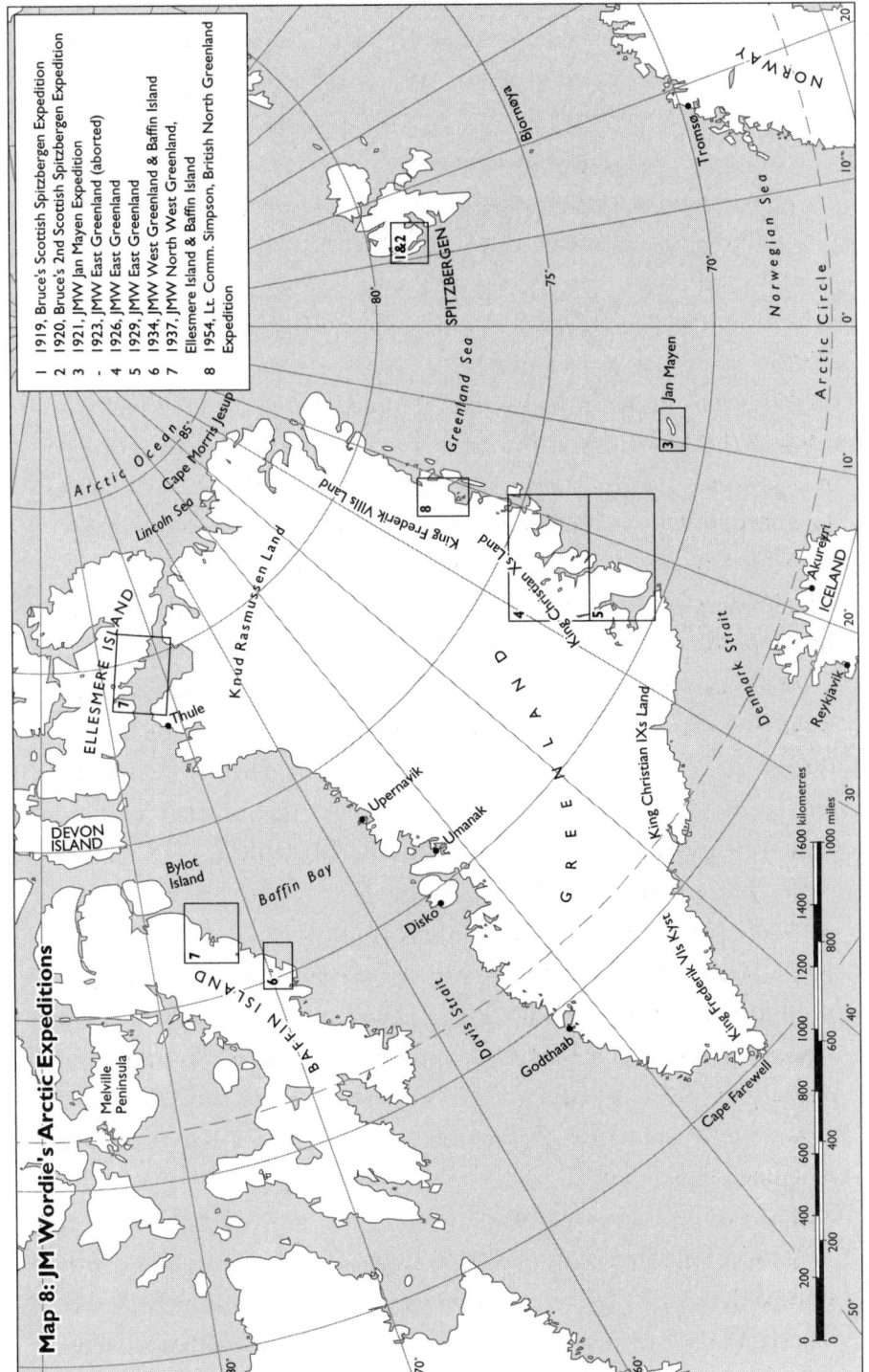

Map 8: JM Wordie's Arctic Expeditions

1   1919, Bruce's Scottish Spitzbergen Expedition
2   1920, Bruce's 2nd Scottish Spitzbergen Expedition
3   1921, JMW Jan Mayen Expedition
–   1923, JMW East Greenland (aborted)
4   1926, JMW East Greenland
5   1929, JMW East Greenland
6   1934, JMW West Greenland & Baffin Island
7   1937, JMW North West Greenland,
     Ellesmere Island & Baffin Island
8   1954, Lt. Comm. Simpson, British North Greenland
     Expedition

NORWAY

Tromsø

Norwegian Sea

Arctic Circle

Bjørnøya

SPITZBERGEN

1 & 2

Jan Mayen

3

Greenland Sea

King Frederik VIIIs Land

8

King Christian Xs Land

4

5

Denmark Strait

Akureyri

ICELAND

Reykjavik

Arctic Ocean

Cape Morris Jesup

Lincoln Sea

Knud Rasmussen Land

ELLESMERE ISLAND

7

Thule

DEVON ISLAND

Upernavik

Umanak

Disko

King Christian IXs Land

G R E E N L A N D

King Frederik VIs Kyst

Baffin Bay

Bylot Island

Davis Strait

Godthaab

Cape Farewell

BAFFIN ISLAND

7

6

Melville Peninsula

1600 kilometres
1000 miles

0   200   400   600   800   1000   1200   1400   1600
0   200   400   600   800   1000

in the Arctic Ocean while searching for the lost Italian navigator, Umberto Nobile, north of Spitsbergen. His body was never found.

Heimland left Aberdeen on 2 July under Captain Karl Jakobsen, the brother of Lars Jakobsen. But the ice conditions in the summer of 1929 were almost as severe as in 1923, when Wordie had to abandon his first expedition to the area. Soon after reaching the pack, radio reports indicated that at least one ship – Koch's *Godthaab* – was already trapped off the east coast of Greenland. *Heimland* moved cautiously but soon encountered a screen of ice blocking the path ahead. On 8 July Wordie gloomily recorded that in the same location in 1926 he had enjoyed the luxury of open water for forty miles. Progress was painfully slow, the ship frequently halted by the pack or swirling fog. For a couple of days the *Heimland* was stationary.

To relieve the boredom, some of the men left the ship to wander round the encircling ice floes and Fuchs, a novice in this environment, came perilously close to a savage death. He absent-mindedly strayed too far from the ship and was suddenly confronted by a towering polar bear just 100 yards (90 m) away. Whittard and Dykes happened to be on deck and quickly realised that Fuchs was unarmed and had no chance of reaching the ship before the bear caught him. Grabbing their rifles, they shot the animal before it could strike the defenceless man. 'Next day we ate bear,' Fuchs recalled.

Several futile attempts were made to break through the ice and reach land and at one stage the rudder was damaged in the struggle. A little later the pressure lifted the *Heimland* out of the water. On one day it required six hours of immense effort to battle through a mere 200 yards (180 m) of ice towards open leads and safety. On another, three charges of dynamite were used in a bid to blast a channel.

But the explosions had little impact and in early August, after four weeks of hard labour, Wordie was resigned to a second defeat at the hands of the ice off the eastern shores of Greenland. He conceded: 'We seem doomed to disappointment. So often we have thought there was only a few more miles to the land and so often been disappointed.'[1]

However the unpredictability of the climate was demonstrated next day when, to the relief of all on board, the *Heimland* finally escaped and broke through to reach Mackenzie Bay. Although cheered by their escape from the ice, the loss of four weeks was a severe blow. The brief Arctic summer was already coming to an end and barely three weeks remained before the party was scheduled to pack up and go home.

Landing was carried out at a more frantic pace than usual and Wordie also reshaped his priorities. He ditched much of the remaining programme and instead directed the party's full effort into penetrating the Franz Josef Fjord and climbing the Petermann.

Captain Jakobsen had his own concerns. The lateness in the season posed a serious threat to the *Heimland*, which risked getting snared by the ice if he took the vessel too deep into the Franz Josef Fjord to land the climbers. Even if he dropped the party off and withdrew, there was no guarantee that the ice would allow the *Heimland* to return to pick up the climbers. Jakobsen decided to take the latter option: to land the men and beat a hasty retreat to safer waters at the head of the fjord, where a rendezvous point was fixed. But in case the ship had to move again, he left behind an emergency cache of food and equipment for two weeks, which was reckoned to be sufficient to enable the climbers to locate the *Heimland* at a second spot outside the fjord at Mackenzie Bay. Jakobsen also took the precaution of leaving a small lifeboat behind.

Fuchs was faintly excited by danger and the prospect of spending a winter on the ice stimulated him. He wrote: 'I keep on feeling how impossible it is to realise my luck in being here to revel and marvel at all these things . . . I wish I had thought of wintering . . . it would have been great fun and very cheap, especially as I could hunt . . .'[2]

A more realistic Wordie quietly assembled his party and began the march towards the Petermann Peak. The six-man team comprised

Forbes, Wakefield, Courtauld, Fuchs, Varley and himself. It was planned to be a ten-day trip, mainly because of the difficulty of crossing the dangerous Nordenskjold Glacier, which barred their path to the mountain. With time short it promised to be a hectic rush. Fuchs described it as the 'Petermann Dash' and on the eve of departure posed the question in his journal: 'When will we be back?'

Wordie took a huge risk in the interests of speed by deciding to cut food and fuel down to a minimum. On the second day out, lunch consisted of one biscuit, two sticks of chocolate and six lumps of sugar.

It was a very demanding hike across difficult terrain, first up the Riddar Glacier, then across the four-mile wide Nordenskjold Glacier and finally a slow ascent up the lower slopes of the mountain. Each man carried a pack weighing around 37 lb (17 kg) and without the luxury of porters it was tough going, especially as the men were not in prime condition after weeks lazing around the *Heimland* in the pack ice. Wordie reported: 'It was hard work up the hill – a month's inactivity on the ship was hardly the best preparation for an expedition like this.'[3] The march was far more demanding than expected, especially as Wordie had underestimated the amount of fuel needed to melt ice for drinking water. He soon reported being 'miserably thirsty'. The dehydration lasted for several days until some of the men went back to fetch more fuel.

Crossing the crevassed Nordenskjold Glacier, which runs along the lower slopes of the Petermann and drains west-to-east into Franz Josef Fjord, was particularly arduous. 'Very stiff work indeed,' Wordie said. The party pushed themselves hard, fully aware that there was precious little time to waste in making the climb and getting back to the ship. 'Heavy packs and rather low spirits,' Wordie added as they reached a height of 6,000 ft (1,800 m) near the Petermann.

On 10 August Wordie almost suffered a fatal fall down an 800-ft (245-m) gorge. But in scrambling to safety, he dropped his pack

Map 9: Nordenskjold Glacier & Petermann Peak, East Greenland

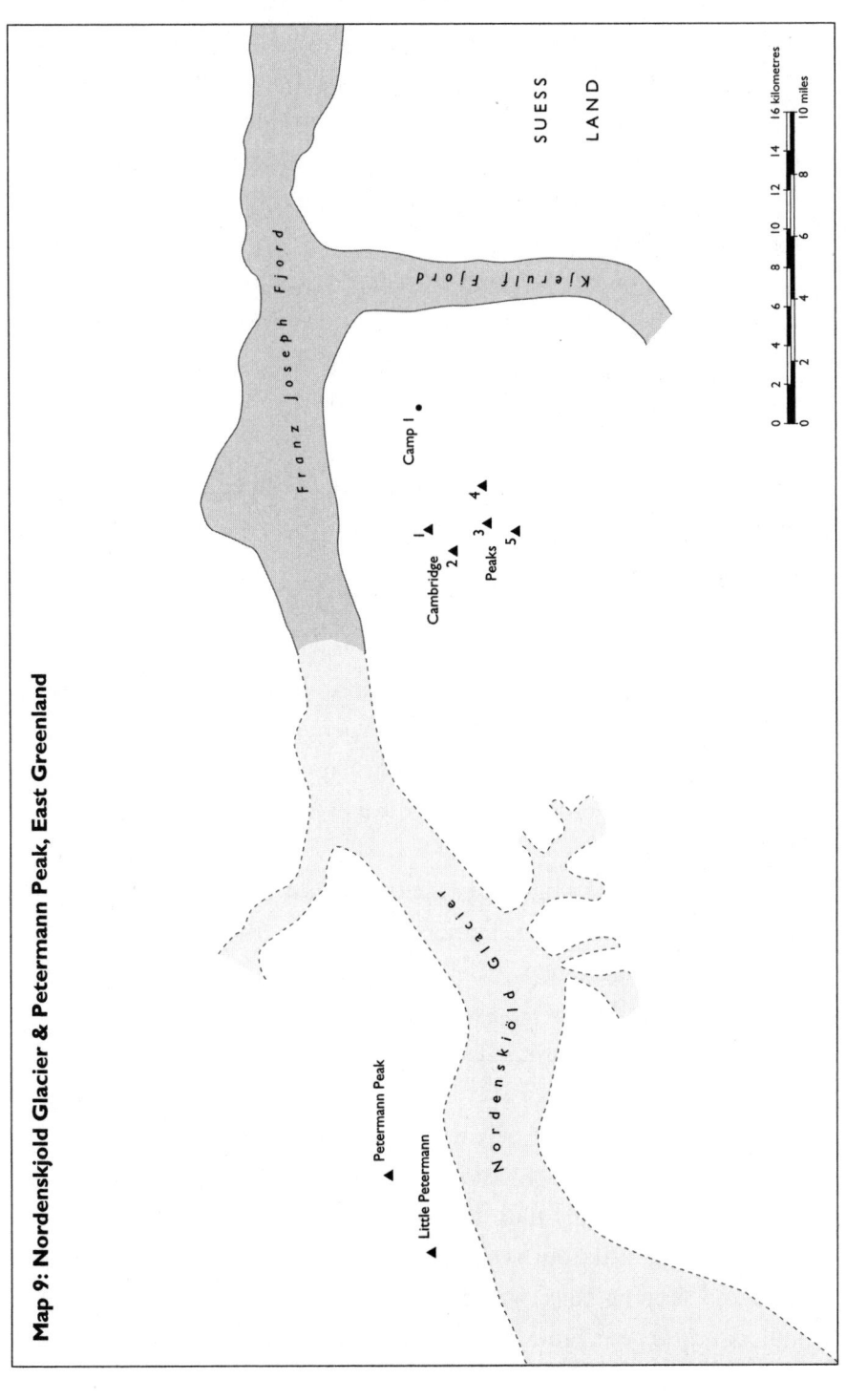

Franz Joseph Fjord

Kjerulf Fjord

SUESS LAND

Camp 1 •

Cambridge 1 ▲

2 ▲

Peaks 3 ▲

4 ▲

5 ▲

Nordenskiöld Glacier

Petermann Peak ▲

Little Petermann ▲

0 2 4 6 8 10 12 14 16 kilometres

0 2 4 6 8 10 miles

over the edge and Fuchs dryly observed: 'One had a very good idea of what one's own body would look like flying through the air.'[4] Although the men were roped together, there was always the danger of a heavy fall. Once Courtauld slipped and fell the length of his rope and was only saved by a quick-thinking colleague who jammed his ice-axe into the snow.

Wordie's typically undemonstrative leadership was crucial in navigating the men towards their goal and in maintaining morale in potentially difficult circumstances. Courtauld noted: 'It's all very well to toddle along in the rear and carry weights, but a very different thing to find the way.'[5] At night they collapsed wearily into their tents, hungry and bitterly cold. Temperatures one night dropped to 14° of frost and snow fell continuously. Fuchs could only write: 'Dead beat and damn cold.'[6]

Varley, the doctor, was the first casualty of the dash to the mountain. His boots split apart and he was forced to remain behind alone in a tent. It was a difficult decision to leave a man, particularly as Varley lacked any mountaineering experience and was also unsure of the route back to the ship in the unhappy event that he became separated from the other five. 'He was very sporting about it all,' Wordie wrote.

In the distance, worsening weather could be seen approaching and winds roared to such ferocity that it was feared the guy ropes on the tent might snap. 'Icicles formed in our beards and faces lost all feeling,' Fuchs reported. Lunch was a paltry serving of tea and oatmeal in ice water. Alarm rose when Wordie and Courtauld suddenly disappeared in the swirling mists. But after an anxious wait of several hours the pair stumbled into camp.

Wordie assessed the situation, with the season closing in and the weather unremittingly foul. He felt the only chance of reaching the summit was to strike out as fast as possible. All surplus gear, including tents and sleeping bags, was stashed at 7,380 ft (2,200 m) and a last mug of hot tea was brewed before the final assault on the mountain.

Petermann Peak, named after a German geographer, was thought to be the highest mountain in the Arctic. Payer and Copeland, who first saw it in 1870, speculated that it rose to at least 11,000 ft (3,300 m). Now a lightly-equipped team of tired, hungry climbers were preparing to make the first full ascent. Climbing proved fairly straightforward, despite the strong winds. At 9.15 on the evening of 15 August, the five men paused for a break within 100 ft (30 m) of the summit. A strong gale was blowing and all reported being bitterly cold in sub-zero temperatures. 'My boots froze solid on me and my face lost all feeling,' Fuchs wrote. The situation now called for decisive leadership and Wordie had to make a difficult decision. He was concerned about the atrocious weather and believed that the final stage of the climb was too dangerous to be attempted with fewer than three men roped together. It meant heartbreaking disappointment for two men, Fuchs and Courtauld, who were ordered to remain behind just 100 ft from the summit.

Wordie, Forbes and Wakefield moved up, taking an hour of exhausting effort in poor half-light and lacerating wind to cover the final 100 ft to the top. Frostbite nipped their cheeks. A little below the summit Fuchs and Courtauld heard the cheers of celebration above the wind. It was 10.30 on the evening of 15 August and the summit area was so narrow that the three men did not have enough room to build a little cairn to record their achievement. A brief note was left in a tin, but taking photographs in the dim light was impossible. Wordie said the three men felt 'almost powerless with the cold'.

A few feet below a deeply disappointed Fuchs recorded that a Force 8 gale (39–46 mph) was blowing and that he had never been so cold in his life. 'I am furious at not having got up to the top after coming all this way. I do call it a bit hard,' he wrote.[7] Wordie attested the height of the Petermann at 9,650 ft (2,895 m), far less than anticipated. But it was a stiff, exhausting climb and the hardest part, negotiating a swift and safe passage back to the ship, was still ahead.

Descending the mountain should have been a lot easier than the ascent. But the men were tired and food was running dangerously low. A swift descent was essential. The gale made the initial steps hazardous, but nevertheless they managed to reach an unconcerned Varley, who was sleeping peacefully when the climbers came down. He had spent the time mending his boots.

The journey back to the ship proved far more difficult than many expected, with freezing temperatures and strong winds hampering their progress. While Wordie glossed over the dangers in his official report, it is clear that retreat down the Petermann was a close-run thing and that the party came near to disaster. Any further deterioration in the weather would have had serious consequences for the tired, cold and hungry party. In his private journal, Fuchs wrote: 'Food has almost run out and it is imperative that we reach the ship as soon as possible.'[8]

Courtauld was struggling badly and a fresh crisis arose when Forbes collapsed. 'Absolutely done for and [he] got into a very nervy state,' Fuchs reported. Wordie decided that Fuchs should remain behind with Forbes to ensure he did not freeze to death. It was a crucial decision, which undoubtedly saved the life of Forbes. In his journal Fuchs explained: 'Had I not [stayed with him] I am sure he would have laid himself quietly down and frozen. If we had lost him it would have been serious, for the rest of us would have had to look for him without food and without being able to cook, as he had the utensils.'[9]

Soon after food ran out and urgent action was needed. Varley volunteered to swim across a freezing pool on the Nordenskjold Glacier to retrieve some pemmican which had been discarded on the way up.

Danger was never far away and once the men were so desperate to save time they crossed the side slopes of a snow dome of instead of going over the top. Fuchs conceded that this route risked triggering an avalanche but added, 'we got away with it.' Wordie suffered his own brush with danger by crashing through a crevasse, leaving only his head and shoulders visible. As he struggled to free himself, a box of matches in his pocket suddenly burst into flames and he was torn between escaping from the crevasse or dousing the fire in his jacket. His colleagues dragged him out, put out the flames and quickly resumed the descent.

Wordie now took another difficult decision, electing to make a hurried dash for the ship, covering the last 20 miles (32 km) in a single day because food was so low. It was a gruelling 14-hour slog, punctuated by only short rests. 'If we sat down, we were too tired to get up,' Wordie said. The final frantic descent down perilous glaciers and snowy slopes alone took over six hours. Wordie conceded that the men were 'absolutely played out' when they finally clambered on board the *Heimland*. Fuchs admitted: 'We were all pretty done.' Courtauld wrote: 'If getting to heaven is half as good as getting on board *Heimland*, it will be worth trying for.' On the ship the Norwegian seamen noticed that all six climbers had 'bowed backs and a slow step'.

What Wordie did not immediately appreciate was how close the party had come to missing the ship and being forced to undertake another gruelling march. While they were scrambling down the mountain, Jakobsen had grown concerned that the *Heimland* would become trapped in the ice and had decided to withdraw to more open waters. Barely an hour before he was ready to sail, the six climbers stumbled back to the ship. It took the men several days to recover from the fatigue and all nursed minor strains and injuries. Forbes and Fuchs suffered badly from nightmares. For six consecutive nights Forbes was found sleep-walking around the ship hallucinating about falling down crevasses. Wordie chose not to divulge the difficulties. On 20 August he cabled Hinks at the RGS with the news that the Petermann Peak had been climbed for the first time and concluded with the cheery sign off: 'All well'.

Only three days later the ship made an unsuccessful attempt to reach Cape Mackenzie at the head of the Franz Josef Fjord, the second rendezvous spot chosen for relief if the *Heimland* had been forced to retreat from the original meeting place. It was fortunate that Jakobsen waited an extra hour for the climbers to return. As the ship approached the area, the pack off the cape was thick and impenetrable and Jakobsen immediately abandoned all attempts to reach the shore. Instead, he turned the vessel towards home.

Wordie, at forty years of age, had been pushed to the brink by the scramble up and down the Petermann. When *Heimland* docked at Aberdeen on 9 September, a small posse of pressmen greeted the party and photographs taken on the quayside showed clearly the strain of the expedition. Wordie looked thin and hollow-cheeked. For the first time, he showed signs of ageing and weariness. But the exertion had not affected his performance in extreme circumstances, particularly the difficult decisions taken at critical moments, such as leaving Fuchs and Courtauld behind near the mountain top. Fuchs reported: '. . . his steady manner gave us all the confidence in his leadership.'[10]

Wordie's official report gave little away, largely ignoring the hazards and close brushes with disaster. He kept his report strictly formal and offered virtually no indication of the dangers the men faced.

Koch, the leading authority on Greenland, led the applause for the expedition, which had struggled against the clock from the very start and was conducted at a feverish pace. He said the expedition had opened up new territory to the west of Franz Josef Fjord and taken the first steps towards a 'completely altered conception' of East Greenland's geography. Longstaff, a knowledgeable and experienced climber, was among those who recognised the extent of the difficulties and the narrow line between success and failure. He said:

I think only mountaineers will realise what a very big job it was to get to this mountain. That sort of thing takes a lot of sticking, especially when one really never gets a good meal from start to finish. Every mountaineer will take his hat off to those who reached Petermann Peak.[11]

Fuchs took a more prosaic view, which more accurately reflected the dangerous finale of the trip. He declared that the 1929 expedition had been a 'memorable baptism of ice'. Wordie stuck to the official line.

HOPES
DASHED

Wordie's links with Shackleton were resurrected in the early 1930s. Among the young men who approached Wordie for advice about Arctic exploration was Shackleton's son, the 22-year-old Edward Shackleton, who was following his father's footsteps onto the ice. Edward, an Oxford graduate, initially wanted to take a small party to Spitsbergen and went to Cambridge to see Wordie. Wordie told him that several other expeditions were expected in Spitsbergen that summer and urged him instead to switch his attention to Ellesmere Island (then known as Ellesmere Land) in the Canadian Arctic, where chunks of the territory were still unexplored. Shackleton gladly accepted the advice and sailed north in the summer of 1934. Unusually for university expeditions of the time, Shackleton's party over-wintered in the region and returned in 1935 after a successful trip. 'On an expedition,' he wrote, 'the mind is stimulated to a degree which in civilisation it may never attain.'

The Arctic was buzzing with activity in 1934, with Britain alone sending four separate expeditions, including a team under Martin Lindsay, which was crossing Greenland. Wordie, too, was heading north for the seventh time.

His reputation was now at its zenith and his expeditions and expertise begun to attract more attention. In the early 1930s his reputation on the international stage was confirmed when the respected McGill University of Montreal approached Wordie to become Chancellor. It was a tempting offer but Wordie turned down the opportunity to work abroad. Peter, his fifth child, was born in 1932 and Wordie always insisted that his children should be educated in Britain.

The 1934 expedition was somewhat untypical for Wordie. It was an uncharacteristically high-profile event, it afforded lavish advance press coverage and was followed closely at home through a series of regular despatches wired back from the ice. At five months, it was also likely to be the longest of his series of journeys to the Arctic. But it was also a disappointingly lacklustre affair, which was thwarted by poor weather and excessive ambition. Another feature was that it contained the lowest proportion of Cambridge men of any of his expeditions. Only five of the nine-man party – Baird, Paterson, Dalgety, Ritchie and Wordie himself – were associated with the university.

The geographical aims of the 1934 voyage were also a little more vague than his earlier expeditions, although the project did include a large programme of scientific work, ranging from geology and mapping to archaeology and ornithology. Wordie, characteristically precise and well-prepared, described the expedition's overall plans as 'an open programme'.

The expedition, perhaps more than any other led by Wordie, was a gamble from the start. For the first time he planned to explore the west coast of Greenland, past the northerly settlements at Upernavik and on to Cape York in the treacherous Melville Bay. One key target was to reach Cape York during the nesting season for the snow goose, the knot and other Arctic birds.

The ship was then scheduled to cross Smith Sound to Ellesmere Island – near to Edward Shackleton's base – and head south along Baffin Bay before penetrating Lancaster Sound, the gateway to the North West Passage. However, the full itinerary and the hope of catching the nesting season meant departing early from Britain and reaching the upper west coast of Greenland when ice conditions were highly unpredictable. It was a toss-up whether the ice would have left Melville Bay so early.

The vaguest part of the venture was the entry to Lancaster Sound, where dozens of ships, mostly British, had begun their failed attempts to conquer the North West Passage from east to west. It was the boldest target of Wordie's life, perhaps even more audacious than his attempts to climb Everest in 1922.

By the 1930s only one ship – Amundsen's *Gjoa* – had sailed through the gruelling waterway. The experienced Longstaff, who was travelling on the 1934 expedition, was brutally frank about their chances. He told reporters on the eve of departure that the prospects of navigating the North West Passage were '10 to 1 against it'.

However, the expedition had caught public attention and newspaper coverage portrayed the small, privately-funded venture as something far grander in scale and ambition. For some it invited comparisons with earlier heroic voyages. Many papers gleefully leapt at the prospect of a British party finally defeating the passage, which had proved a graveyard for the nation over more than three centuries. The object of Wordie's expedition, thundered one newspaper, was 'the finding of the North West Passage' while others said the men were gloriously 'following in Franklin's footsteps'. The comparison with Sir John Franklin's catastrophic search for the North West Passage was hardly encouraging. Franklin's 1845 expedition in the *Erebus* and *Terror* was the biggest single disaster in the history of Polar exploration, the two ships disappearing in the ice with the loss of all 129 men.

Wordie always maintained a strong interest in the passage and had read extensively on the subject. It was Amundsen's book on his historic first-ever navigation that encouraged his interest in adopting new methods of exploring. In later life he collaborated with Richard Cyriax on an article in the *Geographical Journal* to commemorate the centenary of Franklin's terrible expedition.

The 1934 expedition expected to be away for five months but because of the obvious hazards Wordie sensibly took enough supplies for the men to survive for eighteen months. In charge of the ship, once again, was Captain Jakobsen, who commanded his own sealer, *Heimen*, a 129-ton motor-driven vessel which had replaced the ship of the same name that had carried the Cambridge party to Greenland in 1923. Among the crew was Jakobsen's 14-year-old son, Thorvald, who was getting his own baptism of the ice.

The nine-man landing party included Longstaff as zoologist and medical officer and Lieutenant W.E. Fletcher, a naval navigator who was destined to die in 1941 while searching for the lost woman aviator, Amy Johnson. The surveyor and geologist was Pat Baird and Sir John Hanham, the nephew of New Zealand's Governor-General, Lord Bledisloe, went as botanist. Tom Paterson was the archaeologist, M.H.W. Ritchie was official photographer and the ornithologists were Harry Hanham and C.T. Dalgety, who had been with Watkins some years earlier.

Heimen left Aberdeen in May 1934, sailed past the southern tip of Greenland and up the west coast to the settlement of Upernavik. However, 1934 was a long winter and the worst fears about an early departure were soon realised when stubborn ice blocked progress north. The ship was forced to remain in the port for a frustrating ten days.

Even in mid-July, when the waters were expected to be more open, northerly progress was still blocked by ice. An irritated Wordie recalled that the whalers in the past had managed to travel across Melville Bay as early as the first week of June.

While stuck at Upernavik, Wordie took the opportunity of gaining a panoramic view of the ice conditions by climbing the 3,560-ft mountain, Sanderson's Hope. He was joined at the summit by Longstaff, Hanham, Ritchie and Baird. But the view from the top was disappointing, a field of heavy pack stretching for twenty-five miles into the distance. 'Ice prospects not of the best,' he wrote in his diary. 'All wondering if we can get northwards or not.'[1]

Time was critical if the expedition was to complete its full programme; although Upernavik was finally left after nine days, progress north was very slow. By 4 July the ship was at Wilcox Head, where a fresh disappointment awaited them. From the Head, Wordie reported that the ice in Melville Bay was unbroken as far as the eye could see. The *Heimen* made painfully slow progress north but managed to enter the lower reaches of Melville Bay, where the vessel was again checked by the ice. A little later the ship was driven back to the south by the ice and by early August Wordie abandoned attempts to reach Melville Bay.

All that remained was a possible crossing of Baffin Bay to Ellesmere Island, but a despondent Wordie confessed: 'We have in a way already shot our bolt.' By 4 August *Heimen* was back at Upernavik. Despite Wordie's pessimism, the ship did manage to beat against a raging gale and cross the bay to the north-east shores of Baffin Island (then called Baffin Land). To their astonishment word reached the party that two ships – including one carrying Shackleton – had successfully penetrated Melville Bay. 'Our trouble all along has been that we were much too early,' a disappointed Wordie wrote in his diary on 12 August.

For the next two weeks the party roamed along the coastline, examining various inlets, correcting some false map references and studying a number of native settlements. But when the first autumn frosts were encountered at the end of August it was decided to set course for home. By 15 September the *Heimen* was back in Aberdeen.

The results from the three-and-a-half month excursion were worthy but unspectacular. Little new had been learned. Wordie put the best possible gloss on affairs by emphasising that some useful geological specimens had been collected and decent relics of early Eskimo life had been found. Dalgety, the ornithologist, summed up the sense of anti-climax and confessed that all the birds seen during the trip were 'comparatively well known'. The expedition, he concluded, was 'a very great disappointment'.[2]

In truth the most notable achievement was a modest consolation prize: Longstaff and Baird made an ascent of the Devil's Thumb, a well-known 2,000-ft (600-m) pinnacle on Greenland's west coast which over the years had served as a valuable landmark to passing whalers. They hoped to be the first to make the climb. But even this was tinged with disappointment because a small cairn was discovered at the top, indicating that an unknown climber had beaten them to the summit. However the achievement of Longstaff and Baird in reaching the summit came perilously close to being overshadowed by an unexpected controversy.

The Devil's Thumb is an upright, phallic-like rock and in preparing the expedition's official papers for the RGS it was discovered that some irreverent prankster had named it 'Wordie's Prick' on the map. Fortunately, the reference was spotted at the last minute on the page proofs and the map was hastily withdrawn from publication.

Scottish heritage, a subject close to his heart, became a major diversion for Wordie after returning from the disappointing trip to West Greenland. He had long taken a close interest in his heritage and was among a group of far-sighted Scots who wanted to preserve the country's natural environment for future generations.

One particular interest was the fate of Glencoe, the site in the Highlands of the infamous massacre of 1692. He was introduced to the area by his father during childhood trips to Appin, which is a good day's hike from Glencoe. He also understood the special importance of the site to the Scots.

Wordie had shown an interest in preserving Glencoe as early as the 1920s, helped by the support of his sister Alison and a friend, Manny Forbes. Wordie and Alison went to the lengths of making an unofficial survey of the area in 1924 and later began to generate interest in the scheme among influential and wealthy members of the Scottish Mountaineering Club. His initiative was given fresh impetus in 1931 when a group of Scottish conservationists helped create the National Trust for Scotland. Glencoe soon became an early target of their ambitions and the opportunity to acquire the site for the Trust arose in 1935 when the owner, Lord Strathcona, put the historic estate up for sale.

Wordie was among a group of Scots who rallied support to buy the estate and prevent it being developed for commercial exploitation. He joined the two major figures, Arthur W. Russell, law agent to the Trust and Percy Unna, President of the Scottish Mountaineering Club, who lobbied and successfully raised money to buy important tracts of land in the area.

It was a prodigious effort, which between 1935 and 1937 succeeded in purchasing almost 13,000 acres of the glen, including the massacre site, the neighbouring Dalness Estate and Bidean nam Bian (peak of the pelts), the highest peak in the area. Unna, Russell and Wordie raised funds through contacts at the Scottish Mountaineering and other climbing clubs, by public appeals and by approaching wealthy Scots living abroad. But Unna's intervention was the most decisive, including the moment in 1937 when he personally gave £5,000 (£150,000 today) of the £6,500 (£195,00) needed to buy the magnificent Dalness Estate.

Another valued supporter was the philanthropic Pilgrim Trust where Wordie had some old connections. The Pilgrim Trust had allotted £4,000 (£125,000 today) in 1931 towards the cost of building the Scott Polar Research Institute's new premises in Cambridge and it was soon recruited to help with the Glencoe project. The Glencoe initiative was among the earliest and most innovative conservation schemes and has served as a valuable model down the ages. Its simple but effective ideal was summed up in the 1937 appeal for funds to buy the Dalness Estate which decreed that the land be maintained, 'in its primitive condition for all time with unrestricted access to the public'.

A LAST ARCTIC
VOYAGE

By the time much of the Glencoe area had been preserved Wordie was in a position to resume active exploration and finish the task left undone from the unhappy 1934 excursion. In 1937 Wordie prepared to return to the Arctic. He was forty-eight years old and making his eighth and final voyage north. Wordie's fierce ambition had not been dulled by age and the point was emphasised by his sweeping plans for the 1937 enterprise. It was by far the largest and scientifically most challenging of all his expeditions.

However, preparations were thrown into some disarray in early 1937 when Wordie was suddenly struck down by an attack of mumps, a rare but highly contagious ailment for adults. To his frustration, Wordie was quarantined at home in Cambridge for three weeks. When normal service resumed, Wordie once again stuck with his trusted formula of using a Norwegian ice-ship and university men for the expedition's shore party. Nine of the ten men travelling north in 1937 – Carmichael, Drever, Feachem, Hunter, Leaf, Paterson, Robin, Lethbridge and Wordie – were former or present Cambridge men.

The target was again Melville Bay, Ellesmere Island and Baffin Island. But the scientific programme was more diverse than before. The total cost of the undertaking, estimated at £3,400 (about £100,000 in today's terms), was also higher than earlier voyages. Some £1,900 (about £56,000 today) of the expenses were met by the individual members of the expedition but the broader scope of the scientific work called for more outside help and the remaining £1,500 (£44,000) came from third party grants. Cambridge and

Edinburgh universities made small awards and lent some equipment to the expedition, while the Royal Society contributed £800 (£24,000) towards costs.

Apart from the customary geological and archaeological investigations, the most unusual feature was a plan to conduct a major study of the cosmic rays in the earth's upper atmosphere by using high altitude balloons in an area along the east of Smith Sound, which was then close to the Geomagnetic North Pole.

The chance to make observations arose when Wordie was approached by Paterson from the 1934 party. The idea attracted the attention of two specialists, E.G. Dymond, a lecturer at Edinburgh University, and Dr Hugh Carmichael of St John's, who also agreed to join the expedition.

Dymond and Carmichael spent months perfecting their equipment in readiness for the trip. Carmichael's included a lightweight ionisation chamber with an electroscope and a camera and Dymond's was a modified Geiger counter set with wireless transmission. Sir George Simpson, the outstanding meteorologist from Scott's last expedition, arranged for specialist weather and air measuring equipment to be loaned from the Air Ministry's observatory at Kew and some four tons of oxygen cylinders were taken along to inflate the 8-ft (2.4-m) diameter balloons. A feature of Dymond's equipment was that the results of the investigations were transmitted by radio and the apparatus would not have to be recovered. Ian Hunter of Corpus Christi was recruited to handle radio communications.

The expedition's plans to explore the Arctic heights came at a time of growing interest in high altitudes. Manned flights had climbed to over ten miles (16 km) in the mid-1930s and unmanned meteorological balloons had risen to 25 miles (40 km) in the search for a better understanding of the upper atmosphere. But knowledge of higher altitudes above the Arctic was scanty, while the stratosphere above the region was practically unknown. Only a few balloon flights had been made in West Greenland, including some in 1920 by Paul-Louis Mercanton, Wordie's old sparring partner from the Beerenberg.

Paterson and Tom Lethbridge, on his third Arctic visit with Wordie, travelled with the expedition primarily as archaeologists to study Eskimo culture and history. Angus Robin, a geology student and president of the Cambridge Mountaineering Club, was part of the geological team along with Harald Drever and Derek Leaf. Dick Feachem looked after botany.

Wordie again turned to the Norwegian sealers for his ship, hiring the 172-ton motor sealer, *Isbjorn*, from Tromso under Captain Albert Bergersen, who was making his first visit to high northerly waters. The ship, Wordie told the newspapers, was 'an excellent ice-crasher'.

Wordie's faith in Norwegian vessels and crew for his Arctic trips was unshakeable, even if it occasionally rankled with some British shipowners, who felt he should be supporting national interests. But Wordie trusted Norwegian ships and considered that the Norwegian seamen possessed an expertise with the ice that was second to none. Teddy Evans, Scott's deputy on the *Terra Nova* expedition, once said the Norwegians were the 'princes of the ice and sea', a sentiment that Wordie would have recognised. National pride or interests did not enter into the equation.

One man who disagreed was Captain Kenneth Mackenzie, a disgruntled ship-owner who believed that Wordie should support British seafarers. Mackenzie approached Wordie during preparations for the 1937 voyage with the offer of a British ship and appealed directly to his national pride. His vessel, he said proudly, was 'a British ship and [with] a British crew'. Wordie was unmoved, even though he accepted that there were advantages to having a British crew. But he instinctively felt that the Norwegian ice-masters were more suited to the task of navigating in the hazardous Arctic waters, particularly Melville Bay and Smith Sound. Mackenzie was furious and in a fractious exchange of letters accused Wordie of being 'somewhat prejudiced' against British ships and insisted: 'I would not put any foreigner before a picked crew of Britishers.'[1] Wordie responded with the frosty riposte: 'I would very much like to see an English crew and I think it would be of national importance but I am afraid the day is not yet.'

Wordie did not make the same mistake as he had in 1934 when he entered the ice too early in the season. *Isbjorn* left Leith on 27 June and soon discovered that ice conditions were mercifully easier than in 1934. Good progress was made towards Baffin Bay and the expedition launched its first balloon flight at Godhavn on the west coast of Greenland. As the ship worked its way northwards, more balloon flights were made, reaching impressive heights of between 12 and 20 miles (20–30 km). Ironically, the unexpected absence of ice curtailed their work. It was intended to measure the differences in radiation from land and sea by raising some balloons offshore from passing ice floes. But this proved impossible and a further problem was the persistent fog which hampered flights.

Isbjorn travelled north past Upernavik to Thule, before crossing over to the seldom-visited cluster of Cary Islands. The islands, which are located midway across Smith Sound, were first spotted by William Baffin in 1616 and the notoriously difficult surrounding waters had deterred other visitors to the area.

Wordie approached the islands with the warnings of Captain Adams, an old Dundee whaling captain, still fresh in his memory. The veteran Adams met Wordie shortly before *Isbjorn* left Scotland and handed him a stern warning about the area: 'Don't go in among the Cary Islands.' *Isbjorn*'s Captain Bergersen was sufficiently concerned about the area to send a small motor boat ahead of the ship as a pathfinder and to crawl among the collection of islands at a rate of 2 mph (3.2 kph). A safe anchorage was found between Isbjorn and Middle islands, but a mixture of very high winds and swirling fog ended all hopes of launching a series of balloon flights. The brief stop allowed the expedition to conduct a rudimentary sketch of the islands, which corrected earlier misleading maps of the area. But annoying banks of fog prevented Wordie making a full survey or taking astronomical fixes.

The expedition carried on, crossing Smith Sound to Cape Sabine on the eastern side of Ellesmere Island. In the distance they could see Camp Clay, the desolate spot where Greely's horrifying expedition had made their last stand in 1884. 'A very hard and stony spot,' Wordie noted. His interest in the site was stimulated by a chance meeting with Brainard, a survivor of the grisly episode, in the days before *Endurance* sailed for the Weddell Sea in 1914. But pack ice prevented any attempt at landing and inspecting the site of the darkest episode in America's Polar history.

Leaving Lethbridge and three others to dig for Eskimo remains at Turnstone Beach, the *Isbjorn* turned north for the Bache Peninsula to conduct some geological work and visit the farthest outpost of the Royal Canadian Mounted Police. The huts were abandoned but Wordie left some walrus meat for John Wright and David Haig Thomas, two university explorers who were due to visit the area a year later. The trip to the Bache Peninsula, which lies a few minutes above 79°, was a notable achievement for Wordie. It was the farthest north – around 750 miles (1,200 km) from the North Pole – he ever reached. But he chose not to mention it in his diary.

Isbjorn picked up Lethbridge's party and turned south down the coast of Ellesmere Island, crossing Jones Sound. At Cape Sparbo, close to the entrance to the sound and known to the British as Cape Hardy, the archaeologists made some unexpected finds. Inside one of the abandoned Eskimo houses Lethbridge discovered a cartridge case, two buttons and pieces of oak timber. It was, they concluded, material left from one of more than thirty expeditions sent to search for the lost Franklin party almost eighty years earlier.

Elsewhere, the archaeologists came across the remains of a camp made by Dr Frederick Cook, the American who bogusly claimed to have reached the North Pole in 1908, a year ahead of Robert Peary.

Although there were some doubts about the site of Cook's camp, Lethbridge's scrutiny confirmed that they had uncovered the correct location. 'We can therefore claim to have trodden in the footsteps of the master,' he mocked.[2] Cook, a highly capable Polar explorer but a flawed character, had spent an appalling winter at Cape Sparbo in 1908–09 after his supposed return from the Pole. It was at Sparbo that Cook completed the notes and measurements on which his phoney claim to the Pole was based.

Wordie was intrigued by the Peary–Cook controversy and must have been fascinated by the find at Sparbo. One reason for the fascination was that privately he believed that neither Cook nor Peary had reached the Pole. Both men, he decided, had lied about their journeys.

Wordie was reluctant to become embroiled in the long-running dispute about the rival claims and rarely voiced his opinions in public. However, he once allowed his guard to slip and was reluctantly dragged into the controversy.

The affair arose in 1925 when Wordie was approached by Henry Lewin, the author who was writing about the Cook–Peary row, which he called *The Great North Pole Fraud*. Lewin wanted guidance from Wordie about travelling across the ice, a theme which went to the heart of the controversy and posed the greatest threat to Peary's claim to have reached the Pole. Wordie was unequivocal in damning Peary. He told Lewin in a letter: 'I have the greatest doubt whether Peary ever reached the Pole.'[3] After a later more measured study of Peary's account of the 1909 Polar journey, Wordie wrote again to Lewin pointing out that the American had averaged a daily distance of well over 23 miles (37 km) in 45 days over particularly difficult ice conditions in the Arctic Ocean. 'These figures are quite astounding and sufficient to make one suspect his accuracy,' he concluded.[4] Publicly, Wordie was more equivocal. In an article written for the *Geographical Journal*, he talked of Peary's 'great triumph' and added: 'Peary's great achievement was to have travelled over hummocky and often active pack-ice far from land at a speed far beyond his predecessors.'[5] However, Wordie's normal reserve was shattered when he discovered that Lewin was planning to identify him in the book as an expert witness casting doubts on Peary's claim. Wordie was horrified, having assumed that his comments were confidential. In haste he pleaded with Lewin to keep his identity a secret and the author backed down. When the book was finally published in 1935, Wordie's trenchant opinions were attributed to a 'distinguished oceanographer'.

Wordie became involved in the controversy a second time when Rudolph Francke, a German who travelled with Cook on the fictitious 1908 journey, also asked for help to settle the dispute. Shortly before the 1937 expedition sailed, Francke made an emotional appeal to the Canadian government asking them to persuade Wordie to support the Cook case by establishing the truth of the mythical 'Bradley Land'. Bradley Land was the Arctic equivalent of the now discredited Morrell Land in the Weddell Sea. Cook always maintained that he discovered the new territory at around 85° in the Arctic Ocean. His book, *My Attainment of the Pole*, even included a chapter on discovering the island and a 'photograph' of the new land.

According to Francke, the key to Cook's claims of reaching the Pole was to establish the existence of Bradley Land. But Bradley Land does not exist and Wordie bluntly refused to help. He dismissed Cook's theory of finding new land by telling the Canadians that the falsified photograph did not inspire confidence in Cook's claim and declined to have anything to do with Francke's appeal.

Wordie had his own controversy to handle while sailing back towards Baffin Bay. Some of his party believed that the unusually good ice conditions that year offered a golden opportunity to repeat the attempt made in 1934 to enter Lancaster Sound and make a dash through the North West Passage. But Wordie refused, partly because he was concerned about the adequacy of supplies and partly because one of the party was feeling unwell. In addition, he had promised

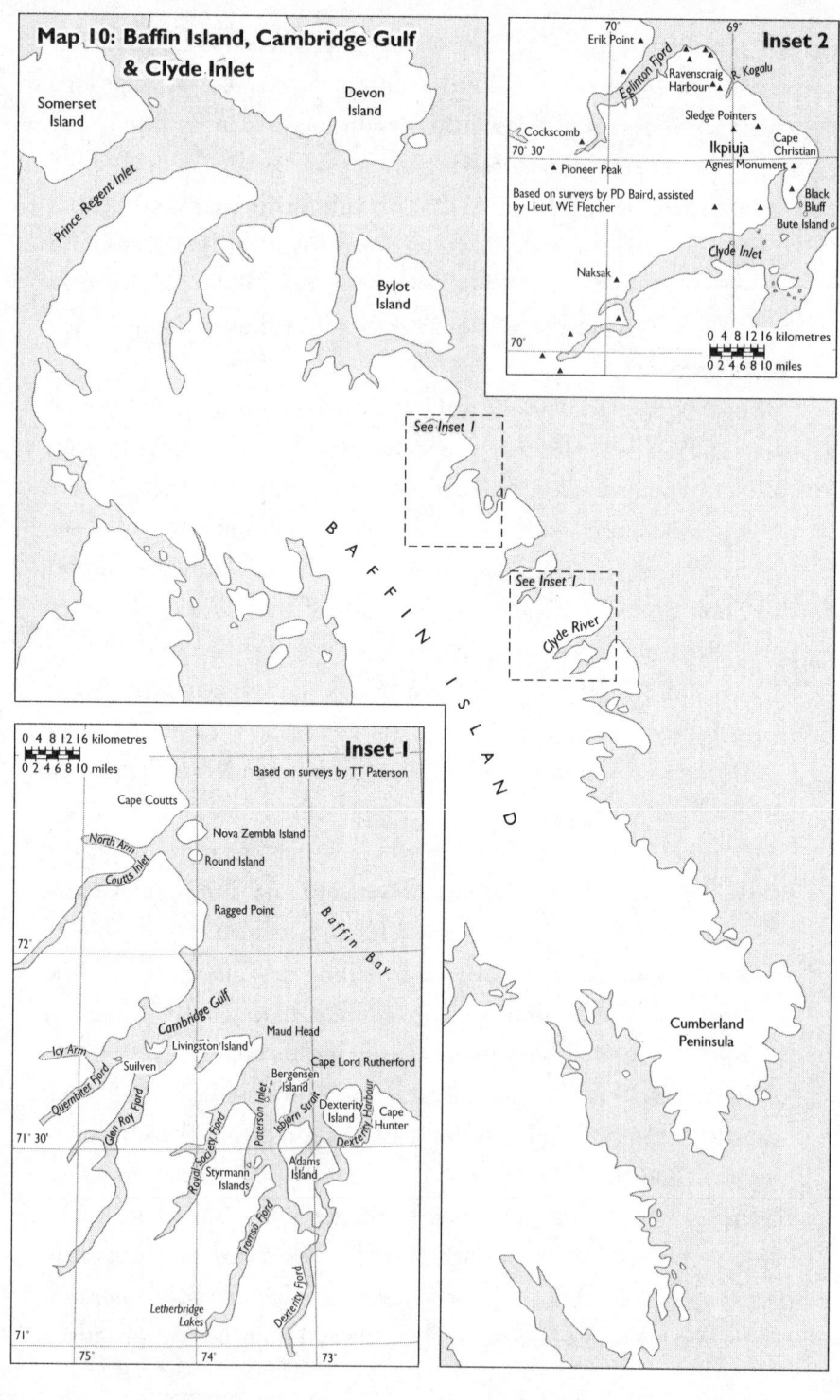

Map 10: Baffin Island, Cambridge Gulf & Clyde Inlet

Somerset Island

Devon Island

Prince Regent Inlet

Bylot Island

B A F F I N   I S L A N D

See *Inset 1*

See *Inset 1*

Clyde River

Baffin Bay

Cumberland Peninsula

Inset 2

70°   69°
Erik Point ▲

Eglinton Fjord
Ravenscraig Harbour ▲   R. Kogalu ▲▲

Sledge Pointers ▲

Cockscomb
70° 30'

Ikpiuja

Cape Christian

Pioneer Peak ▲

Agnes Monument ▲   Black Bluff

Based on surveys by PD Baird, assisted by Lieut. WE Fletcher

Bute Island ○

Clyde Inlet

Naksak ▲

70°

0 4 8 12 16 kilometres

0 2 4 6 8 10 miles

Inset 1

0 4 8 12 16 kilometres

0 2 4 6 8 10 miles

Based on surveys by TT Paterson

Cape Coutts

Nova Zembla Island

Round Island

North Arm

Coutts Inlet

Ragged Point

72°

Baffin Bay

Cambridge Gulf

Maud Head

Icy Arm

Livingston Island

Cape Lord Rutherford

Suilven

Bergensen Island

Quernbiter Fjord

Glen Roy Fjord

Isbjørn Strait

Dexterity Island   Cape Hunter

Paterson Inlet

Dexterity Harbour

71° 30'

Royal Society Fjord

Styrmann Islands

Adams Island

Tromsø Fjord

Dexterity Fjord

Letherbridge Lakes

71°

75°   74°   73°

Dymond that the ship would return to Godhavn for another high altitude balloon flight.

A further important consideration was fuel. Bergerson reported that the *Isbjorn*'s stocks were down to 30 tons, enough for only fifteen days' steaming before turning for home. It would be close but Bergerson was prepared to take the risk. Despite the protests, the *Isbjorn* turned south, leaving the North West Passage for others. In his diary, Wordie explained: 'It was very hard to pass Lancaster Sound today and not go west. Such a complete absence of ice means that we could easily reach Melville Island and probably Banks Land. We have the fuel, but not the provisions for the risk entailed; the captain is as keen as any for the attempt.'[6]

Isbjorn pressed on south to the north-east of Baffin Island, where 600 miles (1,000 km) of new coastline and six new fjords, ranging in length from 40 to 60 miles (64–100 km), were discovered in the area around Cambridge Gulf. To Wordie the ice-free fjords with steep 2,000-ft (600 m) cliff faces were strongly reminiscent of Scotland's terrain and the analogy was reinforced a little later when the crew of the *Isbjorn* caught 2,000 salmon in a spectacularly successful fishing expedition.

The circular voyage of East Greenland, Baffin Bay, Smith Sound and north-east Baffin Island was completed when the *Isbjorn* returned to Godhavn on 10 September. A final balloon fight was made and the party turned for home on 15 September.

However the voyage home came close to tragedy when an experiment with gunpowder went badly wrong and caused an explosion. Leaf took the blast in his face, but the injuries were not sufficient to warrant a visit to hospital.

The port of Leith was finally reached on 1 October and the party broke up, generally satisfied in a job well done. But the success of the mission was partly overshadowed eighteen months later by news that Captain Bergesen and his entire crew were lost in the ice.

Wordie's final Arctic voyage, his most versatile enterprise, was roundly applauded. It was a comprehensive success, adding knowledge in every field it touched. The expedition had mapped 600 miles of new coastline in Baffin Island and prepared the most accurate charts yet of the obscure Cary Islands. It had penetrated six new fjords and determined that Eskimos had first reached Greenland from Alaska by way of Smith Sound and Baffin Bay some 800 years earlier.

The atmospheric studies had also made a valuable contribution to the growing understanding of high altitude radiation. Six successful flights and about twenty pilot flights were made, reaching heights of between 18 and 20 miles (up to 32 km). Only a few years later the work of Dymond and Carmichael was put to good use in wartime communications and Wordie was able to write: 'So our pioneering efforts are now helping to win the war.'[7]

Feachem was particularly generous to the leadership of Wordie. He said the excellence of all the expedition's results were a 'minor monument' to the initiative and vision of Wordie. Dymond also revealed that, despite the frequently low temperatures, Wordie had informed him that it was not always necessary to wear gloves while working in the Arctic. Dymond, a newcomer to the harsh realities of the north, looked at the expedition-hardened Wordie and added: 'I would like to emphasise that he was speaking entirely for himself.'

But perhaps the farewell voyage was best summed up in Wordie's own words. In a telegram to Hinks at the RGS he reported the outline details of the trip and finished with the brief unassuming comment which, in a typically understated manner, brought the curtain down on his active career in Polar exploration. He cabled Hinks with the words: 'Most successful journey.'[8]

CHAPTER 18

TOP
SECRET

THE LOOMING WAR WITH GERMANY BROUGHT WORDIE'S ACTIVE Polar career to an abrupt end in the late 1930s. He was forty-eight years old when he returned to Britain from the Canadian Arctic in the autumn of 1937 and was almost certainly prepared to undertake another voyage after the customary three-year break. But all plans were inevitably overshadowed by the growing likelihood of war. What he did not expect was that Britain wanted to make use of his vast experience and knowledge, particularly of the northern and southern reaches of the globe. Even before the first shots of the war were fired Wordie found himself in demand.

In June 1939, three months before war was officially declared, the Admiralty approached the Scott Polar Research Institute at Cambridge looking for help. SPRI was now firmly established as the country's centre of Polar excellence, with Debenham as director and Wordie, who was appointed chairman in 1937, at the heart of operations.

The appeal for help came from Rear-Admiral J.H. Godfrey, Director of Naval Intelligence, who wanted to recruit SPRI to provide the military with more accurate and up-to-date geographical, geological and other essential data on the terrain where the coming battles would be fought. Godfrey understood that reliable maps, more detailed descriptions of the terrain, weather patterns and similar information were as essential to the armies as the weaponry and ammunition they carried into battle. He understood, as one expert later explained: 'Whether the military commander or politician admits or not, it is the intelligent use of geographical knowledge that outwits the enemy and wins wars.'[1]

Godfrey, assisted by the celebrated author Ian Fleming, was equally alarmed to discover that this key intelligence had been allowed to run down during the 1920s and '30s. As war approached in the summer of 1939 Godfrey realised that British soldiers and sailors were likely to be sent to fight with a disturbing lack of basic knowledge about their battlegrounds. His fears were soon realised when it was discovered that bomb squadrons had to rely on an old tourist guide last published in 1912 to locate their targets in southern Norway, and when naval pilots in another attack were forced to use marine charts with no land contours.

Godfrey knew that the pool of knowledge was to be found at universities and schools up and down the land. He first recruited his friend, Professor Kenneth Mason of Oxford University, to produce a number of detailed and confidential handbooks on strategic targets. At Cambridge, SPRI was recruited to work on a wide range of cold-climate issues for the military.

The first task, undertaken in September 1939 within days of the outbreak of war, was to write a hurried geographical handbook for the Admiralty on the feasibility of the Germans establishing U-boat bases in Arctic ports. The knowledge was critical since U-boats from the Arctic would be capable of slipping undetected into the northerly waters around Greenland, where they were beyond the reach of normal air surveillance and free to terrorise the vital supply line of the North Atlantic convoys. SPRI's confidential report helped identify the likely bases and encouraged the navy and air force to conduct more focused searches on enemy bases.

Under Wordie's direction, SPRI became increasingly involved in intelligence affairs, advising the military on a wide range of matters. These included cold-weather clothing and food, a method of converting Nissen huts for use in the snow and a means of devising an effective snow-shoe for ponies. One of the institute's largest schemes was a detailed geographical study in 1940 for a proposed British Expeditionary Force invasion of Finland, though this operation was never launched.

Although the Treasury had some reservations about Godfrey's initiative, approval was subsequently given to expand and formalise the operation. Early in 1941, two bodies were officially formed, one under Wordie at Cambridge and the other under Mason at Oxford, charged with producing a regular series of geographical handbooks for the military. The handbooks soon became known as Blue Books.

Wordie was effectively seconded to the Naval Intelligence Division and the new outfit was established at SPRI's premises in Cambridge, where they remained for the rest of the war. His official role was part-time director to oversee the work, with day-to-day responsibility as editor in the hands of Dr H.C. Darby, a Cambridge geography lecturer. However it was not long before Wordie and Darby began to clash over the work. Darby became furious at Wordie's irritating habit of going behind his back and not informing him of his key decisions. It was, said one observer, a situation 'fraught with difficulty'. Nonetheless, the combined Oxford–Cambridge teams produced a mammoth behind-the-scenes effort, which made an enormous but often overlooked contribution to the war effort. Many years later, the distinguished geographer, Professor W.G.V. Balchin, said there was 'no escaping the essential contribution of geography in any training for the defence of the realm'.[2]

The Oxford and Cambridge teams produced a remarkable fifty-eight volumes of handbooks, which provided invaluable geographical and other useful information on the main theatres of war. The output of Blue Books was so prodigious that the traditional presses of Oxford and Cambridge universities could not cope with the demand and outside printers and binders had to be called in to help with production. Cambridge alone produced thirty separate volumes for the military during the war years.

In their endeavours the Cambridge team was helped by a group of thirty academic geographers, a scattered army of around sixty specialist contributors and countless other individuals who generously gave their expert advice. None of the contributors asked for payment for their expertise.

One of men to whom Wordie was able to turn for advice was his old friend Hinks at the RGS. Although approaching his seventies, Hinks possessed formidable geographic knowledge and experience. He was awarded the CBE for his decisive role in producing comprehensive maps during the First World War; they were so highly regarded that they formed the basis for re-drawing national boundaries at the post-war peace conference.

Many of the men who had travelled on the Oxford–Cambridge expeditions to the Arctic and Antarctic between the wars were active contributors to the handbooks. One of the first handbooks was on Iceland and the contributors included Carmichael, Lethbridge and Manley, who had been on expeditions with Wordie. By the end of the war, it was highly unlikely that there was a single academic geographer – including some serving on active duty – who had not made some contribution to the output of Blue Books at Oxford or Cambridge.

However, Wordie left the Blue Book production line in 1943, partly because of the friction with Darby and partly because he was recruited to another top-secret military operation.

The tension between Wordie and Darby had grown and finally spilled over one day when Brian Roberts, one of Wordie's closest allies, was discovered working on non-handbook material in Intelligence time. Darby promptly gave Roberts a month's notice to quit. Soon after Wordie stepped down as part-time director. Wordie's departure coincided with his recruitment in late 1943 to join a highly-confidential Naval Intelligence venture called Operation Tabarin, which was considered important enough to have been approved by the War Cabinet.

Operation Tabarin was a hurriedly conceived operation designed to reinforce British interests in the Antarctic, including the Falkland Islands, South Georgia and the island chains in the southern waters. It was effectively a wartime extension of the Discovery Committee on which Wordie had served since 1923. Work on the Discovery Committee was only ticking over during the early years of the war and in 1942 Wordie was appointed chairman of the scientific studies, virtually the only work the organisation was carrying out at this stage. In the absence of other activities, Wordie was effectively directing the operations of the Discovery Committee.

As a first step the three key personnel at the Discovery Committee were moved over to the top-secret Operation Tabarin, where they began to develop a fresh strategy for the Antarctic dependencies. Alongside Wordie was his ally Roberts and Dr Neil Mackintosh, an eminent zoologist who had succeeded Kemp as director of research at Discovery. Tabarin and the Discovery Committee were effectively the same, but with the added responsibilities of conducting their affairs with a wartime agenda.

According to one observer, the three men presided over events 'like benign paladins'. Together the trinity of Wordie, Roberts and Mackintosh dictated policy and organised the expeditions which were sent to establish permanent British bases in the region. It was the good-humoured Roberts and John Mossop from the Admiralty who conjured up the unusual code-name for the operation, which was derived from a bawdy Paris night-club called 'Bal Tabarin'. According to Roberts, the name was a reflection of the fact that the men were engaged in 'a lot of night work and the organisation was always as chaotic as the club.'

Operation Tabarin was superficially a scientific venture, an extension of the marine studies undertaken in the 1920s by the original Discovery Committee. But the real purpose was to prevent other nations, such as Argentina or Chile, from establishing a foothold in the area. An active British presence, it was hoped, would also deter the Germans from establishing naval bases which would threaten vital shipping links in the South Atlantic.

The Wordie–Roberts–Mackintosh triumvirate were fully aware that the cloak of scientific endeavour hid a different political agenda, even if Wordie admitted that 'properly speaking' the Committee's role had little to do with political matters. But in a confidential paper to the government, Mackintosh declared that scientific investigations would 'help support territorial claims'. He added, 'It seems important that measures should be taken against encroachment on these territories for they are not only of potential economic value; they are also likely to be of strategic value.'[3]

None of this was new to the government, which was always happy to exploit Polar exploration for political ends. When Rymill's Graham Land expedition was being put together in the 1930s the government could scarcely conceal its delight. The official conclusion was that a visit to a British-designated area such as Graham Land was far better than sending an expedition to an unclaimed region because, 'It strengthens our position in international law.'

Territorial claims in the region were on the increase in the early war years, notably in 1942 when an Argentine vessel, *Primero de Mayo*, claimed possession of Deception Island. The navy reasserted British authority to the island but it was soon apparent that even more friendly nations like Australia, France and Norway were also eager to establish themselves in the area. Ironically, Chile's claim to territories around the Antarctic Peninsula was based partly on the newly formed belief that, geologically, the peninsula was an extension of the Andes – a theory which Wordie had supported in the *Endurance* scientific papers two decades earlier.

Wordie was quickly absorbed into Tabarin, attending weekly meetings at the Colonial Office in the autumn of 1943, selecting the best sites for building bases, advising on equipment and recommending key personnel for the expeditions. One of his earliest recommendations was to extend the philosophy of helping young scientists develop their skills in the field. He recommended that two or three volunteers should be found from the ranks of Cambridge undergraduates, whom he suggested should be paid £175 per year (approximately £4,000 a year in today's terms). He emphasised that while the men would have ample time to develop their own scientific disciplines, it was essential that they should be adaptable and capable of turning their hands to 'any kind of work'. It was hoped that 'any kind of work' did not involve fighting insurgents from Argentina or Chile. Indeed, the first Tabarin parties to the Antarctic in 1943 were urged not to land if Argentine forces were visible. Instead, parties were asked to deliver a strong note of protest at their occupation and then inform the nearest navy ship. 'There is a desire to avoid shedding Argentine blood,' a confidential memo of the time said. In the event, the first Tabarin expedition had some tense stand-offs, although there was no bloodshed.

The first expedition under the Operation Tabarin umbrella duly led to Britain establishing its first permanent all-year-round presence in the Antarctic. It is an undertaking still in operation today under the name of the British Antarctic Survey.

One of Wordie's most important decisions at the time was to recommend the appointment of Lt-Cdr James Marr as leader of Tabarin's first expedition. Marr was known to Wordie and came to the operation with impeccable polar credentials. Marr, a muscular character from Aberdeen, was a 19-year-old member of the scouts in 1921 when he joined Shackleton's last expedition, *Quest*. He later spent considerable time in the south on several other Discovery Committee voyages, including the 1929–30 trip with Mawson in the original *Discovery*. By 1943 there were few people in Britain with as much intimate practical knowledge of the demanding waters around the Antarctic Peninsula and the South Shetland Islands as Marr. With a wintering party of fourteen men, he sailed from London in November 1943 with the aim of setting up two permanent bases around the Antarctic Peninsula and of completing the mapping of the area.

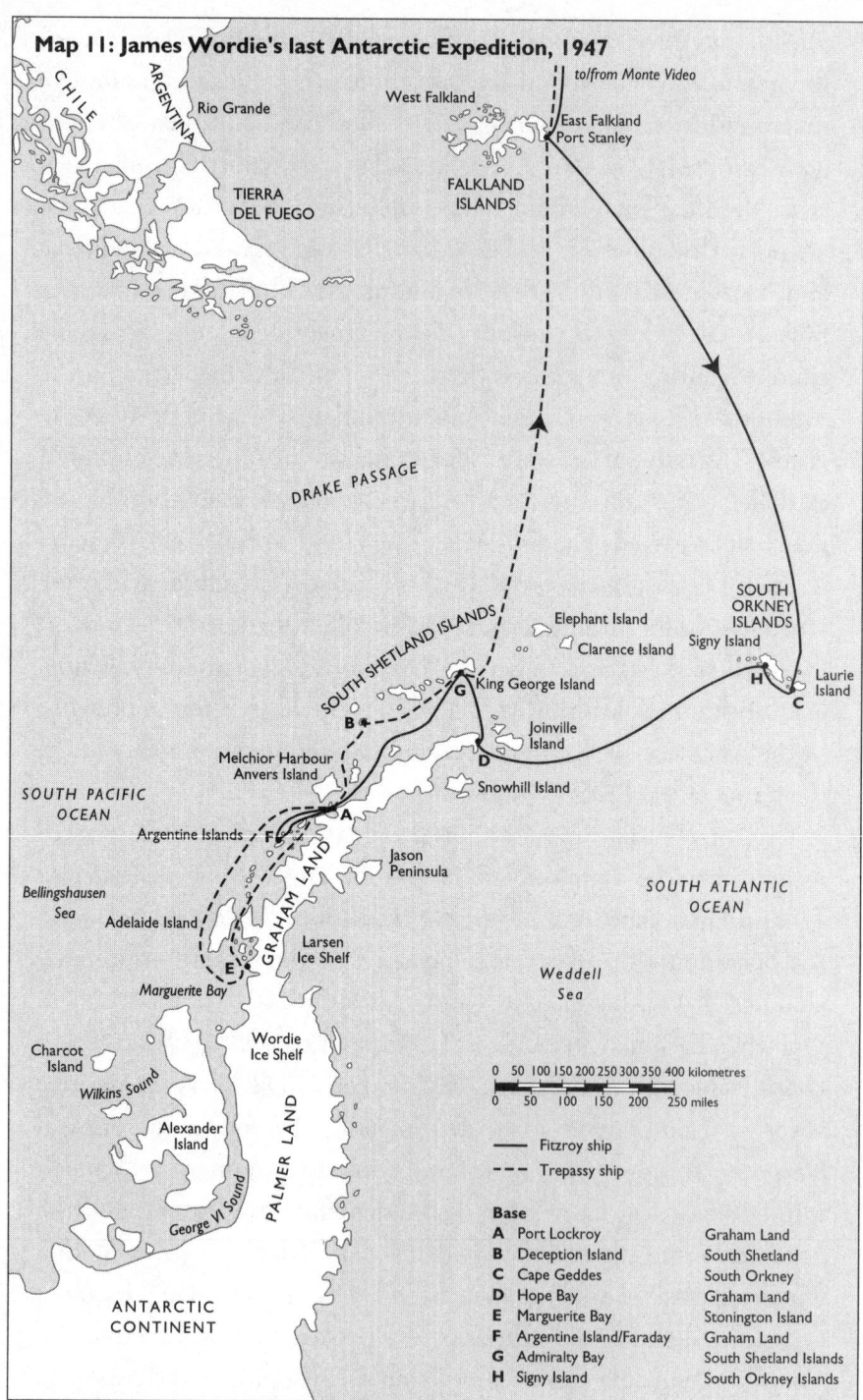

Map 11: James Wordie's last Antarctic Expedition, 1947

to/from Monte Video

CHILE

ARGENTINA

Rio Grande

West Falkland

East Falkland
Port Stanley

TIERRA
DEL FUEGO

FALKLAND
ISLANDS

DRAKE PASSAGE

SOUTH
ORKNEY
ISLANDS

Elephant Island

Clarence Island

Signy Island

Laurie
Island

SOUTH SHETLAND ISLANDS

King George Island

B

G

Joinville
Island

H

C

Melchior Harbour
Anvers Island

D

SOUTH PACIFIC
OCEAN

Snowhill Island

Argentine Islands

F

A

GRAHAM LAND

Jason
Peninsula

SOUTH ATLANTIC
OCEAN

Bellingshausen
Sea

Adelaide Island

Larsen
Ice Shelf

Weddell
Sea

Marguerite Bay

E

Charcot
Island

Wordie
Ice Shelf

0   50 100 150 200 250 300 350 400 kilometres

Wilkins Sound

0   50   100   150   200   250 miles

Alexander
Island

PALMER LAND

——— Fitzroy ship

- - - Trepassy ship

George VI Sound

Base

ANTARCTIC
CONTINENT

A   Port Lockroy   Graham Land
B   Deception Island   South Shetland
C   Cape Geddes   South Orkney
D   Hope Bay   Graham Land
E   Marguerite Bay   Stonington Island
F   Argentine Island/Faraday   Graham Land
G   Admiralty Bay   South Shetland Islands
H   Signy Island   South Orkney Islands

The first base was built on Deception Island, which had been the centre of whaling activity and the last vestige of hope for the castaways on Elephant Island in 1916 had Shackleton not returned with a rescue ship. Meteorological equipment was landed and a magistrate was installed to signal a suitable measure of permanence. The other base was intended for Hope Bay at the very tip of the peninsula in Graham Land, but a belt of pack ice 10 miles (16 km) wide prevented the ship carrying the hut from landing and an alternative site was sought. Instead, the party set up camp on the west side of Graham Land at Port Lockroy on the tiny Wiencke Island, where they found a cylinder containing Argentine claims to the area. The Argentine emblems were unceremoniously removed and a weather station built. Today Port Lockroy is the most popular stop for the influx of modern tourists visiting Antarctica.

A base was finally established at Hope Bay during the 1944–5 season and in the following year further operations were opened at Cape Geddes on Laurie Island in the South Orkneys and at Marguerite Bay in Graham Land, the most southerly point which can be reached by ships in normal waters.

With the end of the war, it was thought advisable to abandon the cloak-and-dagger code-name, Operation Tabarin. 'This spurious secrecy can now be discarded,' Wordie said. In its place came the Falkland Islands Dependencies Survey (FIDS), which was later named the British Antarctic Survey.

The end of the war also brought an increase in territorial claims to the area and a fresh test of Britain's resolve. Both Argentina and Chile established permanent stations around the peninsula in 1947 and the French were setting down roots in Adelie Land. In the same year the Americans launched a massive project under Admiral Richard Byrd, called Operation Highjump, which involved thirteen ships and 4,000 men and laid the foundations for a permanent US base on the continent.

The resumption of normal operations also allowed Wordie to

make a nostalgic return to the Southern Ocean, more than thirty years after being rescued from Elephant Island. In 1946 the Colonial Office, anxious to monitor the progress of FIDS, asked Wordie to tour the area and report back. It was his first voyage to the Antarctic since 1916.

The four-month trip in the ships *Fitzroy* and *Trepassey* was a mixture of routine inspection of the sparse facilities and a dreary round of semi-official functions. There was also the occasional uneasy meeting with ships from both Argentina and Chile which were cruising the area in 1947.

One unusual distraction was provided by the presence of a camera crew from Ealing Studios in London, who were working on the film drama *Scott of the Antarctic*. The producer, Sir Michael Balcon, persuaded FIDS to carry three men to the Antarctic – cameramen Osmond Borradaile and Bob Moss, and David James, an experienced Polar hand who acted as technical adviser to the film – to shoot some background footage for the film in return for help with a proposed documentary. The film-makers had consulted Priestley and Wright about Scott's expedition and persuaded Debenham to read the script for accuracy. But having first-hand access to someone from the heroic age while filming was something that the crew had not anticipated.

The trip also provided an opportunity to formally recognise Wordie's immense contribution to British exploration and, more recently, his role in upholding national rights in the region. The opportunity arose in January 1947 when one of the FIDS base huts, situated on the small Winter Island among the collection of Argentine Islands a few miles to the south of Port Lockroy, was officially named Wordie House. The hut was erected on the site of Rymill's old camp, built during the British Graham Land expedition in the mid-1930s, which had mysteriously disappeared and was presumed lost in a tidal wave. Wordie House, which normally accommodated four or five scientists, operated one of the longest

Fraisgil, the Wordie family home in Montgomerie Drive (now Cleveden Drive), Glasgow

Jane Wordie, mother of James Wordie

John Wordie, father of James Wordie

James Wordie, 1893,
aged four

James Wordie, aged 10 and sister Jean, 12,
pictured in 1899. A little over two years later
Jean was dead from meningitis

James Wordie (front row, second right) with the pipe band of the Glasgow Academy Cadet Corps

James Wordie photographed in 1910,
around the time he entered
Cambridge University

Gertrude Henderson, the wife of
James Wordie, at the age of eighteen,
five years before their marriage

Wordie, pictured in 1923 with his new bride, Gertrude. They were married for 39 years

Endurance party prepares to sail for Antarctica in October 1914. (Back row) Holness and Bakewell; (Second row) McNish, James, Wild, Worsley, Stephenson, Hudson, How and Green; (Third row) Cheetham, Crean, Hussey, Greenstreet, Shackleton, Sir Daniel Gooch (left the ship at South Georgia), Rickinson and Hurley; (Front row) Clark, Wordie, Macklin, Marston and McIlroy. Absent from the picture are Kerr, Vincent, McCarthy, Orde-Lees, Blackborrow and McLeod

Endurance struggles against the crippling ice of the Weddell Sea, January 1915

A rare photograph of Wordie (left) with Sir Ernest Shackleton, taken in
Buenos Aires shortly before *Endurance* sailed into the Weddell Sea

Left. A cross section graphic showing the interior design and layout of the doomed *Endurance*

Wordie (right) with soul-mate Robert Clark in 'Auld Reekie' on board *Endurance*. Above his bunk Wordie kept photographs of his father and sister Alison

Shackleton insisted that everyone share the chores on board *Endurance*. Here Wordie (left) scrubs the floor with bosun Alf Cheetham (centre) and doctor, Alexander Macklin

Trapped. *Endurance* lurches at a crazy angle as the ice of the Weddell Sea tightens its deadly grip

Dry land. After a terrible journey away from the ice, the 28 men from *Endurance* party reached the desolate Elephant Island on April 15, 1916 – their first step on dry land for 16 months. Here they drag the *James Caird* up the rocky beach, with the *Dudley Docker* and *Stancomb Wills* in the foreground

The first hot drink after landing at Elephant Island. (Left to right) Orde-Lees, Wordie, Clark, Rickinson, Greenstreet, How, Shackleton, Bakewell, Kerr and Wild

Castaways. The men who spent four and a half months marooned on Elephant Island. (Back row) Greenstreet, McIlroy, Marston, Wordie, James, Holness, Hudson, Stephenson, McLeod, Clark, Orde-Lees, Kerr, Macklin; (Middle row) Green, Wild, How, Cheetham, Hussey, Bakewell; (Front row) Rickinson. Absent are the invalid Blackborrow and Hurley, who took the photograph on May 10, 1916

Saved. The entire *Endurance* Party re-united in Chile, September 3, 1916, after the rescue from Elephant Island. Wordie stands fifth from the left, next to Tom Crean (sixth left). Frank Wild (eighth left) and Sir Ernest Shackleton (tenth left) are also among the crowd pictured outside the Royal Hotel, Punta Arenas

Local news. A Scottish newspaper, *The Bulletin,* gave its readers a local angle on the dramatic Elephant Island escapade when news of the stranded men reached Britain in June 1916. Wordie (top) and Clark are listed as the party's two Scotsmen, although they were several other Scots on the island

Wordie pictured in uniform after enlisting in the Royal Field Artillery, 1917

Wordie (left) and Lethbridge at the top of
Mount Beerenberg, August 11, 1921

Mercanton (right) stands at the summit
of the Beerenberg with Lethbridge

Returning from Jan Mayen, 1921. Wordie (top).
Left to right: Musters, Richard-Brown, Bristowe, Lethbridge

Wordie in typical pose in the
Arctic during the 1920s

Heimen leaving Bergen, June 1923, on the ill-fated voyage to Greenland. Wordie is third on the right

Expedition ship, *Heimen* trapped off the
east coast of Greenland, July 1923

Wordie (centre) in 1926 on his return from his second trip to Greenland.
Also pictured are D. McI. Johnson (left) and M.A. Barnett

Heimland was stopped by the ice off East Greenland in 1929, leaving less time for exploration
and forcing Wordie's party to make a dash up Petermann Peak

Heimland (left) off East Greenland in the ice alongside the *Gotta*, August 1929

Wordie's party nears the summit of Petermann Peak,
East Greenland, August 1929

Crossing the Nordenskjold Glacier, East Greenland after scaling the Petermann Peak, August 1929. Wordie is leading, followed by Varley, Courtauld and Fuchs

The conquerors of Petermann Peak on board *Heimland* off Aberdeen, September 9, 1929. Left to right: Courtauld, Varley, Fuchs (front), Wordie, Parkinson, Wakefield, Forbes, Dykes, Whittard

Heimen leaves Aberdeen in May 1934 on
Wordie's disappointing expedition to
West Greenland and Baffin Bay

Hunting for game.
Wordie during one of his eight
expeditions to the Arctic

Wordie (centre) pictured at Leith in June 1937 before
leaving on his final Arctic expedition

Wordie in relaxed mood with Tom Lethbridge in 1937, before taking his last expedition to the Arctic. Lethbridge was a close friend who travelled on three expeditions with him

Wordie's expedition ship, *Isbjørn,* pictured at Leith in 1937 flying the Norwegian flag. Wordie always chose Norwegian vessels and crew for his Arctic voyages

Isbjørn fighting the ice near Ellesmere Island in the summer of 1937

Isbjørn (foreground) at Godhavn, Disko Island,
West Greenland in 1937

A portrait of Wordie in 1951 at the height of his powers. He was President of the
Royal Geographical Society and Chairman of the Scott Polar Research Institute and within year
was also Master of St John's College, Cambridge

Wordie (foreground, right) watches as John Hunt, leader of the 1953 Everest expedition, gives the Queen some inside information about the successful climb. The photograph was taken at the first performance of *The Conquest of Everest*, October 1953

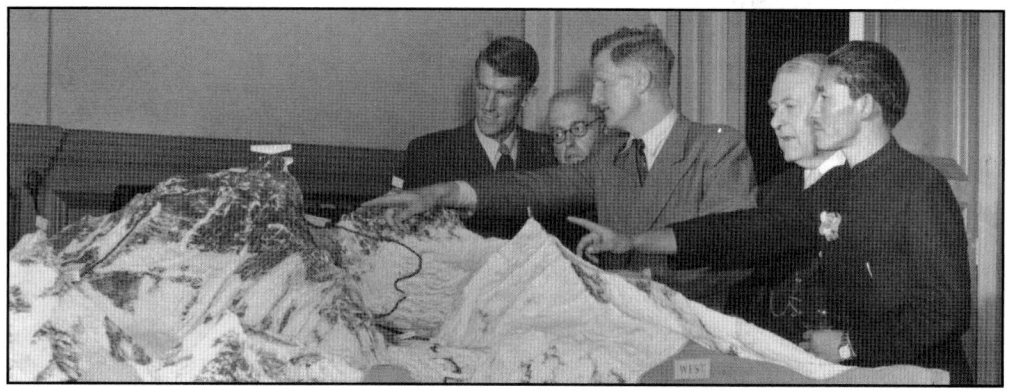

A rare photograph of James Wordie examining a model of Mt Everest with its conquerors, Ed Hillary (left), expedition leader John Hunt (centre) and Tenzing Norgay (right).

Antarctic Club Dinner 1959. Left to right: Sir James Wordie, Sir Vivian Fuchs, Sir Miles Clifford and the Rev. Lancelot Fleming the Bishop of Portsmouth

One of the last photographs of Sir James Mann Wordie, taken at the Master's Lodge, St John's College, Cambridge, 1959

Wordie photographed in the late 1950s, when the strain of his
active life and illness was clearly evident

and most important meteorological observatories on the continent and today is one of the historic sites protected by the international Antarctic Treaty.

Wordie's nostalgic trip allowed him to gain fresh experience of the new generation of scientists who were beginning their careers. Old hands like Wordie were affectionately known as the 'Block & Tackle Brigade', though not to their faces. Wordie could not resist the temptation to point out that the men were living in luxury compared to the conditions experienced on Elephant Island and on other expeditions of the age.

On one occasion a young member of the FIDS team complained that there were no sheets on the beds in the huts. Peering over his glasses in contempt, Wordie snapped: 'Shackleton's men didn't have sheets!' The scientists were not the only people to feel the wrath of Wordie's unsympathetic tongue. Once a student at St John's College complained that the youngsters had to cross the courtyard to visit the toilet or use the washbasin. Wordie stared scornfully at the man and barked: 'When I was with Shackleton we did not wash or clean our teeth for two years – the natural greases kept us clean.'[4]

But the most poignant moment on Wordie's final Antarctic voyage came when *Fitzroy* steamed towards Elephant Island, still as bleak and inhospitable as it was in 1916. 'What a refuge,' wrote film adviser James. 'Just a sheer headland with rocky foreshore and glaciers hanging perilously overhead.'[5]

Fitzroy approached Elephant Island on 20 January, almost thirty-two years to the day after *Endurance* had first become trapped in the ice of the Weddell Sea. Wordie stood quietly on *Fitzroy*'s deck watching through binoculars as the familiar landmarks came into view – initially Cape Valentine, where the first landing was made after the terrible boat journey from the ice floe, and later Cape Wild, where he had spent 4½ months marooned on the weather-beaten beach. 'We were all a bit excited,' he remembered. Some thirty-two years earlier he had written in his diary: 'The fates are against us and it looks as if we were going to have the pack right to the bitter end.'[6] As Wordie's thoughts raced back to the scene of utter deprivation and isolation, the *Fitzroy*'s steward, without a trace of irony, chose the precise moment to announce: 'Tea will be served in the saloon.'

With the ship safely moored off Elephant Island, the party sat down to a splendid dinner of warming soup, generous slices of roast mutton, a sticky sweet, hot coffee and a freely circulating decanter of port. The stark contrast was apparent to all on board. 'Thirty years brings its changes,' Wordie dryly observed.[7]

From about 1½ miles (2.4 km) offshore of Cape Valentine, he could detect the storm beaches where they had first pitched their tents and the protective rocks where the pemmican cases had been stacked. Above the rocky beach was the dangerous scree slope which Wordie and Orde-Lees had tried to climb days after their landfall. 'From out at sea one saw how ridiculous this attempt was,' Wordie wrote in his diary.[8] More chilling to the memory was Cape Wild, where even from 7 or 8 miles (about 12 km) away the glacier, penguin rookery and the 'rocky knob' at the end of the forbidding spit were easily detected with the aid of glasses.

Wordie was struck by an astonishing realisation as the *Fitzroy* steamed along the coast towards Cape Wild. It was, he thought, the first time that he had seen Elephant Island properly. The arrival in 1916 had been in semi-darkness and the trip three days later from Cape Valentine to Cape Wild was made close to the shore. No one was taking in the scenery when the *Yelcho* pulled away from the island after the rescue.

Cape Wild, he now understood, was the only camp site available to the west of the first landing spot, Cape Valentine. But it was also the first sanctuary reached by Wild in his reconnoitre mission and he now realised that a further exploration would have found 'a very different story' for the stranded men. He recorded his initial thoughts in his diary, writing: 'There is a big glacier just south of Cape Valentine, but beyond that is the Cape Walker region with much bare ground, easy slopes and numerous beaches and penguin rookeries. Cape Walker would have been much better than Cape Wild.'[9]

Although Wordie was not suggesting that the Elephant Island ordeal could have been avoided, he now believed that the twenty-two castaways could have been far more comfortable, with perhaps less violent winds to combat, if they had investigated the Cape Walker area. He wrote: 'Cape Walker would have made a splendid camp site . . . and we should have been spared the many months of anxiety at Cape Wild.'[10] In fact, Shackleton had elected to seek a winter refuge to the west of Cape Valentine because he believed that the ice in that area was not likely to block the rescue ship's re-entry to the island. Also the parlous state of the men meant there was only time to seek one refuge. 'It was Cape Wild or nothing,' Wordie reasoned.[11]

Although he did not allow it to show, the emotion of the return to Elephant Island touched the normally imperturbable Wordie. The only outward sign of his feelings arose when Captain Freddie White, the *Fitzroy*'s skipper, offered Wordie the chance to land at Cape Wild. He refused the offer.

Wordie never fully explained to anyone why he did not go ashore. Conditions were fairly good and the temptation to revisit the scene must have been truly enormous. Wordie's diary records the scene: 'The Captain wanted to stop and go ashore but I felt I could not agree.'[12] A little later, when writing up his private notes, Wordie's version of events is slightly different. He wrote: 'It would have been interesting to have gone ashore either at Cape Valentine or at Cape Wild, but time was short and the temptation to land had to be set aside.'[13]

But a truer reflection of his feelings is contained in a personal letter which Wordie wrote that night to his old friend, Hugh Mill. As *Fitzroy* moved slowly away from Elephant Island, he found a private spot and scribbled down a flurry of thoughts about the haunting day when he had relived the horror of Elephant Island. The normally unemotional Wordie told Mill:

> The Captain was very anxious for me to give the order to land either at Cape Valentine or Cape Wild (which was very clear in the distance). But I could not bring myself to agree.
>
> I felt if I did land it should be alone, or with old comrades.
>
> So we held on, but in memory I kept that day when we landed at Cape Valentine and when Shackleton had one of his great moments.
>
> It has been an unforgettable day and I know that you will share with me what I feel.[14]

CHAPTER 19

A GIFT FOR INTRIGUE

THE POIGNANT VOYAGE TO THE ANTARCTIC IN 1947 WAS WORDIE'S last visit to the south and coincided with a major change of direction in his career. After a lifetime in the field, Wordie moved inside to work in the corridors of power. It was a reign marked by great triumphs and major controversies.

The immediate post-war years saw Wordie graduate to positions of authority and influence in Britain's Polar establishment, both at the Royal Geographical Society and the Scott Polar Research Institute. He also built a separate rule at St John's, Cambridge and found time to demonstrate a distinct flair for business.

Wordie had remained largely distant from the day-to-day affairs of the family transport company while he was engaged in active exploration and developing his academic career. But he always kept a close watch on events and in 1947 he was able to make a telling contribution when the new Labour government earmarked his family firm, Wordie & Co., for nationalisation.

Labour had swept to power in 1945 with a promise to roll back the frontiers of the private sector, bringing vast swathes of industry into public ownership. The nationalisation programme, which included the coal mines, power stations, railways and road haulage, was the biggest single transfer of industrial ownership ever witnessed in Britain. Wordie & Co., however, was among the smallest firms caught in the net. Matters came to a head in late 1946 while Wordie was in the Southern Ocean with the Falkland Islands Dependencies Survey. His brother, Willie, cabled to the Falklands with news of the government's plans and Wordie responded by offering a way to avoid a direct take-over by the state.

Wordie's solution was radical. He sent telegrams to Willie in Glasgow urging him to invoke a 90-year-old clause in the firm's business contracts, which obliged one of the original Scottish railway partners from the Victorian age to acquire Wordie & Co. at full commercial value. The clause, which was the inspiration of his brilliant grandfather William Wordie, had been kept up to date over the decades on a rolling six-monthly basis. From a distance of 8,000 miles (12,800 km) in the South Atlantic Wordie saw it as the perfect means of escaping nationalisation. The London Midland & Scottish Railway Company, the successor to the original operators associated with William Wordie, were already close to Wordie & Co. In 1932 the LMSRC purchased a 50 per cent stake in the business and Wordie now urged them to assume full control.

Willie followed Wordie's advice and in 1947, as the nationalisation programmes were being marshalled in Whitehall, the LMSRC was called in to mop up the remaining 50 per cent of shares for a sum of £381,000 (nearly £8,500,000 in today's terms). The government, ironically, was called in to arbitrate in a dispute between Wordie & Co. and the LMSRC over the terms of the take-over deal. Wordie & Co. insisted the business was worth £3 a share but the British Transport Commission eventually came up with a compromise figure of £2 13s 4d (£2.67p) each and the deal was completed before nationalisation took effect in 1948.

The passing of the familiar company did not go unnoticed in Scotland, where the *Stirling Observer* marked the end of an illustrious era by publishing an obituary of the business. Despite Wordie's efforts, the family was not allowed to avoid the full effects of nationalisation altogether. LMSRC had bought Wordie & Co. in exchange for its own shares, and when the railway company itself was nationalised in 1948 the company's shareholders – including the Wordie family – received compensation in the shape of government gilt-edged bonds.

At this stage, Wordie displayed his shrewd eye for investment with a remarkable decision, which had a lasting effect on the family's fortunes. Against most of the prevailing professional advice in the financial community, Wordie insisted that the family should sell the entire holding of government stock and switch the money into a portfolio of ordinary shares. It was a gamble, since shares are inherently more risky than government-backed bonds.

But Wordie's decision proved to be outstandingly astute and ranked alongside his grandfather's inspired move to link his carting operation with the railways. In the half century since the end of the war, shares have out-performed bonds on the stock market by a massive margin and Wordie's advice was worth countless sums to the family.

Wordie's dexterity – his ability to juggle several major issues at once – was fully demonstrated in 1947. While handling the Antarctic visit, nationalisation and his responsibilities at Cambridge and in the polar regions, Wordie was asked to undertake a fresh task for FIDS.

One conclusion from the trip to the Antarctic dependencies was that Britain required a specialist ice vessel to accommodate the expanding scientific operations and to help demonstrate the country's permanent presence in the region. Only months after coming back from the Antarctic he was despatched to America in search of a suitable ship. After a lengthy investigation during mid-1947 Wordie found a 1,000-ton vessel named *AN-76*. The wooden ship, only 194 ft long, had operated as HMS *Pretext* during the war and was returned to the US under the lend-lease agreement. Wordie believed that *AN-76* fitted the bill, and on his recommendation the ship was bought and refitted by the Crown Agents. The vessel was later renamed *John Biscoe* – after the sealing captain who annexed Graham Land for Britain in 1832 – and subsequently served British interests in southern waters for many years.

The purchase of the *John Biscoe* coincided with Wordie's rapid advancement elsewhere within the Polar community. At the age of fifty-eight, when many men were contemplating retirement, Wordie threw himself into his new administrative role with the same energy that had characterised his decades in the field. He rose quickly, joining a bewildering array of official committees and organisations, slowly accumulating more and more power and influence. The links with the RGS, which went back to the days immediately after *Endurance,* were initially the most important. Helped by the clever and powerful Hinks, Wordie was groomed for advancement from the start and their long-standing friendship was undoubtedly a major asset as he progressed through the organisation.

In 1934, Hinks was instrumental in having Wordie appointed as Honorary Secretary of the RGS, which, although a notional position, allowed him to circulate more freely in the rarefied upper reaches of the organisation. He was also unusual among honorary secretaries because he had not retired from active exploration when he assumed the post. It was a position he held for fourteen years until 1948, and it also paved the way for Wordie to be appointed the society's foreign secretary.

A little later he climbed to the very summit of the organisation: the presidency. Wordie was appointed president in 1951 for the customary three-year term. It was a particularly eventful time for the RGS, which was soon centre-stage in the unfolding drama of the race to conquer Mount Everest.

Wordie had come full circle with Everest, having failed to enlist in the first-ever attempt on the mountain in 1922. But as he moved into the president's office, the scramble to reach the summit of the world was reaching its climax. For some it was the last unfulfilled adventure of the Imperial age. For Wordie the mountain was unfinished business. It was also a difficult time for the RGS, which saw Britain's once supreme position in the world of discovery under serious attack. The presumption that Everest was the sole preserve of Empire had been washed away by the 1950s and the stately procession of British climbers to Tibet – 'parties of sahibs' the Dalai Lama called them – was under assault from determined mountaineers with scant regard for the Imperial niceties.

Britain's post-war ambitions for Everest were also thrown into some disarray in 1950 when China invaded Tibet, a move which closed off the traditional route to the mountain from the north. Fortunately, the Chinese occupation of Tibet coincided with a general thawing in relations with Nepal, whose southern approaches to Everest had until that point remained mostly closed to foreigners. Few westerners had even set eyes on the southern outlook, but from 1947 onwards the Nepalese began to allow occasional mountaineering and scientific parties to explore the area. Slowly a new route to Everest from the south was beginning to open up. But the exclusive access to Everest which Britain had enjoyed from the north was gone forever.

While not fully appreciated in London, this also was a moment when the Himalayan climbing environment was changing. In the early 1950s, at precisely the time Wordie became President of the RGS, mountaineering in the Himalayas had entered a new more aggressive and competitive phase. The more combative environment that had existed for decades in the Alps was slowly transferred to the Himalayas as the area was opened to foreigners.

In 1950 a French expedition under Maurice Herzog climbed Annapurna, the giant of the Himalayas at 26,545 ft (8,069 m) – the first time an 8,000-m summit had been conquered. A year later Britain's loss of exclusive rights to Everest was officially confirmed with the stunning news that the authorities in Nepal had turned down Britain's application to send climbing parties to the mountain during the 1952 season. Instead, Nepal had approved an expedition by highly regarded and experienced mountaineers from Switzerland. The only concession was that Britain secured permission to send a party in 1953 which, if the Swiss failed, was likely to be the country's last chance for glory. The French were given permission for the 1954 season and another Swiss attempt was scheduled for 1955.

Wordie became deputy chairman of the Himalayan Committee,

the joint RGS-Alpine Club operation set up to in the 1920s to mastermind the climb. The body, which had been renamed from its original title of the Everest Committee, took the immediate decision to abandon its 'exclusive right' to the mountain. In its place the Committee proposed sending a joint British–Swiss expedition. The Swiss politely refused, still smarting from a snub when the committee had rejected a request for Rene Dittert, a top Alpinist, to join a British reconnaissance trip to the mountain's southern slopes in 1951. Whether Britain liked it or not, a race was developing. The parallel with the contest between Amundsen and Scott for the South Pole in 1911–12 was undeniable and the Himalayan Committee could only sit and await the outcome of the Swiss attempt on the peak.

The Himalayan Committee – and the eager British public – got their wish when the Swiss team narrowly failed to reach the summit. The Swiss, Raymond Lambert and the experienced Sherpa, Tenzing Norgay, reached a height of 28,210 ft (8,600 m), just 84 ft (25 m) above the record achieved by Edward Norton and Howard Somervell in 1924. But they were forced down by brutal winds and biting cold when barely 825 ft (251 m) from the top.

The heartbreaking news for the Swiss reinvigorated the Himalayan Committee, who set about planning for 1953 with renewed energy, knowing that this was Britain's last chance to reach the top first. Larry Kirwan, who had succeeded Hinks as RGS Secretary, wrote: 'We are very determined to make the climb in 1953.'

While there were many key issues to be resolved, the outstanding matter was who should lead the 1953 expedition. The natural choice of leader was Eric Shipton, an appealing figure who had been to Everest five times and was the outstanding climber of the age. Shipton's last visit to Everest was in 1951 when he had led a reconnaissance party exploring the southern access to the mountain and had casually recruited two accomplished New Zealanders to his team, Earle Riddiford and Edmund Hillary.

Shipton, arguably the world's leading mountaineer, fully expected to lead the 1953 Everest party. He was a climber's climber, a man who inspired intense loyalty and respect among fellow mountaineers and whose flair and dash encouraged flattering comparisons with Shackleton. But unlike Shackleton he was not a natural leader. He was informal, notoriously disorganised, and someone who disliked the type of large-scale expeditions that the Himalayan Committee considered would be necessary to scale Everest. A party of ten in the Himalayas, he once wrote, would be 'grossly unwieldy and inconvenient'. In fact, the 1953 expedition took eleven climbers. Shipton was also uncomfortable with the changing mood and more competitive climbing environment, which he abhorred. His old-fashioned values, he once conceded, 'might well seem out of place' in the prevailing climate of the early 1950s. He was also out of his depth when it came to combating the political intrigues and manoeuvrings of the wily gentleman from the RGS and Alpine Club, such as Wordie.

Doubts about Shipton's suitability had begun to surface within the Himalayan Committee during the early stages of planning in 1952. One of the most potent charges levelled against him was that Shipton did not possess the hunger and ambition to lead a successful mission. Shipton, it was said, had showed 'inadequate drive' in 1952 on an expedition to Cho Oyu, a striking 26,870-ft (8,182-m) peak about 20 miles (32 km) due west of Everest. Cho Oyu was meant to be a dress rehearsal for the following year's assault, but it was a disjointed and disappointing venture, which only raised fresh doubts about Shipton's suitability to lead a large-scale operation.

Without consulting Shipton, the Himalayan Committee put out informal feelers to find a replacement. Among those approached was John Hunt, a serving British army officer in his early forties with solid climbing experience in the Alps. Hunt shared something in common with Wordie, having also been turned down for an earlier Everest expedition on medical grounds. Hunt had also been warned against further climbing, just as Wordie had been in 1921.

But Hunt was known to Basil Goodfellow, Honorary Secretary of the Himalayan Committee and an experienced hand in the obscure byways of the Alpine Club and the RGS. Goodfellow hinted that Hunt, a scrupulous planner and natural leader, should be made organising secretary and appointed to the climbing team. However, the appointment of a serving British army officer to the expedition caused minor palpitations in the Foreign Office, to which the post-independence political situation in the Indian sub-continent remained highly delicate. The FO in Kathmandu urged the Himalayan Committee to 'play down' Hunt's military connections and concentrate instead on his mountaineering experience.

Wordie was among the old brigade who felt the committee should bite the bullet and replace Shipton as leader. Helped by Claremont Skrine, a former Asian diplomat, and Harry Tobin, co-founder of the Himalayan Club, the old hands gathered around Wordie and began to out-manoeuvre the increasingly isolated Shipton.

Wordie's misgivings about Shipton may have had something to do with an incident some years earlier. Shipton had visited Cambridge in 1948 to give a lecture at the University Mountaineering Club. At dinner before the talk he told Chris Brasher, the club secretary, that he had always wanted to be a geologist. He asked whether he might be accepted as a mature student at St John's College, where Wordie was senior tutor.

Brasher was enthusiastic about the prospect of bringing the famous explorer and the top mountaineer together and rang Wordie, fixing up a meeting with Shipton at 11 a.m. the next morning. When Brasher came to collect Shipton for the meeting he found him poring over maps with a keen young undergraduate and clearly not ready for his meeting with Wordie. Brasher was agitated and urged Shipton not to be late for the meeting with the punctilious Wordie. 'Oh, cancel it – I'm more interested in this,' Shipton replied.[1] It is not known whether Wordie remembered the slight or whether it weighed on his mind during deliberations over the 1953 Everest team. But he was a man with a strong sense of propriety and the formidable memory of a prize elephant.

Shipton clearly felt that he was losing control and virtually sealed his own fate in July 1952 by making a frank personal statement to the committee, which expressed doubts about his own ability. In his statement, Shipton declared that being involved with a project like Everest could 'easily produce rigidity of outlook' and that someone with fewer inhibitions was 'better equipped' to tackle the climb. 'Was it not time, perhaps, to hand over to a younger man with a fresh outlook?' he asked.

It hardly smacked of the strong, convinced leadership that the committee sought and they seized the moment. As a compromise, it was first suggested that a deputy be appointed. But Shipton had already chosen his own deputy, Charles Evans, a powerfully built brain surgeon with abundant Himalayan experience. When this idea fizzled out, the committee offered Hunt the position as organising secretary. But it was soon clear that Hunt and Shipton – chalk and cheese – would find it virtually impossible to work together.

By September 1952, the leadership remained unresolved and the 1953 Everest expedition was in crisis. Although Charles Wylie, a serving Gurkha officer, was now in charge of organisation under the notional direction of Shipton, Hunt lurked in the background.

In a mood of gathering gloom and uncertainty, the Himalayan Committee called an urgent meeting on 11 September. Wordie knew that drastic – and even highly unpopular – action was now required and that he would be forced to take an unpleasant decision. Shortly before leaving home, Wordie solemnly informed his family: 'This is not going to be a nice day. I have got something nasty to do today.'[2]

Wordie, Skrine, Tobin and other doubters were in the majority as the committee assembled at the Alpine Club in London. The committee chairman, Claude Elliott, was lined up alongside and reckoned that Hunt was the type of 'thruster' that the expedition so evidently needed. But there were notable absentees, partly because the meeting was held at short notice. Among those not present were Kirwan and Lawrence Wager, a veteran of the 1933 Everest expedition, who were defenders of Shipton.

Shipton and Wylie waited in an ante-room while the committee debated the matter in the inner sanctum. According to Shipton, the chief item on the agenda was the deputy leadership and what followed came as a bolt from the blue. Wordie had now hardened in his belief that Shipton was unsuited to the job as leader and should be replaced by Hunt. But he felt that Shipton's experience was important and that he should be retained as expedition adviser, particularly as he had developed a highly valuable working relationship with the Sherpas, who were vital to the team. However, the lengthy discussions only produced another unworkable muddle. Shipton, it was declared, would be co-leader with Hunt up to Base Camp and Hunt would then take over as sole leader for the final assault.

Shipton had been manoeuvred into an impossible position. He could not serve alongside or under Hunt and resignation from the expedition was the only choice. Shipton, in a letter to Wordie, later commented: 'Whether this fantastic proposal was intended to be taken at its face value I cannot say.' The committee voted unanimously for the clumsy compromise and most members withdrew, leaving Wordie, Goodfellow and Elliott to break the unwelcome news to Shipton.

The tension was palpable as the uneasy scenario was unveiled to a slightly shocked Shipton, who promptly offered his resignation if the Committee felt it would help the expedition. At this point a further short break was taken and the Committee ratified its decision to appoint Hunt as leader. Shipton was asked to return, and he found Elliott clearly uncomfortable at the turn of events.

Speaking hesitatingly, Elliott rambled for a moment before Shipton interrupted him by asking outright if Hunt was to be made leader of the expedition. Elliott confirmed the offer to Hunt and a dejected Shipton rose to his feet and left the room, 'absolutely shattered'. Shipton was furious and angrily accused the committee of 'subterfuge and clandestine lobbying'. In a letter to Wordie, he said that the committee 'cannot escape censure' for going behind his back and not consulting him about the change of policy over the leader. He added: 'I find such conduct the more incomprehensible in view of my attitude at the first committee meeting, which surely demanded reciprocal candour and merited some confidence in my disinterested concern for the welfare of the expedition.'[3]

Wordie rarely spoke about the messy affair and was clearly perturbed. Privately, he regarded the sacking of the popular Shipton as among the most unpleasant tasks of his life. He had made the right decision, he felt, but in the worst possible way. Within hours a telegram was sent to Hunt inviting him to lead the 1953 Everest expedition and the controversial decision was endorsed by six votes to two at a fuller Himalayan Committee meeting several weeks later.

The sacking of Shipton, as the committee must have anticipated, caused an outcry among the climbing fraternity, including some who had been earmarked for places on the expedition. Some threatened to resign and Hillary, a straight-talking Kiwi said he could never forgive the committee for the 'boorish way' they fired Shipton. Hillary was particularly concerned that strong-minded climbers, who were well-known for their independence and dislike of authority, would have to endure an unpalatable military-style regime under the army officer, Hunt. But Hunt was an engaging and highly capable leader who soon overcame the doubters and rebuilt morale. Hillary was among the first to embrace Hunt's fine leadership qualities and readily described him as an 'outstanding organiser'.

The heart of operations was to be the RGS, where a special office was established and where Wordie kept a watchful eye on developments. The expedition, with its eleven climbers, was perhaps smaller than Shipton had feared it might be.

One echo of earlier Polar expeditions was the contract which the Himalayan Committee signed with *The Times*, which paid

£10,000 (approximately £160,000 today) for exclusive rights to the story – about half the anticipated costs of the expedition. Hunt was appointed a special correspondent of the paper, a useful ruse which made him an employee and prevented him talking to the many rival newspapers who were anxious to gain an insight into the expedition.

On 26 May 1953 two of the party, Tom Bourdillon and Charles Evans, broke all existing records using the experimental closed-circuit oxygen system and climbed to 28,700 ft (8,748 m), little more than 300 ft (95 m) from the summit. Though they were exhausted and encountering difficulties with their oxygen, the eager Bourdillon wanted to push on. The weather was deteriorating fast and Evans knew the severe risks if they continued. Shouting above the howling winds, Evans persuaded Bourdillon to abandon the climb by warning him that he would never see his wife again if they continued upwards. So they came down.

Three days later, on 29 May, the second assault party of Hillary and Tenzing moved up, the firm snow helping with their progress. At around 11.30 in the morning they looked ahead and saw a snowy dome which was the summit of the world's tallest mountain. Hillary hauled himself onto a flattish area of snow, with nothing but 'space in every direction'. The two men shook hands and Hillary photographed Tenzing on the roof of the world with the flags of the United Nations, Britain, Nepal and India stretched stiffly in the high winds. It never occurred to Hillary to have his own picture taken. After fifteen minutes at the summit, Hillary and Tenzing descended and delivered the first news of the successful climb to their colleagues, George Lowe and Wilfred Noyce. 'Well George, we knocked the bastard off,' Hillary announced.

A more elaborate code was needed to break the news to the rest of the world. In order to conceal the achievement from its rivals, *The Times* correspondent, James Morris, had given each climber a pseudonym and each eventuality of the climb was coded with a special description to obscure the truth. The term 'snow conditions bad' meant Everest had been climbed, while Hillary's code name was 'Advanced base abandoned' and Tenzing's 'Awaiting improvement'. Hunt's hand-delivered message, carried over 180 miles by runners to the remote Indian army radio transmitter at Namche, read: 'Snow conditions bad stop advance base abandoned yesterday stop awaiting improvement stop all well.'

Wordie was at the receiving end of the momentous news. He was one of a select handful of people, including the Queen and the Prime Minister, who knew the secret that Everest had been conquered. Not even the Nepalese government knew. The news was relayed on to London via Kathmandu, finally arriving on 1 June. The following day was the Queen's coronation day and Everest was to be served up as a special present.

Keeping the news under wraps was obviously a strain for Wordie and at home his family could see that he was preoccupied. On the eve of the coronation, the family was gathered at a flat in London, the secret still concealed by the inscrutable Wordie. At 11 o'clock at night, Wordie unexpectedly asked one of his sons to go out and buy the early editions of the following day's newspapers, knowing that *The Times* was going to the break the news in the morning. His son returned with the paper showing the blazing headline: 'Everest Conquered'. A mightily relieved Wordie was wreathed in a broad grin and confessed: 'I had to keep it a secret.'

The political intrigues which marked Wordie's era at the RGS were repeated with greater intensity at the Scott Polar Research Institute, where his time was again marked by major advances and bitter controversies. Wordie had been engaged with SPRI from its earliest days but for much of the first two decades the organisation was led by Frank Debenham and ably supported by Priestley. Wordie's role was more advisory, partly because of his other commitments to active exploration and St John's College. However, there were inevitable tensions from the start. The creators of SPRI, Debenham and Priestley, were regarded as 'Scott's men' and the institute was founded with the specific aim of commemorating Scott. In contrast, Wordie was an unalloyed Shackleton disciple. To that extent, Wordie may have been the outsider at SPRI.

But Wordie's attitude towards SPRI changed dramatically in the late 1930s as his days of active exploration were coming to an end. He was appointed chairman in 1937 – the year of his final Arctic expedition – and soon began to wrest control of the organisation away from Debenham, the organisation's director.

The war and his full-time involvement in Operation Tabarin interrupted his early ambitions for SPRI. But in March 1945, less than two months before the end of hostilities in Europe, Wordie was re-elected chairman and immediately began the task of re-shaping SPRI.

Wordie's ambitions were helped considerably by news that the institute was to receive an unexpected windfall from the government. Early in 1945 SPRI was given approximately £1,500 (£35,000 today) as back rent on the Cambridge premises occupied by Naval Intelligence during the war. Wordie saw this one-off bonus as an ideal opportunity to help finance his grand plans for the institute.[4] Wordie's scheme was to expand SPRI's activities deeper into the field of serious research and teaching, while simultaneously building a library to accommodate both an expanded archive and all the modern material on Polar affairs.

The stumbling block, according to Wordie, was Debenham. Wordie and Debenham, who first met at Cambridge in 1913, had worked well together at the outset. Wordie was an energetic supporter of SPRI in the early days and Debenham backed Wordie when he was elected a fellow of St John's in 1921. But the men grew apart over the years and the relationship cooled further during the war when Debenham was largely excluded from much of Wordie's secret activities for Naval Intelligence or Tabarin.

The two men were similar in their acclaimed scientific prowess, but were quite different in character. Debenham was a gentle cerebral character who flourished in a clubby collegiate environment at Cambridge and disliked confrontation. He was a sensitive person whom Wordie once dismissed as suffering from a form of 'persecution mania'.

In contrast, Wordie was a more combative figure with strong ambitions and a profound passion for intrigue. Wordie liked to exercise control and found it difficult to take a passive role in anything. It was his dictatorial style and penchant for back-seat driving that infuriated Debenham, particularly when Wordie, in effect a non-executive, took decisions without informing Debenham, the institute's chief executive. By the mid-1940s Wordie believed that Debenham was too old for the job and out of touch with the new generation of Polar activists. Nor did he regard Debenham as capable of steering the organisation onto a new footing. 'All of us have been carrying Deb for years and he now knows too much,' Wordie said. Wordie felt that he should be persuaded to resign. It was an opinion shared by Priestley and Roberts.

To help his campaign, Wordie also approached the elderly but influential Mill to take sides against Debenham and encourage him to stand down. 'I hope you will do all you can to persuade Debenham to make way for others,' he once wrote to Mill. Wordie proposed a compromise, which involved Debenham being moved 'upstairs' to the position of honorary director. At this point, Debenham fell ill with emphysema and asked for a long leave of absence from the institute to return to his native Australia for a period of recuperation.

Wordie seized his chance. Lancelot Fleming, another friend of Wordie's from his exploration days, was asked to become acting director while Debenham was away, although Wordie wanted the appointment to be made permanent. 'All will be well when Fleming and Roberts (the new research Fellow) take over,' Wordie told Mill. Towards the end of 1946, after more than twenty-five years of dedicated service, Debenham resigned from SPRI. 'I don't know how I shall bear it,' he wrote, 'it has become part of me, almost an obsession.'[5]

With Debenham removed, the next stage of Wordie's scheme was to obtain long-term government funding to secure the institute's future and to embark on a major expansion programme. It was a moment which brought a sea-change in the affairs of SPRI, building on the early achievements of Debenham and propelling the institute to the status of an internationally-recognised Polar centre. Wordie's fine grasp of financial matters was a crucial factor in helping to transform SPRI. Indeed, placing SPRI's finances onto a sounder foundation was his most notable achievement during his often controversial reign at the Institute. By the end of 1946, Wordie's powers of persuasion had produced a government grant of £1,800 a year (£40,000 today) and this was further extended to £3,000 a year (£64,000) in the spring of 1948. By the end of his chairmanship in 1955, government grants and income from elsewhere in the Commonwealth had reached an impressive figure of £6,000 a year (£90,000).

However, Wordie's success with SPRI's finances could not conceal difficulties elsewhere. Part of the problem was his relationship with Brian Roberts, whose glittering career had developed quickly alongside Wordie's during the 1930s and 1940s. Roberts had also been loyal to Wordie during the battle with Debenham, but he was poised to turn against him in the same way that Wordie had turned against Debenham.

Roberts was a member of Wordie's school of exploration during the 1930s, having participated in two Cambridge expeditions to the Arctic and a voyage to the Antarctic before his twenty-fifth birthday. He worked on Blue Books at SPRI and was a key member of the Operation Tabarin trinity with Wordie and Mackintosh. Wordie thought highly of Roberts and after the war singled him out as SPRI's first-ever research Fellow. He regarded Roberts, a meticulous and enormously hard-working man with a keen sense of humour, as 'absolutely first rate'.

One cause of tension centred on Roberts' role as chairman of the little-known committee tasked with providing an accurate glossary of place names in the Antarctic. By the mid-1940s, a chaotic and confusing system of nomenclature existed. There was no single source for names and many countries had different names for the same places on the map. Typical of the confusion were the conflicting names attached to the Antarctic Peninsula. Britain had originally named it Graham Land, but the Americans called it Palmer Land and others called it Tierra San Martin and Tierra O'Higgins. (It was not until 1964 that all sides agreed it should be generally known as the Antarctic Peninsula, with the northern half known as Graham Land and southern half as Palmer Land.) Roberts embarked on the massive task of bringing order to the haphazard business, which in turn led to his first serious clashes with Wordie.

Both were determined characters and Wordie, who instinctively preferred to stick to the original place names given by the earliest explorers, often disputed changes instigated by Roberts. In turn, Roberts always insisted that Wordie caused him more problems sorting out the place-names chaos than the traditionally more difficult Americans. At the heart of the clash were the basic characteristics of the two men which placed them on an inevitable collision course. Both were highly intelligent, hugely determined and obdurate. Both had an unshakeable belief in their own ability.

Wordie, vastly experienced, authoritative and hugely respected, may have found it difficult to accept that Roberts was his match. The only shred of vanity in Wordie's make-up was an unwavering certainty of his own intellectual superiority. In Roberts, though, he found a serious challenger. The industrious Roberts was a generation younger than Wordie and possessed an encyclopaedic knowledge of the Arctic and Antarctic. Some believed that Roberts was the most profoundly knowledgeable Polar authority in the world. But Roberts was also impatient and obsessive about minutiae, which often made him difficult to work with. Wordie once wrote that Roberts was 'very persistent, almost obstinate and over-anxious to have his own way'. It was a description that could easily have applied to Wordie himself.

One of the biggest disputes between the two heavyweights arose in the early 1950s over the seemingly esoteric matter of what to call large sheets of Polar ice, which at the time had several conflicting names. The confusion was typified by the long-running debate over the giant ice sheet which spills out into the Ross Sea and was the vast amphitheatre for much of the heroic age of Antarctic exploration. It was the arena where Amundsen, Scott and Shackleton had based their expeditions during the heroic age.

The huge flat plain of ice – at over 300,000 sq miles, it covers an area roughly the size of France – was known variously as the Ross Ice Barrier and the Ross Ice Shelf, while some called it the Great Ice Barrier or the Ross Barrier. Amundsen, Scott and Shackleton invariably called it the Barrier.

Wordie was a dyed in the wool traditionalist, who firmly believed that it should remain known as the Ross Barrier, the name given by Sir James Clark Ross in 1841 when it was first sighted. Ross called it a barrier simply because the towering white cliffs presented an insurmountable obstruction to his ships, *Erebus* and *Terror*. It would have been easier, he proclaimed, to sail through the white cliffs of Dover than to penetrate further into the wilderness. As was the custom, the explorer's own choice of name stuck.

Roberts took a more modern view, insisting that the term 'barrier' referred only to the ice-front facing the Ross Sea – the 'white cliffs of Dover' – and that the floating chunk of ice was self-evidently not a barrier to travel since numerous explorers had used it as a highway to the Pole. The whole feature, he argued, should be named the Ross Ice Shelf.

Wordie's opposition to the change of name went back thirty years to the days even before Roberts left school. The issue of what to call the ice sheet had first been raised shortly after the First World War and Wordie took up cudgels in the 1920s. He once told the American Geographical Society: 'I am absolutely against the substitution of "shelf-ice" for "barrier" on charts and maps.' He added:

> At present, shelf ice is on trial among glaciologists. Whatever the original meaning as a hindrance to navigation, it now has an absolutely unambiguous meaning to all Polar travellers. Also, I like the sound; The Great Ross Ice Shelf is far too sibilant. The sound of Barrier is very appropriate. We have also developed what is almost an affection for it.[6]

Some time later he rubbed salt into Roberts' wounds when he wrote a formal paper for the *Journal of Glaciology*, which he provocatively called 'Barrier versus Shelf'. In the article he demanded that the term 'shelf' must be opposed at all costs. Among the editors of the *Journal of Glaciology* was Roberts.

In private Wordie was more forceful and personal about Roberts. At a private lunch at St John's College, he once dismissed his old colleague by declaring: 'This fellow Roberts doesn't really know what he is talking about.'[7] However, Wordie lost the battle of 'Barrier versus Shelf' and Roberts emerged with great credit for sorting out another bit of confusion about Antarctic nomenclature. The ice sheet was duly renamed the Ross Ice Shelf, the name which applies to this day.

Roberts successfully overcame the bitter dispute with Wordie and developed into an outstanding figure in Polar circles, his finest achievement being a highly influential role in drafting the first Antarctic Treaty in 1959. But the pair clashed again later in the 1950s and old Polar hands believe that Wordie never forgot the 'Barrier versus Shelf' controversy.

Wordie plotted against Roberts to block his appointment when the post of Director of SPRI arose in 1957. Wordie was approached to recommend Roberts as director and was unequivocal in his denunciation. Roberts, he bluntly told the university's special selection committee, was not up to the job. In a confidential letter to Professor J.A. Steers of Cambridge University, who was chairing the selection process, Wordie was brutally frank about the shortcomings of Roberts. He wrote: 'I know him to be deficient in the wider outlook but competent in the small details. I think he should be offered one of the lesser posts at the institute.'[8]

Roberts did not get the job, which went to Guy de Robin, who was then working at the Australian National University in Canberra. But it would be wrong to assume that Wordie alone had prevented him from being selected. Those who advised Cambridge not to appoint Roberts included Debenham and the respected Fleming, while Kirwan at the RGS also had reservations about his suitability for the task.

Wordie's choice for the SPRI job was his old friend, Vivian Fuchs, who by the mid-1950s he regarded as 'far and away the most distinguished Polar scientist'. The irony is that Fuchs, unwittingly, was later to be the catalyst for a sequence of events which led to Wordie being removed as chairman of SPRI.

The downfall of Wordie at SPRI can be traced back to the early plans by Fuchs to launch an expedition to cross the Antarctic continent, the goal first proposed by Bruce half a century earlier and beyond the reach of Shackleton. Fuchs, who was known as 'Bunny', first devised his own scheme for a coast-to-coast crossing in 1949 while employed by FIDS and stuck in an Antarctic blizzard. When he returned to Britain in 1950, Fuchs approached Wordie for advice and few were better equipped to dispense wisdom on the subject.

Wordie had been a major influence on Fuchs's life, introducing him to exploration in 1929 and advising him on how to get a job with FIDS after the war. For Wordie the scheme was another important item of unfinished business. But Wordie sensed the early 1950s was not the right time to launch the expedition. He felt the government would not be sympathetic to a plea for hefty State funding of the enterprise at a time of general post-war austerity and he was also concerned about the wider political issues surrounding disputed territorial rights in the Antarctic. He promised to keep his well-tuned ear to the ground in Whitehall and Polar circles and inform Fuchs of the right moment to strike. As a result, the scheme was shelved until 1953 when Wordie was still riding high from the Everest coup.

That same year Wordie went back to Fuchs and suggested that the time had arrived to launch his expedition. He offered his own considerable experience and threw himself into the project with great enthusiasm. Wordie devoted considerable time to the planning, frequently inviting Fuchs to his home, where the pair spent hours studying maps and charts for the proposed Commonwealth Trans-Antarctic Expedition. Outside in the hall, Fuchs's husky dog, Darky, sat quietly.

One of Wordie's most telling contributions was to solve a tricky personal matter for Fuchs, who was finding it impossible to continue planning the expedition and to hold down his job as head of the scientific bureau at FIDS. Wordie had the solution, persuading his old friend Priestley to come out of retirement and assume temporary responsibility for the bureau, thus releasing Fuchs to concentrate full-time on planning the expedition.

Wordie also trawled his connections in Whitehall to find a suitably strong group of people to sit on the Commonwealth Trans-Antarctic Expedition (TAE) committee. His choice of chairman was Sir John Slessor, Marshal of the Royal Air Force, a commanding character who wielded great influence where it mattered. Slessor persuaded the Queen to become the TAE's patron, which paved the way for the Churchill government to back the project with public money and opened doors to funding from other sources, including key Commonwealth countries such as Australia and New Zealand.

Behind the scenes, however, the TAE caused a huge outcry in Polar circles and at the centre of the turmoil was the figure of Wordie. The Polar community was deeply divided by the expedition, even though it offered the prospect of a great British triumph. The deep divisions saw Fuchs and Wordie lined up against heavyweight opponents led by the powerful pair of Roberts and Colin Bertram at SPRI and Kirwan at the RGS.

It was a particularly awkward period since the men had worked closely together for some years and were all well known to Wordie, particularly Roberts. Wordie had also brought Bertram to St John's after the war and was instrumental in him being appointed director of SPRI. But Bertram was among those connected with SPRI who found Wordie a 'devious' character.

The other major opponent was Kirwan, a distinguished geographer, who succeeded Hinks as secretary at the RGS in 1945 and had collaborated successfully with Wordie over Everest. The pair also sat together on the committee arranging the UK involvement in the ground-breaking Norwegian-British-Swedish expedition to the Antarctic between 1949 and 1952, which was the first truly international venture to the continent.

But the two men never struck up a decent rapport and Wordie disliked the tall, mannered Kirwan. Wordie's reservations had first surfaced when Kirwan was being lined up to replace Hinks. Wordie opposed Kirwan's application for the post and instead recommended Andrew Croft to take over. But he lost the battle and Kirwan was installed as secretary in 1945. Wordie was also mildly irritated by Kirwan's behaviour during the debate over Shipton's role in the Everest expedition. While Wordie demanded typically firm action to sort out the muddle over leadership, Kirwan had advocated an unworkable compromise. He disapproved of Shipton's sacking, but supported Hunt as leader of the final assault team, a scheme that was doomed to fail.

The establishment's opposition to the Fuchs-Wordie scheme was multi-layered and involved issues as diverse as the territorial battles in the Antarctic dependencies, stark differences over the scale of Britain's role in Polar exploration and the suitability of Fuchs to lead such an enterprise. It was all overlaid with the unsavoury personality clashes between the key individuals.

Issues were further clouded by events involving International Geophysical Year in 1957, a huge operation which linked twelve nations in a co-ordinated scientific programme on the Antarctic Continent. Fuchs's scheme, in contrast to the governmental activities of IGY, was essentially a private trip and not officially part of IGY. But the TAE overlapped with planning for the international programme and the mixture was further enriched when Wordie, as one of the country's foremost authorities on Polar matters, was appointed chairman of the British National Committee for IGY. Also on the committee was Roberts.

Kirwan, Roberts and Bertram were opposed to the Fuchs expedition on the grounds that the scheme was too ambitious for Britain and should be left to the wealthier Americans. It was felt that the sizeable sums of public money needed to finance the expedition could be spread more effectively across a range of different projects in the Polar field. Another consideration was the long-running dispute with Argentina and Chile over territorial rights in the region. Argentina, for example, was rumoured to be establishing a permanent station at Vahsel Bay and there were hints that an expedition to the South Pole itself was also in the planning stage. Some believed that a sizeable British presence in the disputed territories would send the wrong signals and inflame a combustible situation.

Much of the debate centred on the embarrassing fact that Britain did not possess a specialist ice-ship to transport TAE members or to carry out its wide-ranging responsibilities for the prestigious IGY venture. Roberts, who combined his SPRI activities with an active role at the Foreign Office, argued that it would be humiliating for a foreign-owned vessel to carry the TAE to the Antarctic. Roberts and Bertram insisted that some of the funds being donated to the Fuchs enterprise should be spent on building a dedicated new ice-ship for the nation, which would help meet the IGY obligations and also send a firm signal of intent to Argentina and Chile about the British presence in the area. Roberts also nursed a long-standing ambition to raise government funds for an aerial survey of the Antarctic dependencies and he feared that supporting Fuchs would thwart this aim.

Fuchs, for his part, was slightly bemused by the political intrigue and firmly believed that if the government was supporting his private expedition, it was bound to support British operations in an important international exercise like IGY.

Wordie had a more profound concern. He believed that under the influence of Roberts, SPRI was slowly being manoeuvred into becoming a branch of the Foreign Office and he believed passionately in the institute's independence. He was furious at how the expedition was being used as a political football.

But his most serious charge was that, in pursuit of his Foreign Office agenda, Roberts was deliberately sabotaging Britain's role in IGY. It was a devastating indictment of one of the country's leading Polar authorities and an IGY committee member and it turned up the heat in the increasingly bitter dispute. Wordie disclosed his fears in a private letter written at the time, which declared that Roberts 'completely failed to see the purpose and importance' of the British role in IGY, even though as a committee member he was closely associated with policy. He added: 'He went beyond this and his activities were directed towards preventing the IGY Committee from carrying out its programme and for a time he held up plans for the Halley Bay base. He should have understood its great national importance. This shows his weak side.'[9]

Wordie was not alone in sensing that Roberts was a negative influence. Fuchs also realised that Roberts was aggressively working against the TAE. Publicly he kept his counsel but in a private note written some years later Fuchs recalled that Roberts had begun 'actively to oppose the TAE'.[10] The bitter personal conflict was intensified as it emerged that some members of the Polar hierarchy wanted to remove Fuchs as leader of the TAE. Among those working behind the scenes was Kirwan, who advocated that Fuchs should be replaced by Hillary.

Slessor was a key ally for Wordie and Fuchs and he worked tirelessly to champion their cause. He also managed to disrupt the plotting against Fuchs. Slessor moved quickly to ambush the plotters and spoke confidentially to Sir James Marshall-Cornwall, President of the RGS and a member of the TAE committee. The planned *coup d'état* was summarily abandoned, but even Fuchs never learned what Slessor had actually said to Marshall-Cornwall.

Despite the unpleasantness, Wordie relished the battle. Once he took Fuchs on a secret mission to acquaint him at first-hand with the strength of the forces ranged against them. Late one evening Wordie took Fuchs to the SPRI building in Cambridge where, despite the late hour, a light was burning in the library. Wordie took Fuchs up the stairs where he found Roberts and Bertram deep in conversation. Wordie turned to Fuchs and announced: 'Bunny, I thought you should know those opposed to you.'[11]

Bertram, as Director of SPRI, found it increasingly difficult to work with Wordie, Chairman of SPRI's management committee. He was also concerned that the acrimonious dispute was harming the Institute itself. Bertram wrote to Wordie: 'Over a period you as Chairman of the Committee and I as Director have not appeared to be in full agreement, indeed we are known to have been giving contrary advice. It is essential the Institute presents a united front.'[12]

One sticking point was the decision, almost certainly influenced by Wordie, to set up the expedition within a limited company. It was claimed that limited-company status would enable the TAE to generate more money from the sale of press, broadcasting and book rights. But Bertram totally disagreed with the policy and in 1955 he penned a personal handwritten note to Fuchs which ended with the terse comment: 'Are you a Company Director, a Civil Servant or both?'[13]

Relations between Wordie and SPRI worsened in late 1955 as Fuchs was putting the finishing touches to his expedition. Bertram tendered his resignation as Director but SPRI's management committee refused to accept it while the Institute was going through a separate and delicate reorganisation within Cambridge University.

Bertram saw a way out of the problem by removing Wordie and appointing what he pointedly termed a 'neutral' Chairman of the management committee. The idea appealed to those anxious to settle the dispute and restore the Institute to a more stable footing. One of those approached to lead the management committee was Sir George Binney, Wordie's old friend from Oxford. In late 1955 Wordie was duly ousted after eighteen years in the chair and an association which dated back to the very inception of SPRI.

Wordie's links with the TAE and the IGY were maintained, however. His friendship with Fuchs remained unshaken and he continued as head of the British IGY team until 1958.

Fuchs' expedition was planned on very similar lines to Shackleton's ill-fated venture, involving two parties operating from either side of the continent. Fuchs led the party from the Weddell Sea base and Hillary, who got involved through New Zealand's claims to the Ross Sea area, was in charge of the party based on that side of the continent, and which was scheduled to lay depots for Fuchs's crossing party. The journey, estimated at about 2,000 miles (3,200 km), was slightly longer than Shackleton's intended route but, like Shackleton, Fuchs had estimated that it would take a hundred days to cover the distance. Shackleton had planned a mixture of dog teams and man-hauling for the long journey, while the Fuchs expedition took modified farm tractors and Sno-cat vehicles, whose innovative traction system allowed them to travel over both soft snow and hard ice.

Under the influence of Wordie, Fuchs set up his base at Vahsel Bay, the spot where Shackleton had intended to bring *Endurance* in 1914–15. Appropriately, he named it Shackleton Base and Hillary's quarters at Ross Island were called Scott Base.

The first journey to Vahsel in January 1956 was packed with the sort of drama which provided a disturbing echo of *Endurance*. Fuchs's ship, the 800-ton Canadian sealer *Theron* was trapped in the ice for a month and at home the vultures circled menacingly around Wordie. The strain was apparent on Wordie's face as he waited for news of *Theron*'s fate. There was no more relieved man in Britain when a telephone call brought word that the ship had broken through to Vahsel Bay.

After leaving an over-wintering party at Shackleton Base, Fuchs returned to London and prepared for the main assault in the following season. On 13 January 1957 the expedition fought its way back to Shackleton in the Danish ice-breaker, *Magga Dan* and in November the trans-continental party set out for the first leg of the momentous journey to the South Pole. Despite appalling weather and difficult travelling conditions, Fuchs rolled up to the South Pole on 19 January 1958 on the anniversary of the day when *Endurance* first became trapped in the ice of the Weddell Sea.

At the Pole he met Hillary's depot-laying party, who had arrived a fortnight earlier with barely 20 gallons (91 litres) of fuel in the tractors. After another hard journey from the Pole to the Ross Sea, Fuchs and Hillary finally reached Scott Base on 2 March. The last great land journey on earth, the coast-to-coast crossing of Antarctica, covered precisely 2,158 miles (3,472 km) and took ninety-nine days at an average of 22 miles (35 km) per day. Wordie's unfinished business was finally accomplished.

Fuchs's incredible journey also succeeded in healing the rift within the Polar establishment. The RGS awarded him the Special Gold Medal – only the fourth ever awarded at this point – and SPRI presented every party member with a set of gold cuff links engraved with each man's initials. Roberts, who had worked so hard to stop the expedition, also recognised the extraordinary achievement and was generous enough to applaud the feat. It was a highly satisfactory moment for Fuchs and Wordie. Fuchs remembered: 'I have always thought it to his credit that Brian [Roberts] was gracious enough to tell me that he felt the TAE had, after all, enhanced the British presence in Antarctica.'[14]

The consolation for Wordie was somewhat more tangible: his scientific judgement on the Antarctic was proved correct. Wordie had long held the belief that the eastern side of the fearsome Weddell Sea offered the best access route to the Antarctic mainland around the Vahsel Bay and Coats Land areas. Using his knowledge and experience of the sea ice, Wordie influenced Fuchs' decision to establish his Weddell Sea base at Vahsel Bay.

In the same year he placed his judgement even more on the line by persuading Britain's IGY committee to build Halley Bay Station to the east, about 250 miles (400 km) further along the coast on the Brunt Ice Shelf in Coats Land. Halley Station exists to this day and most notably it was the site where in 1985 British scientists first measured the ozone depletion of the stratosphere above the Antarctic.

It was, appropriately, Wordie's last official association with the Polar territories. It helped establish the largest multi-national programme of scientific endeavour ever put together in the Antarctic. Or, as one observer noted, the IGY operation represented the 'single most significant peaceful activity of mankind since the Renaissance'.

Although accomplished in the modern mechanised age, the Fuchs trans-continental crossing was firmly rooted in the Antarctic's heroic age forty to fifty years earlier and with a huge amount of luck might have been accomplished by Shackleton's expedition. Halley Station, in contrast, represented the modern, scientific era of exploration. The link between the two ages was Wordie, the consummate explorer scientist.

The Polar regions were not the scene of Wordie's final role in public life. His rich and varied life ended, where it began, in academic circles. It is a remarkable fact that while he was coping with the major challenges at the RGS and SPRI, Wordie was simultaneously enjoying a rapid advancement in his status at St John's, Cambridge. Even into his sixties, Wordie remained a driven man.

Wordie first arrived at St John's in 1910 as a 21-year-old mature student and remained at the college until 1959. He was elected a Fellow in 1923 and made Senior Tutor in 1933 at the height of his prominence as an explorer. By 1950, Wordie had advanced to President of the college and was also co-opted to several of the University's powerful bodies like the Council of Senate and General Board.

The next obvious step was to become Master of the College, though Wordie was initially reluctant to make the move. He turned down an earlier invitation, perhaps because of his wide-ranging commitments at the RGS and SPRI. However he received a further call in 1952 following the death of the distinguished Master, E.A. Benians. With reluctance he allowed his name to go forward. A tense vote followed and Wordie made it to the summit of St John's, winning the election by a single vote from the eminent scientist, Sir James Cockcroft, who had been a personal scientific adviser to Churchill during the war.

The curiosity was that Wordie, as President, was officially in charge of the arcane election process, which involved the Fellows of the college locking themselves in the Chapel until a winner was declared. Two ballots resulted in a dead heat between Wordie and Cockcroft and Wordie solemnly called a thirty-minute break before taking the final vote. During this interval one unidentified Fellow changed allegiance, resulting in Wordie winning the election by a single vote. When the counting was finished, President Wordie announced with a straight face: 'It seems as if I have to declare myself elected as Master.'[15]

An immediate consequence was that Wordie and Gertrude vacated their large home in Grange Road after twenty-eight years and moved into the imposing grandeur of the Master's Lodge at St John's.

His period as Master saw some significant changes at St John's, though many regard his assured handling of the college's financial affairs as being his biggest success. This included a highly successful fund-raising exercise which resulted in the Cripps Foundation donating substantial sums to the college.

The Cripps family had made their fortune in the Midlands motor components industry and responded warmly to Wordie's initial appeal in 1956 for funds to repair and expand college buildings. It turned out to be a huge donation. The work was originally estimated at £500,000 (about £7,000,000 in today's terms) and the Cripps family initially agreed to provide £75,000 for the proposed new buildings. The association with Cripps was hugely beneficial for the college and the when the new Cripps Building was finally opened in 1967, the family had contributed a substantial slice of the eventual cost of £1,200,000 (approximately £13,000,000 today).

However Wordie's mastership was not universally popular. Concise and highly-opinionated, Wordie was a formidable presence at the committee table and his reputation for intrigue was seen as positively Machiavellian by the Fellows. He was cautious, conservative and distinctly old-school in an era when many long-standing social values were being challenged by younger reformers. Some colleagues found him slightly unapproachable and someone who kept himself to himself. 'Not clubbable', was one verdict, though the Master by tradition is invariably detached from the ranks. Debenham, who knew Wordie intimately for much of his adult life, once wrote: 'His only fault is ambition.' Another who suffered at the hands of Wordie's scheming cheerfully branded him a 'subterranean bugger'.

A major cause of concern was Wordie's dictatorial style of steamrollering issues through committee regardless of the debate. It was a style first aired in the debating rooms of Glasgow Academy half a century earlier and grimly familiar to those who came into contact with Wordie at the RGS and SPRI. Critics insisted that he was better at deciding on a line of action than on justifying the argument. Fuchs, who was close to Wordie for almost four decades, recalled his unusual technique around the committee table:

He did not often take much part in the discussions, but allowed others to argue. Then he would rather abruptly say, 'Well, we've said enough about that – next item.' Protests at being cut short did not prevail.

At the next meeting, one found that he had personally written the Minutes which represented his views of what the discussions should have led to!

So it was that he almost invariably had his way.[16]

It was not surprising, Fuchs conceded, that some considered him to be 'a little bit authoritarian'.

Another slight cause of tension was his legendary frugality. Wordie never forgot the strict lessons of Scottish prudence handed down by his father, and one episode from St John's typified his behaviour. Shortly after being elected Master, Wordie was asked to follow the college tradition and sit for a portrait, which would hang alongside paintings of earlier Masters. The canny Wordie quickly saw an opportunity to kill two birds with one stone. He already possessed a portrait of himself, painted by Rodrigo Moynihan, a well-known former war artist. The problem was that Wordie thought Moynihan's work was unflattering. He promptly sold the painting to St John's for an undisclosed sum of money and the portrait still hangs on the walls inside the college.[17]

However, the austere façade masked a more complex and often misunderstood individual. Despite his acute intelligence and formidable reputation, Wordie never overcame an innate shyness which often made him hard to fathom. Those who knew him best liked him best. He never sought publicity or fame, even when involved in high-profile undertakings like *Endurance* or Everest. The press was an irritant and he was happiest when remaining in the background, a trait which some critics may have misinterpreted as being brusque and uncommunicative.

A modern-day adventurer with the same impressive record would be a household name and media personality. But the reserved, cautious Wordie would have disliked the present-day cult of the celebrity and the penchant for instant judgements. He was a man of few words, although colleagues remember that what he said was generally worth listening to. He put little in writing, preferring where possible to speak privately and to deliver a verdict in his soft Glaswegian brogue which, in spite of living in Cambridge for fifty years, he never lost. As one colleague remembered, 'Wordie's utterances were always brief and to the point.'

Two other factors worked against Wordie's later career at St John's. On the one hand he was not happy with the bureaucratic responsibilities of being Master. Wordie was not a natural administrator and always seemed to be surrounded by a chaotic muddle of books and papers. 'He appeared to have no filing system,' one associate remembered. But he had a gift for somehow always finding the document he needed amidst the heaps.

His idiosyncratic methods were demonstrated in the early 1950s when he handed over his tutoring responsibilities upon being elected to the Mastership. Standing alongside his successor, Wordie went through the list of names of all his students and described them tersely as either 'a good man' or alternatively 'a strange man'.

The other major issue was his declining health. Wordie was only a few weeks short of his sixty-third birthday when he became Master and his term was marked by increasing bouts of debilitating illness. SPRI's Bertram, who was recruited to St John's by Wordie, recorded his memories of his time as Master. He wrote:

> I think that during his mastership his wits were already failing, more than he realised. He relied, in Council meetings, very largely upon the President, his number 2, in a way not in accordance with St John's customs.[18]

A year later, in September 1959, Wordie stood down as Master of St John's, the last official post he ever held.

CHAPTER 20

THE FINAL
DAYS

THE LAST YEARS OF WORDIE'S LIFE WERE OCCASIONALLY DIFFICULT, with his health failing and the reins of power slipping slowly from his grasp. The consolation was a widespread recognition of his outstanding contribution to the world's understanding of Polar territories.

Oddly enough, the retirement from St John's left Wordie in the unusual position of being homeless. In spite of his fine grasp of business affairs, Wordie never owned a single property in his life and had lived in a succession of homes rented from Cambridge University. The predicament was such that in 1959 Wordie and Gertrude moved into the University Arms Hotel, where they spent a year in cramped quarters before moving into a small flat in Grange Road, near Coton End, the old family home.

The honours, in particular, flowed thick and fast. As early as 1947 he was given the CBE – Commander of the Order of the British Empire – and this was followed by a further accolade in 1957 when he was knighted by the Queen for his services to Britain's Polar activities. Others in the Polar field also recognised his great contribution.

The Royal Geographical Society gave Wordie the Back Grant in 1920 and the Founder's Medal in 1933; the Royal Society of Edinburgh awarded him the Bruce Medal in 1926; and the Royal Scottish Geographical Society presented him with the Gold Medal in 1944. Strangely enough, he was never awarded the Polar Medal for his exceptional record of eight separate expeditions to the Arctic regions. His only Polar Medal arose from his first Antarctic journey in *Endurance*.

Recognition also came from abroad where, significantly, he was elevated alongside some of the greatest figures from the history of Polar exploration. Most notably, the American Geographical Society gave Wordie the Charles Daly Gold Medal in 1952 for services to both Arctic and Antarctic exploration. He was in illustrious company, since previous Daly gold medallists included Amundsen, Koch and Peary.

An unexpected honour came from Norway, where King Haakon personally awarded Wordie the Order of St Olav, the rough equivalent of a CBE in Britain. The medal, which was also given to Glen and Rudmose Brown, is rarely given to foreigners; it was given to Wordie in London in 1943 during Haakon's five-year exile in London while Norway was occupied by Germany.

Hilmar Reksten, the colourful Norwegian shipping magnate, personally recommended the honour for Wordie, Glen and Rudmose Brown. He urged King Haakon to reward their extensive geological, topographical and other scientific work in Spitsbergen between the wars. Reksten said the work had been of 'great importance' to Norway.

What Wordie did not know was that the Norwegian authorities had turned down an earlier recommendation to honour him. Wordie's name was submitted to King Haakon in 1936 but Dr Hoel, a senior Norwegian scientist, blocked the award by telling the king that Britain had not done enough to recognise the research work of Norway's scientists. Reksten rejected his fellow-countryman's accusation and said Hoel probably meant 'insufficient British recognition of himself'.

At home Wordie also received honorary degrees from the universities of Glasgow and Hull and in 1954 he was made an Honorary Fellow of Dublin's Trinity College. The Glasgow Academy, his early school, saluted a famous ex-pupil by making him an Honorary Governor. Another unusual honour came in 1954 when the authorities decided to make a grand gesture by allowing the 65-year-old to say his final farewell to the Polar regions.

The opportunity for a nostalgic last journey arose through his important links with the British North Greenland Expedition under Commander Jim Simpson in 1952–4. Simpson, who was trying to rekindle naval interest in Arctic exploration, turned to Wordie for advice in the late 1940s and found a generous supporter of his scheme. Before long Wordie was installed as vice-chairman of the expedition committee under Sir Algernon Willis, Admiral of the Fleet. Wordie's guidance was crucial and Simpson recalled: 'His wise advice and personal support were invaluable to me. He always seemed to know just the right people, to whom he introduced me, and it was largely due to him that I was able to meet and interest all kinds of influential backers and so eventually to get the enterprise airborne.'[1]

It was probably at the initiative of Simpson that Wordie was invited to make a flying visit to the expedition's field headquarters at Britannia Lake in Greenland on 6 August 1954. 'He was only able to remain for a few hours as the expedition was in the process of being finally evacuated by RAF flying boats,' Simpson remembered many years later. 'I suppose this may possibly have been the last time that he personally took part in an Arctic expedition.' Wordie's brief visit to the Arctic was, indeed, the last time he saw the Polar landscape. By coincidence, it was precisely forty years to the month since *Endurance* sailed from Britain.

Wordie's private life changed little in the later years. He continued regular walking, climbing and stalking – he was an expert marksman – in the Scottish hills well into his fifties and sixties until ill health intervened. His major recreation was the distinctive and ancient game of real tennis, where his major challenge was to find suitable opponents.

His long association with Scottish mountaineering, which dated back to his school days in Glasgow, was capped by his appointment in 1953 as chairman of the British Mountaineering Council. At the same time his influential role in the successful first ascent of Everest led to his appointment as chairman of the Mount Everest Foundation, the charitable body which was set up from the residue of the expedition's funds and since 1954 has awarded approximately £750,000 in grants to climbers.

Wordie's other passion was collecting books, a trait which he also inherited from his father. He built a substantial library of Polar books, which by the late 1950s was probably the most comprehensive library of Polar literature in private hands. The collection extended to almost 4,600 volumes and covered a wide range of Antarctic and Arctic material from the eighteenth through to the twentieth century, including many valuable first editions and rare foreign-language books. At first the books and papers were spread unceremoniously across the family home or in his cluttered rooms at St John's College. In 1959, at the age of seventy, Wordie decided that the vast collection had finally outgrown his resources and he generously donated it to the National Library of Scotland in Edinburgh, where the books can be found to this day.

There are several permanent memorials to Wordie, who is one of the very few Polar explorers to be commemorated with landmarks in both the Arctic and Antarctic. The most prominent is the Wordie Ice Shelf (69° 15′ S, 67° 45′ W) in the Antarctic, a magnificent glacier which pours into the south-east part of Marguerite Bay between Cape Berteaux and Mount Edgell along the west cost of Graham Land. It was discovered by Rymill's party during the 1934–7 expedition but later investigations showed it to be a confluent glacier and not an ice shelf.

Mawson's *Banzare* expedition between 1929–31 named the Wordie Nunatak (66° 16′ S, 51° 31′ E) near Mount Biscoe and Mount Hurley, and Wordie Point (56° 44′ S, 27° 15′ W) is the south-west tip of Visokoi Island in the South Sandwich Islands, which was charted in 1930 by members of *Discovery II*. In the Arctic, Wordie Bay (approximately 68° N, 73° W) can be found off the west coast of Baffin Island and Wordie's Bugt (approximately 74° 04′ N, 22° 24′ W) lies in the Svarlbard archipelago. The Wordie Glacier (74° 15′ N, 23° 03′ W) flows into the head of the bay. A little farther north at 78° 40′ N, 16° 39′ W lies the mountain region of Wordiekammen.

A posthumous honour, which would have tickled Wordie's wry sense of humour, came in 1980 when his face appeared on a special issue of stamps to commemorate the 150th anniversary of the Royal Geographical Society. He was one of six former RGS Presidents depicted in the selection and he stood alongside some of the most famous names in British Polar exploration, including Sir John Barrow, Sir Clements Markham and his old friend, Sir Raymond Priestley. Wordie would have been especially intrigued to note that the stamp's design did not portray an image from his most famous exploits on *Endurance* or any of his eight voyages to the Arctic. Instead, the stamp featured Fuchs's Commonwealth Trans-Antarctic Expedition – the enterprise so strongly opposed by senior figures at the RGS and the source of so much acrimony within the Polar community.

A different type of memorial was Wordie's extraordinary contribution to British Polar exploration. He was, arguably, the biggest single influence in keeping British interest in the Polar regions active between the two wars and in ensuring that centuries of traditional British influence in the area did not come to an end. In some ways he was a latter-day Sir John Barrow or Sir Clements Markham, the early architects of Polar exploration, though Wordie did not have the same official powers as either man.

Equally important was his role as mentor to a whole new generation of young explorers, who were picked from the universities to be the next ambassadors of the country's Polar heritage. It was Wordie who fostered the burgeoning careers of men like Fuchs, Courtauld and Watkins and it is a powerful testament to his influence that few embarked on a voyage to the Arctic or Antarctic without first consulting Wordie. What they discovered was an enormously generous person, always ready to dispense advice and wisdom or to tap into his unparalleled network of Polar contacts. He was, said one who remembered him well, 'a generous spirit'.

However, Wordie came under increasing strain from ill health as he entered the later stages of his life. By the mid 1950s, he was suffering from difficulties with his prostate gland and underwent major surgery in 1957. Although the operation was a success, the side effects were uncomfortable and disruptive. Further complications set in and in 1958 the 69-year-old Wordie underwent further surgery of having a kidney removed. His last years were often painful and uncomfortable, particularly the last two years. A stroke robbed him of the power of speech and by the late 1950s, as he approached his seventies, Wordie was confined to a wheelchair or forced to remain in bed for much of the day at his home in Cambridge.

Wordie, a prodigious traveller all his life, made his final journey in February 1959. Despite much discomfort, he insisted on travelling to Switzerland for the marriage of his youngest son, Peter, to Alice de Haller. But to his utter dismay, Wordie was not fit enough to attend the wedding of Alison, his youngest daughter, in 1961. The heart problem first detected by the Harley Street doctors in 1921 was an early indication of arterial sclerosis – hardening of the arteries – which became steadily more debilitating.

Gertrude, his wife for almost four decades, was a tower of strength, nursing and comforting him through his final days. His condition worsened in early 1962 and Gertrude, supported by their eldest daughter, Elizabeth, waited anxiously at his bedside in Cambridge.

On 16 January a strong wintry gale was battering his home, the cold driving wind rattling the windows. It was a familiar symphony for the old explorer, and at the height of the storm James Wordie suffered a massive heart attack and died, aged 72.

CHRONOLOGY:
JAMES MANN WORDIE
1889–1962

1889	April 26	Born at 4 Buckingham Terrace, Glasgow, son of John Wordie and Jane Catherine Mann
1894		Attends Westbourne School for Girls, Hyndland, Glasgow
1897		Attends Glasgow Academy
1903		First Alpine climb in Switzerland
1906		Attends Glasgow University
1910		Gains BSc and MA with distinction in Geology Attends St John's College, Cambridge as advanced student
1912		Gains 1st Degree in Natural Sciences
1914		Joins Sir Ernest Shackleton's Imperial Trans-Antarctic Expedition 1914–17
	September 19	Sails in *La Negra* from Liverpool to Buenos Aires to meet *Endurance*
	December 5	*Endurance* leaves South Georgia
1915	January 19	*Endurance* trapped in the ice of Weddell Sea
	February 22	*Endurance* reaches furthest south, 77° S

	October 27	*Endurance* abandoned and camp built on ice-floe
	November 21	*Endurance* sinks
1916	April 9	Lifeboats sail for Elephant Island
	April 15	Party reaches Elephant Island
	April 24	Shackleton and five others leave Elephant Island to sail the *James Caird* to South Georgia
	August 30	Party of 22 rescued from Elephant Island at fourth attempt
	September 3	Survivors arrive at Punta Arenas, Chile
	November	Arrives back in Britain
1917	February	Awarded Silver Antarctic Medal
	May	Appointed 2nd Lieutenant 3/4th Lowland Brigade, Royal Field Artillery
1918	April	Wounded near Armentieres during Battle of Lys Appointed Lecturer in Geology Department, Cambridge University
1919	May-September	Joins Bruce's Scottish Spitsbergen Expedition
1920	May-September	Joins second Scottish Spitsbergen Expedition Awarded Back Grant by Royal Geographical Society
1921	July-September	Sails to Jan Mayen Island Makes first ascent of Beerenberg Elected Fellow, St John's College, Cambridge

1923		Appointed Tutor, St John's College, Cambridge
	March 21	Marries Gertrude Henderson at St Columba's Church, London
	June-September	Leads expedition to East Greenland Appointed to Discovery Committee
1924	January 15	John Wordie, son, born
1925	October 14	Elizabeth Wordie, daughter, born
1926	June-September	Leads expedition to East Greenland
	October	Awarded Bruce Medal by Royal Society of Edinburgh
1927	July 12	George Wordie, son, born
1929	February 24	Alison Wordie, daughter, born
	June-September	Leads expedition to East Greenland Climbs Petermann Peak
1932		Peter Wordie, son, born
1933		Awarded Founder's Medal by Royal Geographical Society
1934		Appointed Honorary Secretary Royal Geographical Society
	June-September	Leads expedition to West Greenland and Baffin Bay
1937		Appointed Chairman of Scott Polar Research Institute
	June-September	Leads expedition to Greenland and Canadian Arctic
1939		Seconded to Naval Intelligence (Polar Regions), Cambridge

1943		Joins Operation Tabarin
1944		Awarded Gold Medal by Royal Scottish Geographical Society
1946		Sails to Antarctic dependencies
1947	January 20	Re-visits Elephant Island
		Awarded Commander of British Empire (CBE)
1948		Elected to Council of Senate, Cambridge University
1949		Appointed Chairman of UK Committee for the 1949–52 Norwegian-British-Swedish Expedition to the Antarctic
1950	November	Elected President, St John's College, Cambridge
1951		Elected President of the Royal Geographical Society
1952		Elected Master, St John's College, Cambridge
		Awarded Charles Daly Medal by American Geographical Society
		Vice-chairman of Everest Committee
1953		Elected chairman of British Mountaineering Council
1954		Appointed Honorary Fellow, Trinity College, Dublin
		Last voyage to polar territories, visiting British North Greenland Expedition at Britannia Lake
1955		Appointed vice-chairman of the Committee for Commonwealth Trans-

Antarctic Expedition under Vivian Fuchs,
1955–58
Appointed Chairman of British National
Committee for International Geophysical
Year
Leaves Scott Polar Research Institute

1957	January 1	Receives Knighthood for services to polar exploration and research
1959		Retires as Master of St John's College, Cambridge
1962	January 16	Dies at Grange Road, Cambridge, aged 72 Ashes interred in the Wordie family lair at the burial ground of the Church of the Holy Rude, Stirling

REFERENCES

Chapter 1

1. A fuller history of the family business, Wordie & Co., can be found in Edward Paget-Tomlinson, *The Railway Carriers* (Terence Dalton, 1990)
2. Alison Stancer (née Wordie), personal recollection
3. Alexander Mann's son, Sir James Mann, became Director of the Wallace Collection and Surveyor of the Royal Works of Art and his daughter, Mary Gow, was a recognised water-colourist
4. Glasgow Academy Roll Book/Honour List, (GA)
5. James Wordie, diary June–August 1903
6. John Wordie, letter to James Mann Wordie, 20 June, 1906

Chapter 2

1. Inventory and will of John Wordie and Jane Wordie (NAS)
2. James Wordie, letter to Alison Wordie, 7 September 1913

Chapter 3

1. Margery & James Fisher, *Shackleton,* p. 125
2. James Wordie, Weddell Sea Log, 27 September 1914
3. Robert Mossman, *The Times,* 5 January 1914
4. Peter Speak, *William Speirs Bruce,* p. 124
5. Sir Ernest Shackleton, *Geographical Journal*, Vol. 43, 1914
6. Sir James Mann Wordie, *The Eagle,* June 1962
7. Wordie, Weddell Sea Log, 4 November 1914

Chapter 4

1. James Wordie, Weddell Sea Log, 26 October 1914
2. James Wordie, letter to Margery Fisher, 6 March 1957 (SPRI)
3. Wordie, Weddell Sea Log, 20 October 1914
4. Wordie, 24 October 1914

5. Wordie, 26 October 1914
6. Wordie, 5 December 1914
7. Wordie, 29 January 1915
8. Wordie, 3 April 1915
9. Wordie, 3 April 1915

CHAPTER 5

1. James and Margery Fisher, *Shackleton*, p. 312
2. Reginald James, letter to Hugh R. Mill, 12 May, 1922 (SPRI)
3. James Wordie, letter to Margery Fisher, 6 March 1957 (SPRI)
4. Thomas Orde-Lees, Trans-Antarctic Expedition Diary, 16 October 1915 (SPRI)
5. *Ibid.*
6. James Wordie, Weddell Sea Log, 28 April 1915
7. Wordie, 20 April 1915
8. Wordie, 17 September 1915
9. Wordie, 25 October 1915
10. Wordie, 27 October 1915
11. Frank Worsley, *Endurance* Journal, 27 October 1915 (SPRI)
12. Wordie, 27 October 1915
13. Wordie, 30 October 1915
14. Wordie, 31 October 1915
15. Wordie, 1 November 1915
16. Wordie, 21 November 1915
17. Wordie, 29 December 1915
18. Wordie, 14 January 1916
19. Wordie, 2 February 1916
20. Wordie, 9 October 1914
21. Alexander Macklin, letter to James Wordie, 10 June 1933
22. Wordie, 27 March 1915
23. Wordie, 22 March 1916
24. Frank Worsley, 'Paper on Animals Killed in the Weddell Sea'
25. Wordie, 6 April 1915
26. Wordie, 9 April 1915

Chapter 6

1. James Wordie, Weddell Sea Log, 10 April 1916

2. Wordie, 16 April 1916
3. *Ibid.*
4. Geoffrey Hattersley-Smith, personal recollection of Walter How; interview with author, 2003
5. Wordie, 21 April 1916
6. *Ibid.*
7. James Wordie, Geological Observations in the Weddell Sea Area (RSE/NLS)
8. Wordie, 21 April 1916
9. Wordie, 25 April 1916
10. Thomas Orde-Lees, diary, 24 April 1916 (SPRI)
11. Wordie, 25 April 1916

Chapter 7

1. James Wordie, Weddell Sea Log, 26 April 1916
2. Wordie, 2 May 1916
3. Leif Mills, *Frank Wild*, p. 249
4. Wordie, 5 June 1916
5. *Daily Chronicle*, 6 May 1916
6. Wordie, 5 June 1916
7. William Bakewell, Unpublished autobiography
8. Wordie, 25 July 1916
9. Wordie, 25 August 1916
10. Wordie, 29 August 1916
11. Wordie, 30 August 1916

Chapter 8

1. Sir Ernest Shackleton, Arrangements for Dealing With and Publishing the Scientific Results, 7 October 1916
2. Papers on the Imperial Trans-Antarctic Expedition:
   James Wordie, 'The Drift of the Endurance', read at the RGS on December 17 1917 and published by the *Geographical Journal*, Vol. 51, April 1918
   — 'Geological Observations in the Weddell Sea Area', Royal Society of Edinburgh Vol. 53, Part I, No. 2, 1921
   — 'Depths and Deposits of the Weddell Sea', Royal Society of Edinburgh, Vol. 52 Part IV, No. 30, 1921

— 'The Natural History of Pack-Ice as observed in the Weddell Sea', Royal Society of Edinburgh, Vol. 52, Part IV, No. 31, 1921

— 'Ross Sea Drift of the *Aurora* in 1915–17', *Geographical Journal*, Vol. 58, 1921

Reginald James, 'Antarctic Pack-Ice and the fate of the *Endurance*', *Discovery*, Vol. 4, No 46, 1923

— Some Problems Relating to Antarctic Sea-Ice, *Memoirs and Proceedings*, Manchester Literary and Philosophical Society, Vol. 68, Part I, No. 7, 1924

Richard Mossman, 'Meteorological Results of Shackleton Antarctic Expedition', 1914–17, *Quarterly Journal, Royal Meteorological Society*, Vol. 47, 1921

See also: Sir Ernest Shackleton, *South*, Edinburgh, Birlinn, 2001

3. Sir James Wordie: 'Profile', *The New Scientist*, 5 December 1957

4. Wordie, hand-written note on Imperial Trans-Antarctic Expedition diaries (undated)

5. Peter Wordie, interview with the author, 2003

6. Wordie, Notes on Visit to the Falklands Islands Dependencies Survey, 1947

7. James and Margery Fisher, *Shackleton*, p. 390

8. *Daily Chronicle*, 4 September 1916

9. Wordie, 'Frank Wild Obituary', *Geographical Journal*

10. Alfred Lansing, *Endurance,* p. 7

11. Wordie, inscription in personal copy of *Endurance* by Alfred Lansing

12. Geoffrey Hattersley-Smith: personal recollection of Walter How, interview with author, 2003

Chapter 9

1. H.J. Dawson, War Office memo, 7 December 1916 (NA)

2. James Wordie to Arthur Hinks, 21 December 1935 (RGS)

3. Wordie to Hinks, 21 February 1918 (RGS)

4. Wordie to Hinks, 8 May 1918 (RGS)

Chapter 10

1. Frank Debenham, *The Quiet Land*, p. 178

2. James Wordie, letter to Sir Ernest Shackleton, 3 February 1920

3. Wordie, diary, 17 July 1919
4. Wordie, diary, 6 August 1919
5. Peter Speak, *The Scottish Spitsbergen Syndicate*
6. *Ibid.*

Chapter 11

1. Sir Ernest Shackleton, letter to The Admiralty, 24 September 1920 (NA)
2. James Wordie, letter to Hugh R. Mill, 6 July 1921
3. Paul-Louis Mercanton, *The First Ascent of the Beerenberg*
4. Wordie, diary, 12 August 1921
5. Mercanton
6. Wordie, diary, 6 August 1921
7. Wordie, telegram to RGS, 12 September 1921
8. *The Times,* 31 October 1921

Chapter 12

1. James Wordie, letter to A.R. Hinks, 6 November 1921(RGS)
2. Wordie, Weddell Sea Log, 15 June 1915
3. Wordie, 28 April 1915
4. D.A. Allan, 'James Mann Wordie: Obituary', *Royal Society of Edinburgh Year Book*, 1961–2
5. For a fuller account of this period see: John Wright, 'British Polar Expeditions 1919–39', *Polar Record*, Vol. 26 (157), 1990
6. Terence Armstrong, 'Sir James Mann Wordie: Obituary', *Arctic,* Vol. 15, No. 2, 1962
7. J. Gordon Hayes, *The Conquest of the North Pole*, p. 202
8. A.R. Glen, *Young Men in the Arctic*, p. 20
9. Sir James Mann Wordie: 'Profile', *The New Scientist,* 5 December 1957

Chapter 13

1. James Wordie, record of conversation with James Fisher, 10 July 1956 (SPRI)
2. Emily Shackleton, letter to Wordie, 7 March 1922
3. Wordie, J. 'Sir Ernest Shackleton, Obituary', *Geographical Journal*, Vol. 59 No. 3, 1922
4. Wordie, letter to Hugh Mill, 15 May 1922 (SPRI)

5. James Wordie, diary, 28 July 1923
6. Wordie, diary, 31 August 1923
7. Wordie, J. *Geographical Journal*, September 1927
8. Walt Unsworth, *Everest: The Mountaineering History*, p. 31
9. Frank Worsley, letter to Wordie, 3 April 1923 (NLS)

Chapter 14

1. Tom Longstaff, *This Is My Voyage*
2. *Geographical Journal*, September, 1927
3. John Ridgway, *Gino Watkins*, p. 25

Chapter 15

1. James Wordie, diary, 3 August 1929
2. Vivian Fuchs, *A Time To Speak*, p. 53
3. Wordie, diary, 6 August 1929
4. Fuchs, East Greenland Expedition Journal, 10 August 1929
5. Nicholas Wollaston, *The Man on the Ice Cap*, p. 84
6. Fuchs, *A Time To Speak*, p. 56
7. Fuchs, Journal, 15 August 1929
8. Fuchs, Journal, 16 August 1929
9. Fuchs, *A Time to Speak*, p. 58
10. Fuchs, A Personal Recollection of James Mann Wordie
11. *Geographical Journal*, No. 6, June 1930

Chapter 16

1. James Wordie, diary, 18 June 1934
2. *Geographical Journal*, October 1935

Chapter 17

1. James Wordie, correspondence with Captain Kenneth Mackenzie, 1937
2. Tom Lethbridge, letter to James Wordie, January 1938
3. Wordie, letter to Henry Lewin, 21 December 1925 (NLS)
4. Wordie, letter to Lewin, 28 January 1926 (NLS)
5. *Geographical Journal*, Vol. 86, 1937
6. Wordie, diary 26 August 1937

7. Wordie, letter to Hugh R. Mill, 1 March 1942 (SPRI)
8. Wordie, telegram to Arthur Hinks, 20 September 1937

Chapter 18

1. *Geographical Journal*, July 1987
2. *Geographical Journal*, July 1987
3. Neil Mackintosh, The Future of the Discovery Committee, 11 October 1943 (NLS)
4. Tony Daltry, personal recollection of James Wordie
5. David James, *Scott of the Antarctic: The Film and its Production*, p. 52
6. James Wordie, Weddell Sea Log, 20 January 1915
7. Wordie, letter to Hugh Mill, 20 January 1947
8. Wordie, diary, 20 January 1947
9. *Ibid.*
10. Wordie, Notes on a Visit to the Falkland Islands Dependencies, 1947
11. *Ibid.*
12. Wordie, diary, 20 January 1947
13. Wordie, Notes on a Visit to the Falkland Islands Dependencies, 1947
14. Wordie, letter to Hugh Mill, 20 January 1947

Chapter 19

1. Peter Steele, *Eric Shipton – Everest and Beyond*, p. 133
2. Peter Wordie, personal recollection of James Wordie, interview with author, 2002
3. Steele, pp. 196–8
4. Scott Polar Research Institute, Committee of Management papers (BAS)
5. Frank Debenham, *The Quiet Land*, p. 193
6. James Wordie, letter to American Geographical Society, 2 April 1929 (NLS)
7. Geoffrey Hattersley-Smith, personal recollection of James Wordie, interview with author, 2002
8. James Wordie, letter to Professor J.A. Steers, 31 May, 1957 (BAS)
9. Wordie, to Professor J.A. Steers, 31 May 1957 (BAS)

10. Sir Vivian Fuchs, letter to Scott Polar Research Institute, 27 January 1988 (PF)
11. Peter Wordie, personal recollection of Sir Vivian Fuchs
12. Colin Bertram, letter to James Wordie, 25 October 1955 (BAS)
13. Bertram, letter to Vivian Fuchs, 22 April 1955 (BAS)
14. Fuchs to Scott Polar Research Institute, 27 January 1988 (PF)
15. Professor John Crook, personal recollection of James Wordie, 2003
16. Sir Vivian Fuchs, personal recollection of James Wordie, 1994
17. Crook, 2003
18. Colin Bertram, personal recollections of James Wordie, 1994

Chapter 20

1. Jim Simpson, correspondence re James Wordie, 1998–2000

APPENDIX
JAMES MANN WORDIE
WEDDELL SEA LOG,
1914–16

NOTE: THIS IS AN ABRIDGED VERSION OF THE DIARY OF JAMES WORDIE, which opens on 27 September 1914 and closes on 1 December 1916. Entries were not made daily and events of several days or weeks are often encapsulated into a single entry. The grammar, punctuation and spelling have been faithfully reproduced.

Items in brackets [ ] have been added for explanatory purposes.

James Mann Wordie sailed from Liverpool on 19 September 1914 in the *La Negra* and arrived in Buenos Aires on 10 October to join the *Endurance,* which had left England in early August. *Endurance* departed from Buenos Aires on 26 October and reached South Georgia on 5 November. After a month of preparation, *Endurance* sailed from Grytviken for the Weddell Sea on 5 December 1914.

5 December, 1914. A dull morning gradually cleared into a fine day as we steamed south eastwards. A northerly breeze has sprung up and our square sails were accordingly hoisted. We bowl along at a good pace therefore and feel that as regards weather we are very lucky.

6 December. An uneventful day. During the night the wind stiffened, so that when I went to take my turn at the wheel from 4–6 am there was a big following sea. Steering was pretty difficult. The noon position was Lat. 56° 36′ S, Long. 32° 36′ W: this represents a run of 182 miles since noon yesterday to which has to be added 24 miles done yesterday morning; i.e. 206 since leaving Grytviken.

7 December. On leaving South Georgia a course was followed which would have led to our passing south of Thule Island, the most southerly of the

Sandwich Group. However there have been fears lest the pack should be met north of that latitude, and, that, in adopting a more westerly course, should such have been the case, we might not easily find a way among the almost uncharted Sandwich Group. Hence at 6.0 pm last night our course was changed to a more easterly direction, so that we should pass through the Group between Saunders and Candlemas Islands, the latter the more northerly of the two.

Yesterday's moderate gale still blows and sends us bowling along. The day's run was very good again – 190 miles. At noon the water temperature was as low as 30° F.

[Tom] Crean was on the wheel during the 1st Dog and it was my duty to relieve him while he went in to tea. It was about now that we entered the real pack ice; very loose pack of course, but it meant continual alteration of the course.

8 December. As a result of the manoeuvres last night the day's run has only advanced us eastwards. Our position at noon was Lat. 57° 7′ S, Long. 25° 1′ W: That is to say a little further north than at the same time yesterday.

A new amusement was started this evening – firing short 1 ft arrows at passing whales. The date, etc, is scratched on the arrow just before it is fired off from the gun; the object of course is to learn something about whale migration if possible.

9 December. When I turned out at eight it was to find an almost calm sea, leaden in colour; no large icebergs were in sight, only small pieces. The wind had practically dropped and under sail were hardly making more than one knot. [Robert] Clark took the chance of lowering a net to 40 fathoms before breakfast and made a good haul. The water temp. at noon today was only 32° F. This, taken with the small number of bergs, may mean that the pack is very far to the south on this longitude.

The day's run was 92 miles. Probably these ninety odd miles were got with only one ton of coal consumption. The 'Endurance' gets more speed proportionate to the coal consumption than any ship that has hitherto gone South – never more than about 4 tons a day when at full speed.

(Later) The unexpected has happened – we have encountered the pack once more. There was a feeling of absolute silence; snow was falling; and there we stood, the strangers to such sights on the after deck, the old hands forward at the bridge.

11 December. We avoided the pack; it proved a wise move for in the next 30 hours we were able to make a SSE course in absolutely clear water. The day's run (Dec 10th) was good – 125 miles. We lowered the old Grytviken pram from the rigging this morning and Chippy [Harry McNish] has already set to repair it; it will probably be an entirely new boat by the time he is done.

13 December. There has sometimes been difficulty at the wheel in hearing orders on the bridge, more especially when the dogs are barking. A small telephone was proposed, but found impracticable. Chippy however got over the difficulty by putting a semaphore-like erection on the bridge; and now all shouting, to and from the wheel has stopped.

We are all very pleased with the progress that has been made and moreover there are one or two other signs that open water may not be far off.

14 December. Between 5 and 6 in the morning the ship was almost held up by what the Boss [Sir Ernest Shackleton] takes to be bay ice. He takes it to be bay ice which has broken out this season; but this seems almost impossible: I think myself that it broke out last season, probably in March; this would accord well with the drift of Filchner's ship 'Deutschland' which started to drift north in March and took nine months to reach these latitudes.

15 December. Bad fortune has been our lot today. The going all yesterday afternoon was pretty heavy, though there were some good leads after supper; between nine and ten at night however a strong wind blew up – about 25 mph – which has blown ever since; the policy therefore has been not to advance into the ice, but merely to keep the ship head on to the wind; consequently we no longer move relatively to the pack round about, but drift with it, in this case about 10 miles NW for tho' 6 miles is the net loss. It is singularly annoying to have to remain stationery like this all day but there is no other course till the wind goes down.

16 December. What I myself saw when I came up deck was a sight not soon to be forgotten. In the foreground loose floe and leads of blue water. Such a day was not to be lost. [Frank] Hurley had his cinema going almost all day on the foreyard. At about 8.15 pm we got clear of the pack; from the crow's nest no ice is to be seen to the south. One goes to bed in high spirits.

17 December. Last night's hopeful outlook proved in the end a trap; by 9.0 pm we were in pretty thick ice once more. The ice opened out again about 4.30 and the Boss directing matters from the bridge, she has forged ahead pretty steadily since then.

I must confess not to be able to understand the meaning of these immense floes among which we have now to navigate. I noticed a large iceberg completely cemented in pack. It looks then as if this ice has been formed not very far off, else it would have been more broken up. If so the amount of ice we will have to penetrate may be endless.

20 December. The noon position showed lat. 62° 42′ S long. 17° 50′ W, a backward drift of 6 miles; we are in the same position as on Friday [18 Dec], but further to the E.

In the evening before supper we had a rare game of football on the snow. It was pure farce of course; in places the snow was very soft and a man racing after the ball would often go head over heels.

21 December. Today we have experienced the lowest air temperatures of the voyage: 22° F at 4 am; 23½ at 8; 25½ at 12 noon; 25 at 4.

24 December. We made a splendid run today of 70 miles and found ourselves at noon in lat. 64° 32′ S, long. 17° 12′ W. This was due to the very favourable ice conditions of yesterday continuing all last night and today. The floes I notice are on average much smaller now, while the patches of water remain as big as ever – often 5 miles across.

The outlook therefore on Christmas Eve is very hopeful. We are all in good spirits and some half dozen fellows have been singing in Clark's cabin to the accompaniment of [Leonard] Hussey's banjo.

25 December. We had long been looking forward to Christmas Day and now it is over under the best of conditions. To begin with we have another good run of 71 miles (today's and yesterday's runs taken together show a bigger mileage than the whole ten previous days); our noon position was lat. 65° 43′ S, long. 17° 24′ W.

There is reason to be proud of the way in which 'Endurance' has got through the pack up until now; there is no doubt that her success is due to her small size, which allows her to follow twisting leads quite easily; bigger ships might have been held up for weeks in the places we have been. Our coal consumption still remains low – the Engineer's estimate is 40 tons since we left Grytviken on Dec 5th.

As a preparatory to Christmas a good many of us had baths in the engine room last night; the amount of room was nil, but the situation not unromantic – the red glare of the furnace doors when opened was the only light. We all got our presents too in the shape of small carborundum stones and for the more important people strops – these, presented I believe to the Expedition, had been thoughtfully held back for this occasion by [Thomas Orde] Lees.

The wardroom was decorated with some signal flags and the King's Union Jack was out up later in the day. Not to be beaten I stuck up my Scottish Lion in Clark's cabin.

Our Christmas dinner was held at 12.30 and did us credit; Turtle Soup, Whitebait, Jugged Hare, Plum Pudding and Mince Pies, Figs and Preserved Fruit. The drinks were Rum and Raspberry-vinegar.

28 December. We have been practically stationery since Friday (Xmas Day). Yesterday the temperature was in and about 21° F and a bitter wind blew all day. Today however is much milder and we notice that round the ship the ice is now very thin – which is good augury for our future progress.

A notable feature of nearly three weeks in the pack is the very scanty amount of sunlight which we have experienced. [Alf] Cheetham says he has never been in the pack like this before.

30 December. Our watch were out early cleaning down the decks. Afterwards I stripped and got a bucket of sea water thrown over me. This was the first time I had tried a cold bath so far south, though [Alexander] Macklin and Clark have several times done it; it was very successful and will be repeated but one needs to have got up a circulation beforehand scrubbing down the decks; I don't think it would be safe to have such cold water thrown over one when just out of bed. The sea water temperatures average 29° F.

31 December. We thought ourselves lucky in making a run of 51 miles; the noon position was lat. 66° 47′ S, long. 15° 45′ W. So we are across the [Antarctic] Circle at last. Being Hogmany I have opened a tin of Currant Bun, which will be consumed later in the evening at the small sing-song.

1 January, 1915. At twelve those on the bridge wished each other a good New Year. When I went below we sang 'Auld Lang Syne' in the Rookery. And that was all. The English not regarding the New Year as a festival meant that today was as any other day, even in regard to meals. The day's run was highly satisfactory – 59 miles.

2 January. A really wonderful run of 124 miles: noon position lat. 69° 49′ S, long. 15° 35′ W. We might almost say that we are out of the pack. What we experience now are great numbers of icebergs of all sorts and stretches of ice showing strong pressure: some of these latter might be as much as 10 ft high.

4 January. The wind has almost gone down; what there is now from the south. We steam slowly about, but seem quite unable to get out of the cul de sac in which we have landed ourselves.

I have been looking more closely at the pebbles got from the Emperor Penguin on Dec 31st; the quantity is almost double that I got in the Emperor on Dec 17th. I notice two kinds of granite, a grit, purple sandstone, very nicaceous sandstone and two kinds of dyke rock.

6 January. Progress has not been good. The noon position yesterday was 70° 28′ S, 20° 8′ W showing a run of 62 miles over a period of 48 hours. Yesterday afternoon the leads got steadily worse and finally at 10.30 pm the ship was tied up to a floe, it being fully expected that we might stay there two or three days even.

8 January. The result of a week's manoeuvring is still in doubt: that is to say we are not yet through the band of heavy pressure ice. Position at noon lat. 70° 0′ S, long. 19° 0′ W. The latitude is the same as Sunday 3rd, but the longitude is further west. Do we conclude therefore that the edge of the thick pressure has gone westwards, thus making more land water off Coats Land? Can all this pressure come from a bay E of Coats Land?

9 January. Last night a more SE course was taken and this or a slightly more easterly course was held all night: with the result that we struck open water this forenoon. A week has been lost therefore by taking a SW course instead of a SE one. Of course there was ice then all over what is now open water: the ice has gone off northerly and westerly.

Today is the anniversary of the Boss's 'Farthest South' in 1909.

10 January. An important date in our voyage – Coats Land was sighted about 5.30 tonight. It was a great sight – barrier and open water as far to the SW as we could see.

11 January. Coats Land then is an actuality. What we have seen is land to the NE; about 80 miles of barrier, low in the NE, averaging 100 ft in the SW; then a deep easterly night backed by land, up to 2000 ft in height.

14 January. The sun shone brilliantly all day – the fourth day's sunshine since we left Grytviken forty days back.

I am numbering off the contents of the Emperor Penguins' stomachs as if they were land deposits. The stomach of a young Emperor caught on Tuesday night has given a good deal of amusement: there is about ½ lb of pebbles, the biggest having a maximum dimension of one inch.

We have all enjoyed an Antarctic summer day and are in great spirits.

15 January. During the night an easterly breeze shifted the heavy pack, which caused us to tie up on Wednesday night. So at six this morning the ship was once more under weigh. Noon position 74° 30′ S, 25° 48′ W – a run of 26 miles. During the morning we were some little distance from the barrier; but after midday we got quite close. Shortly after three o'clock we at last passed a berg to leeward of us, whose length exceeded 20 miles.

16 January. I shall not soon forget the sight on deck at midnight: the sun shone feebly through cloud; a strong wind was blowing; a fair amount of brash and small floes were about; and through them the ship went dodging at full speed like a yacht, the Boss working the telegraph on the bridge like a madman. Before turning in I got a glorious sight of new land, land never seen before.

17 January. We remained all night in the lee of a berg where the sounding was made in 136 fathoms. We have remained in the same position all day, allowing the wind to take us round in circles and then steaming slowly back to the lee of the berg. Beyond shelter a strong E wind is blowing, rocking the ship up and down like a cork. The endless glaciers on the land are continually in sight.

18 January. The wind moderated during the night: at 6.30 accordingly the ship made slowly to the SW; later in open water all sail was hoisted and she made rapid southing. At noon we were in 76° 27′ S, 29° 46′ W, a run of 20 miles; we were then 104 miles from Vahsel Bucht, where Filchner landed.

There was just time before lunch for a bath in the engine room; and then into clean clothes afterwards. As I got a haircut from the carpenter

[McNish] yesterday, I am now equipped for the month's hard work with no spare time which will follow the selection of a landing place.

19 January. [The day *Endurance* was beset in the ice.] Last night after some battling in the pack, we finally stopped among convenient small floes about 10.30. We did not reach this haven without a struggle; on going to the wheel at eight, the ship was just being pushed into a thick floe preparatory to gaining a good lead; we were soon stuck however in heavy brash and the two floes closing we became practically nipped in the ice. The engines however kept going for about an hour and a half and finally we won through. It was a lucky escape: screwing pack can be very dangerous.

We have lain in the same position all today – 76° 34′ S, 31° 18′ W. The NE wind, which has caused the trouble, is still blowing: it helped us some days ago: now it has heaped all the ice at the head of the Weddell Sea. The appearance of the ship amongst the ice is as if we had put back the clock three weeks.

20 January. The fates are still against us and it looks as if we were to go on having pack right to the bitter end. The NE wind has been blowing all day, for the sixth day on end. I got in a big washing in the morning, foreseeing that, once the base is settled on, there will be little chance if any of getting such jobs done till the depots are laid. [Hubert] Hudson got a sight at noon and found that we have drifted two miles to the north since yesterday. This is a good sign, showing that there is an offset to the persistent NE wind which is piling up the ice at the head of the Weddell Sea.

22 January. A blizzard blew all day yesterday accompanied with a heavy snow fall and a noticeable rise in temperature. The spirits of everybody were considerably depressed and the Boss began to talk of making west when it cleared; should he adopt this course, it will be all in favour of the geological work.

The floes were pressing in on us: on the ship itself there was little effect as the pressure came diagonally, but there is always the danger of the rudder being jammed, either hard to port or hard to starboard. Finally at night the pressure eased off, much to our relief.

Hudson got an altitude at 5.0 pm; by double altitude – not a very reliable method – he finds that we have drifted 28 miles SW since getting jammed here. One hopes this is correct. Being tied up so near our goal is very disappointing.

24 January. The breeze has gone round through S to W. There are wild remarks being made that we will never get out of our unpleasant position, but I don't think it will be so bad as that. Vahsel Bucht is 60½ miles away in a S 13° W direction. I suppose we will gradually move round and come up the west side of the Weddell Sea.

25 January. Last night about midnight a lead opened not far from our bows. The Boss stayed up all night, hoping for events, but nothing happened. After breakfast it was decided to make an effort to reach the lead and then go west. While steam was being got up <u>all</u> sail was hoisted: it was the first time this had happened. We had hoped for much from the steam, but it achieved nothing. At dinner time the attempt was given up and there was not one on board who was not bitterly disappointed.

Good observations both yesterday and today show that we have drifted 3½ miles to the E in 24 hours. There is still hope of our becoming free: constant changes are going on in the lead beyond our bows.

26 January. The lead beyond our bows seems to be closing up, but we are still hopeful of changes in the floe. The wind today was for the most part E and N. E. Noon position – 76° 50′ S, 33° 42′ W.

27 January. We are beginning already to feel the pinch of being so long held up here: we have run out of seal meat both for ourselves and the dogs. The latter are going on short rations and this, with the cold, may explain the whimpering that has been going on all day.

The wind went round to the SW about mid-day and the square sails were set accordingly; we have not broken out however and there seems little if any chance in the pack ahead of us. The noon position was 76° 50′ S, 33° 47′ W.

29 January. Yesterday a wave of depression seemed to come over everybody on board: it was soon noticed that it was best not to get in the Boss's way. It certainly looked as if we might not get out of this floe before the winter and might spend the next nine months drifting north.

The dullness yesterday was somewhat relieved by finding a passable footer pitch not far from the ship: we had two games, a small one in the morning and an exciting one just before tea in which a good many of the forrard hands joined. It helped to put everybody in a good humour and clear away the depression which had been settling down. Noon position 76° 46′ S, 33° 50′ W.

31 January. Yesterday and today have shown no change in the ice conditions: the winds have been light or none at all and the temperature has if anything been higher. Today ice melters were arranged, and it is now part of the duty of watches to keep these filled. They are three in number: a large one just over the fo'c'sle skylight, a copper tank in the galley and the hut tank above the wardroom.

Today's relaxation has been in the shape of a good hard footer match (seven-a-side) between 4.30 and 5.30: honours were equally divided.

2 February. A sounding was taken in the afternoon: a noon obs. made in the lat 76° 49′ and the longitude worked back from today was 34° 14′ W. The depth was 516 fms [fathoms] that shows as we drift S and W we are getting into ever deeper water. Snow fell in the evening. We all turned in hopeful of a blizzard and perhaps freedom.

One wonders where we will finally be when we leave the ice or stop drifting with winter's approach. At present the Boss has in mind, should we leave the ice within the next day or two, to sail straight for the glacier whose front we passed so romantically early in the morning of the 16th. Should he do so, it shatters my hopes of a party going to explore the western mountains.

5 February. This morning (Friday) a change had taken place: the wind had gone round to the NE again – the favourable quarter. It snowed thickly all day.

Just before twelve I was aware of the box, on which I was sitting reading a volume of the Encyclopaedia, moving over to port and then back to starboard. In a minute a tremendous cheer was heard from the bridge above and a pell-mell rush was made for the deck. It was quite worth a cheer for a crack had opened lengthways along the ship and was rapidly becoming wider.

Instantly all was activity and orders were at once given to start the fires again: (for a fortnight one has been out altogether and other kept so low that only one ton of coal is used in ten days). Then to help things on the jibs were hoisted and the topsail unrolled, there being something of a struggle by everybody to get a hand on the ropes.

The wind, now in the east, caused a pretty considerable list to port. It was a very excited party then that sat down to dinner immediately after.

Steam was made ready in the afternoon, but it was still too thick to proceed. Moreover the leads had closed, though we still lay free in a big pool. We are all in high spirits, as we feel that at least we have got space in which to butt the floes when the weather clears.

6 February. Observed noon position 76° 55′ S, 34° 30′ W. There was practically no change in the state of affairs during the night; snow fell intermittently. From the crow's nest there is ice all round, with here and there some pools of water. Life has already become more abundant and this evening there were five or six Crabeaters [seals] swimming in the water to the stern.

9 February. A thick fog all morning and a cloudy afternoon prevented any observations being taken. Only a small strip of thick pack seemed to separate us from a string of pools and a passable lead beyond.

Steam was got up accordingly and an attempt made to get out of the pool in the afternoon, but it failed: we found great difficulty in breaking even the four day old ice of the pool in which we were lying; then we butted the thick pack, but with little apparent effect and finally gave up when it was seen that the lead has closed.

11 February. Observed noon position: 76° 50′ S, 34° 40′ W. The south wind, from which we were hoping so much, almost died away during the night, which for the rest was very cold, the mercury falling below zero. Some pools had appeared a little distance ahead so steam was got up in case a lead should open. It proved fruitless, but the steam was used to bring the ship into a slightly different position, more suitable for landing on the floe.

14 February. A great and a strenuous effort is being made to get out: looking back on what we have done this morning and afternoon, I think we will manage, even though it should take two days to do so. Our object is to reach a bad lead, which is probably 300 yds distance away; this bad lead ultimately becomes a good lead which runs as far as the horizon.

Work was undertaken systematically and the young ice of the pool cut up into triangles: these were then propelled to the stern of the ship with boat-hooks, poles, etc so that as the ship came gradually forward these broken pieces filled up the space behind her. A great ice saw which was made over a week ago was found impracticable: indeed Cheetham achieved far more with a small hand saw.

When we knocked off for a rest, we had at last got the ship round the corner, so that the head was now pointing south. We tried the trick of jumping in unison on the after deck ('sallying' is I think the technical term) but it was of no avail.

There was nothing for it now but to cut the ship out again: this was speedily done and she once more went astern on her own steam. I think she will get out: beyond the thicker ice at which she is still butting there is a pool of young ice which we can cut through and beyond that a crack leading to the lead.

15 February. Work started again immediately after supper: one gang set to work cutting out the young ice of the frozen pool ahead; some 5 or 6 others were employed rafting back the pieces of broken floe. The ship butted steadily at the thick obstruction and considerable progress was made. Such was the progress that at 8.0pm we thought the ship would manage to reach the frozen pool by her own efforts.

(Later: 5.0pm) Immediately after dinner we set to and rafted off what was left of the bridge, so that by three o'clock the ship's head was well up into the pool. But in attaining so much, we had also brought it about that there was little or no space left now for the ship to manoeuvre in.

About 3.0 o'clock Wild, McIlroy and the carpenter went over to the lead, thus making the first close inspection of our destined route. Then the Boss, Wild and the Skipper [Frank Worsley] went out. They brought back a report that to complete the cutting out would be impossible: so all the tools were brought on board and a pretty despondent crowd went in to tea. We were beaten by time and lack of coal and the low temperatures.

Between us and the lead there is very heavy pressure; we could get out in ten days but then the engines would have to be on the whole time. Further there is already a foot of young ice on the lead we are aiming at: by the time we got there then, there would be too great a thickness for the ship to break through.

16 February. The Boss took yesterday's defeat very well, I thought: he was in the best of spirits today and gave orders for a proper football match to take place this afternoon. At noon I went over with Clark to the lead, now frozen, which was the goal of our efforts yesterday. It was quite frozen over. It now looks as if there was considerable danger attached to going out on such thin ice: a Killer Whale has come up through the ice in the lead and been blowing there ever since.

Outlook tonight seems good: a great lead to the N and E is fast opening; if only the floe with the footer field, it being its field, should move, then we will be free, but free merely by retracing our steps of the last two days.

18 February. Movement of the ice in the lead to the E.N.E. fell away to nothing yesterday and the wind gave no sign of freshening. Killers [whales] still present and prevented measurements of the thickness of the sea ice being repeated.

20 February. Noon observed position: lat. 76°, 57′ S long. 34°, 35′ W. Already most of us getting reconciled to the prospect of having to winter here: what the future may hold is problematical, but the Boss reconciles himself with the chance of the drift taking us nearer the land or at any rate nearer the barrier to the S.W., whither we have been trending. I myself think a good sledging route to the land would be on the frozen lead to the S.E. and S. of the ship.

22 February. The ice averaged 7½–8 inches thick. This afternoon saw the first efforts at placing the dogs in teams and trying them at sledging: the two teams of 5 were out and gave a good account of themselves: it was a relief to know that the dogs can pull.

24 February. Noon position 76°, 57′ S, 34°, 37′ W. Sun now sets well before 10.0 pm: a glorious sunset last night, which probably persisted till sunrise.

26 February. Noon position 76°, 55′ S, 34°, 58′ W. Work began yesterday at landing the dogs; by dinner time all the port side kennels had been emptied, the dogs tethered to a wire on the floe and the kennels dismantled. Today the starboard side was cleared of both dogs and kennels.

The decks have an unusually bare look now and already this afternoon cases were being stowed there out of the hold, preparatory to clearing the latter altogether, as it will make our winter quarters.

27 February. This morning a further step was taken in the direction of preparing for winter: the wood of the hut was removed from the port side of the hold; a selection was made of timber suitable to make a hut for six men – this was placed on deck; the rest of the timber was passed into the coal bunkers. At the same time a fair number of cases were taken up on deck. Soon all the cases will be out of the hold, which will then be ready to be transferred into winter quarters.

In the afternoon there took place a general distribution of clothing – a serious enough occasion, the Boss and Marston having been preparing for it all day. Socks and mits galore, felt boots for use indoors, heavy underclothing and sweaters; the socks of all sorts, Shetland, Harris tweed, sleeping, skiing, etc; the mits also varied culminating in a large pair made of dogskin. The Burberry windproofs were already distributed yesterday.

1 March. Now that we are into March, hope of the ship being freed has now been given up; but for all that we might still break out; after a long interval without much wind a strong gale is now blowing from the N.E. much resembling that which got us into this corner. After a week of very cold weather, the turn has at last come. I suppose we have averaged well below zero in the last four days – the lowest recorded temperature was -18° F. Last night however the minimum was + 11° F, today's noon temp. +15°. As a result the inside of the ship is hopelessly damp and miserable.

3 March. One of the heaviest dogs – Saint – was found in a stiff and numb condition: it was brought into the wardroom and revived considerably: cold cannot have been the reason – its breathing showed some internal trouble. The dog died during the night and a post mortem showed appendicitis. The number of dogs is now reduced to 62 and 4 puppies. A game of footer in the evening, the snow being rather thick for hockey. These games make a fine ending to a day's work.

5 March. Today's [position] 76°, 53′ S, 35°, 29′ W. Bitterly cold; today's noon temp was – 12° F.

A certain routine is gradually going to be evolved. Every morning Clark and myself go off and open the dredging and sealing holes. Ice measurements continue to be interesting but are attended with considerably more labour as the ice gets thicker. Sounding today 561 fms.

This evening after tea the Boss announced the winter arrangements and the divisions into cubicles. Clark and myself have the furthest aft cubical on the starboard side. It looks as if the winter were to be merely a drift NNW and the prospect of sledging now fades slowly into the background.

9 March. A latitude was taken yesterday and gave 76°, 45′ S; today's position is 76°, 46′ S, 34°, 31′ W. We are in practically the same position as we were in a few days after getting nipped. Yesterday two more dogs had to be shot; they were both suffering from worms of a rather curious type which seems to have got a hold on many of the dogs. Three more seals were shot yesterday, the third being brought in today. The total since we were caught in the pack is now forty six: of these the last seem all to be Weddells, which may be ominous of a migration.

13 March. The wind shifted to NE on Thursday night, the temperature rose slightly and last night there was a mild blizzard. The blizzards we have got so far have all been mild: there is nothing terrifying about them, rather a certain picturesqueness and attraction.

Hurley has already painted the sign for our cubical – 'Auld Reekie'; putting that up over the lintel was the first step at decoration; we followed it up today by putting up a long shelf for books above my bunk. Today in the hold the table was rigged up, and the last of the linoleum put down.

15 March. Yesterday saw the start proper of life in the under regions. This meant the start of a fresh routine: breakfast is now at nine, lunch with soup at one, a cup of tea at four, and dinner at six. At meals one is just a little cramped by the uprights supporting the upper deck, but that is really a very small inconvenience.

19 March. The Skipper got a noon position yesterday – 76°, 53′ S, 36°, 42′ W showing that in a week though on the same latitude we have gone about 16 miles to the west. It was found worthwhile accordingly to take sounding; 606 fms; glacial mud.

20 March. Noon position 76°, 48′ S, 37°, 42′ W. That is 15 miles N 70° W of where we were two days ago. During most of this time a pretty stiff S.W. gale has been blowing, but without a snow-fall. There is still some trouble among the dogs. The number is now below sixty but Macklin says there are fifteen more of them in a weak condition.

21 March. I was pretty tired and would have been glad to have turned in, had not the Boss asked Clark and myself along to his cabin for coffee.

He has just had the Shore Party Library of about 300 volumes put in there and is going to start a habit of entertaining a few people there every evening, this being the first of the sort. The Boss himself gets little sleep at present, such is his anxiety over the changes in the ice; the night watch is now doubled and a report is made to him every hour.

23 March. A sounding was taken and showed that the water was still shoaling – 419 fms. The noon position was 76°, 36½′ S, 37°, 45′ W.

26 March. The water is still shoaling very rapidly: a sounding after breakfast gave 380 fms. By jerking on the [dredge] wire as it came up we locked on to a big catch and such it was – rich not only biologically, but also geologically, for the heavy weight was due to two huge boulders, one a reddish grit weighing over 70 lbs, the other about one-third of the size, a fossiliferrous limestone. Here was treasure indeed.

29 March. Noon position 76° 24½′ S, 37°, 48′ W. I was in the crow's nest for the first time in many days – a wonderful sight: the berg, to which we once sledged, now far off and great stretches of young sea ice; where the latter was viewed in the face of the sun, it was just as if a river were meandering over mud flats.

31 March. Expecting a depth not far different from that of yesterday, we were striving to get a sample at 300 fms depth. Much to our surprise and delight, far from reaching 300 fms., we struck bottom at 256 fms., from which a sample was got instead. Such a shallowing since yesterday is sufficiently exciting: already there are wild suggestions about the proximity of land to the west.

3 April. There have now been two soundings since the finding of the unexpected shoaling on Wednesday; both show approximately the same depth, 262 fms. Yesterday, 264 today; it seems pretty clear that we are now on the continental shelf.

At 4 am when out observing, I was struck by the rumbling noises coming from out on the ice aft: I was convinced that heavy pressure was going on, and was able to verify this afternoon that such had been the case.

An important change took place yesterday in the dog routine. All the feeding and exercising is now in the hands of six men – Wild, Crean, Marston, McIlroy, Macklin & Hurley. Change the Boss for one of these and I think the personnel of the transcontinental party will be complete.

5 April. After much waiting we at last got a position yesterday – 76°, 9′ S, 37°, 50′ W. The northerly course was somewhat disappointing, but not unexpected, looking to the series of nearly equal soundings. Yesterday's soundings, eg was 250 fms. Today's 245 and previously to that we had 264, 262 and 256; obviously we have been drifting N just on the edge of what is possibly a continental shelf. The day, in spite of the sun, was the coldest we have had – 22° below zero.

10 April. The great complaint these days is the dullness of the weather. With only a fortnight to go now until the sun leaves, one would like to get what little sunshine is possible every day. So far, however, this month has only afforded one clear sunshiny day, and in the whole of March there were only five. A sounding gave 253 fms. which was better news.

14 April. Yesterday's position was 76°, 4′S, 38°, 37′ W. A sounding gave 212 fms. And the deposit might almost have been called sand. Naturally we all commented on the probable nearness of the land. A few days more and we shall all be very disappointed if we do not sight land.

18 April. The soundings have not differed very much, all being between 190 and 200 fms. During these days there have been entertainments such as a lantern lecture by Hurley last night on the Mawson expedition; it was followed by 'Sweethearts and Wives' in a humble way.

Today happened to be Wild's birthday and following the general custom a cake and a bottle of whisky were passed round after dinner. A comparison of ages took place naturally, in which the average age is 33. The youngest of the party are Kerr (second engineer) 22, James 23, Hussey nearly 24, Macklin and myself nearly 26, Hurley 29 and Clark 32. The average age was considerably raised by Cheetham and the carpenter. Tom Crean, old as he looks, is only 38.

22 April. The clear weather has enabled accurate positions to be worked out; in two days the ship drifted about 26 miles to the south of west. After a long interval, the dredge was once more lowered today: about 400 fms. of wire were let out in a depth of 180 fms. When brought in just before tea the haul proved the richest in stones of all the previous hauls; several hundred pebbles up to 3 ins across embedded in glacial mud and sand.

25 April. Yesterday we were in lat. 76°, 2′ S, 41°, 17′ W; and on Friday in 76°, 3′ S, 41°, 3′ W. On looking back I find we were beset on Jan. 19th in lat. 76°, 34′ S, 31°, 18′ W. We have therefore made 4 miles of westing for every 1 northing; a continuation of this course will take us towards Graham Land well south of Snow Hill, but more probably our course will become more northerly by then.

27 April. Position 75°, 45′ S, 40°, 55′ W. During the last two days we have suddenly started to move rapidly northwards and this in spite of lighter winds than on the days previously. The northerly drift is somewhat disappointing; I for one would much rather be going westwards.

Though my birthday fell yesterday, the celebration did not take place till today. As in all cases, the latter consisted of cake and spirits at the close of dinner.

28 April. Position: 75°, 38′ S, 40°, 46′ W. Hopes that the shoaling water was to lead us ultimately to land seem now to be rapidly dissolving. Today finds us as far north as we have been, but the water is now shallower than 174 fms. Approach to land should mean rapidly shoaling depths; the soundings we have been getting during the last week can only point to a submarine plateau.

I must say that we are being well fed at present and differ markedly in one respect from previous polar voyages; the men get exactly the same food as we do aft – a scheme which effectively bottles up all would-be complainers.

30 April. Dull skies have reigned for two days now, accompanied by high temperatures (plus 10° to 20° F); a light wind, refreshing rather than cold, has blown most of the time so that work out of doors has been very pleasant. Another dog died during Tuesday night. The number is now reduced to 50 plus 8 healthy puppies. It has been decided to feed the remaining dogs well despite a restricted supply of dog food: a full ration can only be kept up for five months.

As regards our own supply of seal meat the outlook is good but not exciting. Hussey and myself were employed weighing it very carefully this morning: the total came out bigger than expected – 790 lbs. As the amount of fresh seal meat used per day for hands averaged about 6 lbs, we will just manage to last the spring four months hence.

2 May. On looking back I find no seals have been obtained since March 10th when six were got.

3 May. Today was the last day on which we could have looked for the sun, but it never appeared. Some 70 days will now go by before we see it again.

6 May. Today has seen the culmination of Emperor Penguin hunting – 9 were secured today for the larder; taken with 2 yesterday, 1 on Tuesday and 3 on Monday, we now have 30 days fresh meat for the ship's company.

7 May. Position 75° 7′ S, 41° 2′ W. Since yesterday we have drifted 8 miles in a direction N 66° E. This easterly component was disappointing, as we were just beginning to appreciate the importance of the northerly drift which has gone on now so rapidly for ten days. We are now rapidly making up on Filchner's track, [Wilhelm Filchner's *Deutschland* drifted in the Weddell Sea during 1912] but it would be much more useful if we could follow a course well to the west of his track.

12 May. The drift almost due north, which has held for the last fortnight, seems now to have come to an end: it is as well as it began to look as if ultimately we might merely duplicate Filchner's northerly drift. Barring the blizzard, the only interest these days is the continued shallowness of the soundings. The minimum was reached on Monday – 152 fms.

15 May. It was somewhat startling to find that we were in 75° 23½′ S, 42° 0′ W – we had gone nearly half a degree in a backward direction. A new development, arising no doubt from the blizzard, is the appearance of new water spaces in almost all directions round the ship. This has considerably curtailed the radius in which the dog teams can manoeuvre.

18 May. Position 75° 23½′ S, 43° 8′ W. We would have liked to have seen the position farther to the west, but yesterday's contrary winds which still prevailed this morning account for the failure to do so. However there is a rumour of land today and I myself think it is well founded.

21 May. Unfortunately it [land] has been at no time clear enough to get a second bearing to it; otherwise its distance could be fixed. The soundings remain consistently shallow – 155 fms.

Each day now seems to have its period of almost hysterical laughter. Last night everybody had their hair cut short like Germans with very amusing results.

I had an unexpected stroke of luck on Tuesday night when on night duty: on that night we installed a new ice melter made by the ingenious Hurley – result plenty of hot water for washing and having a hot bath. Formerly the greater part of the heat went up the chimney outside the melter: now it circulates <u>inside</u> the Methylated Spirit drum: the copper coil too almost doubles the amount of heat playing on the base of the melter.

24 May. Position 75° 22′ S, 44° 50′ W. Our tendency to remain in such high latitudes has its disappointing side. Our chance of drifting north during the winter and breaking out next spring or summer is slowly diminishing. After a long interval we had some songs again on Saturday night. There was Alf Cheetham singing 'Teddy O'Neill' and 'False Flora' and Chippy 'Robbie Burns' and 'The March of the Cameron Men'. Wild sang 'Ford of Kabul River' and 'Forty Years On'; and others also contributed.

26 May. Today's [position] 75° 14′ S, 43° 58′ W: the reason is not far to seek – a moderately strong wind blowing from the SW. Not till today has there been another chance of looking once more for the 'island' of the 18th: today it was not visible which strengthens the view that it <u>is</u> an island.

29 May. Noon position: 74° 55′ S, 43° 45′ W. The northerly drift seems well started now: but how long will it continue ? Filchner's meteorological observations show a very high percentage of S and SW winds in June, July and August. So it may well be that we will experience the same conditions; if so, farewell to all hopes of discovering western land this season.

Soundings moreover show much deep water now: today 204 fms; yesterday 197 in 74° 59′ 44° 0′ W; Thursday 187 in 75° 4′, 43° 55′ W. When the soundings of the last three months are plotted out it becomes evident that we have crossed a broad submarine bank running E.N.E. – W.S.W: should our northerly drift continue we may now look for ever deeper water. (The problematical island of cone shape has now definitely been abandoned).

1 June. In the matter of temperature we seem to have been very lucky last month – an average of – 2° F according to Hussey; now from Filchner's reports we find he got – 8° F in May although he was 180 miles north of our present position. There were 37 – 39 ins [thickness] of ice and on the top of that about 7 ins of fairly hard snow.

10 June. We have had three days now of clear skies with little or no wind, but of course low temperatures – always about – 20° F. Today we are in 74° 25′ S, 44° 30′ W. Despite the calm weather there has been considerable pressure at different places in the leads.

13 June. The soundings are still very uniform – between 250 and 260 fms. The Skipper and I had considerable trouble with the theodolite and finally had to stop with only one longitude sight secured. The result is 74° 29′ S, 45° 15′ W. The southerly position is disappointing; we had looked for a big advance west with little or no change in latitude.

15 June. There have been several discussions lately as to which dog team is the fastest: the matter was finally settled this morning in the form of a race from the Khyber Pass to the ship – 700 yards. All the sledges carried about 700 lbs including driver – not a bad load for seven dogs. Hurley's team led by 'Shakespeare' was the favourite and covered the distance in 2 minutes, 26 secs. Wild's lightweights however beat this by 10 secs and were easy winners, to the general surprise.

20 June. Lat. 74° 36′ S, long. 46° 12′ W. Today we are still better off from the point of view of Morrell Land and Graham Land enthusiasts: we are farther west today than any previous ships sailing in the inner Weddell Sea. If we can only keep this up our forced wintering in the pack will not be so fruitless after all.

25 June. There have been two days of strong SW winds with the result that the ship which was in 74° 21′ S, on the 22nd is in 73° 57′ S today: this of course was very gratifying and a nasty pill for the pessimists to swallow. To our great joy the soundings are showing shallower water. 262 fms on the 22nd – we all thought we were leaving the continental shelf and drifting north into deeper water; but yesterday we got 249 fms. and today 239.

28 June. All our longitudes for the last three months are considerably out – we are more than a degree to the west than we thought: yesterday for instance our longitude was 47° 22′ W. Water today was deeper again – 255 fms.

4 July. Position 74° 9′ S, 48° 57′ W. Though twenty miles W of the last position, yet we had hoped perhaps to be in 50°W, for during the week almost all the winds have been favourable. What is it that prevents going north? – perhaps grounded bergs holding up the pack.

9 July. The soundings of the last few days have all given the same depth – 192 fms: and yet in the interval we have moved not a little: it looks as if we were on a plateau, not a sloping continental platform.

14 July. The last few days have seen a succession of strong winds from different directions. To our surprise on getting up this morning we learnt that the wind was SW but it was rather a shock on going out to learn how strong it was blowing. It is a proper blizzard – the first real blizzard we have had – so strong that even if it is taking us northward we would like to see it stopped.

The Boss is naturally very nervous and the least unusual sound sends him up on deck immediately: under these circumstances he is not the best of companions for a nightwatch.

Curiously enough the temperature still remains at -30° F: low temperatures with a blizzard are unknown on the Ross Sea side; they tell me today that the probable reason for our experiencing such low temperatures with a blizzard is the absence of high land to the SW and W which would have the fohn effect and so raise the temperature. Does this throw light on the possible southern extension of Graham Land? Perhaps the mountains of West Antarctica bend away out to sea and never reach King Edward VII Land.

15 July. The blizzard proper has stopped. Immediately after breakfast all hands, Burberry clad, issued out on the floe armed with shovels to dig out the dogs. Some were buried under 5 ft of snow, others not so much, whilst on the starboard side Judge's kennel was the only one at all snowed up: (like a wise old dog he had preserved a breathing hole with his nose).

17 July. I took a sounding at 2.0 pm – 196 fms: yesterday the depth was 202 fms; [position] today 73° 38′ S, 48° 38′ W. In 3 days we have made over 30 miles of northing and fortunately very little easting; so the blizzard has paid in spite of all the anxiety it has caused.

23 July. Position 7° 18′ S, 48° 0′ W. The last 24 hours have been full of anxiety and for very obvious reasons – cracks have formed in the ice very close to the ship. A very elaborate system of watches prevailed last night:

the Boss, Wild and the Skipper acted as chiefs in 4 hour spells, whilst all the afterguard took 1 hour turns.

This morning we did what should have been done at the very start – placed an emergency stack of sledging provisions on deck in case the ship should be suddenly nipped. This store on deck is purely a precautionary measure; should the boat be nipped (and it is very unlikely) there is sure to be time to get a good deal more out of the hold.

25 July. A rough latitude by the Skipper places us north of the parallel of 73° S. We are likely to improve on this very considerably during the night, for a strong wind is blowing from SW. Spite of that our course seems to be NNW.

The wind suddenly freshened in the afternoon and a rapid shearing movement started along the port crack. It was sufficiently alarming, for the pressure forrard was now intense. We have never seen pressure like it before – our outer line of defence was going and floes both old and young seemed to be crumbling up like paper.

The possibility of the ship being crushed and a boat journey to Graham Land in the summer ensuing was once more mooted. The afternoon was a black one and the Boss's look far from encouraging.

26 July. Position 72° 51′ S, 47° 40′ W. Things are much quieter now; the wind has died down to a mere breeze, but still some shearing goes on among the floes.

The great event today was a 10 minutes glimpse of the sun – an infinitesimal portion of the upper limb, seen today owing to the refraction being 2 mins 29 secs instead of 2′ 9″. It has only been absent 79 days. There is naturally rejoicing among the optimists who had wagered much chocolate that the sun would return before the end of July: the more scientific people have now to pay up, blaming refraction and the great SW winds of the last ten days.

1 August. The anniversary of the ship's departure from London fell today, but it has been too exciting a morning to be pleasant. At 8.30 am a SW – NE crack opened not more than 10 yds from the ship's bows: it was naturally viewed with considerable apprehension but was still only 3 ins broad at 10 am.

I was on messman duty in the pantry about half a hour later when a loud crack was heard and the ship seemed to heave in her berth. Slipped on a Burberry and was on deck in a few minutes – a NW–SE crack ran right across the ship and was starting to open. Dogs were hurried on board and tied to the ship's rail; sledges and loose gear, barring petrol cases, were thrown on deck. We had just got the dogs on in time: the gangways were pulled up and we stood a minute or two watching developments. Soon the ship took a list to starboard and we knew that she was breaking out of her berth. The list to starboard was followed by a list to port, some heavy floes having driven under the ship on the latter side.

Rumblings and groanings as the ice pressed against the ship were audible all morning, reminding one of the butting efforts of the ship during her journey through the pack, but now we were on the defence and were forced to let the ice do the attacking. The ship righted herself before lunch and was lying snug and true in a new berth: it was relief to know that the ship had suffered pressure and been none the worse.

The time till lunch has been spent by the scientists getting together their notebooks and by everybody putting on or having handy such clothing as they deem necessary. The Skipper of course has made a point of having chronometers, sextants and tables handy should we be called on suddenly to desert the ship. Our course probably would be to wait on the floe till summer and then try to reach Snow Hill in Graham Land in boats.

This morning there were few who thought otherwise than that we should be camping on the floe this very evening, but the way in which the ship withstood the pressure was wonderful, and the tension between decks is considerably relieved.

2 *August.* This morning the first consideration was to take on board four days ice supply, in case the blizzard should be of long duration, or work on the floe be rendered impossible for some reason or other. The ship has apparently suffered little from the pressure; the rudder is slightly sprung, and may need some repairing.

4 *August.* Yesterday and today the carpenter has been busy making new kennels to relieve the confusion on deck. Each kennel is made large enough to hold two dogs, which can be partitioned off if necessary. The number of dogs was still further reduced yesterday by shooting 4 of the weaker and older ones: one of them however – 'Sandy' – was found to be quite healthy, and a regrettable mistake seems to have been made.

5 August. A proper sounding has at last been obtained, but after much trouble. Bottom at last was got at 1,146 fms.

8 August. On Sunday evenings it has been the rule all through the winter to have a gramophone concert: the records would have played much oftener, were we not short of needles, but though well over a hundred records were brought, the needles seem to have been entirely overlooked.

14 August. The Skipper took a snap latitude with the sextant about 5.0 pm today: it shows us to be in 70° 55′ S. The depth was found to be 1550 fms.

16 August. We have at last reached 50° W long., and this in spite of light SW winds during the last days. It was a lovely day of sunshine: all the dog teams were out, Hurley took photos, James a declination and Marston even did some painting out of doors.

17 August. While we were out on the floe, the Skipper superintended a sounding: the depth is now 1676 fms. which effectively rules out Morrell's Land about this latitude and which he placed ever so much farther east.

24 August. Position 70° 12′ S, 50° 15′ W. On Sunday afternoon the wind went SE and has remained there with varying strength ever since. The Boss that morning was busy marking with old tins a route through the pressure to the berg ahead. In the afternoon I followed his route with James and Macklin to where it ended – at a pressure hummock nearly 30 ft high.

27 August. Last night had its alarming side, but only for a short while. About 2.0 am like everyone else I was suddenly wakened by a noise like the rush of feet in the tween decks. Then in a few minutes came the call – All Hands on Deck. It did not take long for us all to tumble out on deck: a crack had formed partly in the line of the ship and it was necessary to hurry on board puppies, sledges and odd gear.

30 August. Fresh cracks in the ice seem quite the rule now, but no longer cause the alarm they once did – everything is on deck now except the sledges. Such is the altered view of matters that the hourly watches need no longer be kept on deck; an occasional look now and then is all that is required.

1 September. Shortly before midnight, Clark being on watch, the crack which meets the ship at the stem, opened out as much as 2ft. Clark says that with the help of a hurricane lamp he could see in the inky water the thick masses of ice under the ship. James from his instruments notices a very slight change in the tilt of the ship; but we <u>all</u> notice a few doors are now stiff to open and shut.

10 September. There has been a sudden rise in temperature today, whose explanation is still to seek. From zero or below it the mercury suddenly jumped up to +23° F at 9.0 am today.

Taken with the cracked state of the ice – a new crack formed last night running from the foremast out on the starboard beam – it looks as if a general break up of the pack were not far off: perhaps we may see it within a month from now.

15 September. A cold snap seems to have set in: the days are sunny barring Sunday (overcast and blizzardy) and the temperature well below zero. Favourable winds are again the rule and we now seem to be shooting north again at a passable rate. The Skipper got sights to the sun from his sextant today and makes us 69° 33′ S, 50° 51′ W.

17 September. A year ago today – on Friday 18th September 1914 – Wild, James and myself went down to the docks at Liverpool and saw the dogs put on board the 'La Negra'.

A year has gone and we have practically nothing to show for it. Had we been favoured with a successful year – gone sledging, opened up new country – I suppose it would have been different but I confess to a certain feeling of shame at our failure: and this was heightened yesterday when I read in a paper dated Sept. 21st that one of my best friends at Cambridge, R.C.F. Powell had been killed in action; he was an only son.

19 September. There seems to be an end for the present of the northward drift: on Friday the wind was E during the day and NE at night: yesterday there was a short period of southerly winds; today again the wind is NE. Probably the wind direction has some connection with the temperature: at present it is above zero and feels almost too warm.

For a week no one [has talked] of anything but the war. What had happened ? Would peace be declared by now ? and so on were the futile questions which we tried to answer at meal times. But we had too little information to keep the subject going for long: and now the unending question: When shall we get out ?

21 September. Position 69° 36½' S, 50° 35' W. Thinking that we were farther west (probably in 51° W) we were interested on sounding yesterday to get only 1856 fms, i.e. 6 fms deeper than on Sept. 6 in 69° 54' S, 50° 26' W.

24 September. [Wordie climbed a 100 ft high berg, called the Stained Berg] As far as the eye could reach there was nothing but pack and berg, but from this unusual height the ground plan of the pack was made unusually clear: it seemed as if cut up into small allotments separated by pressure hedgerows.

28 September. We suddenly started on a westerly drift yesterday under the influence of a strong E.N.E. wind. The wind had dropped this morning, then suddenly rose from the S.E. after breakfast and is now a moderate breeze from the S.W. The Skipper thought we were fully as far west as 51° 30' W., i.e. 15–20 miles west of the last sounding in a not very different latitude. The depth is – 1876 fms.

30 September. Early yesterday afternoon a crack formed along the snow filled trench, 2 ft broad, whose formation first started on Aug. 27th. It was about 3ft broad when we turned in. Between half past two and three the innocent crack became a lead 10 yds broad. This resulted in a sharp attack by the ice on the port bow: about 3 ft of pressure formed here a little forrard of the foremast. It was a more determined assault even than that at the beginning of August: at least it has told more on the ship; there was a heap of refuse and tins on the floor of the cabin shared by James and Lees; the bulkhead of the 'Billabong' has bulged out some inches and the linoleum on the port side forrard of the Ritz is thrown into fore and aft folds.

The bag [of seals] is 5, i.e three weeks dog food; it has come none too soon. Today therefore may be set down as the date on which the seals returned – they left us, excepting stragglers, on Mar. 22.

At lunch we could do nothing but talk about the return of the seals and chances of the ship being free; at tea however we were once more harping back to the chance of the ship being crushed and of attempts being made to reach Snow Hill in boats.

4 October. At least a month's seal meat for the dogs has been secured: result – a disinclination on the Boss's part to secure all the seals available, under the impression that seals will be available <u>every</u> day. To show how false this idea is, it may be mentioned that no seals were got today – one of the finest for a long time from a weather point of view.

10 October. The amount of open water now visible from the crow's nest is very encouraging. Hardly a day goes by without some fresh water appearing in the pool on the port beam. Last night too from the crow's nest a long lead could be seen about 2 miles away going right round from E to SW. There is every sign therefore that the floes have loosened more or less on all sides (and this in spite of contrary winds): a break up may not be very far off.

12 October. Under the altered conditions, the pool of young ice on the port beam has melted. The ship is encompassed in all directions by patches of open water and water skies. The outlook is distinctly promising.

14 October. The ship is once more free. Immediately after dinner the crack running aft on the starboard counter was seen to be opening; all sledges, etc were immediately brought on board; and in about 10 mins it was seen that there were a few inches of open water along both the port side and starboard side. Then with a bump the ship lost her list to port and heeled over just a trifle to starboard – the latter owing to internal reasons. The lead gradually opened and shortly after 8.0 pm was over 2 yds in breadth; towards the ship this is represented by 1½ yds open water on the starboard side and 2 ft on the port side.

Since then there is a further change: the ship is free and the rudder apparently in good order but for the twist in the upper part. When the ice parted however it was seen that the propeller was horizontal instead of being upright; efforts are accordingly being made in the engine room to put this right, to prevent damage should the ice close up again.

The open water round the ship within a radius of 200 yds is now very considerable.

15 October. The open water beyond the bows gradually widened and at the same time the lead along the line of the ship. A rising SW wind soon drove the bows against the ice on the starboard side, whilst the stern of the ship was pressed hard against the ice on the port quarter.

It was not a pleasant position: at midnight therefore the Boss and those on deck hoisted the spanker; this soon brought the stern round and gradually drove the ship backwards along the lead aft. At a right angle corner some 100 yds away from the original position she came to a stop hard against the ice and the spanker was brailed in. Gradually however the lead widened and the wind, driving on the yards, gradually brought the bows round and drove her up the lead at right angles (i.e NW) some 2–300 yds.

I doubt if the new position is a safer one: should the lead along our old position close, it will mean a certain amount of shearing in the narrow one in which we now lie.

16 October. From the mast head the Skipper made out a long lead running for at least six miles in a northerly direction from the ship's old position. To reach this lead was by no means difficult in spite of the thin ice covering formed since Thursday night. The Boss therefore made an important decision – to get steam up and try to get free. Personally I think we were going to light the fires a trifle early considering there are only 35 tons of coal left.

19 October. On Sunday [Oct 17] the ice so pressed the ship that at stern she rose over 3 ft out of the water; then yesterday there came more pressure so that she lay right over almost on her beam ends on the ice.

The ship, to judge by the sounds, was being exposed to a sort of bombardment: she finally listed about 5° to port, having I suppose a natural tendency that way at present. On the floe things looked somewhat serious, for much snow was piled up against the sides and the pressure was still continuing. All hands were ordered out on the floe with picks and shovels, and a start was made to dig fore and aft trenches about a yard from the ship's side.

At 4.45 pm slowly but surely the ship heeled right over to port: all sorts of weird noises came up from the engine room and then with a rush all the unsecured dog kennels slid to leeward. The big kennel amidships, which holds eight dogs, went down with a bang and we all thought some dogs had been killed, fortunately this was not the case.

The lead in which we lay was completely closed, so that the ship, raised a little above its normal level on Sunday, had no other course but to heel over on to the ice. She took a list of fully 30° in 5 seconds. Its an ill wind that blows nobody good – Hurley was immediately out on the floe photographing the ship from every possible position.

24 October. Since Wednesday [Oct 20] there has been unfortunately no big enough change in the ice conditions to effect our escape: small changes there have been especially on Thursday and again yesterday. These changes consisted merely in the opening and closing of various cracks and leads.

The ship's company however holds itself in readiness for a big change. One of the engine fires goes continuously, replenished I am told almost entirely by blubber and ashes from the bogies.

The ship's officers are in pairs, 4 hours on and 8 hours off; the rest of us have not quite so much to do, but are liable to be called upon more often – 4 on and 4 off. Result – none of us have undressed for four days, for orders were given that during night watches on deck the afterguard would remain dressed, but could sleep in the wardroom if they kept their boots on.

25 October. At 6.45 pressure of an ugly sort started on the port side: all hands ordered out with picks and shovels. All gear brought on board at quarter to seven. The pressure was now getting worse. But just then the ship seemed to be driven back by the floe ahead, and as luck would have it there was no place for the rudder to go; it was too great a twisting strain; the rudder post came away from the planking on the starboard counter – we had developed a serious leak.

In a few minutes we were preparing for the worst. Clothing and sledges were now being passed up on deck and any sledging provisions not already there.

It is Greenstreet's business with the forrard hands to have the boats ready. We are warned to get our notebooks etc. handy in case we should have to leave the ship. This does not take long as I have always kept notebooks and essential gear handy for an emergency.

At 9.30 pm more pressure started; the afterguard was ordered on to the floe to dig a second trench on the port side 8 yds away. We now learn that the water has stopped gaining: and much is hoped from the carpenter's coffer dam on which he is now working hard, harder than anyone else on the ship.

There have been a few intervals of pressure since last night, enough to raise the ship still more at the bows so that she is well up on to the floe there; but all this does not improve the position aft, where the strain must be tremendous. Things look a bit more promising now; the sun is shining for one thing and we are hoping that coffer dam will be a success.

26 October. We are not out of danger yet, though there is every probability that the carpenter's bulkhead will be a success. We got the water under control fairly easily last night; from 4.0 pm onwards both Downton and bilge pumps were working continuously. We spent the morning completing the emptying of the after hold and I understand that there are only snails left there now.

As the ship lies at present she is very awkwardly placed. The pressure ridge athwart the bows (representing the lead in which she once lay) runs slantwise across the ship at the position of the foremast: should shearing begin there we should be hopelessly placed; indeed any farther pressure in our present position would be extremely dangerous.

27 October. I am afraid this will be the last entry in this diary: we left the ship this evening: it still floats but has been so badly damaged by the pressure of the last 24 hours that it will never float again once the ice opens. I am making this entry seated in a tent on the floe, having for companions Wild, McIlroy and the carpenter. I look to the former of these to pull us through.

The programme of the future is simple: to discard <u>all</u> unnecessary gear – my gold watch may have to go; to sledge and boat westwards to land; and once there to try and make Snow Hill.

Here is what has happened since yesterday afternoon. After dinner a trench was dug round the stern: before completed, a <u>strong</u> shearing pressure came upon us. The leak got worse and all hands came on deck; ordered to stand by the falls.

This would be about 7.45 pm: a few minutes later we were lowering the boats and preparing to put provisions, clothing and sledges ashore. Practically all hands were employed on the latter job from 9 till 11: with three others I spent this interval at the bilge pump.

At intervals the pressure was repeated: a bulwark was stove in. Result: leak not so bad and we are able to hold it with the engine and bilge pumps. There was a note of despondency when we threw ourselves on our bunks, clothes, boots and all: wakened 4 –5 hours to do a half hour spell on the bilge pump; suction frequently got.

This morning several hands were told off to help Chippy caulk aft. The 'old hands' stowed the gear on the floe properly on sledges and got most of it weighed. With several others I was on the pumps all morning: at the time certainly none of us thought the end was near.

There is no open water in sight, but the pool aft of the winter position where we might have stopped remains a sheet of young ice. All round there are lines of working pressure.

At 2.0 pm the pressure started which has given the ship its death blow. It drove us along the crack athwart the bows, raising the stern clean out of the water: the rudder and propeller were buried in a maze of pressure blocks – a sorry sight they were in.

Then came the news – the water was gaining on us, though all three pumps were working. Orders given to put dogs out on floe: we then knew that matters were serious. And so till 4.45 we had a spell o' for tea.

At 6.0 pm still heavier pressure began: the ship was tossed up aft. Orders came to leave the ship. All sorts of gear goes over on to the floe. The water is now up to the level of the boilers. We do hard work on the floe for some hours, shifting everything to a stout floe on the starboard bow. Cook [Charles Green] goes back and prepares a dinner which we eat between 9 and 10 pm. Assemble on floe: Boss explains situation and we turn in.

Everything has come too quickly to make us pause to regret: that will come in the future. From now on the work will be frightfully hard: we have three boats each weighing about 1500 lbs.

Chippy tells me from his bag that the keel went during the pressure.

28 October. Uneasy night: changing position owing to cracks. Water now up to galley level by morning. Awful night of suspense. Foremast went and mainmast about 7 am. Fresh change of position a little more to east. Discarding gear all day. Noted last night how floe was heaving (owing to pressure) before it cracked.

29 October. Arranging gear: cutting down continues. Have 48 days full rations for 28 men. Chippy gets boats arranged on sledges ready to start: only two boats now. Skipper's sights show we have gone 7 miles in two days (i.e. since leaving the ship) in the right direction.

We are going to steer for Robertson Island.

On board ship things in awful state; no deck-house; alleyways stove in; water above main deck except in Rookery; some gear was got out such as wood for Chippy, a chest of tea, some meteorological notes and Wild's farthest south diary 1908–1909.

30 October. We have started the great journey and are now in Camp 2. The pioneer sledge (Boss, Hudson, Hussey and self) got away about 1.15 pm the Boss shouting out 'Now we start to Robertson Island, boys'. (to which all hands raised a cheer).

Made 1 mile NW: 200 yds.

Snow fell in night with E NE wind: a dull day of drifting snow. The men relayed two boats. Ship in sight to SE, the Blue Ensign at the gaff, where the Boss hoisted it on Wed. about 7.0 pm.

31 October. Snow fell all night: high temp. Looked like clearing in aftn: so made W NW ¾ mile over young pressure to camp on old floe. Deep soft snow: hard going.

Order of teams: Pioneer sledge (Boss, Hussey, Kerr, Rickinson and self); 5 dog teams which make two journeys (Greenstreet drives Tom's pups); Wild and Hurley's teams haul whale boat with ease – a problem solved; men pull the lifeboat.

Camp (3a) about 4.0 pm snow falling fast and very damp. Bad light all day. A seal killed in afternoon – 4 days food for men and dogs.

1 November. A complete change of plan has been made: to sledge to the land dragging boats will be too big a task. Today, therefore, we moved to camp 3b (Ocean Camp) about 300 yds to the W on the old floe: and here we will stay, providing the floe does not break, till the summer leads form and we can take to the boats. (This may not be till several months are over)

The majority of us were employed in the morning shifting camp; weather thick and snow very deep and soft.

Meanwhile, the dog sledges went back to the ship and brought up all the available food left at the camp there, while two dog teams brought the third boat along, a bit damaged since its abandonment. In the afternoon some men went back to the ship to try and get food there – little success; masts were cut away, the mizzen tearing up the Rookery; McIlroy got me some books and clothing from the latter place with no little difficulty.

2 November. A strict tally of provisions made today – we have not much to come and go on. The Boss at last realised that we may not get out of the pack for several months – perhaps six.

More salvage was made at the ship, chiefly of firewood with a little food: unfortunately most of the latter was under deep water.

Three seals were killed today – and every inch of them kept.

A lovely day of sunshine: got sleeping bags and socks properly dried.

Sights show that we are in 69° 7½′ S, 52° 5′ W, farther W than we have ever been before.

3 November. More gear brought up from the ship chiefly wood and tackle. It is hoped to reach 'The Billabong' tomorrow where the food lies under water: then we shall be in clover; at present we have only 1 lb a day for six months for all hands.

We must prepare for emergencies, lest the pack should not open this year.

4 November. Prospects are much brighter today. Ship's position is 69° 1′ S, 51° 57′ W. So we go gradually N in spite of light wind.

But the great event of the day was the getting of stores from the Billabong: the first load to reach us consisted of walnuts, curry powder and figs – not very sustaining: but better came later – rice, suet, hams, sugar in plenty and last of all, what we wanted most – flour. There is much else besides; in fact the whole outlook at the camp is now changed; instead of meagre ration – we should have full whacks now.

5 November. The salvage work at the ship is now practically finished and it has been well worth the trouble – men working up to their knees in water retrieving stores from the Billabong with boat hooks. Today we got 30–40 cases of flour and some cases of jam; we are now well supplied for several months.

Dog pemmican for breakfast nowadays, ½ lb per man. Full rations today. Things look more promising.

Was over at the ship in the afternoon: looks like a trawler from a distance. There is little left unsmashed – the wardroom nothing but wreckage: salvage going on through a great hole on port side. Managed to retrieve a few more things including some notes and a few books to read till the final move from our present camp.

7 November. We have had two days blizzard from SE and still it continues to drive us towards the land. The sun shone fitfully and enabled a position to be got – 68° 50½′ S, 52° 27′ W.

The Boss is arranging for the provisions salved from the ship to last three months at full ration: he hopes that the ice will open by then. If not, he talks of leaving the boats – an event which I hope will never happen.

8 November. Postn. 68° 39′ S, 52° 20′ W. Squared up the tent a bit: it is now provided with a wooden floor and is sunk about 8 ins below the normal level: thus we get warmth and additional space.

10 November. Seal hunting is now the order every morning. Yesterday four teams radiated out, but returned empty, bar one which had secured three penguins. Today the hunters had better luck – two seals and a baby in the morning, and two more tonight.

With Hudson walked over to the ship in the afternoon and did some 'looting': not much left but cast off clothing. Have gradually retrieved most of my gear, such as binoculars, etc.

11 November. An idea of the way in which we feed:

Yesterday:	9.0 am	Halibut Kedgeree ½ mug
		Coffee 1 mug
	1.0 pm	Two large oatcakes
		Tea ½ mug
	6.0 pm	Penguin and salt beef hoosh 1 mug
Today:	8.0 am	Friend seal steak
		Tea 1 mug
	1.0 pm	Doughboy and jam: Cocoa 1 mug
	5.30 pm	Liver and ham 1 mug
		Cocoa 1 mug

The wind seems to be easterly: waterskies all round: outlook very promising.

13 November. From this distance it is evident that the ship is sinking fast – only the funnel shows now: in another 24 hours it may be gone.

Camp seems a cheery place now: Hussey plays his banjo almost every night after hoosh and gradually draws forth some singers. A good many books were rescued from the salvage operations – most of the Encyclopaedia and the majority of my own books from the Rookery: so for the present we do not weary over much at these days of inactivity.

14 November. After turning in last night (about 9.0 pm) some sounds of pressure were heard. But where ? I thought they were on the north side of the old floe – 100 yds from the camp: certainly some cracks there have closed with disturbance. But Wild says there are big changes between us and the ship – shearing along a crack with broadens to the E. The ship has gone down about 6 ft at the head.

16 November. The carpenter began altering the whaleboat today: the timbers of the motor boat are being used to raised the gunwales about 1 ft: part of the bow will also be covered in: when finished we will have a seaworthy boat capable of holding all hands.

19 November. At breakfast Wild was saying that we <u>must</u> get some seals today: it is the dogs that are so pressing, for most of the best meat is being stirred for ourselves. And luck was on our side, for the day's bag came to three seals and 1 Emperor [penguin], the last being my share of the kill.

21 November. Today saw the last of the ship. A few minutes before 5.0 pm, just as the last of the dogs had been fed, came a shout that she was sinking: we all rushed out and posted ourselves where best we could see her a mile away. The stern was right up till she almost made an angle of 45°: but her head was going down all the time and about ten minutes after the first alarm, the last of the stern sank from view.

So she completes her first and last voyage, and sinks beaten in fair fight only after a fine struggle.

23 November. We have drifted nearly 4 miles W since yesterday and about 2° to the West. A very careful watch was kept all day yesterday on the bergs, particularly the Stained Berg: apparently they were drifting N faster than we were. West must wait before drawing conclusions however.

24 November. Wild and a party went across to the position where the ship sank today, travelling over the sea ice with considerable difficulty. Nothing whatever of the ship is left. Position 68° 28′ S, 52° 30′ W

27 November. The winds still blow from the S but with some easting in the last 24 hours. Position – 68° 18′ S, 52° 24′ W

28 November. It seems practically certain that we will leave the floe, when the day comes, in three boats. Provisionary crews (11, 9, 8) have been made out and the boats already christened 'James Caird' (Whaler), 'Dudley Docker' and 'Stancomb Wills' (Cutters) – three of the chief subscribers to the expedition.

The Boss and Wild are in charge of the whaler, which since the carpenter has strengthened it, can now hold 4 tons: it is the flagship and has just had a mizzen added. Worsley and Greenstreet take the second boat and Hudson and Crean the third; the latter may or may not be taken all the way.

3 December. Lat. 67° 57′ S. A general move of all the tents except the cookhouse was made yesterday morning: owing to the soot from the stove, the traffic, etc, the snow had begun a rapid melt – about 2 ft had gone this way. Then in the afternoon four seals were killed not far off.

5 December. A year since we left South Georgia. A brisk wind has been blowing for 24 hours.

9 December. Yesterday's sight showed us to be in 67° 44½′ S, 52° 5½′ W – 1 mile of northing in 24 hours spite of contrary winds.

Yesterday morning in clear sunshine – a light northerly breeze – the 'James Caird' was pulled over to an open lead and launched. The six dog teams drove up and their cargoes were stowed on board: 11 men took their places in the boat: she now has a full load = three tons and there was 2 ft of freeboard left.

Then an experiment was made: how long would it take to land all the stores and haul her up on the ice ? it took exactly 5½ minutes. We now know our limits, should we have to hustle some in a closing lead.

12 December. Position 67° 30′ S, 51° 34′ W: thus far we have got after 3 days of blizzard. Everyone is well pleased with the turn events have taken: the pack appears very much more open: the arrival today of a flight of 5 Antarctic Petrels and the finding of some Adelie Penguins are also taken as a good omen.

There must be plenty of land water now after these winds, but what of the area between ?

16 December. The favourable winds continued but it was not till yesterday that another position could be got – 67° 8½′ S, 52° 3½′ W.

Today we have gone north 4½ miles and improved on the westing just a trifle. Below are our distances last Sunday from various points of land compared with what they were when the ship was abandoned on Oct.27th in 69° 5′ S, 51° 32′ W.

	27th Oct.	12th Dec.	15th Dec.
Paulet Island	N17W: 346	N25W: 257	N24W 234
Snow Hill Island	N25W: 312	N35W: 229	
Cape Dundas	N20E: 534	N25E: 448	
(South Orkneys)			

Last night was the 50th which we have spent on the floe: we are averaging just a little over 2 miles a day towards Paulet Island.

21 December. A big change has taken place in our plans: in a couple of days we shall start sledging westward. This decision was come to today as a result of a scouting trip which the Boss made six miles westwards with a dog team today: he reports numerous bad stretches, but on the whole a succession of big flat floes.

He estimates that we shall be able to 2–3 miles a day: a month of that, supposing the floes maintain their present average drift, would put us within 100 miles of Snow Hill at the end of January.

Further, this has to be said for the plan: the food consumed during this period will be independent of our sledging provisions proper: so that all we do is pure gain, and more than that, should the pack never open sufficiently to make a boat journey possible.

The real reason for this change of plan, I think, is that the Boss is afraid we may drift NE and perhaps never reach Paulet Island.

22 December. The plan still goes on, with this change: between 4.0 & 8.0 am tomorrow the two boats will be taken by man haulage about ¾ mile west to the first big floe – i.e. over the roughest part of the way explored yesterday.

We have simply gorged today on all sorts of dainties which would otherwise be left behind: now people turn up their noses even at strawberry jam: for breakfast ham and sausages; for lunch baked beans and corned beef; for dinner jugged hare, apricots and cream; in addition unlimited milk, jam and pickles.

23 December. We set out shortly after 5.0, relaying the two boats westwards: we got them both before 8.0 to an old floe about 1½ miles away, crossing on the way a floe of young ice about ½ mile broad. Tents were struck after breakfast, and taken over by the men on the 15 ft sledge: the dog teams then brought over all the sledges and the galley gear. All turned in a little after midday at Camp No 4.

24 December. We have had our first setback, but it looks now as if we could manage to get ahead again. We left Camp 4 between 9 and 10 last night, but first of all Greenstreet had gone back to the old Camp with his dog team and left a notice there in the 'Stancomb Wills' (which will probably float out some day) telling how the 'Endurance' was crushed, that all were well and that our object is Paulet Island.

Broke a road through two bridges and finally reached an old floe ½ mile across: thus the boats were relayed about 1 mile altogether before 1 am.; the dog teams looked after a dozen or so of sledges., But then we were checked by an open lead ¼–½ mile ahead. Nothing for it but to camp (No 5) and have a good sleep from 2–8 this morning.

25 December. We were roused about 2.0 this morning and got under way 1½ hours later. The dog teams dealt with 14 sledge loads in relays, while the men relayed the boats, now lightened and emptied of all superfluous gear. We had done just 1½ miles when we stopped for lunch; after lunch we did another mile with practically no difficulty at all.

Course NW by W. Noon lat. 67° 3′ S.

26 December. The first half mile was over the old floe, on which we camped, pretty hummocky however in this direction and with numerous sastrugi. Then on again over rough and smooth patches for 1–1¼ miles to where we are now camped. No progress was possible after lunch. Camp No 7.

27 December. Camp 8. Made good about 2 miles, first over tortuous young ice with open pools, then 200 yds of bridge making at the lunch camp, then one mile of young pressure floe, apparently but recently cemented.

The skipper had trouble with the carpenter today whilst sledging: tonight the company assembled on the floe and ship's articles were read.

28 December. Our best day so far – 2½ miles and that in spite of a bad beginning. Before lunch we crossed about ¾ mile of pressure, thin ice and slush: much road making; finally lunch on a thick floe which cracked after the galley was set up.

29 December. Camp 11. The tale is no longer a pleasant one – we have retreated. The Boss was not at all hopeful yesterday morning: a scouting effort had shown nothing but slushy damp ice for three miles ahead. So we relayed the boats back to what will likely be a fairly permanent camp.

The floes have not really opened much, but the Boss at any rate has changed his mind yet once again: he now intends waiting for leads, and just as firmly believes he will get them, as he did a week ago that the ice would be fit for sledging the boats at a rate of ten miles a day.

30 December. Position: 67° 0′ S, 52° 46′ W. We are in our farthest west at last, and the skipper says a little of the progress that way is in addition to what we have sledged from Ocean Camp.

Five seals in all were killed today, which has helped raise our spirits somewhat, which are none too high since the sledging journey has been stopped.

The reason for the stoppage was as much the fear of further damage to the boats as the bad state of the ice. Today, however, the Carpenter recaulked the 'Dudley Docker' and it will be soon be fit for a sea journey.

31 December. The ice of our present floe is just 7 ft thick, overlain by about 3 ft of snow of which some 3–4 ins is frozen to ice under water.

1 January, 1916. Completes a year south of the Antarctic Circle.

The day's bag is 1 Emperor, 6 seals and a Sea-Leopard, the latter a great fellow about 12 ft long. It pursued Lees while he was out scouting for seals this morning, its long sinuous body giving it speed; fortunately he was on skis and could out-distance it but how a man on foot would have fared in the deep soft snow we don't know.

3 January. Seals have been so numerous that we have practically stopped hunting them: we must have three weeks supply of blubber in hand. Spite of NE winds observations show that we drift gradually northwards.

5 January. Thick misty day: but a position was got in the morning 67° 2′ S, 52° 32′ W – the 7 miles is accounted for by yesterday's northerly wind.

11 January. A general break-up seems not far off: Hurley, who was out on ski this morning, reports floes between our camp and our furthest west as much broken up.

14 January. Position 66° 57′ S, 52° 41′ W.

Some important developments took place today: the Boss suddenly got anxious over the absence of seals which has held for some days, i.e. a possible shortage of dog food.

Now there seemed to be only two alternatives as regards our leaving – either we do it in the boats (and therefore do not require the dogs) or else, should the pack not open this season, we will have to remain in camp till April, when it will be a case of making to the land as fast as we can with only one boat: in the latter case dog teams certainly would be useful, but on the other hand we ourselves require the seal meat to feed us till that date, and so keep intact the seven sledge loads of Bovril rations: I think we should manage them with man haulage, as after all it is the boat which decides the pace, being the weakest link in the chain.

The decision was made this morning to shoot most of the dogs this evening: Wild's, Crean's, Marston's and McIlroy's teams were led out of camp just before hoosh tonight and shot by Wild. I think we have done right, but one cannot help regretting their loss.

In the course of the day we moved camp about ¼ mile SE to a larger, but I think thinner floe. I distinguish it now as Camp 12.

Hurley and Macklin have gone off with empty sledges tonight to try and reach Ocean Camp – if they manage, our food supply will be replenished very considerably. Ever since we stopped the sledging effort, many of us wanted to make such an attempt for that very reason. And now it comes, because the Boss realises that the pack may not open this season.

But the season is not late yet: not till the end of February should we give up hope of getting away in the boats.

15 January. Position 66° 55½′ S, 52° 42′ W. Macklin and Hurley did not get back with their dog teams till 1.0 pm today, but they had succeeded in reaching Ocean Camp: only after a struggle.

At the old camp things are in a mess owing to water. They have brought back all the cereals, a good deal of dog pemmican, 90 tins of jam, 2 cases of dry milk, some potted meats and sundries. The trip has been well worth the trouble and fatigue.

17 January. Three seals were killed yesterday, and four today. We are now left with only two dog teams – Greenstreet's and Macklin's: Hurley's were shot and buried yesterday.

19 January. A blizzard continued all day yesterday, blowing from SW by S: we have nearly completed 72 hours of strong wind. At times the wind has been very strong, possibly 50 mph and all along there has been a thick drift along the ground.

The ship was beset on this date a year ago.

21 January. Tonight sees the completion of five days of strong wind from the SW by S: the velocity has averaged 20–25 miles an hour, usually accompanied by drifting snow.

The drift far exceeds all our anticipations – we are in 65° 43½ 'S; the northerly component amounts to 72 geographical miles.

Life in camp is not unpleasant during these days of blizzard: probably the only drawback is the increasing dampness of the tent floors. I while away three hours with Greenstreet this morning walking round the floe. Such is the general routine for most of us in the forenoons; in the afternoon one reads a little and plays bridge; as soon as evening hoosh is over down go the bags and one can read for the rest of the evening in warmth and comfort.

23 January. Position 65° 35′ S, 52° 12′ W. The skipper has worked out the bearings and distances to the points, one of which we would like to reach.

Snow Hill   N59° W   146 [miles]
Paulet Island N40° W   153
Cape Dundas N36° E   357

26 January. Visited the tilted berg beside Camp 8 this morning: from the top of the old Galley at Ocean Camp could just be seen according to the Skipper: the rest of the view was not very encouraging – ice almost everywhere with only here and there pools of water. One thing is evident: our camp is pitched on the best floe within miles: all else is a conglomeration of small floes.

27 January. At present we look like being short of blubber, for seals are ill to find and much more difficult to bring in owing to the state of the pack. Already owing to lack of fuel we are cut down to one drink a day, in the morning: for the other meals only one stove is kept going.

Great efforts are made to prevent our food programme becoming monotonous: for instance, there were rice fritters for lunch yesterday, and semolina pudding the day before: at breakfast the changes are rung on Beauvais and dog pemmican and seal steaks: while at night there is always hoosh, of which Adelie penguin stew (especially in the leg) seems to be the favourite variety.

31 January. 65° 16½′ S, 51° 57′ W. Two days of contrary winds have set us back a little, but fortunately we have lost very little westing.

As regards seal meat we can last six weeks, but the blubber will only last five. Before then the pack will surely have opened, or else gone very far north.

2 February. 65° 14½′ S, 52° 18′ W. A red letter day – the third boat has been brought up from Ocean Camp. It has taken a long time to persuade the Boss to this move, and I doubt if he would have done it, had it not been for the general feeling in camp: its importance is obvious, should we fail to reach Paulet Island.

4 February. Today it is blowing a blizzard almost S by E – the wind could hardly be in a better quarter: we shall make some westing as well as northing. Yesterday's distance to Snow Hill was 127 miles.

7 February. 65° 2′ S, 53° 3′ W. Tonight the wind seems to be almost due N. By good luck sights were got today and show us farther west than we have ever been before. We are now 109 miles from Snow Hill and Paulet Island bears N40°W 114 miles.

I measured the thickness of our floe with a boat hook at the edge this morning: the ice is just over 6 ft thick; on top this there is 18 ins of snow.

12 February. Rough sites place us in 64° 47½′ S, 53° 15′ W. We were all anxious to get sights, as we have been having a succession of favourable winds from SE, S by E, S by W and so on.

The blubber estimate made at the end of January seems to have been a false one: at present we have only 7–8 days fuel, and have had to cut ourselves down to one hot drink a day (at breakfast). Matters were helped by a big Weddell [seal] being killed this morning – the first seal got for a very long time now.

17 February. 64° 57′ S, 53° 15′ W. Since we have been in Camp 12 (Patience Camp) Adelies have not been common, the reverse of our experience at Camp 11b: indeed the few penguins we have been getting seem mostly to be Emperors.

Today there has been a change: no less than 68 Adelies have been caught and killed for the larder; what this sudden invasion means is a mystery, but the skins will come in very handy now that we are running so short of fuel. Bird life has certainly been very common during the last week, due probably to our being so much nearer the land.

20 February. Yesterday morning cleared somewhat and allowed us during the day to make an extraordinary large haul of Adelie Penguins; taken with a few more got this morning, the total is roughly put at 300. One would like to know why all these penguins have suddenly invaded us; (about 15 skins a day keeps the galley fire going).

Sights show us to be in 64° 57½′ S, 52° 54′ W. There is now little anxiety to know what the wind is going to do next, as the season is now getting late.

23 February. 64° 45½ ′ S, 53° 19′ W. Seals are more numerous again, 3 yesterday, 2 today: but penguins are not so numerous – I understand about 70 were killed today and a little less than that yesterday. We now have enough meat and fuel to last at least till the end of May, I think; but before that date we can hardly be still on the floe, unless our luck is of the very worst.

28 February. 64° 31′ S, 53° 20′ W. Completes the fourth month on the floe.

Never have we fed so well since leaving Ocean Camp. Our spirits were further raised by two seals being got near the floe – a Weddell and a Crab.

Life on the floe these days would be very pleasant were it not for the dreadful uncertainty of what our future is going to be.

The afternoons during the last fortnight have been given over to sewing and I have now completed a shirt and trousers made out of the Cameron tartan plaid which Alison got me in Oban before I left home. With the approach of colder weather, any extra clothing will be only too welcome.

We are only 86 miles from Paulet Island today. So near and yet so far.

5 March. 64° 9′ S, 53° 14′ W. Things none too cheery. Yesterday we were 55 miles to Darwin Island (one of the Danger group): the sooner the better if we are to make land this season.

A new factor has come on the scene. The Skipper thinks he has seen Mt Haddington several times and Mt Percy yesterday for the first time. The former should be visible 80 miles off (if the height is correctly stated): we are about 120 miles off if our chronometers are correct. It may be a berg, but we all hope it is the land, for if so we are farther west than we imagine.

10 March. 64° 0′ S, 53° 9′ W. This forenoon two very profitable hours were spent stowing the sledging provisions in the three boats, dividing the food so that each boat had a variety of every kind. Now that we have three boats there will be ample room.

11 March. A brisk SW breeze accounts for the good-run north: a NE current probably accounts for the large amount of easting we have made.

This afternoon to our great joy leads opened all round the floe, especially to the NW. The interesting thing about this opening is that it is not confined to one side of the floe but seems to be all round: the ice therefore is free to open.

If the prospects are as favourable tomorrow morning as they were this afternoon, we shall start in the boats at once – lash and stow and 4.30 and try to be off by 7.0 am.

12 March. After all we have not got away yet: things were too tight again this morning, but not so tight as they have been, so there is every hope.

Our food this month has been almost entirely meat diet. For breakfast we have friend seal steaks six mornings a week, something with a little fried blubber in addition; on the seventh morning there is a dog pemmican hoosh. The Sunday lunch has been liver and ham for over a month: on other days we have penguin legs or penguin steaks, generally with a dog pemmican bannock: lentil soup now makes its appearance once a week – on Wednesdays. The evening hoosh rings the changes on curry, turtle cup, soup squares, vegetable or dog pemmican, varieties of stewed seal meat: once a week there are steaks.

On this diet we seem to be growing fat, but some day it may get rather monotonous: before that happens we hope to make land.

14 March. It has been blowing a blizzard nearly 24 hours from SSE: everybody is in high spirits although we are pretty sure to be north of the latitude to Paulet Island when it stops.

16 March. We spent yesterday morning digging out the sledges, some of which were buried in drifts nearly 3 ft deep left by the blizzard. Of water opening there was next to none and it is the same today. The blizzard apparently tightened the pack again.

Again a blubber scarcity: it was discovered yesterday that there were only 1½ skins left. Cooking was cut down, stews were to be the rule. But today a seal came up on the floe and was killed.

17 March. 63° 35′ S, 53° 22′ W. A somewhat disappointing position, as we had thought that such a strong blizzard and such persistent SE winds (it still blows from that quarter) would have done more for us. One is driven to suppose that the ice is being hard pressed against the land.

22 March. 63° 19′ S, 53° 26′ W. Short commons start today. It was found yesterday that we had only 10 days blubber left: the meat estimate varies from 30–40 days. So now we get only two hot meals a day.

For this shortage bad management is to blame, as for months past many of us have urged the prudent course of laying in more meat, <u>while it was available</u>. These rations give each man about 1500 calories per day.

23 March. 63° 15′ S, 53° 29′ W. At last we have really sighted the land. The honour belongs to the Boss, who sighted it in the west about 8.30 am. What we saw was a dark mass, very far off, whose surface one would describe as very uneven: clouds covered its highest part: two white patches weew visible, perhaps glaciers on an otherwise rocky land.

At 3.0pm the Boss came running into camp, shouting that all Joinville Land was in sight. It was so – a mountain range bearing W ½ N to W by N. Not seen for long as cloud soon came down, but of its existence positively no doubt.

24 March. 63° 13′ S, 53° 24′ W. Joinville Land very clearly seen this morning from 7.30 onwards. The highest summit, which we call Mt Percy, has twin peaks; to the north of it are two conspicuous domes and then much farther N another small rise.

It has been a delightful warm day. Most people were glad to get the chance of washing their feet in the snow. I stripped and turned my undergarments in, having worn them without change for five months.

Provided our chronometers are right we are 32 miles from the NE Danger Island, 45 from Pt Moody and 60½ from Mt Percy.

27 March. 62° 58′ S, 53° 10′ W. Today we start short rations – due mainly to the shortage of fuel. The fire is on in the morning only to provide about ¾ pint of hot milk per man; for breakfast each man is served out with ½ lb of cold dog pemmican: what he has left over he eats for lunch with a biscuit and three lumps of sugar. The night hoosh consists of flakes of meat, with generally soup squares or turtle cup added: it will not be fully cooked, only so to speak made palatable.

28 March. It has been raining this morning – a N wind: the dampness makes one feel much colder than actual low temperatures, particularly about the hands.

Short commons now: ¼ lb dog pemmican and milk for breakfast: one biscuit and six lumps of sugar for lunch: and for dinner a half cooked hoosh.

A party will go back to Ocean Camp, now 8 miles away, whenever the pack permits, as there is much dog pemmican there are some oddments. With that extra food we can hold on for six months at the present ration.

Cannot confess to being <u>very</u> hungry on the short ration.

30 March. The most anxious day we have had since the ship was crushed. Shortly after 5.0 am a crack opened not more than 5 yds S of the galley: before the half hour the Boss had called everyone to stand by. Some of the meat was on the far side of the crack and had to be brought over: others were employed getting the sledges moved farther away from the edge; then all hands hauled the boats over more to the NW.

Then just as we turned in for breakfast a crack opened out below the 'James Caird' and one of the sledges; we rushed over and soon had them hauled back to safety.

Ice thickness. Just outside our tent it is 8 ft 4 ins thick; at the crack by the galley it is over 8½ ft thick. Permanent watches have commenced – 4 hours on and 4 hours off; by this means enough men are always available to shift a boat or sledge.

The two remaining dog teams were shot this afternoon: the meat of the five puppies has been kept as a precautionary measure; the other dogs were not in too good health.

31 March. A bad latitude shows us to be 63° 6′ S: due of course to all these northerly wet winds. Now the wind is S and the temperature much lower. Things are stiff and frozen and very uncomfortable.

70 Adelies were got this morning; but we were cut off from our camp for two hours by opening leads. The 'Stancomb Wills' had been launched for us, but was hurriedly hauled out of the water as there was a danger of it being nipped by the moving floes.

1 April. Yesterday we had some <u>fresh</u> fish for lunch, the pick of about 60 undigested fish found in the stomach of the Sea Leopard shot on Thursday – white sweet flesh and very agreeable.

2 April. Just about 8.0 pm our tent was awakened by the sound of an opening crack; we thought it was under the tent, as a matter of fact it was only a yard away from us. All hands were immediately called. By 8.45

we were able to turn in again, only the worse by being a little wet about the feet.

Our position today is 62°33′ S, 53° 37′ W. It is most favourable and everybody is in very high spirits. Clarence Island is only 83 miles away, bearing N 2° E.

3 April. 62° 24′ S, 53° 45′ W. The wind is now E: we have made an astonishing drift considering the lightness of the wind and contrary winds during the night. There must be a pronounced real current carrying us north and open water very near. The pack is very loose and we seem to be leaving all the bergs behind us.

Another Sea Leopard was shot today – we are now well in hand with blubber and are now getting some of it as food again. So that everybody may be ready and fit for a sudden call, our food ration is now normal again.

4 April. Two Crabeaters were shot this morning and a third escaped. So just when the dog pemmican was coming to an end, we were able to go off sledging rations altogether, barring sugar, and return to three hot meals a day – seal steaks, fried blubber, fully cooked hooshes and so on.

We have fuel to last us nearly two months and meat for much longer. Before that we will have taken to the boats, I feel sure.

5 April. 62° 14′ S, 54° 29′ W. We were a bit anxious during the night and everyone slept fully dressed ready for a sudden call. No lack of food now.

6 April. A present we are in great fear lest the ice should carry us through the gap between Elephant Is. and King George Is., for beyond that there is only open sea. But it looks very much as if we would be carried through the gap, in spite of currents and prevailing NE winds in Bransfield Straits, for we are not far off the latitude of King George Is. as it is.

7 April. 62° 8′ S, 54° 22′ W. Again a day of surprises, for what is apparently Clarence Island was distinctly seen this morning. It had all the appearance of Ailsa Craig seen some 15 miles away, but this snow pyramid must be nearly 60 miles distant.

There was a pronounced swell this morning, but it has now gone down. The wind is due SW. Compare the higher temp. today with the cold when the wind was NW: does this mean that the ice is to the NW, i.e. that the Weddell Sea ice is going through the gap W of Elephant Island?

8 April. 62° 6′ S, 53° 49′ W. Since yesterday WSW winds have prevailed: the position is disappointing; a current seems to be carrying us rapidly eastwards.

In spite of that Clarence Is. is much clearer today: very steep ice slopes seem to prevail, but the summit of the island is dome shaped. Those who were out also saw Elephant Island bearing N 14 W to N 21 W: the Skipper counted no less than ten mountain tops.

The pack is much looser today: a very heavy swell in the forenoon.

9 April. At last we have left in the boats. According to the Skipper we have made good 6 miles NW.

Last night between 6 and 7 another crack formed across the floe – at right angles to a heavy swell – cutting off two boats. One felt it was high time we were away. At 8.0 am the ice was really drift ice (the floes having during the last week been reduced by swells to the requisite size – ours was less than 100 yds across).

After breakfast everything was lashed up and stowed, and the tents struck for eventualities. Then about 11.0 am another crack formed across the floe, diagonally across the site of the Boss's tent. The pack being still open, it was decided to leave as soon as lunch was over.

At 1.30 pm all the boats had been loaded and we were under way, not without a little excitement. Rowed in spells till 6.0 pm through pure drift ice with only one or two thicker pieces. Easy work on whole. Tide rip at 3.0 pm, when east of a barrier berg, caused a little commotion, but we made away from it to the NW. Two or three whales blew round the ship.

SE wind all day and mild. Camp 13, where we now are, is only some 50 yds across.

'J. Caird'	'Dudley Docker'	'Stancomb Wills'
Boss	Worsley	Hudson
Wild	Greenstreet	Crean
Vincent	Cheetham	How
McArty	McLeod	Bakewell
McNeish	Macklin	Rickinson
Clark	Kerr	McIlroy
Hurley	Holness	Stevenson
Wordie	Lees	Blackborrow
Hussey	Marston	
James		
Green		

10 April. The Skipper thinks we have made good about 10 miles NW today, exclusive of drift: there has been a strong easterly gale.

Before noting today's doings there are some odd things of yesterday, of which there was no time to write in the gathering dusk. First of all land was clearly visible all morning, black rocks being seen with the naked eye for the first time: accurate bearings were taken to Clarence Isl.

We disembarked on to a level floe about 70 x 35 yds in gathering dusk and turned in. A false alarm about 8.0 pm and then a real crack right across the floe between 10.0 and 11.0. It passed right under the men's tent, and two men went into the water whilst much gear was wet. The Boss's tent and the Caird were isolated: quite an exciting time getting them over.

After that there could be no more sleep: personal gear was stowed in the boats: only cases left on the floe: so all of us stood by to wait for daylight.

We got under way at 8.0 am a strong E wind making it none too pleasant: some dumping of gear before we left the floe: but once we were away we landed on big open water stretches, and finally absolutely open water at 11.0 am.

We only had open water till midday: then a thin tongue of pack made us go several miles W; finally we got through, only to find the water too rough and stormy: so we retreated and hauled up on an isolated old pressure floe in our rear at 2.0 pm.

A thick day: land at no time visible: we have no idea where we are.

16 April. We landed on the NE point of Elephant Island yesterday, all dead tired after four very anxious nights in the boats, especially on Thursday and Friday, when there was very great danger of not only the 'Stancomb Wills' but also the 'Dudley Docker' being swamped.

During these days in the boats there was no time to write any connected account: a few words each day on a slip of paper are all I have to go by in writing this narrative on the last five days -

On Monday night [10–11 April] we slept sound, feeling comparatively safe on an old hummocky floe, some 35 x 50 yds: so much can exhaustion do.

A very heavy swell got up and effectively imprisoned us. All stood wearily by waiting for an opening – would it be big enough to let us get away? Boats could not live among heaving ice like this: it was swaying like a switchback.

Just when we had almost given up hope of the ice releasing us that day, a very considerable opening formed about 1.0 pm We had the boats launched and filled in not much more than half an hour, and were lucky to get leads and openings in the heaving ice big enough to prevent any chance of colliding with floes.

The wind was blowing strong from NE: the Skipper calculated a drift of 30 miles W in 24 hours, So our course should be SW for King George Isl. But first we must clear the pack by going SE: this the 'Caird' and 'Docker' we able to do fairly easily under sail – our most used means of progression – but the 'Wills' could not work to windward under the 'Caird's' jigger and even under oars was very slow getting up – due partly as well to bad steering through the ice.

Consequently by the time we headed SW, it was beginning to get dark, and farther progress was impossible. We hardly made any advance on this today.

We came up and secured to a floe and had a drink of hot milk. The day's food: ¼ lb of dog pemmican and a biscuit for breakfast; nut food and biscuit for lunch: breakfast and a biscuit for supper. So far we have always managed hot milk in the morning and evening.

Warned by the previous night's experience we did not land on the floe. The boats kept close together out in the open water: two men at a time were at the oars in hourly spells so as to keep the boats always in clear water and keep gradually going SW.

It proved a wet miserable night: to sleep in the bottom of the boat on rough cases with wet feet and damp clothes was only possible owing to our being tired.

Wednesday morning came with a beautiful red dawn. The well had gone down; everything quiet and peaceful, and it was a joy to run about on a floe while hot milk was being got ready. A sight not to be forgotten was the blaze of the blubber stove in the darkness of the dawn and the cheering effect it had on our spirits.

So that morning we sailed in the sunshine feeling that all was well: our clothes dried on us and things seemed good.

Then came noon with the position 62° 15′ S, 53° 3′ W: and our spirits instantly fell: here after rowing and sailing west; and after three days easterly winds, we had actually failed to gain ground. We were actually nearer Joinville Land and Hope Bay than King George Island.

Why this strong easterly current ? Would we be able to make any headway against it ? The only thing was to keep SW and see how much progress we could make with the current. But the afternoon sight only gave 53° 10'.

At night, later than usual, we tied up to a heaving floe, but too late and dangerous to take the blubber stove ashore. Hot milk was made with a Primus. The 'Docker' made fast to a hummock, whilst the 'Caird' and the 'Wills' made fast to her. We settled down below an awning for an unpleasant night.

Between 7 and 8 pm the wind suddenly changed to SE and drove the boats against the heaving floe. A very cramped and cold night trying to sleep on the 'Caird'.

On Thursday the 13th we got under way almost before daylight. Our course was now clear, to run before the wind for Elephant Isl. the sea not nearly so rough and I believe we have made as much as 30 miles in the right direction.

The night was very cold and there was consequently a very considerable formation of pancake ice, the floes averaging a foot at the most. For 3 or 4 miles we sailed due NW through a maze of bergy bits – hummocky lumps free from snow and well washed by water. By noon we had left the pack and were in open sea. We had taken just 4 days to get quit of the pack, but really easterly currents had driven the pack away from under our feet, for as events showed we were in about the same position as ten days previously in heavy pack.

In the morning Hurley made some milk on the Primus with ice brought on board the night previous; there was also enough water over to give each man a mug of tepid breakfast ration. For the rest of the day most of us felt inclined for biscuits. For in the afternoon the sea became much rougher; the water froze on the oars and the sides of the boats.

We were in an awkward position; no water and a very hazy idea of our locality, for the longitude the day before might have been wrong. No stinting of food, so that their [the men's] strength might be kept up.

And so we settled down to a very cold stormy night. It was well that we did not follow Worsley's suggestion of sailing on during the night: the boats would to a certainty have been separated.

21 April. To a narrative of five days, which I was unable to finish writing last Sunday, must now be added that of another five, marked by great hardship and suffering – a fight for shelter. We are now camped at Cape Wild, some 6 miles WNW of Cape Valentine, where we first landed.

The night of Thursday, 13th, proved terrible enough: in the 'Caird' owing to more freeboard we were not so very uncomfortable, but the 'Wills' and 'Docker' suffered much from water coming on board and freezing over everything.

A slippery iced oar was lost on the 'Wills' and one man went overboard, having slipped on a frozen thwart: he was lucky enough to be pulled on board again before the ships drifted away from him in the dark.

On the 'Caird' we got some sleep in a well forrard in spells of four men at a time. I got some sleep in the late evening and then remained out on top from 9.0 pm to 4.0 am, the only shelter I had being an overcoat thrown over my head; I was fairly warm: not so everybody. Went to sleep sooner than a man can say knife.

About 5.30 on Friday 14th whilst in a drowsy state I could hear those on deck saying that land was visible to the NW – Clarence Isl and Elephant Isl they thought. Everybody was smiling – land in sight and bright sunshine. Marston especially looked very fit on the 'Docker'; but two of the crew (Macklin and Greenstreet) had frostbitten feet. Blackborrow was badly frostbitten on the 'Stancomb Wills'.

The wind has now gone SW and soon fell very light, so that sails were useless. So we fell on the oars in spells of one hour and one hour off. Elephant Island was our mark, somewhere about the centre – 30 miles distant I suppose when first sighted.

But the rowing was none too brisk – we had no water, had been 24 hours without a drink. But fortunately we had on board a sack of seal meat, and this we started to eat raw for the water in contained – nearly 60% of the whole, so the Boss said. Plenty of raw seal meat, unlimited nut food and biscuits was what we fed on all day, for the sledging rations were much too dry, and no one would face them.

In the afternoon we made very slow progress: there was no life in the rowing: the Boss became annoyed and finally stopped towing the 'Wills' He threw himself into the work at the oars with fierce energy, but it was of no avail.

We had stopped making any headway at all about 6.0; a current seemed to be driving us off the land, towards the E. The wind went NW, and things looked pretty black: 10 hours rowing had brought us only within 8–10 miles of Elephant Island.

The only course open to us now was to try and make the NE point (Cape Valentine) under oars during the night. Then a fortunate thing happened: the wind went to the SW again and freshened and we were able to pick a course for Cape Valentine under sail.

We [the *James Caird*] took the 'Wills' in tow whilst the 'Docker' had orders to keep as close to us as possible. The wind was now blowing stronger than ever: we had Clarence Island some 6 miles to leeward, should we fail to make Cape Valentine.

It was a fearful night and much water came on board. The 'Dudley Docker' was soon lost sight of, whilst the 'Stancomb Wills' behind us complained bitterly of the seas she was shipping.

On Saturday 15th (a day that none of us are likely to forget) about 5.30 am, Wild suddenly shouted that there were cliffs on the port bow and that he was going to gib. There was a sudden scurry on board and I was wakened in the well by a foot being planted on my face.

But the rocks were not so near as imagined, and we were able to keep our course. We had been on the one to reach from 7.0 pm till now; progress to windward and against a current probably had been very slow. But now after a second rough night our spirits rose, for we had <u>not</u> missed the land after all.

In the dawn we slowly crept under oars NE along the coast looking for a landing place. Glaciers and steep cliffs seemed to deny us the right.

Finally about 8.0 am we were at Cape Valentine, marked by a prominent stack and outlying skerries. Meantime we were all crunching pieces of ice, broken from the glaciers and picked up as they drifted past us, for we were frightfully thirsty – 48 hours without water. That had been our fear during the night – to be carried out to sea without any water.

The Boss went on board the 'Wills' and had a closer look at the coast: we did not wish to risk the 'Caird' too near. Whilst he was away the 'Docker' came up from the S, and raised a cheer when they saw us, for they had passed a much worse night than we had: the Skipper had broken down under the strain – Macklin and Greenstreet took the helm.

It was a big relief to everybody to know that all three boats were here without a man lost. The Boss said little; his motto has always been never to split the party, but last night this was unavoidable.

We now proceeded to land at Cape Valentine, the Boss, the Skipper, the cook and Hurley went on board the 'Wills' and helped her crew take her up a small creek in the rocks, whence it was easy to put her cargo out on the rocks.

She then made trips to and fro under Tom Crean's charge, taking our cases ashore. I went in with the first load and was soon busied carrying cases up from the rocks to a storm beach under the stack, for our landing places was no more than a storm beach.

It took us from 9 till noon to get everything landed, for we were short handed: in the 'Wills' only two men were fit to do anything. Blackborrow, the stowaway, who had been ordered to land first, was helpless with frostbitten hands and feet: some were nearly as bad.

Some fellows moreover were half crazy: one got an ice axe and did not stop till he had killed about ten seals: another began eating raw limpets and dulse, although during the last two days there had been absolutely no restriction to food. None of us had suffered like this in the 'Caird' and to us it now fell to do most of the work.

Hot milk was going soon after we landed and on this we quenched our thirst, not so bad since we had been able to crunch floating ice earlier in the morning. Shortly after noon we were able to haul the 'Wills' and 'Docker' up from the creek; and then the 'Caird' was brought up over the rocks a little farther S, two oars being broken in the process.

We had got a footing on the land but not much more. Three shingle beaches are backed by steep cliffs and screes, up which there is no escape should a storm come.

The thing which pleased us most was the abundance of life. There were about ten Weddell seals when we landed, and a few more came up during the day. There is a colony of Ringed penguins on a fin shaped rock beyond the creek; Gentoos were found about the shore, apparently visitors; Paddies, Shags, Cape Pigeons and Skua gulls were all very common and together with the penguins kept up an incessant din all day.

We were all pretty busy squaring up in the afternoon: everything seemed confusion and one's clothes were hopelessly wet. All cases and important gear were placed on the highest beach; tents were then pitched on the intermediate beach, in our case with some difficulty, as the hoops had been put out a few days back: we managed to make some sort of shelter with oars and boat hooks.

A big meal of seal steaks and then we turned in shortly after 5.0 pm for as sound a sleep as a man can get. Hourly watches had to be set in case of a high tide. One still felt a heaving motion after four nights tossing about in the boats.

One thing above all was absolutely necessary – to find a proper camping place: Cape Valentine was too risky should easterly gales come our way. Wild accordingly took the 'Dudley Docker' westwards with a crew of four shortly after noon.

I did not see her leave, for the Boss had sent Hurley and myself SSE along the shore to see if there was any camp site in <u>that</u> direction. Our quest was useless (indeed we could not go very far owing to the tide).

The Boss sent me out with Lees up the cliffs behind to see what was on top. We had a stiff climb up a scree for about 300 ft, a less enjoyable scree I have never been on: on top I slipped but checked myself with the ice axe about 100 ft lower. Then we climbed for about 50 ft over uncomfortable rocks, made still more treacherous by a thin coating of snow. Our boots were not properly nailed and we had no rope: to go on was unsafe, so we beat a retreat. Climbers could certainly reach the top, but certainly not such a party as ours.

When darkness came the 'Docker' had not come back, so a blubber fire was lit, which would be visible through the gap between the stack and the cliffs. Shortly after 8.0 pm a hail was heard and we all turned out to welcome the returning crew and to haul the 'Docker' into safety on the beach. Great was our joy to hear that Wild had found a decent camping place about 6 miles to the W – apparently the only possible place they saw. Marston told me he thought it would be quite easy to get inland from this new camp site.

All hands were called to lash up and stow about 5.0 am on Monday, 17th. The three boats were launched before 6.0, while the tide was full. I just had time to finish hoosh – full breakfast ration.

The 'Caird' leading, we now rounded the skerries and rowed westwards. So far the weather not so bad, and the wind SE. But just as we rounded the second cape our troubles began. Fierce gusts swept down off the land, proper 'willy-was', and it was all we could do to reach the cape, round it and get in under the land. Then came a hard pull for life, hugging the land and making less than a foot at a time. I felt as if I had been hours on the fo'c'sle head tugging at the cumbersome oar. So we gradually pushed on, having lost sight of the other boats in the thick weather: weathered what we call the Castle Rock and finally reached our destination more exhausted I think than by the previous boat journey. All the boats were reached before 5.0.

Our first remark on landing was that this looked a very windy spot. Hot Bovril and a hoosh of sledging ration and then to sleep.

Thursday 18th April was Wild's birthday, the most uncomfortable he has ever spent, he says, for it was blowing a fierce blizzard from the SE, and our battered tent was filled with snow. The Boss intends to call this spot Cape Wild after its finder: that his birthday should fall next day and the weather be so wild make the name still more suitable.

The most alarming feature of the day was the departure of all life – penguins, seals and sea-elephants: for we had calculated on killing when we wanted and on not having to lay up a store. We do not anticipate the weather being good enough here for meat to keep.

About 8 of the party are broken down and unable for work, some of course merely disheartened by the bad weather. The Boss is wonderful, cheering everyone and far more active than any other person in the camp.

In the afternoon a big flock of Gentoos appeared and all hands mustered round and killed over 100. A seal was also killed during the day. We turned in wondering if the weather would ever be fine at Cape Wild.

Yesterday (20th) was however a somewhat better day – squalls from WSW alternating with fits of sunshine, giving landscapes such as Turner would paint.

All hands were ordered to lash up and stow about 8.0 am; dejected men were dragged from their bags and set to work, barring those too badly frostbitten such as Hudson and Blackborrow.

Everything is now subordinated to getting the 'James Caird' ready to put to sea. Chippy, aided by old McLeod and Marston, made a start, even though the weather was bad, putting in some strengthening beams, and preparing to deck her, barring a small cock pit.

We all hope she will be ready by Sunday or Monday, when a crew consisting of the Boss, Worsley, Crean, Chippy, Vincent and McArty will sail her to South Georgia, and bring back the 'Undine' or a whaler to rescue the rest of the party before the end of May, perhaps as early as the middle of the month, if they have any luck.

The Boss had been talking of getting a hut built up here for all hands but it seems almost impossible: the labour of bringing the stones up would be immense, and really it is the least sheltered part. Far more feasible seems the plan to dig into a slope of dead ice at the end of the S end of the shingle spit: here at any rate a proper galley and shelter of some size could be got.

Chippy has got the 'Caird' nearly decked, but the canvas has still to go on: some hands were busy sewing it today, finding it hard to do so as the ⌐anvas had been drenched with sea water and then frozen.

Most hands were busy skinning the penguins killed two days ago; a fresh kill of about 30 was made this afternoon, but the Gentoos seem easily scared, else more might have been got. A Weddell seal was killed in the afternoon.

Hands much cheerier now despite the weather: Blackborrow the only real invalid; should amputation be necessary he may be taken to Georgia in the 'Caird', as delay is dangerous.

23 April. Two tasks absorbed all hands today – work at the boat and work on the ice cave in the neve slope at the S end of the spit. The 'Caird' will probably sail tomorrow, the carpenter having made immense progress today and the boat being now almost completed. The ice cave has been started as we must have shelter from such weather; by tomorrow some men should be able to sleep in the cave.

Streams of pack were seen to the E today, causing a little disquiet in view of tomorrow's boat journey.

Two Weddells were killed this morning: Gentoos come up in flocks every day, and a few Ringed penguins appear every now and then. I think we are now safe as regards food.

25 April. The 'Caird' sailed yesterday forenoon after being launched and loaded under as exciting circumstances as could be wished for.

Chippy hastened on the completion of the 'Caird' and Marston looked out clothing for the boat's crew: others were filling bags of ballast and collecting rounded stones. The two breakers, each holding 18 gallons, had been filled with fresh water by the night watchmen; they were brought down to the beach with about a month's provisions made up as follows:

200 S rations of 9 ozs
100 B rations of 8 ozs
90 lbs Nut food
60 lbs Antarctic No 1 biscuits

Sugar, salt, Trumilk, Viriol, etc

Mthyl. Spirit and Paraffin.

At 10.30 all was ready and the 'Caird' was put in the water, empty, barring Worsley, Vincent, McArty, Tom and carpenter, all on deck. Just then rollers got up and before they could get her righted and away from the beach, she had listed, shipped some water and slipped two men overboard.

It was an anxious moment, as she is our only hope: matters were made worse by the carpenter trying to climb in, whilst those on her failed to trim the boat. When she was finally righted and away from the beach, she was being worked with only one oar. The 'Wills' was immediately launched and sent out the ballast, that being the oversight which nearly wrecked the 'Caird'.

The breakers aboard, the 'Caird' soon had out her jib and mainsail, while we on the shore stood by and gave three cheers; it was answered from the ship, but we never heard them, only saw them waving their arms. She set sail about 12.30, with a favouring SW wind: stream of pack far on the northern horizon is not likely to trouble her.

She faces a journey of about 800 miles to South Georgia through the stormiest belt of seas; should all go well we expect relief in a month's time.

Both bays to E and W are filled with loose drift ice; the 'Caird' did not sail a day too late.

Before turning to Wild summoned all hands and explained the situation; the prospect of our being here 6 months should the 'Caird' not reach South Georgia; the need for economy in food, and so on. He has the confidence of all hands, his reputation during the boat journey being enhanced twofold.

27 April. We are all wet and miserable. And apparently there is very little can be done to improve out condition. The ice cave which was to mean so much is dripping wet.

I worked all morning at the ice cave, where considerable progress was made.

It being my birthday I was given the afternoon to myself, and spent it on top of the rock making outline sketches of the surrounding scenery. I took the opportunity of hunting for exotic rocks in the shingle and found over a dozen pieces of granite, syenite, etc.

Work was pushed on with the ice cave, as we thought of spending the night there. A morning's work, which soaked everybody, showed that that was impossible. We have put the floorcloth across the roof of the tent and are sleeping on wet shingle tonight. There is talk of putting the two boats on our tent site tomorrow and trying to house more hands in that way.

The great danger now will be lest the meat store should go bad; not only the damp, but the Paddy birds also are the enemy. We are keener than ever for relief, even those such as myself, who would like to explore a bit before leaving.

By now the 'Caird' must be 200 miles nearer South Georgia. We hope she does not share the E wind and rain which we got today. It is typical Highland rain, which has soaked us to the skin; we have no change and not even dry bags to get into.

1 May. Another four days have gone, all full of incident and worthy [of] longer notes than are possible.

We struck our tent before breakfast. Then all hands turned to and levelled our tent site, and built walls at either end of the gut. Before lunch we got the 'Stancomb Wills' raised and turned over: after lunch the same was done with the 'Dudley Docker': the keels are 6–7 ft above the grounds. Then it was a case of trying to make the walls wind tight, and of stretching canvas along the sides; Marston officiated the latter job.

It was a pretty rough shake down for the night; four men on the thwarts of the 'Wills', three on the 'Docker', the rest of us on the deck. Our hope was to be no wetter that night, and a little drier every succeeding night.

It was a tiring days work – for most of us carrying flat stones for wall building. But there is no doubt this form of shelter is better than the cave – barring a great storm coming on.

Wild is proving a first rate leader.

But the night was none too pleasant, for a blizzard came on from the SW and soon found the weak spots in our wall. In the morning everybody was covered with at least 2 ins of snow.

Things were livened up indoors by the bringing in of the small blubber stove which Hurley made at Ocean Camp. It stands in the triangle between the sterns of the boats: from now on we shall always be black with smoke, but we hope at least dry.

As regards food Wild has some serious words to say in the forenoon:

there had been at least three cases of food being stolen, the temptation being easy as there have been too many open cases at the galley. But in spite of that three biscuits were stolen during the afternoon from a case <u>inside</u> the boats. Very strong measures may be necessary.

There are three sick men now in charge – a result of the rigours of the boat journey: Blackborrow has frostbitten feet, which are getting slowly better; Rickinson's heart has been troubling him; the worst case however is Hudson; in addition to frostbitten hands, a general breakdown has set in, and yet he was physically one of the strongest men we had.

A good deal of gear has been lost this afternoon in the gusts. I was a sufferer myself last night; the sledging flag which Alison made flew outside our tent on my birthday [26 April]; I omitted to take it down at sunset and on Tuesday morning it was soaking wet; since then it has been drying on our tent line, till last evening when the line was interfered with by an outsider and now it is gone with much that is more important to others, though to me the flag was more valuable.

Penguin steaks are our standard dish, though yesterday we had sledging rations for a change. As regards meat, we had been getting a little anxious, as neither penguins nor seals have come up for some days. Today, however, some 60–70 Gentoos came up, attracted perhaps by the better weather and such is the skill and cunning which we have now developed, that we practically bagged them all; it meant full rations for all hands for a week and what is of more practical interest a fine hoosh tonight of kidney, liver, etc.

2 May. Has been an absolutely perfect day; a very light breeze from the E: temp of course low. In the afternoon we set to, killed and skinned 30–40 Gentoo penguins. It has been a day fit to cheer anyone: our sleeping bags and gear have profited very considerably.

It looks as if we may fall back on two meals a day; to cook indoors takes double the time. For lunch today a mug of gravy and a penguin rib.

Shall not mind a winter here if we are to get weather like this.

4 May. Today I have at last got specimens collected from the rocks in situ – some dozen or so fairly representative rocks. The rocks are unfortunately very monotonous – metamorphic schists – and the amount of rock accessible is extremely small.

More Gentoos have come up – some 30 yesterday: and a Crabeater seal was killed two days ago when the pack first arrived; I think we are now safe as regards food.

7 May. In the afternoon helped carry stones for wall building at the new galley. The outside galley is now almost complete, ringed with a 6 ft wall and covered with the sail of the 'Dudley Docker': Hurley and Greenstreet have officiated as builders, while the rest of us have carried hundreds of flat stones.

Not for months have we filled ourselves so full as not to be able to eat more, for many said that after lunch they could not go a cake of nutfood even.

31 May. After an interval of at least three weeks I am at last able to make an entry here again. Since Monday the 8th I have been off duty owing to blood poisoning in the right hand (a poisoned tendon sheath, says Macklin) which during the first week was very painful, but fortunately began to mend on the 16th, none too soon as Macklin threatened to begin carving on that date if there was no sign of improvement (no local anaesthetics would have been possible).

It is a convenient date to summarise on, as owing to shortage of fuel, and the non-arrival of a long-expected SW (which would have cleared away the ice and made relief possible at this the most likely time) a further economy has been introduced today – all the cooking is done in the morning, i.e. one hot meal per day.

We were now [11 May] beginning to feel that winter was already on us: and yet the Gentoos were still frequent visitors; the glacier slope this evening was black with birds, probably as many as 1,000.

In the afternoon Wild put up a flagpole on the neve slope and hoisted the Royal Clyde burgee, which will now be hoisted each fine day as a sign to the relief ship.

1 June. [Continuing events of May.] I spent the day [Sunday 14 May] in my sleeping bag, a habit which is now the rule during bad weather, except for those on duty. The reason today was a strong SW blizzard which soon cleared away our great bugbear – the drift ice. It was a fierce gale, the wind carrying away the tops of the waves, and driving spray from the W right over out boats.

With an open sea talk naturally centred on relief, many holding that relief was possible even at that date; most of us however were for allowing a month from the departure of the 'Caird', whilst Macklin always stuck out for June 1st.

2 June. [Continuation of the events of May.] From this date [approximately 16 May] the outside galley was entirely disused and a considerable economy in fuel thus effected. Further it was discovered that penguin skins could be burnt indoors without causing undue smoke – indeed of this nuisance we are now free since the funnel has been properly rigged.

It is a point of honour with each fire peggy to see how few skins he can do the cooking with. Kerr today managed with only 12, but this is much less than usual: the average seems to be 15–16, i.e. with the fire going for 8–10 hours.

I remember Wild saying on the 16th that we would have to wait another week for relief, i.e. till the next SW which we presumed came regularly about every week. But it is idle to prophesy down here.

3 June. Penguins began coming up after midday and finally over 100 were killed and then skinned in the hut; no little excitement; reward 2 lumps of sugar per man. We now feel safe concerning meat and fuel.

5 June. Still no relief. We conclude the Boss has been down and finding close pack has returned. At that rate we can hardly expect a ship before August.

6 June. Today's penguin bag is put at 40. The seal killed on Saturday has set us up in blubber. As a result both yesterday and today the biscuit-sugar lunch has been supplemented by a very generous whack of blubber, yesterday rather oily, but today fried dry and crisp.

8 June. Yesterday's kill of penguins amounted to 71, but that will probably be the end of it for a time, as the ice has come back again. But there is good news to record in the shape of two seals. This morning Hurley killed as big a Weddell as we have seen: the blubber is as much as 3 ins thick: we are well off now for frying and lighting.

Now that we no longer sit round the stove for meals, the bags are down all day, and most of the time indoors is spent in them. Lunch today consisted of a dry biscuit and sugar, plus a novelty in the shape of fried penguin blubber taken from round the lower intestine.

11 June. We seem to have landed a cold snap and are now experiencing proper winter weather. The temp today is +6° F. There was close pack on the horizon, no leads to the NW.

Wild or somebody discovered that it was the King's birthday; so a hot drink of 4 sledging rations was served with steaks, and we duly drank the appropriate health. Realising that the King's health had been drunk on Friday without alcohol, the experiment was made of putting methylated spirit in the milk: but it was a failure, it being Clark's 90% preservative with a fair proportion of wood naphtha, which gave a sickly taste.

However keen alcoholists seemed only too eager to drink other people's leavings and became very merry accordingly.

17 June. Three more days of E wind with comparatively high temperatures. On Thursday it was actually raining.

On Thursday [15 June] the doctors accomplished what would have been pronounced at an earlier date as quite impracticable. Blackborrow had all the toes of one foot amputated, the operation lasting just 55 mins. It was fortunately a mild day and to keep a temperature of 60°F in the hut presented no difficulty. Meantime, those not deemed necessary were turned out of doors for three hours.

21 June. Bays open: occasional lines of stream ice 2–3 miles out with a slow easterly trend. This is apparently the shortest day, with according to Hudson a maximum possible of 5 hrs 20 mins sunlight.

23 June. Midwinter has come and gone with the mildest possible weather: yesterday temp was 30° F, today 33°. There was no ice visible today, the horizon being none too clear.

We settled down to the Midwinter Concert, to which everybody had to contribute. Most of the new songs were of a topical nature: here Hussey and James were very successful, the other efforts being merely commonplace.

Before the singing started three toasts were drunk in methylated spirits (sugared water for teetotallers): The King, The Returning Sun and the Boss and Crew of the 'Caird'. As there was more than one distribution of methylated during the evening some of the party were fairly merry when the concert drew to a close about 9.30.

We were a little bit anxious yesterday at only getting 3 odd penguins with open sea. But today a kill of 66 has shown that such fears are absolutely groundless.

The only shortage now seems to be tobacco and here the forrard hands have been very improvident. Given the same allowance as the afterguard, they had nevertheless exhausted their supply a week ago, and have been a nuisance ever since begging for smokes from the far-sighted.

So yesterday morning Wild, Marston, McIlroy and myself scrapped together half a pound to be distributed among them, and have determined that this shall be the last they shall get. I still have ¾ lb which I hope to make last until the end of July.

25 June. Yesterday we killed 25 penguins. Today just over 30: these numbers are an index of the water condition – open sea. Yesterday it was blowing pretty briskly from a little n of W: streams of pack could be seen 5–6 miles away to the N and W. The heavy sea still prevails – magnificent breakers.

29 June. A large number [of penguins] came up yesterday afternoon and these we killed to the number of 80, not for their meat but for their skins. Our end of the tent now makes a point of collecting the rich fat coating the lower intestine: we then melt it down in a mug in the stove and deal it out among the five of us: it has a sweet taste like melted butter and helps make up for the dryness of the steaks.

However there is talk of blubber now with the latter, as a small Sea-Elephant was killed this afternoon. Probably further slaughter of penguins will now be unnecessary.

Meal hours are now 9.30–10; 12.30–1; 4–5. We now have steaks at nine meals a week, penguin legs twice, two meat hooshes and a hoosh of sledging ration.

4 July. Weather changes seem very sudden and short-lived nowadays. It was very warm when we turned in on Sunday night: by yesterday morning a furious blizzard from SW was raging and it was very cold in the hut. A stream of ice could be seen far out on the northern horizon.

8 July. 35 penguins were killed this afternoon. The total since the beginning of June is about 550: previous to that date, 540 birds were killed.

11 July. A water sky reported to the NE on Sunday night. A NE wind of semi-blizzard nature springing up brought in some pack yesterday morning: the bays were filled with brash and small floes with a fair snow covering – very loose: much open water beyond.

Yesterday's lunch deserves note: a pudding consisting of about 30 smashed biscuits, 4 'S' rations nutfood milk. 30 penguins killed today.

15 July. Today the wind was NE and very warm – temp 31° F: the pack is very much closer – only two small lanes can be seen. A very large fall took place from the glacier this afternoon: had it not been for the ice in the bay and the depth of snow, the wave would have come right across the spit. A piece of ice came away about 100 yds long and reaching from the top to bottom of the glacier face.

Tonight sees the completion of three months since we landed on Elephant Island. 'Sweethearts and Wives' and 'The Boss and the Aurora' were celebrated in the usual way.

17 July. The pack is loosening again, mainly owing to a swell which set in last night. Lanes, however, are not visible, the looseness being pretty evenly distributed through the pack.

20 July. Last night was very muggy and close: there was something in the nature of a thaw inside the boats and owing to bad drainage a pool formed right in front of the stove. So a general clean up seemed desirable: those outside had a very thin time in wet mist: indoors we dealt with the stretch between the door and the stove, removed about 8 ins of dirt and then constructed a trench to the stove, where a large flat stone can be removed and water bailed out at any time.

Today a light NE wind and thick misty weather – very warm.

25 July. Anything for a drink !

It was discovered yesterday that the 'Caird' had left three months ago and that it was our 100th day on the island: so methylated was served to the thirsty ones, now reduced to a half dozen.

A large Weddell was spied on a floe about 10 ft offshore on the W side of the cape. How to bring it in was a problem, but in the meanwhile Wild shot it: an exciting interval while more cartridges were got, as the first two shots were not fatal and the seal in its struggles was getting nearer and nearer to the floe edge. It proved a female with well advanced foetus: hence perhaps the tenacity of life.

26 July. It did not rain all night, rather it blew a strong wind from the W, a warm thawing wind which was like to have washed us out of the hut: some 50 gallons were easily removed thanks to the well left a few days ago and again at 5.0 o'clock some 40 gallons. The water of course came from snow melting on the rocks at the side of the hut.

No pack left, only some floes in the inner corner of the W cove. Temp +32° F. Afternoon bag of 20 penguins.

28 July. The high temp and thaw still holds: this morning and afternoon the bays were clear but the NE wind brought past some streams.

After three days toothache, have given in and allowed Macklin to pull the offender – a back tooth.

1 August. Rain and wet mist for 24 hours, and it still goes on. We are all surprised at the very heavy swell, which seems to show that open water is not far off. Tonight the E cove is reported free of ice.

Two years ago 'Endurance' left the Thames: tonight therefore we have drunk success to the 'Aurora', for us well named the dawn.

3 August. Two days of either rain or snow. We have stayed indoors for three days in succession. There is a heavy surf somewhat deadened by a belt of brash ice inshore about 1 mile broad.

5 August. At last the penguins have come back – 39 were killed today and so relieved the anxiety which was being felt, as we had only skins left for four days firing.

There has been a change in the messes into which we are divided. Some of No 5 mess took exception to Hurley's acting as their server, which he was turning to his own advantage. A rearrangement of messes seemed the only solution.

So the old No 2 mess, which included Rickinson, since we came in the hut, is now dissolved. We are now arranged according to positions in the hut and I now find myself in a sexlet with Hudson and Hussey and the remnants of No 5 mess – Macklin, Kerr and Blackborrow.

11 August. This has been quite the finest day we have had for a long time. I was just preparing to go out at sunrise when Clark who was already out came back with news of a seal on the spit. This was an event, being the first seal up on the spit this season. Soon there were four or five of us out of doors, who immediately set to skin and cut it up.

For, I think, the sixth day now there has been the cheering sight of open sea, low tides and pretty heavy surf.

12 August. Penguin killing has now been stopped, except where it will be necessary: a result of the likelihood of seals being numerous in the near future. Another was killed this morning at the far end of the spit.

It now remains to be seen whether the number of Gentoos will increase now from day to day. For since May we have assiduously hunted every bird that came up, and hardly 3 p.c. can have escaped of some 700 birds killed since it became necessary to slay en masse.

A big improvement during the last week in the cooking. Clark has taken over the duties to give Green a short holiday and well illustrates the proverb about new brooms. The cooking pot for one thing gets cleaned daily, including the frying pan stolen in South Georgia.

Everybody can have his own particular wishes attended in the matter of steaks; and the fried legs are always well-cooked. The only failure seems to have been Tuesday's fried biscuits, which were burnt to cinders. Against this are the triumphs of the hoosh on Thursday and a biscuit pudding today, besides a couple of minced meat hooshes. Fried blubber too is found to be ever so much nicer when friend quite dry and crisp, that state being not unlike bacon fat.

13 August. Went round the coast well up towards the head of the bay; returning went up the slopes in view of the split for about 250 ft – the snow soft and toilsome. Even this small addition to one's viewpoint seemed to make all the difference to the seascape.

Meantime, several fellows were collecting limpets in the pools now made clear by low tide: later on these, amounting to over 100, were boiled in sea water and served round after supper.

17 August. Pack ice reappeared after being thirteen days absent: last night a line of ice could be seen on the NW horizon: today the wind being NE, there was pack of average thickness in the E bay and on the far side of the W bay; beyond was open water.

Every day now sees several hundred limpets eaten before supper: owing to exceptionally low tides, they are easily got. In addition to fried liver, a dulse pudding appeared at lunch today, running to about a plateful per man: it had been allowed to cook all day and looked for the all the world like greengage jam: the taste was somewhat cloying and was all the better with added sugar.

20 August. The nutfood came to an end today, but made a good death of it.

On Friday close pack as far as we could see, the floes on the average of small area but thick: yesterday and today the same, but I notice a slight swell today.

NE winds have held, accompanied by snow and mist. Everything yesterday was as wintry again as could be: but today a semi-thaw and the temp +35° F.

22 August. Heavy snow fell on Sunday night [20 August] – about 8 ins soft and powdery: yesterday almost a return to winter. There was a fair swell: today a heavy sea, were it not for floes and brash.

25 August. Yesterday was a really fine day, but the weather never seems fated to keep up, today being dull and moist. About one fine day a fortnight seems the rule. Today the pack is still looser: water stretches are common and the swell is much less. Six Gentoos were killed yesterday afternoon after a surprising display of agility in landing among the brash.

There is a chance of going short of meat unless the pack clears away. For some days we have had to fall back on penguin meat killed at the beginning of June and now distinctly high.

26 August. Raining all day: temp +35°F.

27 August. It is difficult in these days to invent a new dish, but Greenstreet, cook of the week, achieved it today. The place of nutfood was taken by boiled backbone and seal's head: a very savoury stew all told, especially the head parts.

There was ice this morning for about 4 miles out. A SW wind springing up after noon got it moving and cleared the E bay, but apparently brought up more ice from the W: NW there was ice right up to the horizon.

29 August. The ice is all gone bar streams of very small floes. It must be noted however, that only 6 penguins were killed yesterday and none today. And this is causing us a little anxiety, as our meat store is now considerably reduced: we begin to regret not having killed the penguins which visited us a fortnight ago.

On Sunday last [27 August] the outside galley was cleared of snow: yesterday and today gangs have been busy removing the deep drift on the N side of the hut, lest when the thaw comes, we should be flooded out. Some men shovel; others carry the snow away in boxes and dump it. As there are a limited number of shovels, half are on duty one day, and the other half the next, work only being done in the forenoon.

I was off duty today for this reason, and spent it very pleasantly along the coast to the E. It was a beautiful day, sunny and fresh, with a brisk wind blowing all the time. The colour of the sea seemed varying.

In the morning then I collected dulse and limpets in Cheetham's company: and in the afternoon after some desultory limpeting (it being too cold on the hands) explored along the coast nearly to the head of the next bay.

30 August. On board a Chilian relief ship and making NW to Cape Virgins at 11 knots. I have not yet learned the name of the ship, for all is confused and excited: on all sides we hear of nothing but the terrible war news.

Here then are the day's events:-

All morning about ten of us were kept busy shovelling snow away from the deep drifts on the N side of the hut. Knocked off at midday, and all hands went limpeting, with a view to making a seal-limpet-dulse hoosh. Shortly before 1.0 pm was called away from shelling limpets, lunch being ready.

Then just as Wild was serving out, Marston came to the door asking if we had anything to make a smoke signal, <u>as a ship was in sight.</u>

Lunch was thrown to the winds; all tumbled out of the hut anyway: there she was, what we took to be a whaler, steaming past us eastwards. The smoke signal failed, but there was no need for it, as by now her head was towards us, and she had rung up her flag at the mizzen.

Then came a scurry to get things packed – what we thought worth taking, and get on board. A boat was coming in; and took us off in two journeys.

The end was rather a hurry: none of our rescuers ever saw the hut: the weather seemed changing for the worse: it was best to cut and run. And so all my beach exotics are left behind: the only rocks I have are those in situ. But can one complain ? – My notes are safe, and every man is safe.

The ship was sighted just on 1.0 pm: before two all were on board and the course was set northwards. Then we learnt that this is fourth effort to relieve us; that the 'Caird' reached South Georgia in sixteen days and that the Boss, the Skipper and Tom Crean made a wonderful traverse of the island to Stromness.

Soup, biscuits and cheese were ready in the wardroom by the time we came on board; but nearly everybody was too excited to touch them. Then about 5.0 pm an excellent dinner was provided, the standard being Irish stew which we all fought shy of, except the potatoes. Tinned peaches and white wine deserve mention.

The wardroom, which I suppose normally holds four, is quite crowded out: but dinner was successfully managed in three servings. Then Hussey brought in his banjo. Tobacco and cigarettes circulate like water, especially the former.

My own tobacco was just about petered out; but the men had finished their stock two months ago, and were revelling now in something different from the acrid fumes of senna grass.

I doubt very much if the Chilians could appreciate our concert – their acquaintance with English is very limited. An exceedingly merry evening was spent aft at which apparently the rescued were the sole performers. Here were heard all the 'old' favourites and the 'new' topicals of the hut.

And so, till drowsiness and sheer weariness won the day.

2 September. In the Magellan Straits after a quick and uneventful passage. Thursday was fresh and sunny: yesterday, however, pretty rough: the uneasy motion caught us unprepared and there were few who did not succumb to some form of sea sickness, curiously enough those among us who were seamen by profession being the first to go.

Just after dark last night we were passing through Lemaire Straits. Today we have crossed shallow waters, in sight of land most of the time, towards Cape Virgins. Originally the intention was to land the Boss at Dungerees to send off cablegrams but it was too rough to land tonight and telegraphing is delayed till we reach a small bay just this side of Punta Arenas.

After all, our talked of food has not had the attraction for which we imagined it would.

5 September. Punta Arenas is likely to be our stopping place for nearly ten days, till a ship takes us up to Buenos Aires. A ship left on Sunday homeward bound, but too soon after our arrival for us to go as passengers.

Sunday's doings seem to have excited Chilians as well as English. The 'Yelcho' came through the Straits of Magellan during the night and by daylight we were within a few miles of Punta Arenas. Put in at a cannery at Rio Secco for some hours till warning should reach the town by telephone. Reached our destination about midday, being met by Governor, etc. then through great crowds to hotel, where clothes and a wash were provided. Smoking concert at the English Club at 9.0 pm.

Monday [3 September] saw the beginning of a feverish round of festivities which may prove tiresome. Shopping in the forenoon: in the afternoon a reception at the Governor's.

This morning I managed to slip away by myself and went on foot along a light railway running inland to a coal mine. Got a general knowledge of the country during an eight mile walk.

[Over the following weeks Wordie and the others enjoyed several weeks of celebrations and visits to Santiago, Valparaiso, Montevideo and Buenos Aires. Remnants of the party finally left Buenos Aires on 10 October on board the *Highland Laddie* and picked up several others, including Wordie, in Montevideo. The ship sailed from Montevideo on the night of 11 October for the journey to London. The *Highland Laddie* berthed at Albert Dock, London about midnight, Monday 6 November, 1916.]

BIBLIOGRAPHY

Books

Alexander, Caroline *The Endurance*, Bloomsbury, 1998

Band, George *Everest: The Official History*, Harper Collins, 2003

Berton, Pierre *Klondike*, McClelland & Stewart, 1958

Bertram, Colin *A Biologist's Story*, Bertram, 1987

Bickel, Lennard *In Search of Frank Hurley*, Macmillan Company of Australia, 1980

Bickel, Lennard *Shackleton's Forgotten Men*, Pimlico, 2001

Binney, George *With Seaplane and Sledge in the Arctic*, Hutchinson, 1925

Black, George *The Surnames of Scotland*, New York Public Library & Readex Books

Burton, Robert & Stephen Venables *Shackleton at South Georgia*, Robert Burton, 2001

Crook, Alec C. *Penrose to Cripps*, Cambridge University Press, 1978

Debenham, Frank *The Quiet Land: The Diaries of Frank Debenham* (ed. June Back), Bluntisham/Erskine Press, 1992

Dunnett, Harding *Shackleton's Boat: The Story of the James Caird*, Neville & Harding, 1996

Fisher, Margery & James *Shackleton*, Barrie Books, 1957

Fox, Robert *Antarctica and the South Atlantic*, BBC Books, 1985

Fuchs, Sir Vivian *A Time to Speak*, Anthony Nelson, 1990

Fuchs, Sir Vivian *Of Ice and Men*, Anthony Nelson, 1982

Giaever, John *The White Desert*, Chatto & Windus, 1954

Glen, A.R. *Young Men in the Arctic*, Faber & Faber, 1934

Hardy, Sir Alister *Great Waters*, Collins, 1967

Harrowfield, David *Icy Heritage*, Antarctic Heritage Trust, 1995

Hattersley-Smith, Geoffrey *The History of Place-Names in the British Antarctic Territories*, British Antarctic Survey, 1991

Hayes, J. Gordon *The Conquest of the North Pole*, Thornton Butterworth, 1934

Herbert, Wally *The Noose of Laurels*, Hodder & Stoughton, 1989

Hillary, Sir Edmund *View From The Summit*, Doubleday, 1999

Huntford, Roland *Scott & Amundsen*, Hodder & Stoughton, 1979

Huntford, Roland *Shackleton*, Hodder & Stoughton, 1985

Hurley, Frank *Argonauts of the South*, G.P. Putnam, 1925

Hussey, Leonard *South with Shackleton*, Sampson Low, 1949

Huxley, Elizabeth *Scott of the Antarctic*, Weidenfeld & Nicolson, 1977

James, David *Scott of the Antarctic: The Film and its Production*, Convoy Publications, 1948

Jones, A.G.E. *Polar Portraits*, Caedmon of Whitby, 1992

Kirwan, L.P. *A History of Polar Exploration*, Penguin Books, 1959

Lansing, Alfred *Endurance*, Granada Publishing, 1984

Locke, Stephen *George Marston: Shackleton's Antarctic Artist*, Hampshire County Council, 2000

Longstaff, Tom *This Is My Voyage*, John Murray, 1950

Mair, Craig *Stirling: The Royal Burgh*, John Donald Publishers, 1990

Markham, Sir Clements *Antarctic Obsession: A Personal Narrative of the Origins of the British National Antarctic Expedition 1901–04* (ed. Clive Holland), Bluntisham Books/Erskine Press, 1986

Mawson, Paquita *Mawson of the Antarctic*, Longman, 1964

McGoogan, Ken *Fatal Passage*, Harper Flamingo Canada, 2001

Mill, Hugh R. *The Life of Sir Ernest Shackleton*, Wm. Heinemann, 1923

Mills, Leif *Frank Wild*, Caedmon of Whitby, 1999

Mirsky, Jeanette *To The Arctic*, Allan Wingate, 1949

Morrell, Margaret & Stephanie Capparell *Shackleton's Way*, Nicholas Brealey Publishing, 2001

Mountfield, David *A History of Polar Exploration*, Hamlyn, 1974

Paget-Tomlinson, Edward *The Railway Carriers*, Terence Dalton/Wordie Property Company, 1990

Piggott, Jan (ed.) *Shackleton: The Antarctic and Endurance,* Dulwich College, 2000

Preston, Diana *A First Rate Tragedy,* Constable, 1997

Richards, R.W. *The Ross Sea Shore Party 1914–17,* Scott Polar Research Institute, 1962

Ridgway, John *Gino Watkins,* Oxford University Press, 1974

Rymill, John *Southern Lights,* The Knell Press, 1986

Savours, Ann *The Voyages of The Discovery,* Virgin Books, 1992

Shackleton, Edward *Arctic Journeys,* Hodder & Stoughton, 1937

Shackleton, Sir Ernest *South,* Century Ltd, 1983 (Appendix: *Scientific Work; Sea-Ice Nomenclature,* by James M Wordie; Meteorology by Leonard Hussey; *Physics* by R.W. James; *South Atlantic Whales and Whaling* by Robert Clark)

Shackleton, Jonathan & John MacKenna *Shackleton: An Irishman In Antarctica,* The Lilliput Press, 2002

Smith, Michael *An Unsung Hero – Tom Crean, Antarctic Survivor,* The Collins Press/Headline, 2000

Smith, Michael *I Am Just Going Outside,* The Collins Press/Spellmount, 2002

Speak, Peter *William Speirs Bruce: Polar Explorer and Scottish Nationalist,* National Museums of Scotland Publishing, 2003

Steele, Peter *Eric Shipton: Everest and Beyond,* Constable, 1999

Tenzing, Norgay, *Man of Everest* (As told to James Ramsey Ullman), George Harrap & Co, 1955

Thomson, John *Elephant Island and Beyond*, Bluntisham Books/Erskine Press, 2003

Thomson, John *Shackleton's Captain: A Biography of Frank Worsley,* Hazard Press, 1998

Unsworth, Walt *Everest: The Mountaineering History*, The Mountaineers Books/Baton Wicks, 2000

Wollaston, Nicholas *The Man on the Ice Cap*, Constable, 1980

Wild, Frank *Shackleton's Last Voyage: The Story of the Quest,* Cassell & Co, 1923

Worsley, Frank *Endurance*, Philip Allan & Co, 1931

Worsley, Frank *The Great Antarctic Rescue*, Times Books, 1977

Yelverton, David *Antarctica Unveiled*, University Press of Colorado, 2000

Newspapers, periodicals, etc

A large number of newspapers, periodicals and other publications were consulted in the research of this book, including private collections held by the Wordie Family. The most helpful publications included:

Arctic (Journal of the Arctic Institute of North America)

Cambridge News, Cambridge

Cambridge Review, Cambridge

Countryman

Daily Chronicle, London

Eagle, Cambridge

Evening Standard, London

Geographical Journal, London

Glasgow Academy Journal, Glasgow

Glasgow Evening Citizen, Glasgow

Glasgow Herald, Glasgow

Magellan Times, Punta Arenas

Morning Post, London

Nature, London

New Scientist, London

News Chronicle, London

The Observer, London

The Polar Record, Cambridge

The Railway Magazine, London

The Scotsman, Edinburgh

Scottish Geographical Magazine, Edinburgh

Shipbuilding & Shipping Record, London

Stirling Observer, Stirling

The Times, London

Wireless World, London

Newspaper, Periodical Articles

Allan, D.A. Sir James Mann Wordie – Obituary, *Royal Society of Scotland Year Book,* 1961–62

Anon The Imperial Transantarctic Expedition's ship, 'Endurance', *Shipbuilding and Shipping Record,* 30 July 1914

Anon Sir James Mann Wordie – Exploration's Elder Statesman, *New Scientist,* 5 December, 1957

Anon Sir James Mann Wordie, *The Eagle,* June 1962

Armstrong, Terence Sir James Mann Wordie – Obituary, *Arctic Journal,* Vol. 15, No.2, 1962

Balchin, W.G.V. United Kingdom Geographers in the Second World War, *Geographical Journal,* Vol. 153, No. 2, July 1987

Campbell, James W. Some Local Jacobite Families, *Stirling National History and Archaeological Society,* 15 February 1921

Campbell, James W. The Family of Wordie, *Transactions, Stirling Natural History and Archaeological Society,* 1938

Campbell, James W. The Story of Murrayshall, *Transactions, Stirling Natural History and Archaeological Society,* 20 October 1925

Carmichael, Hugh & E.G. Dymond High Altitude Cosmic Radiation Measurements Near the North Geomagnetic Pole, *Proceedings of the Royal Society,* No. 946, Vol. 171, June 1939

Carmichael, Hugh & E.G. Dymond Upper Air Investigations in North-West Greenland, *Proceedings of the Royal Society,* No. 947, Vol. 171, June 1939

Clark, Robert S. Marooned on Elephant Island, *Aberdeen Grammar School Magazine,* March 1920

Cyriax, Richard & James Wordie Centenary of the Sailing of Sir John Franklin with the Erebus and Terror, *Geographical Journal,* Vol. 106, 1945

Debenham, Frank The Scott Polar Research Institute, *Geographical Journal,* July 1926

Feachem, R.W. The Cambridge University Arctic Expedition, 1937, *Cambridge Review,* 12 November 1937

Feachem, R.W. Wordie's Last Expedition, *Scotland Magazine,* April 1962

Fuchs, Vivian Sir James Mann Wordie – Obituary, *Polar Record,* Vol. 11 (71), 1962

G.H.R.L. Sir James Wordie – Obituary, *The Glasgow Academy Chronicle,* March 1962

Graham, Lascelles 'Old Boys' and Their Stories of the High School Stirling, 1900 (publication unknown)

Keegan, John The Battle of the Lys, BPC Publishing, 1971

Mercanton, Paul-Louis The First Ascent of the Beerenberg, *Echo des Alpes* No. 8, 1924

Morris, David B Robert Louis Stevenson and the Scottish Highlanders, 1929 (Publication unknown)

National Trust for Scotland *Glencoe,* 1994

Paine, Ronald The View From Ossian's Cave, *The Countryman,* Vol. 94, No. 3, 1989

Paterson, P. Bygone Days in Cambusbarron, *Cambusbarron Community Council,* 1981

Paterson, T.T. Physiographic Studies in North West Greenland: Wordie 1934 Arctic Expedition, *Meddelelser Om Gronland,* 1951

Ritchie, M.H.W. The Wordie Arctic Expedition, *The Sphere,* 14 October 1934

Robb, Geo. Carting Department, *The Railway Magazine,* September, 1907

Roberts, Brian Obituary, *Polar Record,* Vol. 19, 1979

Robin, Geoffrey Sir James Mann Wordie – An Obituary, *Nature,* 7 April, 1962

Royal Society of Edinburgh Bruce Memorial Prize: Citation to James Mann Wordie, 25 October, 1925

Russell, George S. Glencoe and Dalness – How It All Began, *Heritage For Scotland,* Vol. 3, 1987

Scott, J.M. James Mann Wordie: Biography (undated, publication unknown)

Shackleton, Sir Ernest The Imperial Trans-Antarctic Expedition, *Geographical Journal,* Vol. 43, 1914

Speak, Peter The Scottish Spitsbergen Syndicate, (Publication unknown)

Thomson, Jessie & Charles Strachan From Castle Rock to Torbrex: Essays on the High School of Stirling, 1962 (publication unknown)

Watson, Francis Sir James Mann Wordie 1897–1962, *Proceedings of the British Academy*, Vol. XLIX, Oxford University Press

Wordie, James My First Ascent of the Alps, *The Glasgow Academy Chronicle*, October 1903

Wordie, James 'Barrier' versus 'Shelf', *Journal of Glaciology*, Vol. 1, No 8, October 1950

Wordie, James Lincoln Ellsworth, *Nature*, Vol. 168, September 1951

Wordie, James The Drift of the Endurance, *Geographical Journal*, Vol. 51, April 1918

Wordie, James Geological Observations in the Weddell Sea Area, *Transactions of the Royal Society of Edinburgh*, Vol. 53, Part 1, No. 2, 1921

Wordie, James The Natural History of Pack-ice as observed in the Weddell Sea, Royal Society of Edinburgh, Vol. 52, Part 4, No. 31, 1921

Wordie, James Depths and Deposits of the Weddell Sea, Royal Society of Edinburgh, Vol. 52, Part 4, No. 30, 1921

Wordie, James Ross Sea Drift of the Aurora in 1915–17, *Geographical Journal*, Vol. 58, September 1921

Wordie, James The Cambridge Expedition to East Greenland in 1926, *Geographical Journal*, September 1927

Wordie, James Cambridge East Greenland Expedition, 1929, *Geographical Journal*, No. 6, June 1930

Wordie, James The Falklands Islands Dependence Survey 1943–46, *Polar Record*, Vol. 4 (32), 1946

Wordie, James Notes on a Visit to Falkland Islands Dependencies, 1947

Wordie, James The Geology of Jan Mayen, Royal Society of Edinburgh, Vol. LIV Part III (No 18)

Wordie, James An Expedition to Melville Bay and North-East Baffin Land, *Geographical Journal*, October 1935

Wordie, James An Expedition to North West Greenland and the Canadian Arctic in 1937, *Geographical Journal*, November 1938

Wordie, James The Ross Ice Barrier and the Shackleton Ice-Shelf, Presidential Address at International Association of Scientific Hydrology Commission of Snow and Ice, 21 August, 1951

Wordie, James The Voyage of the St Roch Through The North-West Passage, 1944, *Polar Record,* No. 30, July 1945

Wordie, James Sir Ernest Shackleton, *Geographical Journal,* No. 3, 1922

Wordie, James Report on Archaean Rocks of Central Spitsbergen, 1919

Wordie, James Report on the Northern Portion of Prince Charles Foreland, 1920

Wordie, James Report on the Tertiary Rocks of Prince Charles Foreland, 1920

Wordie, James Preliminary Report on Certain Areas of Spitsbergen, October 1919

Wordie, James Present Day Conditions in Spitsbergen, *Geographical Journal,* July 1921

Wordie, James Sport and Pastime in the Antarctic, *The Glasgow Academy Chronicle,* October 1919

Wordie, James Frank Wild – An Obituary, *Polar Record,* Vol. 3 (19), 1940

Wordie, James Sir Hubert Wilkins, *Nature,* Vol. 183, January 1959

Wordie, James & Brian B. Roberts The Scientific Results of the Shackleton Antarctic Expeditions, *Polar Record,* Vol. 4, No. 26, 1943

Wordie, James & Arthur Hinks Peary's Journal to the Pole, *Geographical Journal,* Vol. 86, 1937

Wordie, James & Stanley Kemp Observations On Certain Antarctic Icebergs, *Geographical Journal,* No. 5, May 1933

Wordie, James & George Tyrell Memorandum on Future Geological Work in Spitsbergen, 1919

Worsley, Frank Shackleton's Expedition to the Antarctic – The Rescue by Chile, *The Chilean Review,* 1928

Wright, John British Polar Expeditions 1919–39, *Polar Record,* 26 (157), 1990

Archive sources

British Antarctic Survey (BAS)
British Library, London (BL)
Fuchs, Peter (PF)
Glasgow Academy, Scotland (GA)
Glasgow School of Art, Scotland (GSA)
Glasgow University, Scotland (GU)
The National Archive, (formerly Public Record Office) London (NA)
National Archives of Scotland, Edinburgh (NAS)
National Library of Scotland, Edinburgh (NLS)
National Trust for Scotland (NTS)
Riksarkivet (National Archives of Norway), Oslo (NSA)
Royal Geographical Society, London (RGS)
Royal Society of Edinburgh (RSE)
St John's College, Cambridge (SJC)
Scott Polar Research Institute, Cambridge (SPRI)
Scottish Record Office, Edinburgh (SRO)
Stirling Central Library, Scotland (SL)
Alexander Turnbull Library, New Zealand (ATL)

Unpublished correspondence, diaries, interviews, etc
(Unless otherwise stated, documents listed below are in the possession of the Wordie family)

S.Y. *Aurora* Extracts from log book, 1915–16
Bakewell, William L. Unpublished autobiography, (Rajala Family)
Bertram, Colin Memories of James Wordie, 1994
Bonney T. Assessment of *Natural History of Sea Ice in Weddell Sea,* by James Mann Wordie (SJC)
British Antarctic Survey Documents, correspondence re: Operation Tabarin, 1943–97, AD1/D; AD3/1; AD6 series: Scott Polar research Institute, Management Committee Minutes, 1954–58, AD 3/1/AS (BAS)

Clarke, (née Wordie) Elizabeth (Daughter), Personal recollections of James Wordie, interviews with author, 2003

Crook, John Personal recollections of James Wordie, interviews with the author, 2003

Debenham, Frank, Report on James Wordie's expedition papers, 17 August, 1921 (SJC)

Discovery Committee Correspondence, papers, reports 1925–47 (NA) Correspondence, papers, reports 1922–49, see National Library of Scotland (NLS)

Elliott, Frank, Interview re: Falkland Islands Dependencies Survey, 1997, AD6/16 (BAS)

Everest Committee Correspondence, papers, 1921–52 (RGS)

Everest Expedition, 1953, Government correspondence and papers, AIR 8/1733; FD1/8597; FO 371/101/101163 (NA)

Fisher, James, James Wordie: Record of conversation, 10 July, 1956 (SPRI)

Fleming, Launcelot, Letter to Frank Debenham, 18 August, 1945 (SPRI)

Fuchs, Sir Vivian, Personal recollection of Sir James Wordie (undated); Letter to Anne Savours, re: Sir James Wordie, 3 November, 1994; Journal of East Greenland Expedition, 1929 (PF); Correspondence, documents and Committee minutes of Commonwealth Trans-Antarctic Expedition, 1950–58 (PF); Letter to Scott Polar Research Institute, re: Brian Roberts, 27 January, 1988 (PF)

Glen, Sir Alexander, Personal recollections of James Wordie, correspondence with author, 2003

Gregory, Professor John, Report on James Wordie's dissertation for Fellowship, 7 September, 1921 (SJC)

Harker, Alfred, Report on Fellowship dissertation on The Natural History of Sea Ice as observed in the Weddell Sea, 15 October, 1919 (SJC)

Hattersley-Smith, Geoffrey, Interviews with author, 2002

Hurley, Frank, Journal, 1914–17, (SPRI microfilm. Original ML)

James, Reginald, *Endurance,* Final List of Noon Positions, 1914–16

Endurance journal, 1914–16 (SPRI); Letter to Hugh R Mill, 12 May, 1922 (SPRI); Letters to James Wordie

Law Philip G., Personal recollections of James Wordie, January 1995

Macklin, Alexander, Letter to James Wordie, 10 June, 1933; Shackleton: As I Knew Him, speech to Rotary Club, 1959

Markham, Sir Clement, Note to Royal Geographical Society, re: Imperial Trans-Antarctic Expedition, 1914 (RGS)

Marr, John E., Letter to St John's College, re: James Wordie 20 June 1910 (SJC)

McNeish, Harry, *Endurance* diary 1914–16, (SPRI microfilm. Original ATL)

National Library of Scotland, Wordie Collection: 68 Volumes of correspondence, documents, reports including; Discovery Committee papers 1922–49; British Graham Land Expedition 1934–37; MS 9501-68 (NLS)

National Trust for Scotland, Correspondence re: Purchase of Glencoe and Dalness Estate, (NTS)

Operation Tabarin Government correspondence, documents, etc ADM1/18114 (NA); Correspondence, documents, 1943–97, AD6/1 series (BAS) Correspondence, documents, etc (SPRI)

Orde-Lees, Thomas, Trans-Antarctic Expedition 1914–16, Diary (SPRI)

Paget-Tomlinson, Edward Personal recollections of James Wordie, interviews with author, 2003

Parkinson, Mervyn, Personal notes on Sir James Wordie, December 1995

Rae, Joanna, Operation Tabarin, British Antarctic Survey papers, (BAS)

Roberts, Brian, Letter re: Operation Tabarin, 3 December, 1965

Royal Geographical Society, Re: James Wordie; Correspondence, papers, reports, 1917–1960; *Endurance* expedition, Correspondence, papers 1917–19; Everest; Everest/Himalayan Committee, 1921–53, correspondence, papers, (RGS)

Royal Palace, Oslo, Re: The Royal Order of St Olav

Russell, Arthur W., Correspondence with James Wordie re: Glencoe

Russell, George S., Correspondence re: James Wordie

St John's College, Cambridge, James Mann Wordie: Student and Fellow's Record Sheet; Correspondence (SJC)

Scott, J.M., Letter to Reginald James, 7 December, 1949

Shackleton, Emily, Letter to James Wordie, 1922.

Shackleton, Sir Ernest, Letter to James Wordie, 7 October, 1916; Correspondence with Admiralty, re: *Quest* expedition, ADM 1/8595/162 (NA)

Simpson, C.J.W., Correspondence with Peter Wordie re: James Wordie, 1998–2000

Stancer (nee Wordie), Alison (Daughter), Personal recollections of James Wordie

Swithinbank, Charles, Interviews with author, 2003

Vosper, Dr Sydney, Extracts from diary, 1917–18

Wordie, George (Son), Personal recollections of James Wordie, interview with author 2003

Wordie, Sir James Mann, Correspondence, diaries and papers 1889–1962 Including correspondence with: HM Admiralty; BBC; Hugh Carmichael; Richard Cyriax; Government of Denmark, Greenland Department; Harald Drever; E.G. Dymond; Margery Fisher; Launcelot Fleming (SPRI); Arthur Hinks (RGS); Captain Ove Hoegh; Professor Olaf Holtedahl; Walter How (SPRI); Ian Hunter; Gunnar Issachsen; Reginald W James; Dr Lauge Koch; Derek Leaf; Tom Lethbridge; Dr Paul-Louis Mercanton; Hugh R. Mill; Noel Odell; Royal Botanical Gardens, Kew; Royal Society; Pte MacWhirter; Northwest Territories Commissioner, Canada; Angus Robin; Royal Geographical Society (RGS); Robert Rudmose Brown; Arthur W. Russell (NTS); James M Scott; Scottish Spitsbergen Syndicate; Emily Shackleton; Sir Ernest Shackleton; Professor J.A. Steers (BAS); H.J. Wintle (SJC); Alison Wordie; Gertrude Wordie; Jane Mann Wordie; John Wordie;

The Wordie Collection at the National Library of Scotland contains over 4,600 books, journals, pamphlets and maps, and 68 volumes of correspondence and papers, MSS 9501-68; Acc 11483; (NLS)

Diaries, notebooks:

Switzerland 1903

Switzerland 1907

Germany 1911

Canada and Yukon 1913

Switzerland 1914

Weddell Sea log, 4 vols. 1914–16

Spitsbergen 1919

Spitsbergen 1920

Jan Mayen 1921

Voyage of *Elspeth* 1922

East Greenland 1923

East Greenland 1926

East Greenland 1929

West Greenland 1934

West Greenland 1937

Log Book of *Isbjorn,* Baffin Island 1937

Baffin Island 1939

Journal of *Trepassey* voyage for Falkland Islands Dependencies Survey, 1947–48

North Greenland 1954

Glasgow Academy: Graduation records; Roll book/Honours List; Honorary Degree; Correspondence (GA)

Glasgow University: Graduation Records, (GU)

St John's College Cambridge: Student record sheet;

Fellow record sheet; Correspondence (SJC)

Military Service record 1916–19, WO/374/76864 (NA)

Scottish Spitsbergen Syndicate: Papers and correspondence, 1919–20

Transcript of BBC interview, 17 November, 1937

Wordie, Jane Mann (Mother)

Correspondence with James Wordie, 1906–10;

Inventory (ref: SC36/48/229 pp. 457–466) (NAS); Trust disposition and settlement (ref: SC36/51/154 pp. 780–794) (NAS)

Wordie, John (Father), Correspondence with James Wordie, 1906–10;

Inventory (ref: SC36/48/229 pp. 531–536) (NAS); Will, (ref: SC26/51/154 pp. 841–855) (NAS)

Wordie, Peter J. (Son), Correspondence re: James Wordie;

Personal recollections of James Wordie, interviews with author 2001–03

Worsley, Frank, *Endurance* journals 1914–16 (SPRI); Paper on Animals Killed in the Weddell Sea, 1914–16

Films

South, by Frank Hurley, BFI Video Publishing, London

INDEX

Incorporated Society of Carters 2
International Geological Congress,
 1913 20
International Geophysical Year
 1957–58 247
International Polar Year, 1882–83 136
International Polar Year, 1932–33 157
International Whaling Convention
 1946 171
Instituto de Pesca No. 1 95
Irvine, Alexander 'Sandy' 153, 155
Isbjorn 203, 204, 205, 209
Isfuglen 136

Jacobites 1
Jackson-Harmsworth Expedition 125
Jagger, Charles 159
Jakobsen, Karl 184, 185, 191, 197
Jakobsen, Lars 164, 166–67, 172, 174,
 176, 179, 184
Jakobsen, Thorvald 197
James Caird 57, 64, 66–69, 71, 74, 75,
 77–78, 82, 84–85, 86, 90, 92–93,
 94, 95, 101, 104, 116
James, David 220, 221
James, Reginald 'Jimmy' 30, 34, 35, 43,
 46-48, 60, 66, 77, 78, 89, 98, 103,
 107, 108, 111, 112, 113, 114, 128, 132,
 133, 134, 135
Jan Mayen Island 134–35, 136-38, 142,
 145, 151, 154, 164
Johansen, Hjalmar 126
John Biscoe 227
Johnson, Amy 197
Joinville Island 64, 72
Jones Sound 205
Journal of Glaciology 243
Jutland, Battle of 94, 105

Kemmell, Mount 118
Kemp, Stanley 169, 215
Kerr, Alfred 56, 63, 91, 113
King George Island 65, 70
King's College, London 162
Kirwan, Larry (Sir) 230, 234, 244,
 246, 247, 249
Klondike Gold Rush 21

Koch, J.P. 155
Koch, Dr Lauge 176, 184, 192, 258
Konig, Dr Felix 25

La Negra 34
Lack, David 156
Lady of Avenel 130
Lambert, Raymond 230
Lancaster Sound 195, 196, 207, 209
Lansing, Alfred 114
Larkins, Dr 144
Laurie Island 125, 219
Leaf, Derek 201, 203, 209
Leith 127, 204, 209
Lethbridge, Tom 139, 151, 156, 163, 164,
 178, 201, 203, 205, 206, 214
Lewin, Henry 206, 207
Lindsay, Alexander 10
Lindsay, Martin 194
Little Pendulum Island 176
Lochhead, James Bursary 13
London Midland & Scottish Railway
 Company 226
London Zoo 177
Longland, Jack 20, 155
Longstaff, Tom 143, 154, 155, 173, 192,
 196, 197, 199
Lookout Point 81
Lord Mayor's Fund *see* Scott
 Memorial Fund
Lowe, George 236
Ludendorff, General Erich 117, 120
Lusitania 25, 105
Lys, Battle of 118, 120

Mackenzie Bay 185
Mackenzie, Kenneth 203
Mackintosh, Aeneas 30
Mackintosh, Dr Neil 215, 216, 240
Macklin, Alexander 30, 44, 46, 60, 61,
 63, 91, 92, 101, 103, 104, 111, 112, 113,
 114, 116, 132, 145
Maclaren, Bobby 164
Magga Dan 251
Malaspinna Glacier 20
Mallory, George 143, 153
Manley, G. 172, 214

Mann, Alexander 9
Mann, Byers & Co. 4
Mann, Julia 162
Marguerite Bay 219
Markham, Sir Clements 14–15, 25, 261
Marr, James 217
Marr, John 19, 27
Marshall-Cornwall, Sir James 249
Marston, George 30, 32, 37, 44, 62, 75, 80, 84, 88, 89, 97, 103
Martin, James 180
Mason, Professor Kenneth 212, 213
Mathieson, John 126, 130–31
Mawson, Douglas (Sir) 32, 86, 109, 217
May, Jan Cornelius 136
Mayne, L.S. 164
McCarthy, Timothy 66, 84, 121
McGill University 194
McGonagall, William 4
McIlroy, James 44, 45, 46, 54, 61, 91, 101, 113, 114, 121, 126, 132, 145
McI. Johnson, D. 172
McLeod, Thomas 52, 55, 98
McLintock, Sir Leopold 50
McNish (McNeish), Harry 42, 51–52, 54, 55, 57, 58–59, 66, 67, 78, 82, 84, 116
Melville Bay 195, 197, 198, 201
Melville Island 209
Mercanton, Paul-Louis 135–41, 154, 203
Mill, Hugh Robert 25, 48, 107, 134, 158, 159, 160, 177, 223, 239
Mons, Retreat at 105
Morrell Land 109
Morris, James 236
Moss, Bob 220
Mossman, Robert 26, 36
Mossop, John 215
Mount Everest Foundation 260
Moynihan, Rodrigo 255
Mrs Chippy 55
Mylius-Erichson, Ludvig 155

Namche 237
Nansen, Fridtjof 126, 170

Nathorst, Professor 174
National Library of Scotland 260
National Trust for Scotland 199
Nationalisation, Government policy 1946–48 225
Naval Intelligence Division 211, 213, 238
Nelson Line 110
Nepal 142, 229
Nimrod expedition 1907–09 22, 35, 122, 152
Nobile, Umberto 184
Nordenskjold Glacier 174, 186, 190
Nordenskjold, Otto 38, 72
North East Land 156
North Pole 133, 205, 206
North West Passage 20, 146, 148, 195, 196, 207
Northern Exploration Company 126
Norton, Edward 230
Noyce, Wilfrid 20, 236

Oates, Captain Lawrence 'Titus' 173
Ocean Camp 57, 58, 59, 60
Odell, Noel 154, 168
Operation Highjump 219
Operation Tabarin (*see also* Discovery Committee and British Antarctic Survey) 214–17, 219, 238, 240
Orde-Lees, Thomas 31, 41, 44, 48, 63, 69, 74, 80, 85, 90, 96, 97, 99, 100, 101, 102, 103, 111, 112, 114, 128, 146, 222
Order of St Olav, Norway 258
Oxford University 134, 153, 213

Palmer Land 241
Pardo, Luis 102
Parkinson, Mervyn 182
Parry, Sir William Edward 148
Patience Camp 59, 60, 65, 72
Paterson, Tom 195, 197, 201, 202, 203
Paulet Island 38, 53, 57, 58, 60, 64
Peary, Robert 133, 205–07, 258
Petermann Peak 174, 182, 185, 186, 188-93
Petunia 126, 127

Wild, Frank 30, 32, 44, 48, 54, 58, 59, 61, 62, 66, 76, 77, 78, 80, 82, 84, 86–91, 96, 97, 98, 99, 101, 104, 111, 113, 126, 128, 132, 145, 158
Wilkins, George Hubert 129
Williamsfield House 2
Willis, Sir Algernon 259
Winter Island 220
Wohlegemuth, Lt von 136
Wordie & Co. 4, 17, 225, 226
Wordie, (née de Haller) Alice (daughter-in-law) 262
Wordie, Alison (sister 1894–1958) 4, 13, 18, 20, 23, 31, 33, 56, 111, 120, 162, 199
Wordie, Alison (daughter) 182, 262
Wordie, Elizabeth (daughter) 167, 262
Wordie, George (son) 182
Wordie, (née Henderson) Gertrude (wife) 161, 162, 163, 167, 172, 182, 253, 257, 262
Wordie House, Winter Island 220
Wordie, Sir James Mann
Birth 4; Education 10–12, 13–15; First climbs 13; Cambridge 16–18; Yukon 20; Applies for *Endurance* expedition 23; Lends Shackleton money 35–36; *Endurance* beset in ice 41; Relationship with Shackleton 47–48; *Endurance* abandoned 53; *Endurance* sinks 57; Open boat journey to Elephant Island 66; Landing on Elephant Island 78; *James Caird* launched 82; Marooned 86; Rescue 103; Appointed Chief of Scientific Staff 107; Wounded in Battle of Lys 118; Helps form Scott Polar Research Institute 122; Spitsbergen expeditions with Bruce 124; Expedition to Jan Mayen Island 134; Climbs Mt Beerenberg 138; Applies to join Mt Everest expedition 142; University expeditions – a new style of Polar exploration 145; Shackleton Memorial Fund 158; Marriage 161; 1923 Greenland expedition 164; Joins *Discovery* Committee 168; 1926 Greenland expedition 172; Nurtures new generation of young Polar explorers 178; 1929 Greenland expedition 182; Climbs Petermann Peak 185; 1934 Baffin Bay expedition 194; Helps with purchase of Glencoe 199; 1937 Greenland and Ellesmere Island expedition 201; Cook–Peary controversy 205; Seconded to Naval Intelligence 211; Admiralty 'Blue Books' 212; Operation Tabarin 214; Returns to Elephant Island 221; Advises on nationalisation of Wordie & Co. 225; Appointed President of RGS 228; Key role in 1953 Everest expedition 228; Controversy at Scott Polar Research Institute 237; Barrier versus Shelf row 242; Disagreement over Fuchs's Commonwealth Trans-Antarctic Expedition 244; Chairman of Britain's International Geophysical Year 247; Appointed Master of St John's College 253; Honours 257; Last visit to Polar territories 259; Arctic and Antarctic landmarks (Wordie Bay; Wordies Bugt; Gletscher; Wordie Ice Shelf; Wordie Nunatak; Wordie Point; Wordie Wordiekammen) 260–61; Final illness and death 262
Wordie, (née Mann) Jane (mother) 4, 6, 12, 17–18
Wordie, (née Jeffrey) Janet (grandmother) 3
Wordie, Jean (sister 1887–1902) 4, 12
Wordie, John (son) 167
Wordie, John (father 1839–1910) 3, 4, 6, 17–18
Wordie, John (1783–1830) 2
Wordie, Peter (son) 194, 262
Wordie, Thomas 2